HISTORY OF UNITED STATES NAVAL OPERATIONS
IN WORLD WAR II

By Samuel Eliot Morison

I *The Battle of the Atlantic,* September 1939 – May 1943

II *Operations in North African Waters,* October 1942 – June 1943

III *The Rising Sun in the Pacific,* 1931 – April 1942

IV *Coral Sea, Midway and Submarine Actions,* May 1942 – August 1942

V *The Struggle for Guadalcanal,* August 1942 – February 1943

VI *Breaking the Bismarcks Barrier,* 22 July 1942 – 1 May 1944

VII *Aleutians, Gilberts and Marshalls,* June 1942 – April 1944

VIII *New Guinea and the Marianas,* March 1944 – August 1944

IX *Sicily – Salerno – Anzio,* January 1943 – June 1944

X *The Atlantic Battle Won,* May 1943 – May 1945

XI *The Invasion of France and Germany,* 1944 – 1945

XII *Leyte,* June 1944 – January 1945

XIII *The Liberation of the Philippines: Luzon, Mindanao, the Visayas,* 1944 – 1945

XIV *Victory in the Pacific,* 1945

XV *Supplement and General Index*

Also
Strategy and Compromise

HISTORY OF
United States Naval Operations
IN WORLD WAR II

★

VOLUME EIGHT

New Guinea and the Marianas
March 1944–August 1944

From a painting by Albert K. Murray USNR

Admiral Spruance and Staff

Left to right: Captain Emmet P. Forrestel, Admiral Raymond A. Spruance,
Captain B. B. Biggs, Captain Charles J. Moore

HISTORY OF UNITED STATES NAVAL
OPERATIONS IN WORLD WAR II
VOLUME VIII

New Guinea
and the Marianas

March 1944 – *August* 1944

BY SAMUEL ELIOT MORISON

With Illustrations

An Atlantic Monthly Press Book

LITTLE, BROWN AND COMPANY · BOSTON

1964

LIBRARY OF CONGRESS CATALOG CARD NO. 53–7298

Published June 25, 1953
Reprinted September, 1953
Reprinted January, 1954
Reprinted February, 1957

Reprinted May, 1959
Reprinted February, 1960
Reprinted May, 1961
Reprinted March, 1962
Reprinted September, 1964

ATLANTIC—LITTLE, BROWN BOOKS
ARE PUBLISHED BY
LITTLE, BROWN AND COMPANY
IN ASSOCIATION WITH
THE ATLANTIC MONTHLY PRESS

Published simultaneously
in Canada by McClelland and Stewart Limited

PRINTED IN THE UNITED STATES OF AMERICA

To
The Memory of
MARC A. MITSCHER
1887–1947
Admiral, United States Navy

Preface

THIS volume covers five of the most eventful months of the Pacific war, March through July 1944. After describing submarine patrols of this period, and the fast carrier strikes of March and April, we take up the amphibious operations in New Guinea under General MacArthur's command, and carry forward his Southwest Pacific Forces in a series of bold leaps to Hollandia, Wakde, Biak and the Vogelkop. The rest of the volume is devoted to Pacific Fleet operations from the end of the Marshall Islands campaign to the recovery of Guam. The Battle of the Philippine Sea in June, a naval action equal to Midway in tactical interest, and decisive on the outcome of the war, has been told in great detail; for it was the greatest carrier action of all time. In the history of World War II this battle occupies a place analagous to that of Jutland in World War I.

The three assaults into which Operation "Forager" was divided add up to one of the most important amphibious operations in history. Those that we have already described in the Gilberts, Marshalls and New Britain were "sudden death" affairs, in which the enemy was rolled over by one powerful rush. But the Marianas operation lasted two months; it was stoutly and bitterly contested during the whole of that time, changes in the original plans were forced by events, and the greatest flexibility as well as fortitude had to be displayed by the naval and ground forces to conquer or re-cover those rugged and well defended islands.

I participated in Operation "Forager" in U.S.S. *Honolulu* (Captain Harry R. Thurber), flagship of Rear Admiral Walden L. Ainsworth, and began to compile my materials and write my first draft on board that great fighting ship, as the news came in. There has been plenty of time since to correct first impressions! Early in

1945 I visited Guam to go over the beachhead with Marine officers who had participated in that assault. For Part II, I have enjoyed the expert assistance of Rear Admiral Bern Anderson (Ret.), who throughout the New Guinea campaign was a member of the VII 'Phib staff and who, himself, directed some of the important phases of the amphibious assaults. Mr. Roger Pineau, a member of my small staff since 1947, has supplied me with translations of Japanese action reports and other documents, and has done research on specific points. From Tokyo, Captains Toshikazu Ohmae and Yasuji Watanabe have provided very many details and explanations of Japanese movements that are not found in the documents; and our former opponents, Admirals Toyoda and Ozawa, have answered leading questions. Indeed, the coöperation of our late enemies has been so wholehearted as to enable me to give the Japanese side of the Battle of the Philippine Sea in nearly as great detail as ours. Ensign Richard S. Pattee USNR worked up part of the material for submarine patrols and did other bits of specific research. Mr. Donald R. Martin compiled the task organizations; Miss Isabel J. Gatzenmeier of the Naval War College drafted the charts; Miss Antha E. Card did some valuable checking as well as highly accurate typing; and Stephen J. Allen, YN1, assisted us in various ways.

Correspondence and conversations with ranking officers of the United States Navy and Marine Corps who participated in these operations have been frequent; their aid and assistance has been individually acknowledged in footnotes. Rear Admiral John B. Heffernan, Director of Naval Records and History, has given me constant support, encouragement and constructive criticism. Finally, I wish to mention, in all love and gratitude, the constant assistance rendered by my wife, Priscilla Barton Morison, who accompanied me to Tokyo in 1950, and has been both a comfort and an inspiration during the arduous months as this volume neared completion.

As in all other volumes of this series, responsibility for all statements of fact and opinion rests on me personally, and not on the Navy. I wish to express my thanks to the many officers and enlisted men who have pointed out errors in preceding volumes, and to assure them that a new and revised edition of Volumes I–VI, incorporating their corrections and many of their suggestions, is now being prepared.

As the war progressed in the Pacific, the tremendous increase in the striking power of the United States Navy, especially in its air and amphibious arms; the new techniques, weapons and tactics that were developed, and the greatly extended distance of active operations from continental bases, rendered naval operations more vast and more complicated than ever before in history. It has been no small task to bring the New Guinea and Marianas campaigns within the compass of a single volume. I have done my best to relate the essential and important events, to state the main outlines of strategy and planning on both sides, to describe procedures and methods new to warfare, and to preserve some record of the individual deeds of valor and sacrifice by sailors, aviators and ground troops which alone made victory possible.

SAMUEL E. MORISON

Harvard University
December 1952

Contents

Preface   vii
Abbreviations   xxi

PART I

STRATEGY, SUBMARINES AND STRIKES

I   The Pacific Strategy for 1944   3
    1. Two Roads or One?   3
    2. Japanese Counter-strategy   10

II Submarine Patrols, *December 1943–July 1944*   15

III Fast Carrier Strikes on Palau, Hollandia and Truk,
    22 March–30 April 1944   27
    1. Strikes on Palau, Yap and Wolcai   27
    2. Strikes on Hollandia, Wakde-Sarmi, and Truk,
       30 March–30 April   34

PART II

THE CONQUEST OF NEW GUINEA

IV The Southwest Pacific Organization   45
    1. The Supreme Commander and His Subordinates   45
    2. Southwest Pacific Specialties   49
       a. Seventh Fleet Air Power; *b.* Engineer Spe-
       cial Brigades; *c.* The Assault Pattern; *d.* Mo-
       tor Torpedo Boats

V   Dutch New Guinea and the "Reckless" Plan   59
    1. Terrain and Planning   59
    2. The Enemy's Situation   65

VI The Hollandia Operation, *21 April–6 June 1944*   68
   1. Aitape, 22–27 April   68
   2. Battle of the Driniumor River, 1 June–10 August   71
   3. Tanahmerah Bay, 22 April–6 June   74
   4. Humboldt Bay, 22 April–6 June   79
   5. Japanese Reaction and Retreat, 22 April–17 May   88

VII Wakde-Sarmi, *May 1944*   91

VIII Biak, *27 May–1 June 1944*   103
   1. Biak-Bosnik   103
   2. Z-day at Bosnik, 27 May   108
   3. The Drive for the Airfields   114

IX The Japanese Reaction to Biak (Operation "KON"),
   27 May–13 June 1944   117
   1. Decisions and Air Strikes   117
   2. First Reinforcement Attempt, 31 May–4 June   119
   3. Battle off Biak, 8–9 June   125
   4. A-Go Cancels KON, Biak Secured, 10–22 June   131

X Noemfoor and Sansapor, *2 July–3 September 1944*   134
   1. Noemfoor Island, 2 July–31 August   134
   2. Sansapor, 30 July–31 August   140
   3. New Guinea Epilogue   144

PART III

THE MARIANAS

XI Preliminary Poundings and Final Plans, *February–April 1944*   149
   1. Ladrones-Marianas   149

2. First Call, 23 February   154
3. Plans, Problems and Procedures   157
4. Japanese Preparations to Defend Saipan   167

XII Approach and Bombardment, *10 May–14 June 1944*   170
1. Rendezvous and Approach, 10 May–10 June   170
2. Fast Carrier Air Strikes, 11–13 June   174
3. Pre-landing Bombardments, 13–15 June   179
4. The Underwater Demolition Teams   183

XIII Saipan, *15–21 June 1944*   186
1. D-day Battle, 15 June   186
2. Beachhead Secured, 15–17 June   199
3. Shore Advances and Counterattacks, 17–21 June   206
4. *Phelps's* Adventures, 16–21 June   210

XIV Battle of the Philippine Sea, Preliminaries, *3 May–18 June 1944*   213
1. Operation A-Go, 3 May–13 June   213
2. The Japanese Submarine Offensive, 14 May–4 July   222
3. "Forward to Decisive Victory," 12–15 June   231
4. Strikes on Iwo and Chichi Jima, 15–17 June   237
5. Feeling Each Other Out, 15–18 June   240

XV Battle of the Philippine Sea, the Action, *19–20 June*   257
1. "The Great Marianas Turkey Shoot," 19 June   257
  a. Guam-Rota Phase, 0530–1000; *b.* Ozawa's Four Massive Raids, 1000–1450; *c.* Mop-up on Guam, 1449–1845
2. The Submarines' Contribution, 19 June   278
3. Moving Westward, 2000 June 19–0500 June 20   282
4. The Air Battle of 20 June   288
  a. The Approach; *b.* Twilight Air Battle, 1840–1900; *c.* Night Recovery, 2045–2300

XVI   Battle of the Philippine Sea, Conclusion, *20–24 June*   305
  1. Stern Chase, 20–22 June   305
  2. "Operation Jocko," 24 June   311
  3. Victory   313
  4. Plane Losses   319
     a. Japanese; *b.* United States

XVII   Saipan Secured, *21 June–9 July 1944*   322
  1. The Pattern of Air and Naval Support   323
  2. The Struggle for Mount Tapotchau, 21–26
     June   330
  3. The North End Cleared, 27 June–9 July   334
  4. Conclusion   337

XVIII Logistics for the Marianas   341
  1. Conceptions and Principles   341
  2. Food and Fuel   343
  3. Ammunition   346
  4. Shipping and Stretchers   347

XIX   The Fight for Tinian, *24 July–1 August 1944*   351
  1. Plans and Preparations, 12–23 July   351
  2. J-day, 24 July   360
  3. Tinian Taken, 25 July–2 August   364

XX   Guam Recovered, *June–August 1944*   371
  1. A Deferred Operation   371
  2. First Phase of the Assault, 21–28 July   382
     a. Northern Sector — the Asan Beaches;
       b. Southern Sector — Agat Beaches and
       Orote
  3. Island Secured, 29 July–10 August   398

Appendix   I   Hollandia Task Organization   403

Appendix   II   Naval Forces Engaged in the Cap-
                 ture of Saipan and Tinian   407

Appendix III Forces Engaged in the Battle of the
Philippine Sea 412
1. United States, 19–20 June 1944 412
2. Japanese Forces in Operation
A-Go, 1–20 June 416

Appendix IV Naval Forces Engaged in the Capture of Guam, *21 July–10 August
1944* 418

Index 423

List of Illustrations

(All photographs not otherwise described are Official United States Navy)

Admiral Spruance and Staff   *Frontispiece*

Rear Admiral William M. Fechteler USN   48

Rear Admirals Crutchley and Berkey   49

Hollandia and Sansapor: 88–89
     A Lake Sentani field after air strikes, 21 April
     Coast between Humboldt and Tanahmerah Bays, 22 April
     Assault troops landing from LCIs at Sansapor, 30 July
     LSTs unloading at Beach Red 2, Tanahmerah Bay, 21 April

Saipan and Tinian from the Air, 29 May 1944:   176
     Magicienne Bay and Aslito Field
     Charan Kanoa

Commander Robert H. Isely USN   177

Saipan: 192–193
     The initial landings, 15 June
     The Charan Kanoa beachhead, 25 June
     Marines fighting on Saipan

Admiral Soemu Toyoda   216

Vice Admiral Jisaburo Ozawa   217

Vice Admiral Marc A. Mitscher USN: 232
     On bridge of *Lexington*
     Lieutenant Commander Ralph Weymouth reports

Part of the Mobile Fleet during the Battle of 20 June: 233
     Cardiv 1 mancuvering under air attack

Rear Admiral Richard L. Conolly USN   376

Major General Roy S. Geiger USMC   377

Orote Peninsula and Asan Beachhead: 400
    Orote Peninsula and Apra Harbor, Guam
    The Asan beachhead after the landings

After the Battle, U.S.S. *Lexington:*   401
    Burial at sea

List of Charts

Movements of Fast Carrier Task Force, 22 March–4 May 1944   35

Hollandia Operation, General Area, April 1944   62

Aitape   71

Tanahmerah Bay, 22 April   76

Humboldt Bay, 22 April   80

Wakde-Sarmi, 17–18 May   93

Wakde Island, Landing Plan, 18 May   100

Geelvink Bay and the Vogelkop   105

Biak Island, Bosnik and Airfields, 27 May   109

Movements of Japanese Forces "KON" Operation, 30 May–11 June   121

Night Action, Stern Chase, 8–9 June   128

Noemfoor Island, 2 July   137

Sansapor and Vicinity, 30 July   142

Theater of Operations "Forager" and "A-Go"   153

The Greater Marianas, 1944   163

Saipan, Positions for the Landings, 15 June 1944   188–189

Saipan, Schematic Diagram of Northern Half of Assault Waves   191

Saipan, Landings and Progress, 15–21 June   204

Japanese Submarine Operations and the Exploits of *England*, 15 May–16 June   226

Battle of the Philippine Sea, I   242–243
  Movements of Japanese Fleet; Japanese and American Air
  Searches, 13–17 June, 1944

Battle of the Philippine Sea, II   248–249
  Fleet Movements and Searches, 0000 June 18–0300 June 19

Standard Disposition of Task Force 58, Morning of 19 June   259

Battle of the Philippine Sea, III   262–263
  Fleet Movements and Searches, 19 June

Japanese Attack Disposition, 19 June   264

Battle of the Philippine Sea, IV   270–271
  "The Great Marianas Turkey Shoot," 0300–1500 June 19

Battle of the Philippine Sea, V   275
  Track of U.S.S. *Lexington*, 19 June

Battle of the Philippine Sea, VI   288–289
  Fleet Movements and Air Attack on Japanese Fleet, 20 June

Disposition of the Japanese Fleet at Time of Air Attack, 1840
  June 20   293

Battle of the Philippine Sea, VII   306
  The Pursuit, 0500–2400 June 21

Saipan Secured, 22 June–9 July 1944   323

Tinian, July 1944   352

Guam, July–August 1944   372

Guam, Landings and Beachhead 21–28 July   384–385

The Pacific Ocean Areas of U.S. Naval Operations,
  1944–45   420

Abbreviations[1]

Officers' ranks and bluejackets' ratings are those contemporaneous with the event. Officers and men named will be presumed to be of the United States Navy unless it is otherwise stated; officers of the Naval Reserve are designated USNR. Other service abbreviations are USA, United States Army; USCG, United States Coast Guard; USMC, United States Marine Corps; RN, Royal Navy; RAN, Royal Australian Navy; RAAF, Royal Australian Air Force.

A.A.F. – United States Army Air Force
AKA – Attack cargo ship; APA – Attack transport; APD – Destroyer-transport
AP – Armor-piercing; SAP – Semi-armor-piercing; HC – High capacity; HE – High-explosive, all shells
ATIS – Allied Translator and Interpreter Section, Far East Command
BB – Battleship
BLT – Battalion landing team
CA – Heavy cruiser; CL – Light cruiser
C.A.P. – Combat air patrol
C.I.C. – Combat Information Center
C.N.O. – Chief of Naval Operations
Cominch – Commander in Chief U.S. Fleet; Cincpac-Cincpoa – Commander in Chief Pacific Fleet and Pacific Ocean Areas
C.O. – Commanding Officer
Com – As prefix, means Commander
CTF – Commander Task Force; CTG – Commander Task Group
CV – Aircraft carrier; CVL – Light carrier; CVE – Escort carrier
DD – Destroyer; DE – Destroyer escort; DMS – Destroyer minesweeper
DP – dual-purpose

ESB — Engineer Special Brigade

Inter. Jap. Off. — ussbs *Interrogations of Japanese Officials* (1946)

JANAC — Joint Army-Navy Assessment Committee *Japanese Naval and Merchant Ship Losses World War II* (1947)

J.C.S. — Joint Chiefs of Staff

Jicpoa — Joint Intelligence Center Pacific Ocean Areas

LC — Landing craft; LCI — Landing craft, Infantry; LCM — Landing craft, mechanized; LCT — Landing craft, tank; LCVP — Landing craft, Vehicles and Personnel

LSD — Landing ship, dock; LST — Landing ship, tank; LVT — Landing vehicle tracked (Amphtrac)

N.A. — National Archives, Washington, D.C.

N.A.S. — Naval air station; N.O.B. — Naval operating base

O.N.I. — Office of Naval Intelligence

O.T.C. — Officer in Tactical Command

PC — Patrol craft; PT — Motor torpedo boat

RCT — Regimental combat team

SC — Submarine chaser; also an air-search radar

SWPA — Southwest Pacific Areas

TBS — (Talk Between Ships) — Voice radio

UDT — Underwater demolition team

ussbs — United States Strategic Bombing Survey

VB — Bomber squadron; VC — Composite squadron; VF — Fighter squadron; VT — Torpedo-bomber squadron. M is inserted for Marine Corps squadrons

WDC — Washington Document Center document; these documents are mostly now in National Archives

YMS — Motor minesweeper; YP — Patrol vessel

AIRCRAFT DESIGNATIONS

Numeral in parentheses indicates number of engines

United States

B–17 — Flying Fortress, Army (4) heavy bomber; B–24 — Liberator, Army (4) heavy bomber; B–25 — Mitchell, Army (2) medium bomber; B–26 — Marauder, Army (2) medium bomber; B–29 — Superfortress, Army (4) heavy bomber

C–47 — Skytrain, Army (2) transport

Dumbo — PBY equipped for rescue work

F4F — Wildcat; F4U — Corsair; F6F — Hellcat; Navy (1) fighters

OS2U — Kingfisher, Navy (1) scout-observation float plane

P–38 — Lightning, Army (2); P–39 — Airacobra; P–40 — Warhawk;
    P–47 — Thunderbolt; P–61 — Black Widow, Army (2) fighters

PBM–3 — Mariner, Navy (2) patrol bomber (flying boat)

PBY — Catalina (2) seaplane; PBY–5A — amphibian Catalina; PB4Y —
    Liberator (4)

PV–1 — Ventura, Navy (2) medium bomber

SB2C — Helldiver; SBD — Dauntless; Navy (1) dive-bombers

SOC — Seagull, Navy (1) scout-observation float plane

TBF, TBM — Avenger, Navy (1) torpedo-bombers

Japanese

Betty — Mitsubishi Zero–1, Navy (2) high-level or torpedo-bomber

Frances — Nakajima P1Y, Navy (2) land all-purpose bomber

Hamp — Mitsubishi Zero–2, Navy (1) fighter

Irving — Nakajima J1N, Navy (2) night fighter

Jake — Navy (1) float plane

Jill — Nakajima B6N, Navy (1) torpedo-bomber

Judy — Aichi D4Y, Navy (1) dive-bomber

Kate — Nakajima 97–2, Navy (1) torpedo-bomber

Val — Aichi 99, Navy (1) dive-bomber

Zeke — Mitsubishi Zero–3, Navy (1) fighter

PART I

Strategy, Submarines and Strikes

East Longitude dates except for events in Europe, the United States and Hawaii. "King" Time (Zone minus 10).

CHAPTER I

Pacific Strategy for 1944

1. *Two Roads or One?*

THE WAR in the Pacific is gathering momentum. Starting with the Coral Sea battle it has taken the combined South and Southwest Pacific forces two years of almost continuous fighting to break the Bismarcks Barrier and clear the way for an advance along the New Guinea-Mindanao axis.[1] After four more months (April–July 1944), the forces of General MacArthur are poised on the Vogelkop — the head of the New Guinea bird — ready to spring into the Philippines. In the Central Pacific it has taken the Pacific Fleet a whole year after the Midway victory to build up an invasion force, and another eight months to conquer key Japanese positions in the Gilbert and Marshall Islands.[2] Yet, in a little over four months after Eniwetok was secured, the vital chain of the Marianas is in American hands, the Imperial Japanese Navy has been stripped of its naval air arm, the Philippines are laid wide open, and bases have been acquired from which, exactly a year later, the atomic bombs will be flown to Japan.

On the first day of March 1944, when most of the Marshall Islands were secured and the Admiralty Islands were undergoing the second day of invasion by General MacArthur's amphibious cavalry, nobody knew what was coming next. The obvious thing would have been for MacArthur's spearhead to take the Palaus and Nimitz's the Marianas, one or the other forcing the Japanese Combined Fleet to a decisive and fatal action. The two streams of power

[1] See Vol. VI, *Breaking the Bismarcks Barrier.*
[2] See Vol. VII, *Aleutians, Gilberts and Marshalls.*

could then merge, flow toward Luzon or Formosa, and next to the coast of China. The Allies would then be in possession of at least three bases, from which Japan could be severely air-bombed or, if necessary, invaded. There would be no struggle for the Philippines, except perhaps for northern Luzon; that archipelago, like the Netherlands East Indies, should be liberated by the surrender of Japan.

But it was not to be so simple. In the first place, General Douglas MacArthur, Supreme Commander of Allied Forces in the Southwest Pacific Area, firmly believed in the one road to Tokyo, his own; and that the Allies were honor bound to liberate the Philippines en route. He had been encouraged to believe that this route would be followed. At the "Trident" Conference in Washington in May 1943, the Combined Chiefs of Staff had approved a "Strategic Plan for the Defeat of Japan," according to which, after the Bismarcks Barrier had been broken, General MacArthur's command would roll over the back and head of the New Guinea bird into the Celebes and Sulu Seas, there to be joined by Admiral Nimitz's fleet, coming up through the Marshalls and Carolines. In the meantime the Royal Navy would press eastward through Malacca Straits and an Anglo-Indian army with the assistance of China would reopen the Burma Road. The culmination of this triple thrust would be the seizure of Hong Kong and its hinterland, from which Japan could be bombed. In this scheme Admiral Nimitz's Pacific Fleet was given the secondary rôle of securing MacArthur's right flank by seizing the Gilberts, Marshalls and Truk; after which it was assumed, at least by General MacArthur, that the Pacific Fleet and amphibious forces would come under his command and support his major advance.[3]

Fortunately the British and American Chiefs of Staff left war plans flexible. They believed in keeping Japan, the ultimate objective, constantly in mind, but in shifting their steppingstones as the volume and direction of the opposing current might dictate. They never discouraged General MacArthur from pushing along

[3] Vol. VI 6, 8; Vol. VII 79–85.

the New Guinea-Mindanao axis as far as he cared to go. But why must his road be the only one to Tokyo? Why should Admiral Nimitz and the Pacific Fleet necessarily tail along with him through narrow waters into the South China Sea? Why not send them "northabout," on a second and parallel route to Tokyo?

Several factors combined to disappoint the General and please the Admiral, who would have been less than human had he enjoyed a mere supporting rôle. First, demands in the Mediterranean canceled the Burmese operation, and the Royal Navy could not promise to break through the Straits of Malacca until Germany was defeated. That threw the whole May 1943 concept off balance. Second, Admiral Nimitz, in the Gilberts and Marshalls campaigns, had demonstrated that his Pacific Fleet comprised two of the most swift, resourceful and powerful striking forces, the fast carrier and amphibious groups, ever known in naval warfare; to confine them to narrow seas commanded by enemy land-based aircraft would be idiotic.[4] And third, a big long-range bomber about to be born — the B–29 — could very well use an island named Saipan from which to strike Japan.

In American naval strategy, the capture of Saipan began as a gleam in Admiral King's eye. To the Combined Chiefs of Staff at Casablanca on 14 January 1943 he remarked, "The Marianas are the key of the situation because of their location on the Japanese line of communications."[5] Not only Admirals King and Leahy, but many thoughtful officers of the Navy, were convinced that relentless pressure by sea power could defeat Japan short of invasion. They looked on the Marianas as the logical point for an attack on the inner perimeter of Japanese defenses, and also as forward bases for long-range bombing, refueling submarines, and replenish-

[4] Admiral King remembered very well the war game at the Naval War College in 1933, in which the "Blue" fleet pursued the "Orange" into those very waters and got itself "annihilated." E. J. King and W. M. Whitehill *Fleet Admiral King* (1952) pp. 239–42.

[5] Same, pp. 419, 438, and minutes of C.C.S. 56th meeting. I am indebted to the officers in the historical section of the Joint Chiefs of Staff for aid in studying their minutes and those of the C.C.S. There is also a well documented account of strategic planning in Major Carl W. Hoffman *Saipan* (Hist. Div. Marine Corps, 1950) pp. 13–22. For the B–29 see H. H. Arnold *Global Mission* (1949) pp. 476–80.

ing surface ships. They anticipated that American control of the Western Pacific, exercised from these bases, could destroy Japan's capacity to wage war by depriving her of oil, rubber, rice and other essential commodities.

Admiral King may be said to have won his point when he convinced Generals Marshall and Arnold, his colleagues on the Joint Chiefs of Staff, that these islands were the key to the Western Pacific. At the "Quadrant" Conference at Quebec in August 1943, the Marianas were approved as an objective for the Pacific Fleet after Truk, but only as an alternative to the Palaus. In the same report it was recommended that General MacArthur take the Admiralties after neutralizing Rabaul, capture Hollandia 1 August, and go on to the Vogelkop step by step.[6]

General MacArthur was disappointed at this decision to support two roads instead of one. Now that he could see daylight through the Bismarcks Barrier, after 17 months of frustration and struggle, it seemed hard that he should be denied the stellar rôle in the Pacific advance. To be stuck on the Vogelkop, gazing sadly out across the ocean while Admiral Nimitz carried the flag to Japan, was no pleasant prospect.

Since the top strategists agreed to keep war plans flexible, subject to change as the situation developed, General MacArthur might conceivably have had his way; most certainly would have, if the Pacific Fleet had been thrown for a loss in the Gilberts and Marshalls. As it turned out, the balance was tipped the other way, not only by the quick conquest of the Gilberts and Marshalls, but by a new factor that brought the Army Air Force to the side of the Navy.

Admiral King and General Arnold brought this up at Quebec, but Brigadier General Laurence S. Kuter USA of the Joint Staff Planners developed the argument. In a memorandum of 4 October 1943 he wrote, "Current Planning in the Pacific treats the seizure of the Marianas as a subordinate operation," to be undertaken after

[6] C.C.S. 301, summarized in part in Vol. VII 84; slightly changed when incorporated in the final "Quadrant" report to the President and Prime Minister 24 August.

the Celebes and Sulu Sea have come under Allied control. As such, it would not make sense; one might as well forget it. But the forthcoming B–29, the new Superfortress with a radius of 1500 nautical miles when carrying 10,000 pounds of bombs, gives the Marianas new significance. We must secure them as quickly as possible in order to establish B–29 bases.[7] And on 25 October the C.C.S. planners recommended that Central Pacific forces go directly from the Marshalls into the Marianas, which "might be in our hands by July 1944" — as indeed they were.

General MacArthur reacted vigorously against this proposal. At Cairo, on 3 December, his chief of staff, Major General Richard K. Sutherland USA, presented the Joint Chiefs of Staff with a digest of the latest MacArthur plan. According to this, Nimitz after taking the Marshalls should assist the General in pushing through to Mindanao. Sutherland advanced three reasons why a separate Central Pacific advance should be abandoned. It could be carried out only by a series of massive amphibious operations, each of which would take many months to mount; objectives were too far distant for land-based aircraft to be employed in the assault phase; carrier-based aviation could not maintain unrelenting pressure. Thus, he concluded, a Central Pacific offensive could never acquire momentum; it would be a series of starts and stops with the enemy building up to resist faster than we could build up to advance.[8]

There was little trace of the General's ideas in the "Specific Operations for the Defeat of Japan, 1944," approved by the Combined Chiefs at the "Sextant" Conference 3 December 1943.[9] The gist of this document follows: —

Every effort should be exerted to bring Russia into the war at the earliest practicable date.

The concept of the following operations is that of obtaining bases from which the unconditional surrender of Japan can be forced. In

[7] JPS 288, in J.C.S. Records.
[8] Minutes of J.C.S. 133rd Meeting, Annex.
[9] C.C.S. 397 (revised), less the Burma part, which was struck out because of the predicted inability of the British to start it.

addition to the specific objectives, efforts must be made to destroy the Japanese Fleet, to intensify air and submarine blockade of Japan and operations against shipping, and to continue efforts to keep China in the war.

1. *North Pacific.* Build-up in preparation for entry into the Kuriles and Siberia, in case Russia decides to fight Japan.

2. *Central, South, and Southwest Pacific.* "The advance along the New Guinea–N.E.I.–Philippine axis will proceed concurrently with operations for the capture of the Mandated Islands. A strategic bombing force will be established in Guam, Tinian and Saipan for strategic bombing of Japan proper."

3. *China.* Build-up, and establish another B–29 base at Chengtu.

4. *Carrier Strikes.* To be intensified.

"Specific Operations" was supplemented by a tentative timetable which, instead of being delayed as usual, was subsequently speeded up. Entry into the Marianas started 15 June instead of 1 October; MacArthur reached the Vogelkop 30 July instead of 15 August, and three "whistle stops," Hansa Bay, Ponape and Kavieng, and one main objective, Truk, were eventually omitted.

Plan and timetable were communicated to General MacArthur and Admiral Nimitz on 23 December, and the Cincpac-Cincpoa staff held a conference with South and Southwest Pacific representatives at Pearl Harbor in mid-January, at which various combinations were suggested between the Marianas, Truk and Palau. General MacArthur made a final effort to switch the Central Pacific train onto the New Guinea-Mindanao track by sending General Sutherland to Washington in early February, in the hope of converting the J.C.S. But the Joint Chiefs' sights were now firmly fixed on the Marianas.

Three "elder statesmen" of the armed services who reviewed and criticized war plans [10] called for an end to this debate on 15 February. The Navy, or Central Pacific concept is correct, said they; the northern road to Tokyo is the more direct. General MacArthur's concept would not permit the full employment of American naval

[10] The J.C.S. Joint Strategic Survey Committee: Vice Adm. Russell Willson, Lt. Gen. Stanley D. Embick and Maj. Gen. Muir S. Fairchild.

and air superiority, and Mindanao is not on the direct road to any-thing; possession of it would neither open communications to China nor cut the Japanese lifeline to the Netherlands East Indies. We would be faced with a costly series of ground struggles in which Japanese tenacity would exact a heavy toll in lives, before we could even reach Manila.

The upshot of this and other discussions, and of a visit of Admiral Nimitz and Rear Admiral Forrest Sherman to Washington in early March, was a J.C.S. directive to Nimitz and MacArthur dated 12 March 1944.[11] We shall give a detailed summary of this directive, because every operation covered by this volume stems from it.

The J.C.S. have decided that the most feasible approach to Formosa, Luzon and China is by way of the Marianas, the Carolines, Palau and Mindanao. These objectives are to be attained by

1. Cancellation of the Kavieng operation.
2. Early completion of the occupation of the Admiralties and devel-opment of air and naval bases there.
3. Occupation of Hollandia by General MacArthur's forces on 15 April; Nimitz to furnish fast carrier and other fleet cover and sup-port.
4. Neutralization, not capture, of Truk and other Caroline islands by Nimitz.
5. Occupation of Saipan, Tinian and Guam, starting 15 June, and the Palaus, starting 15 September, by Nimitz, with the object of controlling the eastern approaches to the Philippines and Formosa, and establishing fleet and air bases.
6. Occupation of Mindanao by MacArthur supported by the Pacific Fleet, starting 15 November, with the object of establishing air bases from which Japanese forces in the Philippines can be reduced and con-tained "preparatory to a further advance to Formosa, either directly or via Luzon," and mounting air strikes against enemy bases in the Nether-lands East Indies.

This directive, which governed all military movements in the Pacific until October of the same year, was important both for what it included and what it omitted. It firmed up the Marianas operation and assured General MacArthur that he would not be

[11] Cf. Vol. VII pp. 285, 319.

stalled on the Vogelkop. Hansa Bay and Wewak, included in the "Specific Operations" plan of 3 December,[12] would now be leap-frogged in favor of the more important and westerly position of Hollandia, with the aid of Mitscher's fast carrier forces.[13] And an even greater saving of time and lives was effected by the cancellation of planned assaults on Kavieng and Truk. For the Truk carrier strike of 18 February had convinced Captain Charles J. Moore, Admiral Spruance's chief of staff, who convinced Admiral Nimitz, that the installations there were not worth the lives it would cost to assault the atoll.

2. *Japanese Counter-strategy*

Mr. Alexander Kiralfy, briefly reviewing Japanese military history since Emperor Jimmu (600 B.C.), in the periodical *Foreign Affairs* for October 1943, argued that the Japanese Navy would not come out and fight, at least for some time. The Emperor would never risk another general naval action until hostile forces were threatening his capital. Mr. Kiralfy alleged it to be fundamental Japanese strategy to win wars by the Army alone, the Navy's rôle being to protect the Army's communications. In this war, the Japanese Navy was used exactly that way; it might deliver an all-out battle for the home islands, but not until the United States Navy came within shooting distance of Tokyo.

Although the Battle of Midway, one might suppose, had demonstrated that Admiral Yamamoto, at least, had discarded this alleged traditional doctrine for that of Nelson and Mahan, Mr. Kiralfy brushed it off with the remark that Midway Island, not the Pacific Fleet, was Yamamoto's objective.[14] And anyway, had not Yamamoto failed? So his successor, Admiral Koga, would naturally revert to the traditional and hitherto unbeatable Japanese naval

---

[12] See above, p. 7.

[13] Halsey suggested this at a conference with MacArthur at Brisbane, 3 March, according to Halsey's then chief of staff, Rear Admiral Carney (his letter to Rear Adm. Heffernan 1 Mar. 1951).

[14] *Foreign Affairs* XXII 46, 55, 57.

doctrine. After all, Japan had not lost a war since 1592.

Mr. Kiralfy's article had a marked effect on American public opinion. It seemed to answer the question why the Combined Fleet had not come out to fight since the Battle of Santa Cruz in October 1942. Even Admiral Nimitz was impressed by the Kiralfy article. In the discussions at the Joint Chiefs of Staff in Washington on 11 March 1944, he predicted that the Japanese Fleet could not be brought into action "except on their own terms"; he even doubted whether they would engage if we invaded Formosa. Admiral King scoffed at this, and as usual he was right; but Admiral Mitscher admitted in his report on the Battle of the Philippine Sea that on the eve of that engagement there had been a general belief that the Japanese would not come out and fight.

Imperial Headquarters and successive commanders in chief Combined Fleet had very different ideas and intentions. They had always been advocates of the one big, decisive naval battle, as they had planned Midway to be. That concept, in fact, was almost an obsession with them. Had not the sainted Togo thus defeated Russia in 1905? Had not the Royal Navy almost pulled it off at Jutland? [15] It was, however, realized that no battle could be won without carrier planes, and the reason for the Japanese Navy's apparent modesty during the better part of two years was its want of an air arm. Japanese carrier air groups had twice been wiped out, at Midway in 1942 and in the hopeless defense of Rabaul in 1943. Construction of new carriers was being pushed as fast as the limited industrial facilities of Japan allowed; ships of other types were hastily converted to carriers; plane production reached 1700 per month in March 1944; [16] and new air groups, recruiting the elite of Japanese youth, were being intensively trained in the winter of 1943–44.

[15] Cdr. Masataka Chihaya, who graduated from the Japanese Naval War College in 1944, wrote a summary of Japanese strategy for us, after the end of the war, in which he pointed out how the "big decisive battle" concept had dominated war planning and strategic thinking in his arm of the service. Cf. Capt. Atsushi Oi "Why Japan's Anti-submarine Warfare Failed," U.S. Naval Inst. *Proceedings* LXXVIII (1952) p. 601.

[16] USSBS *Japanese Aircraft Industry* p. 155.

Admiral Mineichi Koga, Commander in Chief Combined Fleet, was not a reader of *Foreign Affairs*. He did not realize that he was not expected to come out and fight. He had always intended to seek naval action at the first opportunity, and to fight for the Marianas or Palaus with all he had. The "New Operational Policy" that he urged on Imperial Headquarters in the fall of 1943 provided for a defensive perimeter running from the Marianas through the Palaus and the Vogelkop to Timor, for delaying actions in the Bismarcks, Bougainville, Gilberts and Marshalls, and for engaging the United States Pacific Fleet at an opportune moment, preferably when tied down to the support of an amphibious operation.[17] Well, here was the moment! On 8 March 1944 Koga issued a plan for the Combined Fleet to sally forth and annihilate the Pacific Fleet. This was to be Operation "Z." The moment for decisive action would come when the enemy penetrated the Philippine Sea, either at one of its Marianas gateways, or via the Palaus, or along the coast of Northern New Guinea. Since it takes about six months to train new pilots for combat, new air groups would not be ready before 1 April. By that time, it was estimated, about 500 equipped and manned planes would be available for the carriers, and in addition, another 400 to 500 land-based planes could be deployed to the Marianas and Palaus.[18]

Koga's "Z" plan called for a concentration of all the naval strength that Japan could muster. Detailed plans were elaborated also for ground defenses. It was decided to reinforce the weak garrisons in the Marianas and Carolines with troops from Manchuria, in which Russia had apparently lost all interest. A new army, the Thirty-first, was organized by withdrawing a battalion from each of about 15 regiments then in Manchuria and placing them under the command of Lieutenant General Hideyoshi Obata, who has been described by his opposite number in the navy as "extremely intelligent and, for an army officer, of extremely broad vision."

[17] See Vol. VI 25.
[18] Translations of excerpts from staff diary 31st Army Feb–Mar 1944, Cincpac-Cincpoa Trans. No. 3 Item 12,058 p. 28.

These battalions were embarked for the Marianas in late February.

Dispatch of troops from the Asiatic mainland to the threatened islands was not an easy matter, since Japanese merchant ship sinkings had averaged over 200,000 tons per month since September 1943. And Imperial Headquarters realized that they could not defend the "perimeter" if they lost control of the air, as they had over the Marshalls and Rabaul. So the Japanese planners laid out an ambitious plan for the construction of new airfields and for an increase in their production of military planes. They hoped that ground and air forces could prevent the enemy from taking his next objective, until the time was ripe for a decisive fleet engagement.

Insurmountable difficulties beset the carrying out of these plans. Japan was short of almost everything except man power. Allied attacks and strikes in early 1944 upset timetables and destroyed a great number of planes. And on the last day of March the Japanese Combined Fleet lost its second wartime commander, Admiral Koga. He had decided to move his headquarters ashore from flagship *Musashi*, then at Palau, to Davao in Mindanao. Two flying boats carrying him and his staff took off from Babelthuap on the evening of 31 March. Koga's plane was never heard from again. The other, carrying staff officers, encountered a storm and splashed six miles off Cebu. Rear Admiral Fukudome, his chief of staff, spent two anxious weeks in the hands of natives until he was rescued by Japanese troops.[19]

Admiral Koga's death was kept quiet until 5 May, when the appointment of Admiral Soemu Toyoda as his successor was announced. This distinguished flag officer had performed widely varying duties.[20] Like his predecessors, he firmly believed in joining battle with the Pacific Fleet at the earliest opportunity. With this thought in mind he caused Koga's Operation "Z" to be revamped and issued on 3 May as the "A-Go" Operation Plan. And from

[19] *Inter. Jap. Off.* II 520.

[20] Born 1885, graduated from the Japanese Naval Academy 1905; naval attaché in England after World War I; Commander in Chief Fourth Fleet 1937; Second Fleet, 1938; Chief of the Naval Technical Dept. 1939; C.O. Kure Naval Station and full Admiral Sept. 1941; member Supreme War Council Nov. 1942; C.O. Yokosuka Naval Base May 1943.

"A-Go," as we shall see in due course, stemmed the great Battle of the Philippine Sea.

Although a Grand Escort Command was set up by the Japanese Navy in November 1943 to meet the growing menace of United States submarine raids on merchant shipping, it was so hampered by the Combined Fleet's priorities in ships and matériel, and by the "one big battle" concept, as to be "miserably slighted." [22]

[21] Capt. Oi's article (note 15 above), pp. 595–601.

CHAPTER II

Submarine Patrols[1]

December 1943–July 1944

UNITED STATES submarines were now coöperating effectively with the Pacific Fleet. In the Battle of the Philippine Sea they not only gave Admiral Spruance his best intelligence on the enemy's fleet movements but sank Admiral Ozawa's flagship and another big carrier, and disposed of several destroyers even before the enemy engaged. But these exploits, which will be told in connection with that battle, are only part of the submarine story. Day in and day out, blow high blow low, the underwater boats were hacking away at Japanese merchant tonnage.

In that praiseworthy pursuit they were far more successful in 1944 than before, and for two main reasons. Owing to Allied victories in 1943, Japanese shipping lanes were now restricted to the Western Pacific. Most of all, the technique, "savvy" and general know-how of the submariners improved so fast that the enemy's anti-submarine measures, never good, became totally inadequate.

The American 21-inch torpedo, though never so far-ranging or deadly as the Japanese 24-inch "long lance," [2] became vastly improved by two fundamental changes. First, Admiral Nimitz on 24 June 1943 ordered the super-secret magnetic exploder, cause of

---

[1] Patrol Reports of individual submarines' commanding officers; Office of Naval History ms. "Submarine Operational History World War II"; Theodore Roscoe *U.S. Submarine Operations in World War II* (1949); *U.S. Submarine Losses World War II*, compiled by Comsubpac; JANAC; *Inter Jap. Off.*, and several USSBS interrogations not included therein. For the submarine war in the Pacific hitherto, see especially this History IV 187–234, VI 60–85, and consult indexes of Vols. III, V and VII.

[2] See Vol. VI 195–6.

countless duds and disappointments, to be used no longer. Second, after the Bureau of Ordnance had been exhorted in vain to do something about the erratic contact exploder, Admiral Lockwood, Commander Submarines Pacific Fleet, conducted simple torpedo experiments at the Pearl Harbor submarine base and against the cliffs of Kahoolawe Island. These proved that the spring in the detonator was not strong enough to free the firing pin in a direct, 90-degree hit; it worked only with a glancing or small-angle hit. A few slight modifications in the detonator, invented by ordnance technicians, put everything right. But it was not until September 1943 that the first United States submarine departed Pearl Harbor with dependable torpedoes. And it was no coincidence that before the year's end one of these submarines sank an enemy carrier.[3]

For the entire year 1943 the score — as corrected after the war's end — by United States submarines in the Pacific was 22 warships and 296 *Marus,* the merchant loss amounting to 1,335,240 gross tons. Since Japanese shipyards had produced a little over half a million tons of new shipping in 1943 and captured or salvaged about 100,000 tons more, the net loss was 718,000 tons. In addition, 31 warships and 76 *Marus* had been damaged.

The loss to the United States Navy that year was 15 submarines and 1129 officers and men, a heavy one indeed; yet the three submarine commands in the Pacific, based at Pearl Harbor, Brisbane and Fremantle, had 75 boats on their rolls on New Year's Day 1944, as against 53 on 1 January 1943. And these 75 were almost all fleet submarines, as most of the aged S-boats had been retired to training centers. In the same twelvemonth, Japan lost 23 submarines.

The underwater fleet saw the New Year in with a flock of sinkings — 3000-ton converted gunboat *Okuyo Maru* by *Ray* off Halmahera, 6700-ton freighter *Ryuyo Maru* by *Puffer* in the Sulu Sea, aircraft ferry *Nagoya Maru* by *Herring* in the East China Sea;

---

[3] *Sailfish* (Lt. Cdr. R. E. M. Ward) ran into a returning plane-ferry convoy on the very rough night of 3–4 Dec. 1943, about 250 miles SE of Tokyo Bay, and in a fight that lasted 14 hours, from first contact to end of escorts' depth-charging, sank carrier *Chuyo.*

and *Balao* so crippled *Kiyosumi Maru* that carrier planes finished her off at Truk next month. *Seahorse* (Lieutenant Commander Slade D. Cutter) disposed of five *Marus*, totaling 13,716 tons, around the Palaus between 16 January and 1 February. And the total score for January 1944 in the Pacific was 56 ships totaling 294,902 tons, a record.[4]

In February many boats were detailed to support the Marshall Islands operation and the carrier strikes on Truk and the Marianas. Adding the carrier planes' bag to that of the submarines, the total loss to Japan in February 1944 was 486,000 tons of shipping.

Grayback (Commander John A. Moore), patrolling between Luzon and Formosa, was lost with all hands on 27 February after damaging 17,000-ton *Asama Maru* and sinking 11,500 more tons of shipping. Probably an enemy plane was responsible. *Trout*, the veteran boat which had carried gold out of Corregidor early in the war, was on her eleventh patrol with Lieutenant Commander Albert H. Clark as skipper when, on 29 February, SSE of Okinawa, she picked up a fast convoy (Eastern Matsu No. 1) carrying troops from Korea to reinforce Saipan and Guam. She damaged a new 11,500-ton transport *Aki Maru* and sank 9245-ton *Sakito Maru*, which contained 4124 troops and a crew of 105. Of these, 2504 went down with the ship.[5] But, in the flurry of depth-charge attacks that followed, *Trout* was lost with all hands.

Sandlance (Commander Malcolm E. Garrison) performed a new exploit on her maiden voyage and established a new tradition — that a submarine on her maiden voyage should not only sink merchantmen but top off with a Japanese warship.[6] *Sandlance's* patrol took place in rough waters. En route Pearl Harbor to the Aleutians in February 1944, she encountered two tempests within four days and, when surfaced, became quickly sheathed in ice,

---

[4] This included light cruiser *Kuma*, sunk by H.M. submarine *Tallyho* in the Malacca Straits.

[5] Dispatch Report to Army Gen. Staff; information from Capt. Ohmae.

[6] Others that followed suit were: *Bluegill* sinking CL *Yubari* 27 April (see this History VI 74–75); *Cavalla* sinking CV *Shokaku* 19 June (see later in this volume); *Croaker* sinking CL *Nagara* 7 Aug.; and *Hardhead* sinking CL *Natori* 18 Aug. All were first patrols.

which she could slough off only by submerging. Arriving on station off Paramushiro in the Kuriles 24 February, *Sandlance* found herself completely surrounded by drift ice. A gale cleared the surface but brought a driving snowstorm in its wake. When that passed, the temperature dropped so that the sea water, instead of sluicing off the periscope whenever it was raised, froze over it in a film of ice. Despite these difficulties, Commander Garrison conned his boat along the Kuriles and Hokkaido, knocking off a 3500-ton freighter on 28 February and a much larger one on 3 March, evading all attacks by patrol craft and planes. Eventually he entered the Japan current, when water temperature promptly rose from barely freezing to 70° F. *Sandlance* passed Honshu and down along the Bonins. During the midwatch 13 March, when his sound operator reported echoes, Garrison brought his boat to periscope depth to view a "sight beautiful to behold — worth the past four weeks of battling typhoons, blizzards and icefields. We were completely surrounded by ships." He had run into a second Marianas-bound reinforcement convoy, Matsu No. 2. A full moon enabled him to select the best targets, light cruiser *Tatsuta* and a large freighter. At 0310 *Sandlance* shot two torpedoes at each, then swung 180 degrees and fired her last two "fish" at a second *Maru*. In a jiffy she was surrounded by wildly depth-charging escorts who could not seem to locate her. Garrison coolly kept his boat at periscope depth for fifteen minutes to watch developments. In that time he observed that *Tatsuta* was sinking and that the first *Maru* was burning, decks awash; and he saw *Kokuyo Maru*, victim of his Parthian shot, go down rapidly, bow first. The destroyers then forced him down and kept him down for 18½ hours; after which, with all torpedoes expended, he turned the bows of *Sandlance* toward the Royal Hawaiian Hotel.

Postponing to another chapter the submarines' exploits in Admiral Mitscher's March carrier strike on the Palaus, let us see what happened in the Western Pacific in the month of April. The scorekeepers in Washington by this time had concluded that the Japanese Navy must be getting very short of destroyers. So far, during the Pacific war, it had lost 64, and very few new ones had been built. This meant that, after the assignment of a minimum destroyer screen to the Mobile Fleet, there would be few left to escort merchantmen; and Admiral King decided that it was time to decrease that small number. Accordingly on 13 April he issued an order to Pacific Fleet submarines to give enemy destroyers No. 2 priority as targets, after capital ships but ahead of transports, tankers and freighters.

United States submariners hardly needed this to persuade them to turn on their traditional enemies. *Albacore* sank *Sazanami* on 14 January 1944, *Skipjack* got *Suzukaze* on the 26th and *Guardfish* put *Umikaze* down for keeps on 1 February. On the 10th *Pogy* sank *Minekaze* in the East China Sea, *Tautog* sank *Shirakumo* off Hokkaido on 16 March, and *Redfin* disposed of *Akigumo* 11 April in an attack on a heavily escorted convoy off Zamboanga. And on the very day that Admiral King issued his order *Harder* (Commander Samuel D. Dealey), after a long duel with *Ikazuchi* off the Marianas, was able to add another good phrase to the book of traditional United States Navy sayings: "Range 900 yards. Commenced firing. Expended four torpedoes and one Jap destroyer."

Commander Dealey now took his boat south to patrol Woleai Atoll in the Carolines. After a two-day wait, a freighter and two escorting destroyers sortied from the lagoon, where the enemy was endeavoring to build a new air base. *Harder* chased this convoy from 0825 April 16 to 0400 next day. When ready to fire at the destroyers, she was thwarted by a rain squall that hid them from sight, but neatly sank the No. 2 target, 7000-ton freighter *Matsue Maru*.

Now that the United States controlled the waters of the Gilberts, Marshalls and eastern Carolines, and had broken the Bismarcks Barrier, and with more submarines coming out every month, it was possible to concentrate on enemy shipping lanes nearer Japan. Admiral Lockwood accordingly began a new scheme of submarine operations, known as the Rotating Patrol Plan, in mid-April. Waters still under Japanese control were divided into areas, and submarines were put on a rotating patrol from inshore to offshore, from northern to southern, and from active to inactive areas, in order to give each boat an equal share both of dangers and of opportunities. The areas were given nicknames such as "Hit Parade" and "Marus' Morgue," and their subsections were called after musical instruments, race horses, and automobiles.

During April 1944, the Japanese high command continued its attempts to reinforce the Marianas and Carolines by means of fast troop convoys. United States submariners made a special point of striking these formations, with results distressing to the enemy. On 3 April *Pollack* cut out one of seven transports from convoy Matsu No. 4, en route Tokyo to the Marianas and Truk. Convoy Matsu No. 5 landed its troops safely at Palau around 20 April and formed up for the return passage to Tokyo. Four big transports were escorted by destroyer *Hatakaze* and three frigates. *Trigger* (Lieutenant Commander Frederick J. Harlfinger) picked up the convoy about 35 miles north of the islands shortly before midnight 26 April and tracked it until she reached a position on the port bow. Harlfinger made three separate attacks, firing all but one of his torpedoes and believed that he had sunk at least three *Marus* and an escort. Actually his first attack scored a hit on *Miike Maru*, a former N.Y.K. liner of 12,000 tons, and on *Asosan Maru*, a former Mitsui liner of 9000 tons. His second attack damaged one of the frigates; his third hit again *Miike Maru*, which burned for two or three days and was lost; but *Asosan Maru* was salvaged.[7]

In the meantime Rear Admiral Ralph W. Christie's Southwest Pacific submarines, based at Fremantle in Western Australia, were finding good hunting in the Sulu and Celebes Seas. A convoy called *Take Ichi* (Bamboo No. 1) was carrying a whole infantry division south from Shanghai to reinforce the Japanese positions on the Vogelkop, in the hope that they could stop or at least postpone General MacArthur's return to the Philippines. Off Manila Bay on 26 April, the convoy lost *Yoshida Maru No. 1* to Pacific

[7] *Inter. Jap. Off.* II 490; Japanese Monograph No. 116 (851–127), "The Imperial Japanese Navy in World War II."

Fleet submarine *Jack*. After calling at Manila and steaming safely through the Sulu Sea, unfortunate "Bamboo" on 6 May ran afoul of *Gurnard* (Commander Charles H. Andrews) in the middle of the Celebes Sea. Andrews directed his torpedoes to such good purpose that three transports totaling almost 20,000 tons were sunk, and thousands of soldiers drowned. The losses in this convoy, as we shall see in due time, had a material influence on Japanese strategic plans.

Another severe loss to the Japanese was the 16,800-ton converted tanker *Nisshin Maru*, sunk off North Borneo by *Crevalle* (Lieutenant Commander Francis D. Walker, Jr.) on 6 May. She was a converted "floating whale factory."

The South China Sea was no longer secure for Japanese shipping. Fremantle-based submarines were now pursuing merchantmen from Singapore to Saigon and Hong Kong. *Lapon* (Commander Lowell T. Stone), after a barren month, took 11,000 tons of merchant shipping out of a convoy off Saigon on 24 May. On the same day *Raton* (Commander James W. Davis) sank one frigate and crippled a second near the Tambeland Islands. The two boats were patrolling very close to each other. *Lapon*, having received warning of a Japanese submarine in the vicinity, made the mistake of identifying *Raton* as enemy and fired two torpedoes at her in the early morning of 27 May. Providentially the "fish" exploded short of *Raton*, which got off with a bad shaking and sundry leaks.

Throughout this period, Southwest Pacific submarines continued their former activities of keeping the Filipino guerrillas informed and supplied, and evacuating marooned Americans and endangered Filipinos on the return passage.[8] *Angler* (Lieutenant Commander R. I. Olsen) was ordered in March 1944 to rescue "about 20" Filipinos, on whom the Japanese were closing, from a point on the north coast of Panay. When Olsen surfaced off the rendezvous on 20 March, he was informed that 58 men, women and children had been assigned to him as passengers. After hiding from the Japanese in the jungle for over two years, many of these unfortu-

[8] See VI 85.

nate people were sick and all were undernourished, dirty and lousy; many had tropical ulcers and one woman was expecting a baby. But a submariner is never nonplussed. The entire crew of *Angler*, during the 12-day run to Darwin, was berthed in the after-battery compartment; male passengers in the forward torpedo room, and women and children in the after torpedo room, except that pregnant, nursing and sick women occupied the chief petty officers' quarters. Food had to be strictly rationed and meals for all hands were cut down to two daily. The stench below was indescribable. But the passengers were all landed without a casualty.

Narwhal (Commander F. D. Latta) performed no fewer than seven such missions to the Philippines [9] during the first six months of 1944; *Redfin* performed two, *Crevalle* and *Nautilus* each one; and similar missions to North Borneo were performed by *Tinosa*, *Haddo* and *Harder*. [10]

During May and early June 1944, Pacific Fleet submarines closed in on the shipping lanes that connected Palau and the Marianas with Japan. *Sandlance* on her next patrol got two 3000- to 4400-ton *Marus* singly; and then, in a running fight from 14 to 17 May, depleted a homeward-bound convoy of three more ships, for a grand total of 20,650 tons. *Silversides* (Lieutenant Commander John S. Coye) on 10 May caught a northbound convoy between Palau and Saipan and picked off three *Marus*. Ten days later she sank a thousand-ton auxiliary gunboat, *Shosei Maru*. On 29 and 30 May Coye spotted two convoys in succession northwest of the Marianas; he got two *Marus* out of the first, trailed the second two days before attacking, and then fired his last four torpedoes, which missed. But his contact reports brought to the scene Captain Leon N. Blair's task unit of three boats, which in a series of attacks scored hits that materially aided the Pacific Fleet in the Marianas campaign. "Blair's Blasters," as this trio was nicknamed, consisted of *Shark*, [11] *Pilotfish* and *Pintado*. With *Silversides* helping, they closed in just as the German wolf-packs were wont to do in the

[9] In the 5th and 6th her C.O. was Lt. Cdr. J. C. Titus.
[10] Roscoe pp. 369–72, 514–16.
[11] Second of that name; the first *Shark* was sunk off Celebes in Feb. 1942.

Atlantic and, though twice thwarted by the convoy's zigging away, sank a 4700-ton *Maru* on 1 June. The same day they picked up a second convoy, trailed it for over 24 hours, and torpedoed another 4700-tonner. *Silversides,* low on fuel and without torpedoes, had to pull out for home, and so missed the fun when on 3 June the "Blasters" spotted a fully loaded southbound convoy. Known to the Japanese as No. 3530, this Saipan-bound convoy consisted of seven transports and freighters carrying 7200 men (mostly of the 118th Infantry) and 22 tanks. *Pilotfish, Shark* and *Pintado* took attack positions on the morning of 4 June. One salvo from *Shark* sank 6900-ton transport *Katsukawa Maru,* leaving 2800 Japanese soldiers swimming. The "Blasters" hung on, and next day *Shark's* skipper, Lieutenant Commander Edward N. Blakely, disposed of a 3000-ton freighter and the 7000-ton transport *Takaoka Maru,* the latter with 3300 troops and 11 tanks on board. On 6 June Lieutenant Commander Bernard A. Clarey of *Pintado,* hitherto thwarted by inopportune changes of course by his targets, bored into the midst of the now disorganized convoy to sink a 2800-ton freighter and the 5600-ton transport *Havre Maru,* with 1120 soldiers and the other eleven tanks.

The escorts of Convoy No. 3530 did a good job of rescuing a majority of the 7200 soldiers whose ships were sunk, and landing them at Saipan; but the troops had lost all their weapons and tanks, and thousands of tons of construction equipment; losses which made the American capture of Saipan much less arduous.

In the waters between Mindanao, New Guinea and the Palaus, *Aspro, Bluegill, Pargo* and *Ray* among them sank five *Marus* in May; *Flying Fish* got two on the 25th between Palau and Guam. Off Formosa a wolf-pack composed of *Bang, Parche* and *Tinosa,* under Captain George E. Peterson, broke up a northbound convoy, sinking some 30,500 tons. In and around the Bonins *Burrfish* downed a 6000-ton tanker, and *Spearfish* and *Sturgeon* got themselves each a freighter between May 6 and 11, while *Pollack* picked destroyer *Asanagi* out of a northbound convoy. Another group operated off the Kuriles in May before the ice melted. *Tautog,* which knew those waters well, sank four *Marus; Barb* and *Herring* got two more and a frigate; total, over 23,000 tons. But *Herring* on 1 June was spotted by a shore battery and sunk with all hands by a well-directed salvo.

She was not the only United States submarine that failed to return. *Gudgeon* (Lieutenant Commander Robert A. Bonin), which already had a bag of a Japanese submarine, a frigate and almost 70,000 tons of merchant shipping, left Pearl Harbor on her twelfth war patrol on 4 April 1944 and was never heard from again. *Robalo* (Commander M. M. Kimmel) out of Fremantle was sunk off Palawan 26 July, probably as a result of a battery explosion. Four members of her crew swam ashore but did not survive the war.

Submarine operations during the Marianas campaign will be described in detail in Chapters VIII, XIV and XV below. In brief, Admiral Lockwood's plan for this operation included lifeguarding off the islands struck by Mitscher's fast carrier planes, and patrols to watch the straits and waters through which the Japanese Mobile Fleet would have to enter the Philippine Sea.[12]

Support operations did not cancel all patrols; it was in June and early July that *Tang* (Commander Richard H. O'Kane), which departed Pearl Harbor 8 June, hung up a record for number of ships sunk, and merchant tonnage sunk, in a single war patrol. These exploits were in the East China Sea off the coast of Kyushu and in the Yellow Sea off Korea. Between 24 June and 6 July, *Tang* sank nine freighters and a tanker for a total of 39,160 tons.

As soon as the Battle of the Philippine Sea was over, more submarines were released for the pursuit of Japanese merchant shipping, and the area which Comsubspac named "Convoy College," extending across the East China Sea from Luzon Strait to Formosa and the coast of China, became the scene of great destruction. The "Mickey Finns" (*Guardfish, Piranha, Thresher,* and *Apogon*), a wolfpack under command of Captain W. V. O'Regan, were the first "freshmen" to cross this watery campus, and their five-day

---

[12] Roscoe p. 366. *Swordfish,* of the Bonins patrol, sank DD *Matsukaze* within sight of Chichi Jima 9 June, and a 4800-ton freighter 15 June.

semester, from 12 to 17 July, cost the enemy some 41,000 tons of merchant shipping. They were closely followed by "Parks' Pirates" (*Parche, Steelhead* and *Hammerhead*, Commander L. S. Parks), two of which fought a memorable action.

Off Takao in Formosa, where several Japanese convoy routes converged, *Steelhead* (Commander D. L. Whelchel) sighted a convoy at 1030 July 30 and trailed it all day under heavy air cover, coaching in her nearby classmate *Parche* (Commander Lawson P. Ramage) for a night surface attack. *Steelhead* got in the first hits, on a tanker, at 0332 July 31, just as *Parche* was coming up. One of the Japanese vessels sent up rockets and flares, and from that moment there were plenty of pyrotechnics to light up the scene. "Red" Ramage, on his bridge, could see several large merchantmen and three escort vessels, one to starboard and two to port between his boat and the convoy. Avoiding this pair, Ramage soon found himself in a tight spot inside the screen and directly athwart the convoy's course. A freighter breezed past him at 200 yards, and then took two torpedo hits from *Parche*, which was already engaging two tankers. One tanker disintegrated under four torpedo hits and sank in a matter of seconds; the other managed to keep going after two bow hits.

By that time the convoy was in complete confusion, every ship for herself. Ramage bore right into the midst of them, conning his boat dexterously to avoid collisions and reach good firing positions, striking at one *Maru* after another, missing one that tried to ram him by a scant 50 yards, stopping another head-on with three on-the-nose punches, then swinging ship to finish her off from his stern tubes. By the first glimmer of dawn he hauled clear, after expending 19 torpedoes, at least a dozen of which hit and exploded. *Steelhead*, in the meantime, was not idle; between them this pair of aces accounted for one 10,000-ton tanker, two 9000-ton transports and two passenger-cargo vessels, totaling over 39,000 tons; and several others were badly damaged.

This night battle fought in Luzon Strait during the early hours of 31 July 1944, stands out as one of the most courageous and stubbornly fought submarine actions of the war. Both boats and their crews emerged exhauted but unscathed, although their skippers had stuck to the bridge under intense machinegun and 4.7-inch shellfire from tanker, escorts and armed merchantmen.

By this time, Saipan being secured, submarine tender *Holland* moved up there to afford the submarines a forward fueling and repair base 3600 miles west of Pearl Harbor. With hunting grounds restricted by the westward advance of American sea power, and Japanese shipping accordingly canalized to the narrow seas, convoys became larger and hunting more profitable. In October 1944, 68 United States submarines sank 328,843 tons of Japanese merchant shipping, the highest monthly score of the war; and, after 220,476 more tons had been sunk in November, the total tonnage afloat of the Japanese merchant marine, which had been over five and a half million tons two years earlier, fell to less than two million tons.[13]

In striking contrast to the history of the German U-boats, that of the United States submarine force showed a steady increase both of combatant and merchant shipping sunk, as the war's end drew near. And, in contrast to those of the Allies, Japanese resources were unequal to making up the deficiency.

JAPANESE TONNAGE SUNK BY UNITED STATES SUBMARINES [14]
Last 4 Months of 1943 and First 8 Months of 1944

1943	Number of Warships	Gross Tons	Number of Marus [15]	Gross Tons	Total Ships	Total Gross Tons
Sept.	3	3,085	31	135,540	34	138,625
Oct.	–	—	26	128,088	26	128,088
Nov.	4	3,992	47	228,313	51	232,305
Dec.	3	22,120	33	130,097	36	152,217
1944						
Jan.	3	9,230	53	285,672	56	294,902
Feb.	4	12,092	52	252,016	56	264,108
Mar.	5	8,322	29	121,213	34	129,535
Apr.	9	12,203	24	98,199	33	110,402
May	6	6,960	54	236,700	60	243,660
June	11	76,570	44	189,611	55	266,181
July	8	15,689	40	220,089	48	235,778
Aug.	11	41,089	45	232,028	56	273,117

[13] Roscoe pp. 523–24.
[14] Data from JANAC, corrected by Japanese sources.
[15] In this category are all fleet tankers, transports, and converted merchantmen, as well as freighters and passenger vessels.

CHAPTER III

Fast Carrier Strikes on Palau, Hollandia and Truk

22 March–30 April 1944 [1]

1. *Strikes on Palau, Yap and Woleai*

AS A result of Admiral Mitscher's fast carrier strike on Truk of 17–18 February 1944,[2] Admiral Koga in *Musashi* retired with all forward-based elements of the Combined Fleet to the Palaus. This interesting group of islands,[3] westernmost of the Carolines, lies directly north of Geelvink Bay, 1055 miles west of Truk, and only 700 miles northwest of Hollandia. Any concentration of Japanese naval strength there was a potential threat to the Hollandia operation which General MacArthur wanted removed. A good working-over by the same Task Force 58 that had put Truk out of business was the obvious way to do it. Admiral

---

[1] Action Reports of ships and commands involved, especially Admiral Spruance "Report of Carrier-based Strikes against Palau, Yap and Woleai, 30, 31 March, 1 April 1944," Apr. 8, 1944; and Vice Admiral Mitscher "Action Report, 19 to 28 April 1944–Hollandia Area," 1 June 1944; Craven and Cate *The Army Air Forces in World War II*, Vol. IV; Robert R. Smith *Approach to the Philippines*; Report of Cdr. H. C. Hopkins RN who observed the strikes from *North Carolina*, to the British Naval Attaché, Washington, 3 Apr. 1944; Cominch Monthly Analysis Mar. 1944 Annex A. On the Japanese side, the "*Nachi* Documents," records recovered from cruiser *Nachi*; Japanese Monograph No. 87 (851–34), "Naval Operations in Western New Guinea and the Area North of Australia."

[2] See Vol. VII of this History, chap. xviii.

[3] The Spaniards first called the islands *Los Paláos* after the native praus or canoes. In the 18th century they began to call them "Pelau," the name of the red volcanic earth that covers Babelthuap. "Palau" first appears in Chamisso's account of the Kotzebue expedition of 1817. Capt. Henry Wilson, a British adventurer who was active in the islands around 1783, Anglicized the name as "Pelew," but this form has gradually died out.

Nimitz agreed heartily, and allotted the necessary forces; the Southwest Pacific command coöperating by flying long-range searches and striking Woleai. Photographs of Palau also were wanted for the impending invasion, but the main object of this March strike was to clear the waters and the air between New Guinea and the Eastern Carolines for the big leap to Hollandia.

In moving into Hollandia, General MacArthur and Admiral Kinkaid had to expect powerful interference by Japanese air or naval power from two places only: the Vogelkop airfields and Palau. The first could be taken care of by B–24s based on the Port Darwin airdrome, but the Palaus were not yet within reach of Allied forces. Only submarines had even taken a look at these islands since the start of the war. Intelligence sources indicated that Koror and Makakal Harbors and Kossol Roads were now the most important Japanese naval bases east of Manila and south of Saipan. On Peleliu, one of the southernmost islands of the group, there was an airfield within search distance of Hollandia, and another under construction on Babelthuap, the largest of the Palaus. Thus the Palau strike was primarily a covering operation for Hollandia, secondarily a reconnaissance in force to obtain intelligence for a future amphibious operation.

Admiral Nimitz told Admiral Spruance on 9 March what he expected; Commander Fifth Fleet allocated forces for the strike on the 18th, and on the 21st issued his operation plan.[4]

Practically the whole Fifth Fleet was there — three of the four carrier groups, with an average of 16 destroyers to each screen. Compare the miserly six that had screened each of Admiral Pownall's groups in the strike on Kwajalein only three months earlier!

Despite Mr. Kiralfy's soothing assurances, the possibility that a thrust so deep into the "Greater East Asia Co-prosperity Sphere" would provoke the Japanese Combined Fleet to come out and fight had to be envisaged. In that event, Vice Admiral Willis A. Lee would pull 6 battleships, 13 cruisers, and 26 destroyers out of the

---

[4] Central Pacific Force (the title Fifth Fleet was officially adopted only in April 1944) Plan Cen 8–44 Mar. 21, 1944. These are West Longitude dates.

three carrier groups, form battle line, and engage. One officer ventured to inquire of Admiral Lee how he proposed in the event of a night attack to disengage all these vessels from the carrier groups and form battle dispositions. "Boy, the Jap fleet ain't *intended* to come out during this operation!" was all he got out of "Ching" Lee.[5]

Majuro Lagoon was the assembling point; as early as 14 March the big battleships were there. Fueling and other logistics for so prolonged a thrust into enemy waters were a problem. A support group was formed around Rear Admiral Ernest G. Small's cruisers to remain on call near the Admiralty Islands, with a number of fleet tankers attached, for the last topping-off of destroyers; for destroyers require sustenance about every four days when they are steaming at high speed. In addition, a separate group of seven fleet oilers departed Majuro ahead of the combatant ships in order to fuel them when about one third of the way to Palau, and six more followed the fleet at a respectful distance, to be on call in case a surface action took place.

On 22 March (West Longitude date) this mighty force of flat-tops with their numerous supporters, attendants, escorts and hangers-on sortied from Majuro Lagoon. Avoiding the rhumb line course through the enemy-held Carolines, they made a wide southerly sweep in order to skirt the arc of possible search planes from Truk. But they did not escape attention. On the third day out, 25 March, at 1332,[6] the fleet was sighted by a search plane from Truk, and again at the tanker rendezvous next day. Certainty that the fleet had been sighted produced a sudden change of plan. Admiral Spruance's conviction that he had been detected caused him to push ahead without waiting for late photographic intelligence of Palau. He informed Admiral Nimitz by plane message that the attack would be advanced from 1 April to 30 March. On the 28th all destroyers were topped off from battleships and from the *San-*

---

[5] See chap. xviii for the way this problem was handled in the Marianas operation.
[6] East Longitude date, Zone minus 11 time. The force skipped 24 March, and the rest of the operation is in this time.

gamon-class escort carriers of the Support Group, which there-
upon parted company with the force.[7]

Pacific Fleet submarines made an outstanding contribution to
this raid on Palau. *Tunny* (Commander John A. Scott) and *Gar*
(Lieutenant Commander George W. Lautrup) were sent there
during the third week of March to act as lifeguards for downed
aviators. And they did much more. *Tunny*, on the night of 23
March, picked up surface radar contact on a Japanese submarine,
I-42, on a supply run to Rabaul, with no torpedoes on board. At
2324 *Tunny* began firing four torpedoes, after which Commander
Scott ordered "Take her down." Down she started, but the lanyard
on the conning tower hatch caught between steel and gasket, so
that sea water poured in and Scott had to broach to avoid flooding.
Just as a quartermaster lifted the hatch to release the offending
lanyard, a great shock was felt and "an eerie flash lit up the inside
of the conning tower; for a moment there was some doubt as to
who hit whom," But *Tunny* was all right, whilst breaking-up
noises from *I-42* resolved the doubt. *Gar* rescued eight American
aviators.

By 26 March seven United States submarines were assembled off
the Palaus. *Tunny* was just off Toagel Mlungui (the West Pass),
and *Gar* covered the eastern coast of the islands. On an arc from
north to south, with a radius of 60 miles from Toagel Mlungui,
Tullibee, Blackfish, Bashaw,[8] *Tang* and *Archerfish* took patrol stations.

Their purpose was to intercept any Japanese ship that attempted
to get out from under the carrier strike on 30 March. But fate in-

[7] A Royal Navy observer on board *North Carolina* remarked that fueling under-
way had been so perfected by the U.S. Navy that "no orders whatsoever were
given when securing the destroyers alongside." Admiral Lee's band played sprightly
airs during the process, and ice cream for all hands was passed across to the "cans."
He thought that H.M.S. *Mantelpiece* had come to life: —
> And on all very sultry days,
> Cream ices handed round on trays.

At the beginning of the Pacific war, British observers were inclined to scoff at
American bluejackets' fondness for ice cream; but it was observed that whenever
British tars visited a U.S. ship they made a beeline for the ice-cream bar.

[8] *Blackfish* and *Bashaw* were Brisbane-based boats of TF 72.

tervened. The game was flushed prematurely; the enemy guessed what was coming. On the night of 26 March *Tullibee* (Commander Charles F. Brindupke), patrolling the northern end of the arc, picked up a Japanese convoy of four *Marus* and three escorts. She closed to 3000 yards and fired two. A few seconds later she was taken apart by a terrible explosion, the result of a circular run of one of her own torpedoes. The only survivors were blown overboard. There were several still afloat when Gunner's Mate C. W. Kuykendall regained consciousness, for he remembered hearing shouts; but after about ten minutes all was silent. The only survivor, he was picked up next day by a Japanese escort vessel, and it is from him that we know what happened to *Tullibee*.

More by chance than by design the Japanese shipping in Kossol Roads and other Palau harbors fled through the gap left in the submarine screen by *Tullibee's* loss. Only *Tunny* got in one crack before they escaped.

On the late afternoon of 29 March she sighted four Japanese warships and several merchantmen steaming out of Toagel Mlungui Pass. The combatant force was battleship *Musashi* with Admiral Koga on board, light cruiser *Oyodo*, and two destroyers. *Tunny* ducked under one of them and fired a spread of torpedoes at the battleship. One hit *Musashi* far forward in the chain locker, knocking off the end of her bow and killing seven sailors but doing no damage that could not be repaired at Kure inside three weeks.[9] It seems unfair that after this exploit *Tunny* should be near-missed by an American carrier bomber and have to fight leaks all the way home.

In the meantime, Task Force 58 had good evidence that Palau was expecting them. Between 2000 and 2200 March 28, Japanese torpedo-bombers, not yet fitted with radar, put on one of their oldtime pyrotechnic shows complete with colored flares and float lights. They were beaten off at some expense to themselves but without damage to Spruance's force, and at dawn 30 March the

[9] Tabular Records of Japanese BB movements, WDC 160,624 NA No. 11,791.

carriers reached their launching point about 100 miles from the land.

The Palau Islands may be compared in appearance to a tropical Puget Sound with steep, verdure-covered banks and many small, cliffy islands. Intricate channels and reefs and numerous inlets afford plenty of hiding places for shipping, and puzzle any pilot making his first visit. All day 30 March and half the next, hundreds of planes from the carrier force roamed over the harbors and ranged the shores, strafing and bombing. The Japanese flew in all the fighters they had from Peleliu and Yap, and very many were shot down, although not "over 90" as the pilots claimed. Admiral Reeves's group then proceeded northeasterly to give Yap a good going-over, while Admiral Montgomery's and Admiral Ginder's groups at dawn 31 March took up new launching positions off Palau. Strikes continued through the forenoon and early afternoon of that day.

The mining of two passages to the main harbor by specially equipped Avenger squadrons from *Lexington*, *Bunker Hill* and *Hornet* was an original feature of this raid.[10] The object was to prevent shipping from escaping to sea. At the time the planes began laying mines, about 24 Japanese vessels were in harbor, and 8 already under way turned back in, where they were destroyed at leisure by United States planes. Destroyer *Wakatake* and repair ship *Akashi* stood out to sea. The first was sunk by aërial torpedoes 20 miles north of Palau; *Akashi* hid in a cove but the bombers found and destroyed her. Seventy-eight "eggs" in all were "laid" by the Avengers, and by this means 32 ships were contained in harbor and 36, with an aggregate tonnage of almost 130,000, were destroyed or badly damaged by mines or aircraft.[11] After bottling

[10] CTF 58 Special Report on mining of Palau 12 Apr. 1944. The mines were taken to Majuro by *Terror* from the depot at West Loch, Pearl Harbor, and the detonators installed on board the carriers. The aviators, who did not like this assignment, called themselves the "Flying Miners," with an improvised emblem of crossed shovel and pick-axe.

[11] The postwar score, as given in JANAC, is Patrol Boat 31 (an old DD) and four subchasers, one submarine tender, two net tenders, one aircraft ferry, one MTB tender, seven tankers and six cargo or passenger *Marus*. But Japanese Mono-

up shipping in the harbor, the "flying miners" laid several fields of camouflaged mines with delayed arming in the main pass in order to block the entrance and departure of ships for days ahead. And TF 58 received not a single hit from gunfire, bomb or torpedo.

Admiral Reeves's strike on Yap, the fortified Caroline island about 240 miles northeast of Palau, was carried out according to schedule, but no planes were found there.

On 1 April all three carrier groups converged on Woleai, the Caroline island about 350 miles south of Guam. So few planes were based on this negligible island that the strike produced a minimum of damage, but Woleai furnished the occasion for a notable rescue.

Submarine *Harder* (Commander Samuel D. Dealey), on life-guard duty, was informed that Ensign John R. Galvin USNR had been seen afloat. Fighter planes flew over the submarine and guided her toward the pilot, who was sighted ashore on the point of an islet. Dealey headed in to the lee shore until *Harder* scraped bottom forward, then launched a rubber boat manned by three volunteers, two of whom jumped overboard when they reached the surf, pulled their boat through the breakers coast-guard fashion, reached the pilot and placed him on board. The rubber boat was only recovered through the breakers, and to windward, by Gunner's Mate Paquet swimming a line to it from the submarine, a good 500 yards away. All this under sniper fire from the shore, although bombing and strafing planes did their best to silence it. "A truly courageous accomplishment," as Commander Dealey reported.

Owing to the effective rescue work by seaplanes, destroyers and submarines, 26 out of 44 men from the 25 planes lost in combat during the three days' strikes were recovered. Fortunately the weather became overcast on 2 April, so that the retiring carrier force was able to double back on its outward route, as peacefully

---

graph No. 116, which includes ships under 500 tons, is more comprehensive, listing five more ships totaling 17,566 tons sunk by planes outside the harbors. The 36-ship total amounted to 129,807 tons.

as a tourist cruise. The ships entered Majuro Lagoon 6 April, where they were greeted by Admiral Nimitz and staff members, who had flown in to make final plans for the Hollandia operation.

Technically, the two massive strikes on Truk and the western Carolines within a period of six weeks set up a new standard for carrier warfare, and in the art of concentrated air bombing. The one-strike hit-and-run raid, the last instance of which was Admiral Pownall's on Kwajalein 4 December 1943, had become as dead as the dodo. "Carriers were no longer an expensive weapon for dealing single, sharp blows, but had become efficient machines for keeping aircraft constantly in motion against enemy targets from dawn to dark." [12] And, thanks to the new mobile service squadrons, carrier targets could now be selected almost anywhere in the Pacific that fitted in with the higher strategy.

Spruance's force had only seven days at Majuro for rest and replenishment before it had to sortie to cover General MacArthur's operation against Hollandia.

2. *Strikes on Hollandia, Wakde-Sarmi, and Truk 30 March–30 April*

Allied Intelligence estimated that by the end of March 1944 the Japanese had accumulated 351 aircraft on their three airfields about Hollandia in Dutch New Guinea. Hitherto the V Army Air Force had been able to direct only small night-bombing raids against this future scene of battle, because it had no fighter planes capable of escorting bombers from the nearest Allied airfield at Nadzab. But General Kenney's service command was working on modifications to the P–38s (Lightnings) to give them more fuel capacity and range. On 30 March the V A.A.F. was ready to launch its first big daylight strike. More than 80 Liberators, escorted by 59 Lightnings, hit the Hollandia airfields and caught most of the Japanese planes neatly parked; and next day repeated the raid

[12] Comairpac "Analysis of Pacific Air Operations June 1944," p. 2.

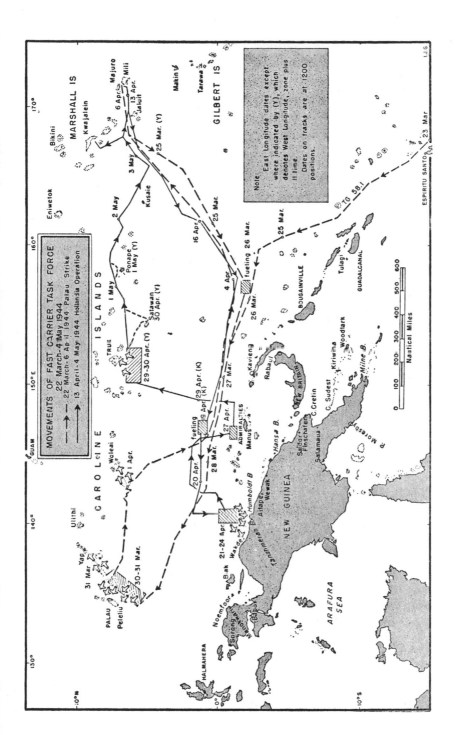

MOVEMENTS OF FAST CARRIER TASK FORCE
22 March–4 May 1944

→ 22 March–6 April 1944 Palau Strike

→ 13 April–4 May 1944 Hollandia Operation

Note:
East longitude dates except
where indicated by (Y), which
denotes West Longitude, zone plus
11 time.
Dates on tracks are at 1200
positions.

with similar strength. The claimed results — 199 Japanese planes destroyed — naturally elated the air force. After two days of bad weather the heaviest raid yet, including nearly a hundred low-flying A–20s, was sent against the Hollandia airfields on 3 April. After this strike Japanese opposition even from the ground was only sporadic. Three more attacks were made on 5, 12, and 16 April, completely knocking out Hollandia as an enemy air base. The aviators' claims of destruction, in this instance, were on the modest side; for, after the airfields had been captured, 340 wrecked planes were counted on and around the strips and an estimated 50 more had been shot down over the jungle, in which their remains were concealed. Some part of this score may be claimed by the carrier-based planes of Task Force 58, which hit the same fields on 21 April, but the V A.A.F. in this instance had left very small pickings for the naval bombers.[13]

Although the J.C.S. had decreed that TF 58 would support the Hollandia operation, Admiral Nimitz made it clear to General MacArthur, on his 23 March visit to Brisbane, that the first duty of the Fifth Fleet, including the carriers, was to destroy the Japanese Combined Fleet if it chose to challenge. Admiral Nimitz evidently hoped that it would, and Admiral Mitscher's operation order to TF 58 shows that the same object was uppermost in his mind: —

This force will destroy or contain enemy naval forces attempting to interfere with the seizure of Hollandia; will, without prejudice to the foregoing task, neutralize enemy airfields in the Hollandia-Wakde area by repeated air strikes by carrier air groups and by surface-ship bombardment if requested, and will provide air support requested by Commander Attack Force.[14]

On its sortie from Majuro 13 April, TF 58 was organized into three task groups. TG 58.1, Rear Admiral J. J. Clark, with carriers *Hornet, Belleau Wood, Cowpens* and *Bataan*, would hit the Japanese airfields and defenses at Wakde, Sawar, and Sarmi, about 120 miles west of Hollandia, between 21 and 24 April. TG 58.2, Rear

[13] *Army Air Forces in World War II,* IV 584, 592–98; R. R. Smith, *Approach to the Philippines* pp. 50–51.   [14] CTF 58 Op Order 5–44.

Admiral A. E. Montgomery, with carriers *Bunker Hill, Yorktown, Monterey* and *Cabot*, would strike Wakde and Hollandia airfields on 21 April and support the landings in Humboldt Bay during the three following days. TG 58.3, Rear Admiral J. W. Reeves, with carriers *Enterprise, Lexington, Princeton* and *Langley*, would hit the Hollandia airfields and defenses on 21 April and then support the landings at Tanahmerah Bay. If the Combined Fleet showed its teeth, Vice Admiral Lee's battle line would be detached for surface action. Tactically this Hollandia sweep of TF 58 was a duplicate of the previous attack on Palau, except that it was prolonged over four days. Captain Paré's support group of tankers trailed along to replenish the fuel tanks of the flattops and their satellites.

The dawn fighter sweep of Rear Admiral Clark's group on 21 April strafed aircraft on the ground at Wakde and made a fighter sweep on Sarmi. The only enemy reaction was light to moderate antiaircraft fire. After five more strikes, in order to make it a sure thing, cruisers *Santa Fe, Mobile* and *Biloxi*, with five destroyers, bombarded Wakde and Sawar airfields on that night, and Clark's planes struck again on the 22nd.

Montgomery's and Reeves's carrier groups also operated with no resistance other than scattered antiaircraft fire. Admiral Mitscher reported somewhat plaintively that "due to the very large number of enemy aircraft previously destroyed by the V Air Force strikes, it is impossible without photographs showing previous destruction, to determine accurately the number of planes destroyed by TF 58." Over 200 airplanes appeared in photographs on the first strike, but there is no doubt that most of these had already been put out of business by General Kenney's fliers. Not a single enemy plane rose from the five target fields to intercept; the only aircraft that heckled TF 58 were naval reconnaissance planes flying from Biak Island, and a few torpedo bombers from there or Sorong.[15] And all that closed the force were shot down or turned back by combat air patrol. These few weak raids were the maximum Japanese effort against TF 58, whose combined losses (operational and com-

[15] Japanese Monograph No. 87 pp. 5–6.

bat) between 21 and 24 April were only 21 planes, and total casualties, 12 aviators. The ships came through without a scratch.

So, if the results of fast carrier participation in the Hollandia operation were slight, the cost was commensurate. The big flattops were not really needed to take Hollandia, and one might conclude that they would better have passed the time resting at Majuro, but for the results of an incidental crack at Truk on the return passage.

Admiral Nimitz had already decided that the time was ripe to give Truk another heavy working-over.[16] Although B–24s from the Central and South Pacific had been making regular calls there for a month, another big raid might knock it out for keeps. Actually the Japanese had heavily reinforced Truk since February, in spite of all these attacks; some 104 aircraft were present on the Moen, Eten, Param and Dublon fields on 29 April.

While his ships were refueling and replenishing off Seeadler Harbor, Admiral Mitscher issued dispatch orders to TF 58 for air strikes against Truk, to be followed by a cruiser bombardment of Satawan Island, about 170 miles southeasterly, and a battleship bombardment of Ponape Island, 380 miles to the eastward.

Early in the morning of 29 April, West Longitude date, an 84-plane fighter sweep was launched from a point about 150 miles from Truk. This was standard tactics to clear the skies of enemy fighters. A fairly heavy cloud cover over the atoll caused the Hellcats to miss some of the 62 planes that the Japanese, warned by radar, managed to get into the air to meet the attack. Nevertheless, on that and the following day, 59 were shot down and 34 destroyed on the ground.

The only important Japanese counterattack, consisting of eight planes, was delivered at 0815 April 30. One managed to get through to drop a bomb near *Lexington*, which did no damage. The following night a couple of snoopers approached Admiral Montgomery's group, but that exhausted the enemy's offensive efforts during this two-day raid. Only 12 planes were still serviceable on

---

[16] For a description of Truk and its place in Japanese strategy, see Vol. VII chap. xviii. For this raid, the USSBS publication *The Reduction of Truk*, based on information obtained there after the surrender, is the best source.

1 May, and nearly all installations that had not been moved underground were destroyed or heavily damaged. Admiral Mitscher had not expected to find many ships at Truk, nor did he; but almost everything afloat in the lagoon, a small patrol vessel, two small freighters and about 20 other small craft, was destroyed. And a Japanese submarine, *RO–45*, which was either trying to escape from Truk or to take refuge there, was caught about 20 miles south of the atoll early on 30 April and destroyed in a combined attack by destroyers *MacDonough* and *Stephen Potter* and aircraft from carrier *Monterey*.

Some spectacular rescues of downed airmen were made during the two-day raid. Task Force 58 lost 26 planes in combat and suffered 9 operational losses. Of the 46 airmen shot down, more than half were rescued, some inside the lagoon. Submarine *Tang*, the boat with an almost fabulous history, had been diverted from patrolling the Palaus to lifeguard duty at Truk, and reached her station off the atoll at 0400 April 30. All day and the next she kept busy locating life rafts and picking up aviators, with fighter planes hovering overhead to point the way and protect her from interference. Three survivors from a splashed Avenger, riding a raft, were recovered around noon. On the morning of 1 May a raft with survivors was sighted from the air inside the lagoon. A float plane from *North Carolina*, sent out to make the rescue, capsized in the choppy sea. Her crew was rescued by a second plane from *North Carolina*, which then taxied out to the waiting *Tang* with the raft in tow and the aviators on board. Altogether 28 downed airmen were rescued from the water by this air-sea team, 22 of them by *Tang;* and, although two scout planes were lost in the process, the crew of one was recovered. Nineteen airmen were lost, most of them because they were shot down over islands or too near shore to be reached. *Tang's* score remained a lifeguard record for over a year, and her performance proved the value of fighter cover in lifeguard operations.

Henceforth, Truk was almost as useless to the Japanese as Rabaul, and routine heavy bomber raids from Eniwetok and the Admiralties took care that it remained so. Seven supply submarines were the only vessels that reached it during the rest of the war. When the Marianas campaign opened, the local Japanese commander shifted his total air strength, a pitiful 14 planes, to Guam.

On the afternoon of 30 April, TF 58 turned eastward to leave calling cards at other Caroline islands. Already, at 0730, nine heavy cruisers had been detached under Rear Admiral Jesse B. Oldendorf to bombard Satawan Island. This bolo-shaped islet, at the southeastern end of Satawan Atoll in the Nomoi group, is just big enough to hold a Japanese airstrip, already unserviceable from earlier land-based bombing raids. At 1532 the cruisers began pouring 800 rounds of eight-inch and 1400 rounds of five-inch shells into the islet. Neither return fire nor any other enemy activity was observed, but an ammunition dump exploded and an oil tank caught fire. The real value of this bombardment, as Admiral Oldendorf observed, was to afford "a welcome change to the crews of the ships participating," bored with numerous alerts that never materialized.[17] Bombardment completed at 1745, the cruisers rejoined TF 58 about 50 miles north of Nomoi.

A similar diversion for the battleships was scheduled for Ponape, largest of the Carolines. A rugged and heavily forested island, 2500 feet high and about 19 miles in diameter, it is surrounded by a coral reef and has a good harbor where the Japanese had a seaplane base and near which they had already constructed an airfield and were building another. For this bombardment, Vice Admiral Lee came out of his "stand by for surface action" position and became active as Commander Battle Line, with six battleships, *Iowa, New Jersey, Massachusetts, North Carolina, South Dakota* and *Alabama*, all mounting 16-inch guns. Each batdiv was assigned a desdiv for screening and for supplementary bombardment, and Admiral Clark's carrier group, reverting to the rôle predicted for carriers in the 1920's, stood by to protect the battlewagons if attacked by enemy aircraft. Airstrips, town and seaplane base were duly bombarded on the afternoon of 1 May, the only opposition coming

[17] Comcrudiv 4 Action Report, Satawan Bombardment.

from antiaircraft guns, which ceased firing when the big shells began to burst. Admiral Lee, after a shoot of 70 minutes, concluded that no worthwhile targets remained, and called quits to avoid wasting ammunition. As at Satawan, the main profit in pounding Ponape lay in giving the ships practice on live targets; and it was the first time that the battle line had been able to function as a unit.

The battleships[18] now joined Clark's group and arrived Eniwetok 4 May. The other two carrier groups had already gone ahead, and arrived the same day at Majuro. Task Force 58 now enjoyed a well-earned rest until it was time to sail for the Marianas.

[18] To which I should have added *Indiana.*

PART II

The Conquest of New Guinea

East Longitude dates except for events in Europe, the United States and Hawaii. "King" Time (Zone minus 10).

CHAPTER IV

The Southwest Pacific Organization[1]

1. *The Supreme Commander and His Subordinates*

ALL General MacArthur's operations at this period stemmed from the Joint Chiefs of Staff directive of 12 March, the genesis and intents of which we have already discussed. Two immediate tasks committed to the Supreme Commander were build-up of the Admiralties as an air and naval base, and the occupation of Hollandia and Humboldt Bay on 15 April 1944. After that, he could seize such positions along the New Guinea coast as he thought desirable, with a view to supporting the Palau operation on 15 September and launching his invasion of Mindanao two months later. Hollandia, Palau and Mindanao were regarded by the J.C.S. as three fixed points between which MacArthur had a free choice of targets and methods.

The anatomy of the Southwest Pacific command was so peculiar and interesting as to require a brief description before we launch into the Hollandia campaign.

General Douglas MacArthur USA, Supreme Commander of the Southwest Pacific Area, was an international and in some respects a supra-national figure. All his forces were American and Austral-

---

[1] Robert R. Smith *The Approach to the Philippines*, a volume in the *U.S. Army in World War II* series which has been at our disposal in ms. and page proof, and Craven and Cate *The Army Air Forces in World War II*, Vol. IV, have been most useful, as has the ms. "Command History, U.S. Naval Forces Southwest Pacific Area," with Admiral Kinkaid's comments; General MacArthur's "Operation Instructions" for each operation, and Admiral Kinkaid's Operation Plans. And the personal experience of Rear Admiral Anderson has been liberally drawn upon.

ian, excepting a few French ships and the valiant remnant of Netherlanders who had escaped the Malay Barrier debacle of 1942. His command was not the creation of a formal agreement. In 1942 the United States, the United Kingdom, Australia, the Netherlands and New Zealand had agreed in principle to a dividing line between two command areas in the Pacific.[2] These governments then agreed to approve directives to MacArthur and Nimitz as issued by the Joint Chiefs of Staff when acting as executive agent for the Combined Chiefs of Staff. The last proviso, however, was a distinction without a difference, since our British allies, and other nations involved, recognized from the first that the United States was paying the piper in the Pacific and had the right to call the tune.

General MacArthur did not set up a joint staff like that of Admiral Nimitz,[3] but a modified Army staff the key officers of which had been with him in the Philippines. Australian Army officers and United States and Australian naval officers were included as technical assistants; but in organization and methods this was a United States Army staff throughout the war. The number of men under MacArthur rose from a few thousand in early 1942 to nearly 750,000 in all services at the time of the Hollandia operation, as against about 350,000 Japanese troops deployed in the area.

The Supreme Commander exercised his authority through three principal officers — Blamey, Kinkaid and Kenney. Allied ground forces were under General Sir Thomas Blamey, Commander in Chief of the Australian Army. For administration and training purposes there was a single command, but in field operations Blamey directed Australian troops only, whilst Lieutenant General Walter Krueger, commanding the United States Sixth Army, directed United States forces. MacArthur brought this about by the simple

---

[2] See this History VI 15 for a chart showing the dividing line. In general, it ran from Hainan to long. 130° E, south through the Philippine Sea to the Equator, east to long. 159° E, and south through the Solomons and east of Australia to the South Pole. The western boundary of the SW Pacific Area, between it and the Allied Command SE Asia Area established in Aug. 1943, was the Indochinese and Malayan coast to Singapore, south through the SE part of Sumatra, SE to lat. 18° S, long. 115° E, and south along that meridian.

[3] For a description of Cincpac-Cincpoa joint staff see Vol. VI chap. i.

device of transferring the Sixth Army, together with Australian components used in each operation, into a special task force called the "Alamo," whose commander reported directly to him; and Krueger commanded the Alamo Task Force until Morotai was invaded in 1944. Neither the Australian government nor General Blamey appeared to object to this arrangement, and it worked very well. The United States Army Service Force, Major General J. L. Frink USA, also stemmed directly from General MacArthur.

Overall commander of Allied Air Forces Southwest Pacific Area, consisting at this time of the V United States Army Air Force, the Royal Australian Air Force, and the Royal Netherlands East Indies Air Force, was Lieutenant General George C. Kenney USA. Major General Ennis P. Whitehead USA, his deputy, moved up forward and directed all elements in contact with the enemy in New Guinea.

Allied Naval Forces Southwest Pacific Area were commanded by Vice Admiral Thomas C. Kinkaid.[4] His forces consisted in great part of the Seventh Fleet, United States Navy, elements of the Royal Australian Navy and a few small Dutch and French war vessels. In brief, this was his task organization: —

TF 73 Commodore Thomas S. Combs, Seventh Fleet Air.

TF 74 Rear Admiral Victor A. C. Crutchley RN. H.M.A.S. AUSTRALIA and SHROPSHIRE with Australian and U.S. destroyer screen.

TF 75 Rear Admiral Russell S. Berkey. U.S.S. PHOENIX, NASHVILLE and BOISE with destroyer screen.

TF 76 Rear Admiral Daniel E. Barbey, the VII Amphibious Force. Transports, beaching craft and vessels assigned as escorts.

TF 70 Special elements operating directly under Admiral Kinkaid. Commander Selman S. Bowling, commanding Motor Torpedo Boat Squadrons, was the most important.

(TF 77 was the designation used by Admiral Kinkaid for the attack force in an operation. Commodore Robert G. Coman, commanding Service Force Seventh Fleet, had no TF number.)

---

[4] For brief biography of Kinkaid see Vol. V this History, p. 88*n*, and for portrait, with General MacArthur, VI 435.

In addition, there were two submarine task forces, Rear Admiral Christie's TF 71 based on Fremantle, and TF 72, Captain John M. Haines, based on Brisbane. Since the conquest of Dutch New Guinea offered no opportunities for submarine action, the underwater part of the Seventh Fleet conducted practically a separate war against Japanese shipping, which turned out to be a very weighty contribution to victory.[5]

With the possible exception of these submariners, there was nobody in the Southwest Pacific command who doubted who was the boss. General MacArthur set up every operation himself, but did not interfere in the tactical execution. In the Southwest Pacific, the first step in planning was "Warning Instructions" by the General to the ground, air and naval commanders directly under him. assigning their specific tasks in broad terms. Upon receipt of Warning Instructions, planning began on the next level of command. General Krueger was the coördinator of plans, but each element of the ground, naval and air forces retained full operational control of its own force, with one exception. Troops embarked for amphibious assault were under naval command until the Army command post was established ashore.

With planning conducted on a coöperative basis, there had to be frequent conferences. As soon as his ground, air and naval commanders had had time to study the Warning Instructions and to outline tentative plans, General MacArthur summoned them to his headquarters — which were still at Brisbane in March 1944 — heard their comments and recommendations and, after digesting them, issued his Operation Instructions. This was the directive. The General's directives did not follow the standard form laid down in Army manuals, but they stand out as excellent examples of military orders clearly and briefly expressed. He told his subordinates in effect, and without flourish, "Here is a job to be done, these are the tools to do it with, and this is the time in which I wish it to be accomplished. You work out the details."

[5] Southwest Pacific submarine patrols of this period are covered in part in Vol. VI chap. vi, in part in chap. ii of this volume.

On a destroyer's bridge

Rear Admiral William M. Fechteler USN

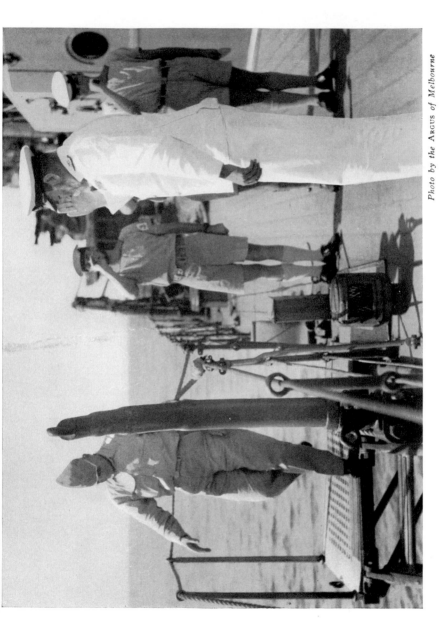

Rear Admiral V. A. C. Crutchley RN seeing Rear Admiral R. S. Berkey USN over the side of H.M.A.S. *Australia*

Rear Admirals Crutchley and Berkey

2. Southwest Pacific Specialties

a. Seventh Fleet Air Power [6]

All land and tender-based aircraft assigned to the Seventh Fleet were under the operational control of General Kenney's Allied Air Forces. Except for two weeks during the Hollandia operation when he had the loan of a few Pacific Fleet escort carriers, Admiral Kinkaid had only nominal control over the aircraft assigned to his fleet. The air arm of the Seventh Fleet, composed almost exclusively of Catalinas and Liberators,[7] began to expand, both in strength and scope of operations, about 1 March 1944. On the 24th, Commodore Combs broke his flag in tender *Tangier,* moored in Seeadler Harbor, from which Patrons 33 and 52 under his direct command began flying routine searches some 500 miles north of Manus. Before the month was out, PBYs raided Woleai in the Carolines for four consecutive nights in support of Admiral Spruance's carrier strike on Palau. At the same time, Liberator Squadron 106, based at Nadzab Field in New Guinea, was flying daylight over-water

[6] Com Air Seventh Fleet and Fairwing 10 War Diaries; "Command History of Fairwing 17"; Craven and Cate *The Army Air Forces in World War II,* IV 570–670; *General Kenney Reports* pp. 337–58.

[7] The Catalina (PBY) was a twin-engined seaplane that had been in service since 1935; the four-engined Liberator (PB4Y-1) was the Navy's version of the Army B-24, modified for overwater search.

Earlier developments, touched upon in former volumes, were: The remnants of Patwing 10 (Catalinas) evacuated from the Philippines and N.E.I. in 1942 with tenders *Childs, William B. Preston* and *Heron,* based at Perth, formed the bulk of Seventh Fleet Air until mid-1943, when, on 27 June, Capt. Thomas S. Combs became Commander Aircraft Seventh Fleet. By 15 Sept. expansion of squadrons and planes enabled Patwing 17 to be commissioned at Brisbane with Combs as wing commander. VP-101 with tender *San Pablo* moved to Samarai in China Strait and began "Black Cat" night radar searches as far as Rabaul and Wewak, attacking enemy shipping whenever encountered; it sank DD *Mochizuki* on 24 Oct. and freighter *Naples Maru* on 20 Nov. 1943, and several others under 500 tons. VP-101 was augmented by other squadrons, some of which based at Port Moresby, where the duties were air-sea rescue and ferrying men and supplies over the Owen Stanley Range to Australian troops at the junction of the Sepik and Yellow Rivers. The Samarai squadrons also did "Dumbo" rescue work around Rabaul, and on 15 Feb. 1944 one Catalina picked up fifteen downed aviators under the guns of Kavieng. The Perth-based Catalinas (Fairwing 10, Captain Howard V. Hopkins) conducted routine patrols and provided escort to convoys and submarines in the Indian Ocean as a detached element of TF 73.

searches along radii of 800 miles from Finschhafen, covering the ocean north of New Guinea up to Biak Island and almost to Palau and Yap. In mid-April Bombron 106 began to move forward to the new Momote Field on Los Negros Island in the Admiralties. All Commodore Combs's squadrons were now placed under the operational control of Major General St. Clair Streett USA, commanding the XIII Army Air Force.

From 1 April 1944, naval air-search operations were conducted from the Admiralties. Searches were extended out to 1000 miles, in order to detect any possible Japanese surface reaction to the Hollandia operation. By mid-June Fairwing 17 included three squadrons of Catalinas, two of Liberators, and one of Ventura (PV-1) patrol bombers, with tenders *Heron, Tangier, Orca, Wright, Currituck* and *San Carlos*.

As new bases in western New Guinea were taken by amphibious assault, elements of Fairwing 17 moved forward. On 12 May *San Pablo* arrived at Hollandia [8] to tend a detachment of Catalinas engaged in night anti-shipping strikes in northwestern New Guinea, and in spotting gunfire for cruisers. On the 26th, six Liberators arrived at Wakde to begin daily search flights over the Pacific. Late in July the range of air operations was further extended when tender *Wright* moved forward to Owi Island off Biak. All the waters of the Western Pacific, from Truk to Mindanao, were now covered by Allied air search; yet, as we shall see, this availed the Pacific Fleet very little in the Marianas campaign.

The operations of Fairwing 17 turned out to be mostly routine; only an occasional contact with a Japanese patrol plane or small ship varied the monotony. And, as enemy aircraft disappeared from New Guinea, "Dumbo" rescue missions diminished for lack of calls.

On 9 July 1944, Rear Admiral Frank D. Wagner — who, as commander of Patwing 10, had caught the full force of the first Japanese offensive in the Philippines — relieved Commodore Combs as Commander Aircraft Seventh Fleet. Early in 1945, when the writer

[8] *Orca* relieved her on the 22nd; *Half Moon* arrived Hollandia 16 May.

met Admiral Wagner on board *Currituck* in Manila Bay, he remarked, "Right back where we started!" It was indeed a long way back from that gallant, hopeless retreat of 1941; but the end was in sight.

b. Engineer Special Brigades [9]

An indirect but beneficial result of General MacArthur's staff being an Army staff was this: the Army's "web feet," the Engineer Amphibian Brigades, cold-shouldered by the Navy in other areas, were welcomed here. These brigades were born as a result of competition between the armed services.

The United States Army, though a late convert to the theory of the Navy and Marine Corps that the next war would require amphibious operations on a scale never before contemplated, felt that the prewar ship-to-shore amphibious exercises held at Culebra and elsewhere were inadequate.[10] Army planners, admitting that ship-to-shore technique must be used in long-range amphibious operations, insisted that in order to beat Japan there must be plenty of shore-to-shore operations as well, in which troops are embarked in the same landing or beaching craft from which they are discharged on enemy beaches.

In April 1942, after the Japanese had swept through the Western Pacific with their specially designed landing craft, the Army called for the construction of thousands of landing craft and the training of men to use them. That was a bad time for the Navy to undertake such a program, when German submarines were raising havoc on our Atlantic seaboard and the Battle of Midway had not yet been fought. So, in May 1942, the Joint Chiefs of Staff gave the United States Army responsibility for initiating and developing an "am-

[9] Based on the ms. history by James Mullican "Amphibian Engineer Operations," Vol. IV of "Engineers in the Southwest Pacific, 1941–45," lent to us by the courtesy of Army Engineers' historical office in Baltimore; the anonymous *History of the Second Engineer Special Brigade*; Brig. Gen. William F. Heavey *Down Ramp* (1947); Brig. Gen. D. A. D. Ogden, "Our Business Is Beachheads" *Military Engineer* June 1945.
[10] See I lv–lvii and II 12–23 of this History.

phibian" program with the British shore-to-shore procedures as model. The Army handed the job to its Corps of Engineers, and within a month the newly created Engineer Amphibian Command was established at Camp Edwards on Cape Cod. Plans were made for several amphibian brigades, each to consist of approximately 360 officers, 7000 men and 550 landing craft — 36-foot LCVPs and 50-foot LCM tank lighters [11] to be trained for shore-to-shore operations. The Atlantic Coast was combed for yachtsmen, fishermen, small-boat operators, sailors and engine mechanics, and Army service records were scanned for men with the right background and experience. Each brigade included three boat and shore regiments, and each regiment was designed to furnish the shore party and water transportation for one division of troops.

The first of these new organizations to be sent to the Southwest Pacific, in November 1942, was the 2nd Engineer Special Brigade.[12] Colonel (later Brigadier General) William F. Heavey of the Corps of Engineers United States Army commanded this unit throughout the war. General MacArthur liked having his own fleet of landing craft and asked for two more amphibian brigades. Accordingly the 3rd ESB (Brigadier General David A. D. Ogden USA) began to arrive in October 1943, and the 4th (Colonel Henry Hutchins USA) followed in May 1944.

The ESBs' shakedown operation was the occupation of Nassau Bay, and in the Lae-Salamaua and Finschhafen campaigns they obtained good battle training. General Heavey, knowing that naval officers would view his command as an amateur effort to do a naval job, and that many soldiers, too, were skeptical of "amateur yachtsmen," did everything to prove his men's competence. Without basic naval training, the ESBs had to learn about water transportation the hard way, but learn they did. Their boats took part in assault landings, usually making the run to the objective from an

[11] Four brigades were organized in the United States and two others activated in England, to take part in the Normandy landings. In March 1943, when the Navy had a breathing spell, the J.C.S. gave it sole responsibility for future operation and maintenance of amphibious craft. Existing Army amphibian units were not disbanded, but no more were authorized.

[12] Name changed from 2nd Engineer Amphibian Brigade in March 1943.

Army embarkation point under their own power, sometimes catching a ride on transports and cargo vessels. For the landing forces they unloaded the assault shipping and organized supply dumps, developing expert shore party teams which were very successful in solving these eternal problems. Once the beachhead had been seized, the ESBs provided local transportation and lighterage for the follow-up or consolidation phase of the operation. Since New Guinea lacked roads and the jungle was dense and full of swamps, water transportation was both heavy and vital. Frequently the ESBs would arrange brief shore-to-shore movements at an hour's notice in order to get troops around some terrain obstacle, as was done in Sicily by the Navy in the summer of 1943.

Beach parties are often confused with shore parties, but the two had very distinct and different functions. The former were the traffic policemen of the beach, waving boats into the right spot to land, ordering them retract when empty, and seeing to the evacuation of casualties. VII 'Phib organized and trained eight beach parties, each consisting of three naval officers and 18 men. Their relation to the ESB shore parties was very close, and the two coöperated effectively.

Severe demands, and the engineers' resourcefulness, produced many innovations. They equipped LCMs with 20-mm and .50 caliber machine guns, converting them into "flak boats" which delivered antiaircraft protection at the beaches and could double as gunfire support craft. Launchers for 4.5-inch rockets were mounted on landing craft and dukws for support work, and the rocket dukws, especially, soon came to be a familiar and highly valued part of every landing force.

By March, 1944, the ESBs were proved and experienced members of the amphibious team in the Southwest Pacific.

c. The Assault Pattern

The VII Amphibious Force began life in 1943 with one flotilla of 336-foot LSTs, one of LCIs and one of LCTs; one attack transport (APA), one attack cargo ship (AKA) for training purposes, and, a little later, a division of converted destroyer transports (APDs). As the Force grew in size, the number and types of beaching craft increased. They always remained the most important shipping used in Southwest Pacific amphibious operations. The landing ship dock (LSD), which could preload dukws, amphtracs and landing craft and launch them by flooding, also played an important part. A pattern of boat movements and landings, built around numerous echelons of beaching craft, was early laid down, and improved upon in all future operations.

For a sand beach landing, the initial assault troops were generally transported in APDs and landed in the ramped landing craft (LCPR) that these ships carried; but amphtracs (LVTs) and dukws, manned by the engineers, had to be used for initial landings over drying coral reefs. After the assault waves came landing craft disgorged from an LSD, carrying tanks and shore party engineering equipment. Next there would be several waves of the 157-foot landing craft infantry (LCI) spaced so that each wave could beach, debark troops and retract before the next was due. Bringing up the rear, about one hour after H-hour, were six or seven LSTs loaded with troops, vehicles, and bulk supplies, so planned that each could be unloaded before nightfall.

Depending upon the size of the landing force for a given operation, and the distance from rear area staging bases whence it had to be moved, any and every type of beaching craft might be used for the follow-up echelons, which, at three- to five-day intervals, supplied and built up the newly seized objective. This process continued until the Army Service Force could assume responsibility for logistic supply of the new base with its own merchant shipping.[13]

Planning and directing these numerous assault and build-up movements involving amphibious shipping was a function of VII

[13] At Hollandia, for instance, follow-up echelons in amphibious shipping were scheduled for D-day plus 1, 2, 4, 8, 10, 12 and 20. There were 11 merchant ships in the D plus 8 echelon. The D plus 12 echelon consisted of 7 LSTs for Aitape; and 26 LSTs, 12 LCTs towed by LSTs, and 2 merchant vessels for Humboldt Bay.

'Phib escort vessels — destroyers, destroyer escorts, frigates, patrol craft (PC), subchasers (SC), and small minesweepers (YMS) — were assigned by Admiral Kinkaid to the operational control of Admiral Barbey.

In New Guinea the 114-foot landing craft tank (LCT) operated in a manner for which it was not designed and of which few could have believed it capable. Living quarters for the crew of two officers and ten men were a small, boxlike compartment intended to house them only during short-haul operations such as crossing the English Channel. But in the Southwest Pacific these craft had to operate continuously in all sorts of tasks ranging from an assault echelon to harbor lighterage, and to house their crews for months on end.[14]

Commander Burrell C. Allen, Jr., who handled the LCT Flotillas, operated from an "apple cart" (APc) as flagship, and by 1 May 1944 had about 90 LCTs under his command, scattered all the way from Brisbane to Hollandia. Plagued by a chronic lack of spare parts and shortage of repair facilities, Commander Allen had to call on the natural ingenuity of American bluejackets to keep enough craft operating to meet the many and varied demands for their services.

Commander Homer F. McGee had 35 landing craft infantry (LCIs) in his Flotilla 7 by 1 May 1944. Three had been converted to rocket-launchers, but the rest performed their planned troop-carrying function. In assault movements they were used to transport infantry with personal equipment. Originally designed for the cross-channel lift between England and France, they were not intended for long hauls; but in New Guinea they were used whenever and wherever large numbers of troops were involved. Only 157 feet long, they were crowded and uncomfortable at sea with the standard complement of 183 troops embarked, and very unpopular among the GIs.

The LCI rocket gunboat, a favorite with VII 'Phib gunfire sup-

[14] See this History VI 376–77 for the fine performance of LCTs in supporting the Arawe Task Group.

port officers, began to be used about the same time that the converted LCI(G)s were appearing in the South and Central Pacific. The idea of mounting rocket launchers on naval craft came from the Royal Navy. By removing the ramps from an LCI and mounting launchers in battery along the gunwales, enough for a salvo of 288 4.5-inch rockets could be installed. First tried at Cape Gloucester, the rocket LCIs were a spectacular success.

LST Flotilla 7,[15] Captain Richard M. Scruggs, provided the backbone of VII 'Phib amphibious movements. From D-day until Army Service Force took over, these big beaching craft ran shuttle between rear area bases and the objective, ferrying troops, vehicles and supplies. Between runs, any LST available might be found staging troops and equipment from the deep rear to forward bases.

One United States and three Australian attack transports (APAs) were regularly assigned to VII 'Phib, and six more were lent by Admiral Turner for the Hollandia operation. Although APAs bore their share of the overall load of the operations, Admiral Barbey did not look on them with great favor, because in comparison with LSTs and LCIs they were slow to unload, and vulnerable. Nevertheless, the fast tempo of MacArthur's thrusts and the heavy demands of base development crowded even the assault waves, and required that every type of lift be used.

d. Motor Torpedo Boats[16]

One of the interesting and baffling things about naval history is the way in which a type of ship or weapon designed for one purpose turns out to be useless for that purpose, but very useful for another. Destroyers were originally "torpedo-boat destroyers." Soon there were no torpedo boats left to destroy, but the destroyers are still indispensable. The original function of aircraft

[15] One group of Flotilla 7 (12 LSTs) was manned by the Coast Guard.

[16] "Command History of Motor Torpedo Boat Squadrons, Seventh Fleet"; Robert J. Bulkley ms. "PT – A History of Motor Torpedo Boats in the United States Navy"; War Diaries of PT squadrons and Action Reports of individual PT boats.

carriers was to provide an "air umbrella" for the Fleet; but in this war the carrier became the offensive vessel *par excellence*, and the battleships, originally designed to fight enemy battleships, became protectors of the flattops or bombardment ships. Motor torpedo boats were designed to sneak up on enemy warships at night and torpedo them; but around Guadalcanal that function turned out to be futile, when it was not suicidal.[17] Presently in the Central Solomons, and simultaneously in New Guinea, a new use was found for the PTs. Armed as gunboats — their torpedo tubes rapidly becoming a sort of vermiform appendix for lack of employment — they harried and broke up Japanese alongshore barge traffic which, by reason of the American command of adjacent waters, had become the enemy's only surface supply line.[18]

Each PT unit commander directed all operations of the boats in his zone. Every day he prepared two dispatches, one reporting results of the night before, the other setting forth what he intended to do the following night. All these were collated by Commander Selman S. Bowling [19] and sent out in general messages to all interested commands, naval, army and air; and the MTB commanders kept a liaison officer at headquarters both of Alamo Force and V Army Air Force. These "intents" and "results" messages, as they were called, provided a simple means of keeping each Allied armed service fully and promptly informed of what the PTs were doing. On a lower level, each PT task unit commander constantly telephoned local ground and air commanders, with whom he was expected to coöperate in every possible way and at short notice, his own estimate of his boats' capabilities. This arrangement worked well throughout the New Guinea campaign, but it was not proof against accidents.

In no theater of war were the PT boats more useful than along the coast of Dutch New Guinea. Based on tenders that were frequently moved forward, they ran nightly patrols in search of enemy

[17] See Vol. V of this History pp. 337–40.
[18] See Vol. VI chaps. iv, v.
[19] Relieved Commander Morton C. Mumma, who devised this system, 18 Feb. 1944.

barges, denied water-borne transport to the Japanese (who always seemed to prefer a boat ride, however dangerous, to slogging along jungle trails), and were constantly taking shore batteries under fire. Before an assault they landed and embarked scouting parties who obtained valuable intelligence, and took deliveries of hungry and dispirited Japanese troops from loyal natives. The courage and enterprise of the junior reserve officers who commanded PTs and their crews, were exemplary; and fortunately their losses were few.

CHAPTER V

Dutch New Guinea and the "Reckless" Plan

1. *Terrain and Planning* [1]

BIRD-SHAPED New Guinea, the largest island in the world not dignified as a country or a continent, has also been one of the least known and least wanted parts of the world. A Spanish discoverer in 1545 named the island for its fancied resemblance to the African Guinea. During the following century several Dutch navigators explored the coast, and a number of native chieftains in 1660 acknowledged the Dutch East India Company to be their sovereign. But it was not until 1828 that the Kingdom of the Netherlands annexed the island from the Vogelkop to long. 141° E. During the later scramble for colonial territory, Germany and Britain divided that part of the island not annexed by the Dutch; Germany taking the north coast from the Dutch border to Cape Ward Hunt, together with the Admiralties and the Bismarcks, while the British annexed Papua (the tail of the bird), and the south coast up to the Dutch border. After World War I German New Guinea became an Australian mandate. Hence, in 1941 the island was fairly evenly divided between the British Commonwealth of Nations and the Kingdom of the Netherlands.

Early in 1942 Japan seized key positions along the north coast, but was prevented from occupying Port Moresby by the Battle

---

[1] Besides sources indicated in footnote 1 chapter iii, Allied Geographical Section Terrain Study No. 61 "Area Study of Northeastern Netherlands New Guinea and Geelvink Bay"; Gen. Eichelberger *Our Jungle Road to Tokyo;* Orders and Reports of the principal commanders, especially Generals MacArthur and Krueger and Admirals Kinkaid and Barbey.

of the Coral Sea; and her attempt to seize Milne Bay was balked in August.[2] At the same time General MacArthur, with the aid of the South Pacific Command, began his long uphill climb over the Owen Stanley Range, along the coast of Papua, and through the Bismarcks Barrier.[3] By March 1944 he had control of Papua, the Huon Peninsula, the Admiralties and western New Britain; Rabaul and Kavieng had been neutralized. He was ready to make a spectacular leap over the old international boundary at long. 141° E into Dutch New Guinea.

Dutch New Guinea consists of about 152,000 square miles of rugged mountains covered with heavy rain forest. The coastal climate is hot and humid. Hundreds of different languages are spoken by the natives, who comprise a wide variety of frizzy-haired types, mostly Melanesian. They are regarded as the most savage and ferocious of all Pacific island natives; head-hunting and cannibalism may still be practiced in the more remote mountains. Until 1935 Dutch authority was exercised only at certain coastal points, the interior being largely untouched by Europeans. Then gold was discovered. Concessions were granted to prospectors for gold and oil and the government attempted to settle unemployed Javanese on the Vogelkop Peninsula. But the census of 1936 showed only 204 Europeans in the entire territory.

From Geelvink Bay, over the neck of the bird to the eastern boundary, a 450-mile stretch of coastline, there is only one first-class harbor and anchorage. That is Humboldt Bay, a cup-shaped bight with a clear entrance four miles wide. Hollandia, the name by which the entire section came to be known to American forces, was a tiny settlement at the head of Challenger Cove, an arm of Humboldt Bay, formerly the easternmost Dutch outpost in the Netherlands East Indies. West of Humboldt Bay the Cyclops Mountains rise to over 7000 feet, their steep and heavily forested northern slopes dropping off sharply into the ocean. South of this range and about six miles west of Humboldt Bay is Lake Sentani, a narrow and irregularly shaped body of water 15 miles long. Be-

[2] See this History V 116.   [3] Same, pp. 115–17, and a large part of Vol. VI.

tween the north shore of the lake and the Cyclops Mountains is a plain on which the Japanese constructed three airfields. From Tanahmerah Bay, 25 miles west of Humboldt Bay, a native track led up through the hills and behind the Cyclops Mountains to Lake Sentani. Except for occasional native clearings, the whole region is heavily forested. And on a coastal plain about five miles east of Humboldt Bay, at a place called Tami, the Japanese, early in 1944, began to construct another airstrip.

This Humboldt-Tanahmerah region, with three airfields already built, offered the best site short of Geelvink Bay for developing into an Allied naval, air and troop-supply base. Since it had been of slight importance before the war, little detailed information could be obtained by General MacArthur's staff planners. Reliance had to be placed on maps prepared by Army engineers from aërial photography, which failed to reveal important terrain features that were to prove costly obstacles when the landings were made.

Since air cover and support for the Hollandia operation from Pacific Fleet carriers could be furnished for a limited time only, it would be necessary to provide an air base from which V Army Air Force planes could take over at an early date. The nearest base to Hollandia, Nadzab in the Markham River Valley, was 500 miles away — too far for efficient air support. But General Kenney's planes had discovered and bombed a Japanese airstrip at Tadji, on the coastal plain eight miles southeast of Aitape, about 125 miles ESE of Hollandia. Used earlier in the war to stage planes eastward, it was now lightly held. Aircraft based here would be within easy supporting distance of Hollandia; and possession of the nearby Aitape, though it lacked a harbor, would provide a good roadblock in case the Japanese army at Wewak should try to move west.

For this Hollandia operation General MacArthur's staff had already made preliminary plans before the J.C.S. directive of 12 March 1944, and the Operation Instructions were issued on the 18th. The code name, Operation "Reckless," may have reflected the feeling in Brisbane about making so long a jump deep into enemy-held territory; but the operation itself proved to be any-

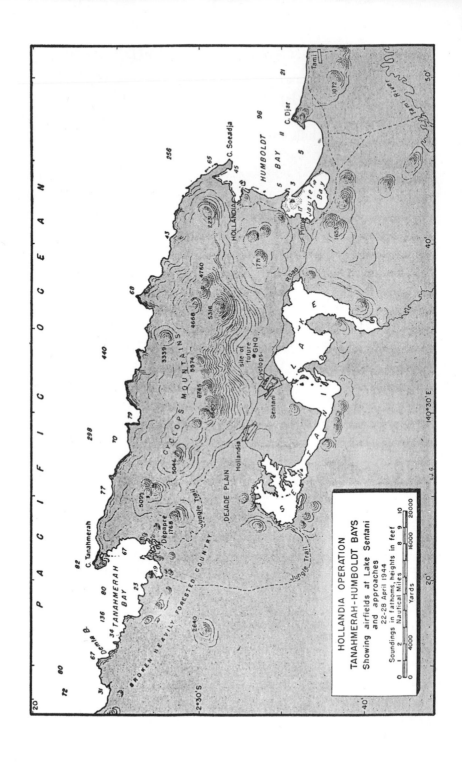

HOLLANDIA OPERATION
TANAHMERAH-HUMBOLDT BAYS
Showing airfields at Lake Sentani
and approaches
22-28 April 1944

Soundings in fathoms, heights in feet

thing but reckless. That it did so prove was in part due to the support tendered by the Pacific Fleet. Detailed plans for Pacific Fleet support were worked out at Brisbane on 25–26 March, when Admiral Nimitz and several members of his staff flew down from Pearl for conferences.[4] All other details were already in the hands of MacArthur's subordinates.

The final plans called for three simultaneous landings on 22 April: in Tanahmerah and Humboldt Bays, and at Aitape. The "Reckless" Task Force to effect the first two consisted largely of the I or "Eye" Corps, commanded by Lieutenant General Robert L. Eichelberger USA, who had brought the Buna-Gona campaign to a successful conclusion. The I Corps was built around the 24th Infantry Division, a regular Army outfit commanded by Major General Frederick A. Irving USA, and the 41st Infantry Division, a National Guard unit from the Pacific Northwest commanded by Major General Horace H. Fuller USA. The 24th would land at Tanahmerah Bay and drive around the Cyclops Mountains to the Lake Sentani airfields, while two regimental combat teams of the 41st landed at Humboldt Bay and moved toward the airfields from the east, making a double envelopment. To the 163rd RCT of the 41st Division, commanded by a seasoned veteran of the Buna campaign, Brigadier General Jens A. Doe USA, was entrusted the assault on Aitape (Operation "Persecution"), where it would be reinforced next day by the 127th Regiment of the 32nd Infantry Division.

Vice Admiral Kinkaid, whose responsibilities forced him to remain ashore near General MacArthur's headquarters, delegated to his amphibious force commander, Rear Admiral Daniel E. Barbey, the detailed planning and actual execution of the naval phases of the operation. Barbey's headquarters were on board *Blue Ridge*, off Cape Sudest, whence he and his staff could easily fly to General Krueger's headquarters at Cape Cretin or to General Eichelberger's at Goodenough Island for conferences.

Barbey's staff carried the burden of three distinct amphibious

[4] For details see King and Whitehill *Fleet Admiral King* p. 538.

operations. Like Turner in the Central Pacific, he decided to take charge of one landing in person; but he was responsible for all three. Rear Admiral William M. Fechteler commanded at Humboldt Bay,[5] and Captain Alfred G. Noble, Barbey's chief of staff, at Aitape.

Composition of naval attack groups and landing forces, tonnage and shipping requirements, and other matters of mutual interest were worked out by VII 'Phib planners in coöperation with the Alamo Force staff. This, in Barbey's opinion, concentrated too much planning at Alamo headquarters; he would have preferred a less centralized system, as in the Pacific Fleet, in order to give the lower levels of command more experience in this important aspect of the art of war. In theory Barbey was probably right, but personality counted more than system, and that of General Krueger made the centralized system work well in the Southwest Pacific.[6]

As an instance of the way things were done, General Krueger conferred at his headquarters on 30 March with the five air and ground force generals and the three amphibious group commanders. After the main conference broke up, Admiral Fechteler and Gen-

[5] William M. Fechteler, b. California 1896, Naval Academy '16; served as junior officer in various battleships and destroyers and later in several fleet and force staffs; officer detail section Bupers to 1943, when he became C.O. *Indiana;* promoted Rear Admiral January 1944, and assigned deputy commander VII 'Phib, later Commander 'Phib group 8, participating in New Guinea and Philippines operations. Asst. Chief of Naval Personnel 1945; promoted Vice Admiral 1946, Com Battleships and Cruisers Atlantic Fleet; Deputy CNO (Personnel) 1947; promoted Admiral and Commander in Chief Atlantic Fleet 1950; Chief of Naval Operations Aug. 1951; C. in C. Allied Forces Southern Europe 1953–56, when retired with rank of Admiral.

[6] [Note by Captain Bern ˉAnderson.] General Krueger's staff was one of the smoothest working army staffs I ever saw. Krueger was in a tight spot as "coördinator of planning." This gave him a dominant but not a command position. He handled the situation tactfully, leaning over backwards to consult with the naval and air commanders he had to deal with in the field. Kinkaid and Kenney were his opposite numbers, but the first delegated the detailed naval planning to Barbey, and Kenney delegated his to General Whitehead, who was "Advon 5" — advanced echelon of V Army Air Force and the working part of that force in New Guinea. As far as his own plans were concerned, Admiral Barbey incorporated every detail of the operation in his plan, much the same as Admiral Turner did, leaving subordinates merely to carry out schedules already decided on. At the target, once the order to land was given, Barbey simply watched, and often turned down a staff officer who wanted to needle subordinates. General Krueger was a thorough soldier, perhaps a little on the hard side. He demanded a high state of efficiency, shunned publicity and was what the correspondents labeled "no color."

eral Fuller, with Captain Bern Anderson (landing craft control officer on VII 'Phib staff and liaison officer to Alamo Force) and three or four others, held a detailed discussion of the Humboldt Bay landings in the mess hall, with charts spread out on the tables. Fechteler outlined his thoughts on the choice of beaches where the landings should be made, the armament and timing of pre-liminary bombardment, and other important details. General Fuller seemed to be in complete agreement, offering a few suggestions all of which were good. Within half an hour the minds of these two key officers, who had never before met, were in accord; every essential detail was decided, and such pleasant personal relations were established that later changes were made with good grace.

2. *The Enemy's Situation* [7]

The Japanese situation at Hollandia in April 1944 stemmed from that Imperial Headquarters decision of September 1943 to which we have often alluded.[8] The decision was to set up a new defensive perimeter running through the Marianas, the Palaus, Western Dutch New Guinea and the Netherlands East Indies, behind which ground forces were to be augmented, airfields built, and naval power assembled. The Japanese hoped rather than expected that all would be completed by the spring of 1944, when they could once more assume the offensive and "annihilate" both MacArthur and the Pacific Fleet. Hollandia, hitherto neglected, would be built up into a major air and supply base fed by a chain of bases in western New Guinea; the Palaus would be the staging point for troops and supplies moving south from Japan. Unfortunately for Japan, the weight of the growing Allied offensive in the Pacific forced her to make revision after revision, and the New Guinea link in the perimeter chain was again and again forced back, until it slid off the Vogelkop into the Ceram Sea.

[7] Japanese Monograph No. 90 (851–60) "The A-Go Operation 1944"; Japanese Monograph No. 87 (851–34) "Naval Operations in Western New Guinea and the Area North of Australia"; *Inter. Jap. Off.* II 287–90, 409–10; R. R. Smith *The Approach to the Philippines.*
[8] See especially this History VI 22–26.

Imperial Headquarters, apparently agreeing with General Mac-Arthur that the New Guinea-Mindanao axis was the proper line of Allied advance, believed in November 1943 that the General would launch a major drive along the north coast of New Guinea at no distant date. The war lords of Japan were much more concerned over this expected move than with the actual seizure of the Gilbert Islands and the Torokina beachhead on Bougainville. They poured army and air reinforcements into New Guinea and made a partial army reorganization to meet the MacArthur menace. The Second Army,[9] Lieutenant General Fusataro Teshima, with headquarters at Manokwari on the Vogelkop Peninsula, was given in December a new infantry division from China and the 7th Air Division from Ambon. His zone of responsibility was extended to Wewak in March 1944, when two more divisions were ordered in from China. The Eighteenth Army, Lieutenant General Hatazo Adachi, was already in eastern New Guinea. On 25 March Adachi was ordered by Teshima to withdraw his army – three badly battered infantry divisions [10] – overland and to concentrate on Hollandia. But Adachi stalled, for he was convinced that the next Allied landing would take place at Hansa Bay. He did not know that the Joint Chiefs of Staff in faraway Washington had decided to bypass that position. Naturally, General MacArthur did all he could to confirm Adachi's conviction. During March and early April 1944, Wewak was heavily bombed by General Kenney's Allied air forces with a pattern suggesting preliminaries to a landing. On the night of 18–19 March, and again on 10 April, destroyers *Daly, Hutchins, Beale, Mullany* and *Ammen* made bombardment sweeps off Wewak and, covered by V Army Air Force fighters, off Hansa Bay and the nearby coast.[11] Motor torpedo boats patrolled actively at night; dummy parachutists dropped near Wewak; submarines left empty life rafts to drift ashore, suggesting the presence of reconnaissance parties.

[9] Not to be confused with the Second Area Army, General Korechika Anami, with headquarters at Davao, who was over Teshima.
[10] Exact figures are unobtainable, even in Tokyo. Estimates varied from 45,000 by GHQ to about 75,000 from scattered Japanese sources.
[11] CTG 74.5 and 75.5 (Capt. McManes) Action Reports.

General Anami in Davao, who was senior to both Teshima and Adachi, was disturbed at the latter's reluctance to pull up stakes and hike westward. He sent his chief of staff to Wewak on 12 April to act as expediter. In consequence of this visit, on 22 April, when the Allies landed at Aitape and Hollandia, two regiments of the Eighteenth Army were already on their way thither by jungle trail.

The Japanese naval force in New Guinea had the dignified name of Ninth Fleet, with Vice Admiral Yoshikazu Endo as commander. But it was little more than a token force of subchasers, minelayers and barges, with about 300 ground troops. Combined Fleet, preparing for the big decisive naval battle, had no intention of intervening in this area.

Japanese air power in Dutch New Guinea was fairly strong in the early part of 1944, but it did not stay so after 30 March when General Kenney's V Army Air Force began daylight raids on the Hollandia airfields. Kenney's fliers caught the Japanese aircraft parked wing to wing, and in short order wiped them out. The 6th Air Division general was relieved in disgrace.

The senior Japanese ground commander at Hollandia was Major General Kitazano, who had arrived from Wewak only ten days before the landings. What happened to him thereafter is unknown; but on 22 April General Teshima of the Second Army ordered General Inada of the 6th Air Division to assume the ground forces command.

This confused and confusing reorganization within Japanese commands, and the attempted rapid redeployment of troops and aircraft, may explain why nobody had any plans for the defense of Hollandia. But the Japanese were not much good at defensive planning anyway, often being content to issue merely exhortative commands to "annihilate" the enemy on the beach. In any case, the enemy situation gave the "Reckless" Task Force a far easier assault than any Allied commander had imagined that it could be — one vastly easier than the taking of the Marianas a few months later.

CHAPTER VI

The Hollandia Operation[1]

21 April–6 June 1944

(Operations "Reckless" and "Persecution")

1. Aitape, 22–27 April

FROM the naval point of view, MacArthur's triple-pronged leap into central New Guinea was a single operation, and the largest of the war in the Southwest Pacific.[2] Admiral Barbey was in overall command of the whole thing, excepting the fast carrier strikes that we have already described in Chapter III; either Barbey or one of his deputies exercised local command at each beachhead until the landing force commander established headquarters ashore. The main divisions were the Western Attack Group for Tanahmerah Bay, the Central Attack Group for Humboldt Bay, and the Eastern Attack Group for Aitape.

For security against air attack, Barbey laid out a circuitous route for the expeditionary force, which would require four or five days to accomplish. The LCIs left the staging areas a day ahead of the transports and spent a night in Seeadler Harbor to afford the troops a chance to stretch their legs ashore. April 20, at a point 50 miles northwest of Seeadler, at 0700, rendezvous was made by all the assault forces including Admiral Ragsdale's eight escort carriers

[1] CTF 77 (Rear Adm. Barbey) Action Report, War Diary and Op Plan 3–44; CTF 78 Action Report, and those of Rear Adm. Fechteler for Humboldt Bay, and Capt. Noble for Aitape; Gen. Krueger "Report of the Hollandia Operation"; R. R. Smith *The Approach to the Philippines;* "Amphibian Engineer Operations"; Heavey *Down Ramp;* Eichelberger *Our Jungle Road to Tokyo.*

[2] Comprising 215 vessels, including beaching craft. See Appendix I for complete task organization.

with their screen of 17 destroyers. Their function was to provide anti-submarine and combat air patrol for TF 77 during the balance of its outward passage, and close air support for the landings at Aitape.

Captain Noble's Eastern Attack Group broke off from the main convoy in the evening of 21 April and, with the escort carriers, headed for Aitape. Two fast destroyer minesweepers, *Hamilton* and *Perry*, went ahead to sweep the transport area, arriving on schedule at 0500 D-day, 22 April. H-hour was set for 0645.

The 1200-yard long landing beach at Aitape, designated Blue, lay in front of a village called Korako, and barely a mile from the Tadji airstrip. Here a group of islands two to four miles off shore forms a partially protected roadstead. These islands, the long stretch of featureless coast on each side of Beach Blue, and the town of Aitape might have been bristling with concealed enemy guns for aught Captain Noble knew; and the need of covering a long shoreline and four islands in one 30-minute bombardment by six destroyers gave his planners a severe headache. Every vessel that had a 3-inch gun or better was drafted to help. Destroyer transports had to double as bombardment ships as soon as their landing craft were away; even the converted Liberty ship *Etamin* had four assigned targets for her two guns, one 5-inch and one 3-inch.

At 0630 naval gunfire was lifted for ten minutes while planes from the escort carriers bombed and strafed the beach area.[3] This proved to be more than sufficient. Allied Intelligence had over-estimated enemy strength at Aitape as 3500 Japanese, including 1500 combat troops. A check-up after the landing showed that in the entire area on D-day there were about 1000 men, of whom only 240 were combat troops, the rest were service troops who took off into the bush when the shells began to fall.

Under cover of bombardment, landing craft of the assault waves assembled near control vessel *SC–648*, 5000 yards off shore. The starter, whose word they awaited for leaving the line of departure, was that well-known character "Red" (Captain John W.) Jamison,

[3] CTG 77.3 (Capt. Noble) Action Report.

who had won his web-feet off Fedhala in the autumn of 1942.[4] As Commander Special Service Group, he was control officer for directing landings and unloading and Captain Noble's deputy, responsible for everything after the landing craft left the ships. This was a flexible and simpler system of controlling the landings than the elaborate scheme worked out by Admiral Turner, which we shall describe when we reach the landings at Saipan. But it might not have withstood a situation where tough opposition was encountered at the beachhead.

The Aitape landing was made in nine waves on a two-battalion front. Moderate surf caused several landing craft to broach, but scattered rifle fire was the only enemy opposition encountered. The troops found breakfasts still cooking and bunks in disorder, left by the fleeing enemy. By nightfall the principal objective of the Persecution Task Force had been secured at a cost of two killed and thirteen wounded.

Shortly after noon on D-day, No. 62 Works Wing of the Royal Australian Air Force was already ashore, figuring out how to rehabilitate the Tadji airstrip. The Aussies worked around the clock for nearly 48 hours, when the strip was ready to receive 25 P-40s of No. 78 Wing, R.A.A.F. At the same time, United States Army Engineer Aviation Battalions 872 and 875 started laying out and building a bomber strip, but that was not ready for use until 15 June.[5]

The second echelon, carrying the 127th Regiment, 32nd Division, arrived 23 April. Unloading proceeded with only minor accidents to overloaded and bogged-down vehicles. A regiment of the 3rd Engineer Special Brigade provided the shore party, assisted by a small naval beach party. Lack of enemy opposition resulted in so few calls for air support that on the afternoon of 23 April half the escort carriers were sent to Manus for fuel and provisions, and at sunset next day the rest were released and proceeded to Hollandia to take over close air support from the fast carriers. The only Japanese air reaction occurred shortly before midnight 27 April, when three planes came in undetected at low altitude and made a torpedo hit on *Etamin*, starting several fires and explosions. The damage control party got these in hand, but *Etamin* with almost half her

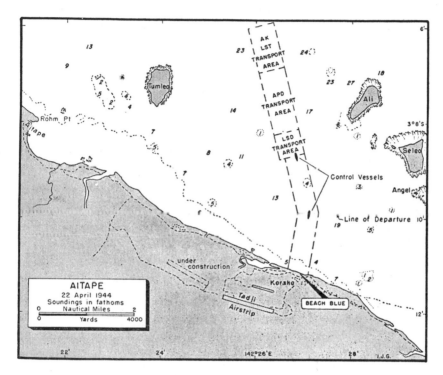

cargo still on board had to be towed to Finschhafen. This was the only serious damage suffered by any naval vessel during the entire Hollandia operation.

2. *Battle of the Driniumor River, 1 June—10 August* [6]

Although out of place chronologically, we must here describe briefly a campaign that inevitably followed the Allied landing at Aitape.

[6] *The Approach to the Philippines* chaps. vi–viii; War Diaries of PT Squadrons involved; Cdr. R. J. Bulkley's PT History pp. 316–26; CTF 74 Action Report.

Even as Persecution Task Force was consolidating positions around Aitape, General Doe and the 163rd RCT were tagged for another landing at Wakde, 120 miles west of Hollandia. They were relieved by the 32nd Division, whose commander, Major General William H. Gill USA, arrived 4 May. He organized a defense perimeter around the airfields, and for two months the only military activities were patrols to find out whether General Adachi, commanding the Eighteenth Army at Wewak, 90 miles east of Aitape, was up to anything.

He was. This Japanese general had a mind of his own. When ordered, on 2 May, to move by jungle trail back of Aitape and Hollandia to western New Guinea, Adachi came up with what he thought was a better plan, to attack General Gill's forces at Aitape; and his superiors accepted it. He hoped to launch his attack on 10 June, but weather, Allied ground patrols, aircraft and motor torpedo boats patrolling the coast — factors which reduced the Eighteenth Army to hand-carrying its supplies — delayed him a full month. Even so, he was able to muster some 20,000 troops for an attack, launched on the night of 10 July, against Allied positions along the Driniumor River. And that river lies only 18 miles east of Aitape.

Allied Intelligence had kept abreast of Adachi's preparations. Patrols operating eastward along the coast and across the Driniumor River maintained contact with advance elements of the Japanese. By the end of May, General Krueger was convinced that an attack was coming. The Supreme Commander offered him a reinforcing division, but it was not until 21 June, when captured documents revealed Adachi's detailed plans, that the 43rd Infantry Division was ordered up to Aitape, from New Zealand, and the 112th Cavalry and 124th Infantry Regiments were sent in from eastern New Guinea.

Persecution Task Force, now built up to almost three-division strength, rated corps status; and Major General Charles P. Hall USA moved in with XI Corps staff and assumed command at Aitape on 28 June. In the meantime, a line of resistance was set up along the Driniumor River. Intelligence reports indicated that at least one Japanese division had been moved forward from Wewak to within five miles of the stream, but Allied patrols could find no evidence of so large a troop concentration. After a reconnaissance in force on 10 July also discovered nothing, General Hall at 2330 so informed Alamo Headquarters. Fifteen minutes later he was involved in the biggest and bitterest jungle battle in New Guinea since the Buna-Gona campaign of November–December 1942.

At 2345 Japanese light artillery opened up on Allied positions along the river, and ten minutes later Japanese troops opened a series of screaming attacks. Lieutenant Colonel Edward Block USA, commanding the 3rd Battalion 127th Infantry, had fortunately alerted his battalion to expect this assault, and the first attacks were repulsed with heavy loss. But during the night the Japanese succeeded in breaching a 1300-yard gap in the Allied lines. From that time for a full month there followed an intricate pattern of give-and-take tactical moves and actions at battalion and even company levels in the thick jungle between the coast and the foothills of the Torricelli Mountains, six miles inland. Adachi, though suffering heavy casualties, pressed his attack, throwing two divisions into the battle. The heaviest weight of defense and counterattack fell on General Gill's 32nd Division, which had also taken the brunt of the fighting at Buna. The 112th Cavalry and 124th Infantry Regiments, and the 169th Infantry of the 43rd Division, also suffered heavily.

Allied naval forces also had a part in this action. PT boats under Lieutenant Commander Robert Leeson USNR operated along the coast between Aitape and Wewak and, together with Allied aircraft, prevented the Japanese from supplying their troops by barge. They also broke up troop concentrations along the coastal road and trails. On 10 July Admiral Kinkaid ordered Commodore John Collins RAN over from Seeadler Harbor to cover the PTs, which were being harassed by shore batteries. He arrived 13 July with H.M.A.S. *Australia, Shropshire, Arunta,* and *Warramunga,* and

U.S. destroyers *Ammen* and *Bache*. Meanwhile the developing Battle of the Driniumor broadened his mission to supporting the troops. In his conference with General Hall and the air and PT commanders it was decided that the Navy could best aid by interdicting Japanese truck traffic behind the lines in the direction of Wewak. From 14 to 24 July, when Commodore Collins's task force was withdrawn to cover Sansapor, the cruisers and destroyers ranged the coast, bombarding targets, some of them three or four miles inland, assisted during daylight by R.A.A.F. spotting planes from Aitape. Destroyers worked with PT boats at night searching for barges and trucks as far east as Karawop, 14 miles northwest of Wewak. There was little or no return fire and results are difficult to assess, as many of the targets were in deep jungle; but prisoners and observers alike spoke highly of the accuracy of the bombardment. General Krueger expressed his deep appreciation for the naval assistance.[7]

Exhaustion of ammunition and supplies of all kinds, brought about by the interdiction of his supply lines and the unremitting pressure by General Hall's corps, forced Adachi back from the Driniumor on 9 August. He had sacrificed about half of the 20,000 troops thrown into this futile attempt to recapture Aitape but it had cost the United States Army 400 killed, and about 2600 wounded, to thwart his effort.

3. *Tanahmerah Bay, 22 April–6 June*

Plans for the Tanahmerah Bay part of Operation "Reckless" had to be revised radically on the spot, because most Allied information about the hinterland was wrong. A prewar Dutch colonizing project in that area had failed, and by 1941 all the colonists had abandoned it; but there was supposed to be an excellent trail, graded for road development, between Depapré village at the head of Tanahmerah Bay and Lake Sentani. Unfortunately this

[7] Commo. Collins "TF 74 Diary of Proceedings 11–25 July 1944."

trail had never progressed beyond the mind of some Dutch engineer.[8] United States submarine *Dace* (Commander B. D. Claggett) landed an Australian scouting party, led by Lieutenant G. C. Harris RAN, near Tanahmerah Bay on 23 March in the hope of obtaining firsthand information on the terrain and its defenses. The local natives appeared to be friendly but gave away the scouts' presence to nearby Japanese, who attacked the party while it was trying to make its way inland, killed four members including the lieutenant, and forced the others to hide out in the jungle until after the landings.[9]

From aërial photography two landing beaches were selected for Tanahmerah Bay. Red 2 on the eastern side of the bay was 800 yards long with flat land (hopefully supposed to be dry) extending 1500 yards inland; Red 1 lay at the head of Depapré Inlet, a narrow cove fringed with coral and dominated by hills. Landing craft could beach here only at high tide (the range was three feet) because a coral reef blocked the inlet. There was thought to be a road connecting the beaches, besides the hypothetical road to Lake Sentani, supposed to be passable for wheeled vehicles and capable of rapid improvement. Unfortunately, because the Japanese defenses were supposed to be concentrated at Humboldt Bay, our operation plan called for the main thrust from the coast to the lake to be made here by General Irving's heavily reinforced 24th Division. General Eichelberger planned to set up headquarters and land most of his service troops and reinforcements on Tanahmerah Bay. After tactical plans had been completed, a new set of aërial photographs revealed the error in some of these terrain assumptions; but General Krueger ruled that it was too late to change.[10]

---

[8] Allied Geographic Section SWPA *Terrain Study No. 61,* p. 33.

[9] General Eichelberger in *Our Jungle Road to Tokyo* pp. 130–34, describing this incident in detail, states that Lt. Harris and part of his group landed first to reconnoiter; on being discovered by natives, he flashed a prearranged signal to *Dace* not to land the rest of the party and to send in for him; but the signal was misinterpreted and the rest of Harris's party went in by rubber boat. Cdr. Claggett, writing to Capt. Anderson 25 Sept. 1952, said that this misinterpretation was news to him; he received the signal to land the balance of the party, and did so. After waiting two days without word from Harris's party, *Dace* returned to Manus with little information.   [10] General Krueger Report p. 20.

So the mistaken plan still held when Admiral Barbey's Western Attack Group, after an approach in the dark of the moon over calm, unruffled seas, sighted the Cyclops Mountains rising up at dawn, 22 April. By 0500 the ships began to ease into their assigned positions. At 0600, just as day was breaking, Rear Admiral Crutch-

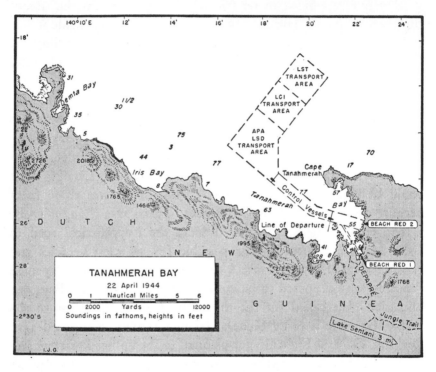

ley's Australian gunfire force, screened by six United States destroyers, began bombarding the Red beaches and the dominating terrain. Bombardment completed at 0645 without provoking enemy reaction; Crutchley ranged the coast and pulverized Japanese barges and supply dumps in Demta Bay.

By the time the naval bombardment ended, Admiral Barbey had decided that there were no Japanese defenders on Tanahmerah Bay; and that was correct. Strikes by TF 58 planes were canceled, but a closely timed bombing run to explode possible beach mines was carried out.

Under cover of the bombardment, Captain Paul A. Stevens's transport group (*Henry T. Allen, Carter Hall*, H.M.A.S. *Kanimbla* and *Manoora*) lowered the Army Engineers' boats. Captain Stevens observed that "Considering the limited experience in working with transports, the ESB crews handled their boats in a commendable manner." The main landing was made by two regiments of the 24th Division on a two-battalion front, in seven waves. One hour after the first had landed, seven LSTs beached dry-ramp. Everything went smoothly. Scattered rifle and machine-gun fire from the flanks, soon silenced by alert destroyers, was the only resistance encountered.

Beach Red 2 proved to be excellent for LSTs but a trap for foot soldiers and engineers, since only 30 yards behind it lay an oozy swamp, impassable even on foot. There simply was no way to get men or vehicles off this beach except by the way they had come; they might as well have landed at the base of an unscalable cliff. The confidently expected road to Red 1 did not exist, and after the engineers had worked a day and a half to build a road they had to admit that it couldn't be done in less than eight days, even though the distance between the beaches was only a couple of miles. So, by the time the LSTs began to disgorge vehicles, tanks, antiaircraft weapons and 155-mm guns, the beach became so congested that most of the vehicles had to be left on board and their loads manhandled ashore. Obviously there would be no room for General Eichelberger's headquarters or for the reserve and service troops yet to arrive.

General Irving, who landed at 0930 to take command ashore, quickly realized that a prompt and radical change of plan must be made. The smaller landing at Beach Red 1, where an infantry battalion was set ashore by LVTs and LCMs, worked out successfully and afforded some chance to relieve the pressure on Red 2; but this beach was only a hundred yards long and the approaches in Depapré Inlet, foul with coral heads and reefs, needed work by engineers before they could be used by beaching craft. Landing craft could cross the reef inside the inlet for about an hour at high water, and only two LCMs could beach at once; LSTs could not even enter. But Red 1 was exploited to the limit, amphtracs worked all day shuttling troops and supplies from landing craft lying-to outside.

The troops at Beach Red 1 met no opposition when landing. In the maze of trails and crisscrossing tracks behind Beach Red 1, they spent an hour trying to find the "road" to Lake Sentani. It proved to be only a narrow, winding trail climbing the hills in a series of hairpin turns, and passable only by foot. By nightfall D-day, patrols had penetrated eight miles inland, meeting only occasional rifle fire, but they were getting close to positions where a large enemy concentration was reported.

General Irving decided to transfer troops from Red 2, where they were completely useless, to Red 1 by ESB boats. During the day two battalions were thus shifted across the bay, and at 1730 the Marine tank company, too, was transferred. But the tanks never got off the beach at Red 1, and were finally evacuated on 4 May and returned to the parent organization.

Embarked in one of the small minesweepers of the Special Service Group was a naval demolition party which went to work on the coral in Depapré Inlet and blasted a channel to a village near the mouth so that landing craft could beach there. Then they started blasting out a boat channel to Red 1. By 30 April it was 500 feet long and 60 feet wide, with 14 feet of water. Only then could the LVT-shuttle across the reef be suspended and LSTs enter.

General MacArthur, embarked in cruiser *Nashville*, arrived at Tanahmerah Bay at 1320 on D-Day. General Krueger, who had been watching the show from destroyer *Wilkes*, went on board, together with General Eichelberger and Admiral Barbey; and at 1500 this distinguished party landed on Red 2. General Irving gave them a spot account of progress and problems, and they had a firsthand view of the unloading snarl. After an hour's inspection, General MacArthur re-embarked in *Nashville* and left Tanahmerah Bay to look in on the situation at Aitape.

During the forenoon of 23 April it became obvious that the main landing for Operation "Reckless" could not continue at Tanahmerah Bay. Red 1 simply could not handle the huge quantity of vehicles, equipment and supplies that were ready to be unloaded. To complicate matters further, a cargo vessel, two transports and seven LSTs were due to arrive next day, full of men, vehicles and supplies. Fortunately the 41st Division was making better progress at Humboldt Bay than had been expected, and was moving rapidly toward Lake Sentani. About noon on the 23rd, at a conference between General Eichelberger and Admiral Barbey, it was decided to shift the main effort to Humboldt Bay. General Irving, with the two regiments and other elements already ashore, would remain at Tanahmerah and continue the drive up the narrow jungle trail toward the airfields.

Weather and terrain, far more than the Japanese, blocked this advance. The troops were strung out in single file, meeting small groups of Japanese who conducted a skillful delaying action for the first day or two. Ammunition and supplies had to be carried on men's backs, for no vehicle of any kind could negotiate the trail. Air drops of supplies had to be canceled because of heavy rain. Nevertheless, the van of this column reached the westernmost airfield at Sentani on 26 April, and made junction with elements of the 41st Division which had come up from Humboldt Bay. The double envelopment was complete. But it took three months for engineers to complete a vehicular road from Depapré Inlet to Lake Sentani.

4. *Humboldt Bay, 22 April–6 June*

The general pattern of the landings in Humboldt Bay was similar to those at Aitape and Tanahmerah. Here the terrain limitations were known and appreciated well in advance. Near Hollandia Village, on the delta of a small river that empties into the northern arm of the bay, the ground rises sharply from a shoreline fringed with coral, and not provided with suitable landing beaches. But there is a narrow sand beach (White 1)—about 700 yards long, with clear approaches, some two and a half miles south of the village—which looked barely possible. Only a 70-yard depth of dry land separated it from a swamp, and the only exit lay around

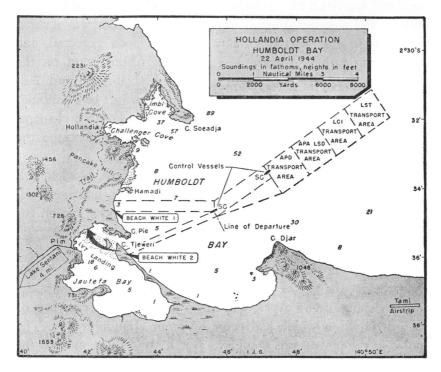

the base of Pancake Hill, a flat-topped eminence covered with kunai grass, where the Japanese had placed antiaircraft batteries.

About a mile south of Beach White 1, Cape Pie, with a 150-foot hill on it, forms the northern side of the narrow entrance to Jautefa Bay. On the other side of this entrance is a long, feature-less sandspit named Cape Tjeweri, upon which the only other possible beach within Humboldt Bay was located. Designated Beach White 2, its one exit lay along the sandspit in the opposite direction from Lake Sentani.

Jautefa Bay is entered by a narrow, winding channel with less than ten feet of water, which could accommodate only small landing craft; but at a place called Pim within this bay was a small jetty at the end of a road built by the Japanese, which led over a hill to Lake Sentani. This was the route by which the enemy supplied his airfields from the sea, when he could use the sea. Since Pim could be approached only by water, or by a native trail from Hollandia, its capture seemed very important to General Fuller, and his assault plans were so drafted as to make best use of this difficult and unsatisfactory terrain. The main landing would have to be made on Beach White 1 as the only place where LSTs could beach. One battalion would land on the southern beach (White 2), using amphtracs and dukws, then cross Cape Tjeweri, splash through Jautefa Bay, and make a final landing near an open slope covered with kunai grass northwest of Pim.

Admiral Fechteler's task group peeled off from Admiral Barbey's around midnight 21 April and shaped a course for Humboldt Bay, which it reached on schedule at 0500 April 22. While the transports lowered boats, Admiral Berkey's six destroyers and three light cruisers eased into positions to deliver prelanding bombardment, while control craft took their assigned stance to mark boat lanes and line of departure 6000 yards off Beach White 1.

It was still dark under the overcast as these preparations went on, since sunrise came at 0634 and twilight near the Equator lasts only about twenty minutes. A gentle northeast breeze hardly ruffled the sea, smooth as a lake except for a slight ground swell. From the inner control vessel, *SC–743* with Captain Bern Anderson embarked, thousand-foot-high Cape Djar rose steep two miles on the port quarter; the lower Cape Soeadja, three miles on the starboard beam, took shape as day broke. The scene might have been completely peaceful had not fires along the shore reminded the observer that TF 58 had done business there the day before and that grim events might be unrolling. There was no time to relax and watch a beautiful dawn break over a tropical harbor.

Promptly at 0600 the three cruisers opened fire with their main and secondary batteries on targets in Hollandia, along Beach

White 1, and on the headlands behind the entrance capes. After half an hour the destroyers, closer in shore, took over for 15 minutes and continued firing on the far flanks even after H-hour, 0700; the beach itself was reserved for air strikes from the fast carrier planes. Cruisers and destroyers together fired 1600 rounds of 6-inch and 3700 rounds of 5-inch shell before H-hour. The air strikes were handled by Support Air Controller (Colonel William O. Eareckson USA) who was with Admiral Fechteler in destroyer *Reid*. Bombing and strafing runs were made on targets that dominated both beaches, and two flights of Avengers laid anti-mine and anti-personnel bomb patterns by intervalometer over Beach White 1. During the bombardment destroyer-minesweepers *Long* and *Hogan* entered the bay and made an exploratory sweep. No mines were found but, since Bill Fechteler believed in all the preliminary bombardment he could get, *Long* and *Hogan* turned-to and sprayed the beaches with their 3-inch and 20-mm guns. The bombardment drew no reply, and the enemy attempted no interference with landing preparations.

The main landing was made in eight waves on Beach White 1, by the 162nd Infantry 41st Division, preceded by two LCIs which launched rockets at Pancake Hill to knock out the antiaircraft guns. One infantry company landed on White 2 to secure Cape Tjeweri, over which 18 LVTs, carrying elements of the 186th Infantry Regiment, would later roll in order to cross Jautefa Bay and place their passengers on the grassy slope northeast of Pim.

Japanese on the spot were completely surprised. Warm food and tea being prepared for breakfast in a number of coconut-log and earth dugouts behind Beach White 1 indicated that its defenders had fled when the naval bombardment began, a fact later confirmed by prisoners of war. Only an occasional rifleshot or machine-gun burst greeted the assault. "The headlong flight of the enemy at the appearance of the Aitape and Hollandia Task Forces," observed General Krueger, "was an event unparalleled in the history of our campaign against the Japanese. Not only did the majority flee without a show of resistance, but those who remained to fight failed to offer any type of resistance we have come to regard as characteristic of the Japanese." Moreover, a relatively high percentage of Japanese surrendered. No fewer than 611 were captured at Hollandia, and 98 at Aitape. On one occasion, sixteen soldiers waited alongside the road for an Allied truck to pass, stepped out before its headlights, and gave themselves up to the driver. Incidents like that were exceedingly rare in the Pacific war.[11]

Within an hour of the landing Pancake Hill was occupied by American infantrymen, who found there three 75-mm antiaircraft guns, one of which had survived the bombardment without a scratch. General Fuller assumed command ashore about 0900; and at 1000 General MacArthur landed from *Nashville* on Beach White 1 for a close look at the operation.

By midafternoon troops had reached all D-day objectives and were in possession of the hill dominating Hollandia. The infantry company which landed on White 2 stayed there to guard against counterattack, and at 0715 LVTs carried two companies across cape and bay to the landing place near Pim. By nightfall the heights above Pim had been taken and liaison had been effected along the trail to Hollandia with troops from White 1. All at a cost of six men killed and 16 wounded.

Beach White 1 happened to be the center of a major Japanese supply dump. Piles of bombs, ammunition, provisions and supplies — even airplane engines, soon wrecked by souvenir hunters — were neatly stacked along the beach. The LSTs could beach dry-ramp or nearly so, but the usable land between beach and swamp was narrow and already almost filled with Japanese matériel. Before anyone could use the only exit, which led into high ground behind Pancake Hill, the engineers had to bulldoze a roadway and begin clearing dispersal and dump areas. Within a few hours the beach was heavily congested. An engineer aviation battalion, landing

[11] Gen. Krueger Report p. 40. It would be interesting to learn whether the preliminary air bombing had taken the fight out of the Japanese, or was their morale low for other reasons? Certainly the short naval bombardment cannot take all the credit.

with its equipment in the afternoon of D-day, not only added to the snarl of vehicles in the exit lane but compounded the problems of the shore party by churning up the sandy track leading off the beach so that it could be used only with great difficulty. Nevertheless, by nightfall D-day *Westralia* and seven LSTs had been unloaded on Beach White 1, and some 4200 tons of ammunition, drummed fuel, rations and other supplies were stacked up between and around the Japanese matériel already there. More than 300 vehicles also had been put ashore.

After it became clear that the initial landings were progressing smoothly, Admiral Fechtler's rocket-equipped LCIs started cruising around the bay looking for targets. Late in the afternoon Commander Dwight H. Day, in charge of the rocket group, spotted two turbaned individuals standing in the open near a burning Japanese dump and gesturing as if they had something to communicate. Beaching one of the LCIs, he learned that these men belonged to a group of about 120 Sikhs captured at Singapore who had been brought to Hollandia as laborers. At the beginning of the naval bombardment they had been told by their Japanese masters to take to the hills and await the repulse of the Americans. Next day the entire party of Sikhs came down to the same spot and were evacuated for eventual return to India. About 125 nuns and missionaries of several nationalities also were rescued at Hollandia.

By the close of 23 April the 186th Infantry had reached a point about halfway to Lake Sentani, while the 162nd Infantry had taken Hollandia and fanned out into the high ground behind and beyond, mopping up scattered enemy parties. Aircraft from TF 58 stood by to render aërial support, but had few calls as targets were exceedingly scarce. No organized resistance developed anywhere ashore.

A fire in a Japanese dump near the north end of Beach White 1, started by Allied air bombers before D-day, was indirectly the cause of the only contretemps in the Humboldt Bay landings. The busy shore party did little or nothing to put it out. An effort was made by the Navy beachmaster to get a YMS near enough to use her fire hose, but she could not reach it and the fire continued to burn throughout 23 April and into the night. At 2045 a single Japanese plane, using this fire as a point of aim, dropped a stick of bombs into the area which started several more fires. The shore party tried to check them by building a firebreak, but a large Japanese ammunition dump exploded and sent burning bombs soaring hundreds of feet into the air with a tremendous pyrotechnic display which amazed and alarmed the sailors lying off shore. The fire then spread quickly all along the beach, burning fiercely through the night with numerous explosions which sent out shock waves for miles. A number of ESB boats bravely worked into the beach through falling debris and flying shrapnel to evacuate troops; without their prompt and generous action the casualties of 24 killed and 100 wounded would have been much higher. Over 60 per cent of all rations and ammunition that had been landed on 22–23 April — twelve full LST loads — was destroyed. Fires burned and explosions erupted on White 1 until 27 April, when the engineers returned to clean up and rebuild.

All this made 24 April a hectic day in Humboldt Bay. Five LSTs arrived on schedule with men, supplies and equipment; two APAs and seven LSTs diverted from Tanahmerah Bay, one with General Eichelberger's headquarters, also arrived. And all twelve LSTs were scheduled to leave the same day in order to pick up more loads. Early next morning at high tide, eleven LSTs were driven onto White 2 full speed, but had to drop ramps in three to four feet of water. By nightfall, after extreme efforts by the shore party, all but two were completely unloaded. Since the dry ground behind White 2 was even narrower than on White 1, before long it too was congested with vehicles and supplies. Eventually the whole beach was cleared by ESB boats shuttling matériel into Jautefa Bay, and before another echelon arrived at Humboldt Bay, White 1 was again usable.

Task Force 58 had now completed its assignment. Admiral Mitscher sent a representative by air so to report to Admiral Barbey, and to announce his impending return to the Fifth Fleet. General Eichelberger has stated that he wished to ask higher authority for a TF 58 strike on a concentration of Japanese planes at Manokwari on the western side of Geelvink Bay; that Admiral Fechteler and Mitscher's representative backed him up but Admiral Barbey refused to go along; and that the same Japanese planes "certainly raised hell with us later at Biak." [12] Manokwari, however, was already being worked over by B–24s flying from Darwin, and Admiral Barbey's attitude was based on the Mac-Arthur-Nimitz agreement that Task Force 58 must be released a fixed number of hours after the landings in order to meet future commitments in the Central Pacific. [13] Actually there were few if any Japanese planes then at Manokwari, because as soon as TF 58 appeared off Hollandia the Japanese began pulling out to Sorong and beyond, well out of Mitscher's long reach. The planes that "raised hell with us at Biak" were staged in much later.

In the meantime the troops had been making steady progress toward the airfields. On 24 April the 186th Infantry was placed on half rations and ordered to conserve ammunition as a result of the beach fires, but by noon it had reached the shores of Lake Sentani. Here, Japanese troops were encountered. The Engineer Special Brigade met this situation by moving amphtracs over the road from Jautefa Bay to the lake, where on 25 April they were used to carry troops by water around enemy positions. The nearest airfield, Cyclops, was taken in the morning of 26 April, and by nightfall Sentani Field was in the bag and contact had been established with the 24th Division, which had already moved into the third field, Hollandia.

On 30 April, twelve LCTs arrived at Humboldt Bay in tow of LSTs. By this time the Army's supply situation at Lake Sentani was serious, owing to the beach fire and to a temporary breakdown of transportation over the single road from Jautefa Bay. The

[12] *Our Jungle Road to Tokyo* p. 118.
[13] Letter to Capt. Anderson, 8 Aug. 1952.

Air Force had flown in some supplies from the rear area, but far from enough; and it wanted a fighter strip built as soon as possible.

Near the coast at Tami, about four miles east of Cape Djar, there was a partially built Japanese strip which had not figured in the plans. At a conference between the operations officers of Generals Eichelberger and Kenney and Captain Anderson on the morning of 30 April, it was arranged to use the recently arrived LCTs to lift an aviation engineer battalion from Beach White 1 to the beach off Tami. The movement started immediately. Early that evening word reached us that these LCTs were being fired upon by American troops at Tami, and the lift was accordingly suspended until daylight; but next day this gunfire was found to have come from Japanese who had filtered through. It became necessary to move in a battalion of infantry to protect the beaching point. Tami airstrip was ready 3 May for transport aircraft, which began shuttling supplies, hauled by ESB boats from Humboldt Bay to Tami beach, up to Lake Sentani. Even with this assistance the 186th Infantry had to subsist for three or four days principally on Japanese rice and canned fish.

Capture of the three airfields at Lake Sentani ended the assault phase of the land campaign, but there remained a great deal of mopping-up to be done before Hollandia and the airfields could be securely held. This phase lasted until 6 June, when Army service forces assumed responsibility for the entire area and the operation was officially declared closed. It cost United States forces 152 killed and missing and 1057 wounded. Over 600 Japanese were captured and 3300 killed up to 6 June.

General Krueger made a good conclusion to the Hollandia operation in his report: —

The complete success realized in the Hollandia–Aitape operation clearly proved the soundness of the decision to carry out a scheme of maneuver so patently daring. The Japanese, completely confident in the strength of their base at Wewak, failed utterly to organize their defenses at Hollandia and Aitape against coördinated attacks.

5. *Japanese Reaction and Retreat, 22 April–17 May*

Surprise at Hollandia was complete and overwhelming. Admiral Endo's captured orderly conveyed the spirit of the first Japanese reaction in saying, "When the American bombardment and attack came, the Admiral sat in his chair all morning without saying a word and just looked at the sea." [14] Ninety per cent of General Inada's ground forces were service troops who fled into the hills when the first naval shells began to fall; his only good troops were deployed along the Depapré–Lake Sentani trail, and they were too few to stop the 24th Division.

When word of the landings reached the Japanese army commander at Manokwari, he wished to order two regiments, then stationed at Wakde-Sarmi, to march overland to the relief of Hollandia. His superior officer at Davao vetoed the plan but permitted two battalions of infantry and one of field artillery, which had already started 24 April, to continue. The head of this column had reached a point only halfway to Hollandia on 17 May when Allied landings near Wakde threatened its base. The column was promptly recalled to Sarmi, and thus ended the only effort to reinforce Hollandia by land. [15]

General Inada, having given up hope on D-day, decided to assemble his forces at a village about 15 miles west of Lake Sentani and retire to Wakde-Sarmi overland. The first of nine or ten echelons left this village about 26 April, and the last was on its way by 9 May. About 7200 troops started on this overland trek. Remnants of the first echelon were approaching Sarmi on 17 May when they were greeted by the Allied landings nearby. Wounds, disease and starvation took such a terrific toll of the retreating columns that a bare 14 per cent of the men survived. Of almost 11,000 Japanese troops in and about Hollandia on 22 April, 3300 were killed by Allied forces, 600 were captured and not more than a

---

[14] Eichelberger *Jungle Road* p. 115.
[15] *The Approach to the Philippines* pp. 98–100.

A Lake Sentani field after air strikes, 21 April

Coast between Humboldt and Tanahmerah Bays, 22 April
The plane is a carrier-based SBD

Hollandia and Sansapor

Assault troops landing from LCIs at Sansapor, 30 July

LSTs unloading at Beach Red 2, Tanahmerah Bay, 21 April

Hollandia and Sansapor

thousand reached Sarmi. The rest doubtless sought individual hide-outs in the jungle and most of these too perished miserably.

The 300 naval ratings of the Ninth Fleet in and around Hollandia were also annihilated. During the afternoon of 22 April Admiral Endo began to shift them and his headquarters to Lake Sentani. The last word received at Tokyo from the Ninth Fleet was a brief message at 1415 next day, "The enemy is approaching our HQ." [16] The Admiral probably died by his own hand. Survivors either joined the trek to Sarmi or wandered about in the hills until starvation and disease cut them down. The Ninth Fleet was de-activated and stricken from the rolls of the Japanese Navy on 10 July 1944.[17]

The Fourth Air Army, almost wiped out in the pre-D-day strikes in the Lake Sentani fields, could do nothing. The Japanese based their hopes of delaying the Allied advance on their Navy's 23rd Air Flotilla. This outfit concentrated on building bases in western New Guinea; and by April had airfields operational at Wakde, Biak, Babo in the bird's mouth, and Sorong in the bird's eye. But its total air strength was a 36-plane fighter squadron with 12 reserves, and a 21-plane reconnaissance squadron.

The few and futile attempts of the 23rd Air Flotilla to harass Allied naval forces around Hollandia have already been mentioned in Chapter III. Captain Kamoto, who was on the flotilla staff during this period, explained its lack of activity by the few planes available, the problem of aircraft maintenance, and a generally low quality of men and matériel. He had plenty of fuel, however, for supplies of aviation gasoline had been accumulated for a much larger number of planes than could actually be collected.

About mid-April, when headquarters of this flotilla were shifted to Sorong, Imperial Headquarters, correctly guessing that Biak and the Vogelkop would soon be MacArthur's objectives, made special efforts to reinforce that part of New Guinea. The flotilla's strength was ordered to be built up to 180 aircraft.[18]

Two infantry divisions comprising about 40,000 troops were

[16] Japanese Monograph No. 87 p. 7.
[17] *Inter. Jap. Off.* II 409.
[18] Same, 287–89.

transferred from China to Halmahera, in a convoy designated *Take,* or Bamboo. We have already told, in Chapter II, the sad story of Convoy Bamboo; how one transport was sunk en route to Manila by U.S. submarine *Jack* in April, and three more on 6 May by *Gurnard.* Nearly half the troops on board were drowned before even coming close to their objectives, and those who finally reached Sorong and Halmahera were in no condition to help their comrades in New Guinea.

In the meantime General MacArthur had struck again.

CHAPTER VII
Wakde-Sarmi[1]

May 1944

THE Supreme Commander needed no prompting, nor reference to the J.C.S. directive of 12 March, to push his westward advance along New Guinea as rapidly as possible. Always "his own G–3," General MacArthur had already outlined to his planning staff a series of assaults, all pointing toward the target date of 15 November for Mindanao. Four operations — Wakde, Biak, Noemfoor, and Sansapor — carried Southwest Pacific Forces to the northwest point of the New Guinea Vogelkop, 550 miles west of Hollandia, in a little more than three months.

Admiral Kinkaid's Allied Naval Forces conducted all seaborne aspects of this advance; highly important, as the ocean was the only available road. The battle-tested VII Amphibious Force carried many thousands of troops and thousands of tons of supplies and equipment on schedules that would make any railroad timetable seem simple.

Always in the offing providing cover, or close in shore delivering gunfire support, for every move, were the cruisers and destroyers under Rear Admirals Berkey and Crutchley. They too were veterans in this game. The motor torpedo boat squadrons, as eager

[1] Action Reports of ships and commands, especially Capt. Alfred G. Noble, Commander Eastern Attack Force, and Capt. Bern Anderson, Commander Special Service Unit; Gen. Krueger's Report of the Wakde Operation; Smith *Approach to the Philippines*; Ms. draft "Amphibian Engineer Operations"; *Army Air Forces in World War II*, Vol. IV; W. F. McCartney *The Jungleers, A History of the 41st Infantry Division* (Washington 1948); *History of the Second Engineer Special Brigade* (Harrisburg, 1946); Office of the Chief Engineer, GHQ, Army Forces Pacific, *Engineers of the Southwest Pacific, 1941–45*, I, 172–73.

as the V Army Air Force to secure forward bases, also took a leading part in the breathless race.

Even before Humboldt Bay was assaulted, enough data had accumulated to render that area far less attractive as a major air base than it had first appeared to be. As early as 23 March Generals Kenney and Whitehead recommended that the Hollandia operation be expanded to include Wakde and Sarmi, as essential for their airfield network program. But General MacArthur, who had to take into account many factors other than airfields — shipping and troop availability, for instance — kept to his original plans. His Warning Instructions for Wakde and Sarmi, with 12 May as target date, were issued 10 April, as the transports were loading for Hollandia.

Wakde-Sarmi is a convenient name for an area about 120 miles west of Hollandia on the north coast of Dutch New Guinea. On the east it is bounded by the two Wakdes, low coral islands lying a couple of miles off shore. The real name of the larger and outer one is Insoemoar, but in Allied circles it was always called Wakde Island. Of irregular shape and about a mile and a half long, it was occupied in 1942 by the Japanese, who within a year had built there an excellent coral-surfaced runway, with buildings and revetments suitable for a staging base. Insoemanai, the smaller island, lies inshore of Insoemoar. The bight between them affords a good limited anchorage for shallow-draft vessels, with access to a landing beach extending 500 yards to the south of a small jetty.

Opposite Wakde, on the mainland, is the small village of Toem. Thence the coast trends west and northwest about 18 miles to the village of Sarmi, with an indentation called Maffin Bay about midway between. Along this strip of coastline the country behind the beaches is heavily forested, for the most part flat, and in places swampy. The Tor River flows into the sea about five miles west of Toem. Four miles farther west, across Maffin Bay, the Japanese had cleared the dense bush for an airstrip which was not yet finished; but between that and the village of Sawar they had an airstrip already operational.

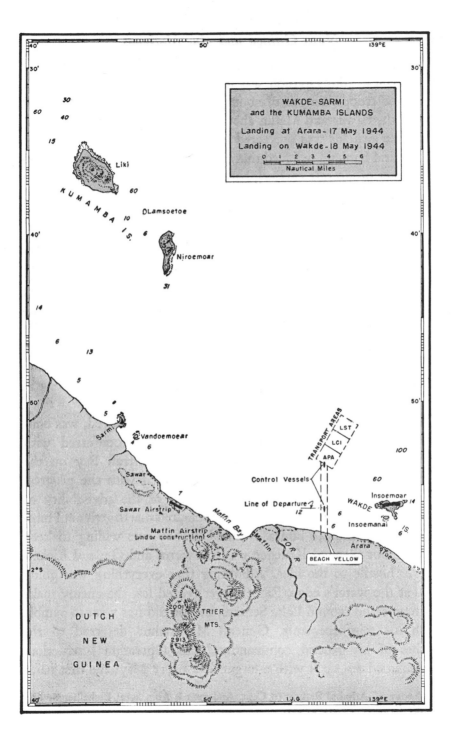

WAKDE-SARMI
and the KUMAMBA ISLANDS

Landing at Arara - 17 May 1944

Landing on Wakde - 18 May 1944

0 1 2 3 4 5 6
Nautical Miles

At Sarmi, a village on a small peninsula, the command post of the Japanese 36th Division was located in the spring of 1944. Its estimated troop strength of about 11,000 was distributed between Sarmi, the Sawar and Maffin airstrips, and Wakde Island. Each of the three airfields was protected by antiaircraft weapons.

Admiral Kinkaid believed that the enemy was assembling a powerful fleet of aircraft carriers, battleships and heavy cruisers in the northern Celebes Sea, and he estimated correctly that the Japanese were not doing this to protect Wakde. A new strategic plan known as the "A-Go," of which we shall hear more, was shaping up. Admiral Toyoda, like his predecessor Koga, sought a decisive battle with the Pacific Fleet, whenever and wherever it should attempt to penetrate the Japanese defensive perimeter that ran from the Marianas through the Palaus to the Vogelkop. Wakde lay outside this perimeter, and Imperial Headquarters proposed to write it off after a desperate defense. But the Allies could never be quite sure of that, and Combined Fleet concentration in Tawi Tawi offered a constant threat to Wakde and succeeding operations in Dutch New Guinea.

Planning for Wakde-Sarmi, as for those that followed, was conducted literally on the fly. When MacArthur conferred with Krueger, Eichelberger and Barbey at Tanahmerah Bay on the afternoon of 22 April, he was so well pleased with the progress already made that he asked their opinion of the advisability of moving right on to Wakde, using the echelons due to arrive at Humboldt Bay within 48 hours. Admiral Barbey was willing to keep moving but General Krueger was lukewarm and General Eichelberger hostile to the idea. Admitting that everything was going well at the water's edge, Eichelberger feared lest the enemy make a strong stand around Lake Sentani, and he did not wish to gamble with his reinforcements. General MacArthur deferred to the wishes of his ground commanders.[2] His Operation Instructions were issued 27 April with a target date of 15 May; the first naval

[2] Letter of Admiral Barbey to Capt. Anderson 8 Aug. 1952; Eichelberger *Our Jungle Road to Tokyo* p. 107.

attack plan was produced on 6 May.[3] Rear Admiral Fechteler was designated to command the naval attack force, Major General Horace H. Fuller, of the 41st Division, the ground forces.

In the meantime two rather disquieting discoveries had been made. Heavy bombers could not use the Lake Sentani airfields, and new aërial photographs revealed that no site suitable for a heavy bomber strip existed in Dutch New Guinea, short of Biak Island. Hence, until Biak could be taken, the heavies would have to continue operating from Nadzab, 440 miles east of Hollandia, or from the Admiralties. Yet the famous 12 March J.C.S. directive declared that the principal purpose of seizing Hollandia was to establish bases whence heavy bombers could attack Palau and neutralize western New Guinea and Halmahera. The need for full speed ahead to Biak was evident. General MacArthur decided to simplify the Wakde-Sarmi operation and move into Biak just as soon as the Wakde airfield could be used by Allied aircraft.

It is relevant here to point out that if the Seventh Fleet had had moving airfields — aircraft carriers — the Wakde "whistle stop" could have been omitted. General MacArthur and Admiral Kinkaid had always wanted carriers, and one of the purposes of Admiral Nimitz's visit to the Supreme Commander in March had been to explain why they couldn't have any, except on a short-term loan as at Hollandia. There were not enough to go around, as the Marianas operation, in which all available CVs and CVEs were employed, proved.

Rear Admiral Fechteler, who now commanded the VII 'Phib in Admiral Barbey's absence,[4] examined the tactical feasibility of assaulting Biak ten days after Wakde. He felt very dubious about it. He was concerned over the lack of photographic coverage. Biak appeared to be surrounded by coral reefs, which enhanced the difficulty of landing. But he concluded that "certain hazards and

---

[3] CTF 77 (Adm. Fechteler) Op Plan 4-44. Both the 41st Div. and the 163rd RCT were still mopping up, at Hollandia and Aitape.

[4] Barbey departed about 1 May for a long overdue leave, and on returning to the Southwest Pacific Admiral Kinkaid detained him in Brisbane to help plan the invasion of the Philippines.

expediencies" had to be accepted "solely because of the strategic urgency of the situation." General Krueger decided on 9 May that General Doe's 163rd RCT (7800 strong) was enough to take Wakde; that the rest of the 41st Division should be saved to seize Biak. With available shipping, at least ten days between the two moves would be necessary. No ships would be available for troop lift to Wakde until 12 May, when a certain echelon would finish landing reinforcements at Hollandia. The urgent necessity of giving the Pacific Fleet land-based air support for its scheduled landing in Saipan on 15 June was also recognized. All these factors put together made it clear that the earliest possible target date for Wakde was 17 May, and for Biak 27 May. General MacArthur approved on the 10th and issued revised instructions; and Admiral Fechteler designated Captain A. G. Noble to command the assault.

On 13 May the assigned beaching craft arrived at Aitape and began loading the equipment of the 163rd RCT, which had been relieved in combat by elements of the 32nd Division only one week before. Two transports and 11 LCIs embarked the assault troops two days later, and the whole attack group assembled at Hollandia on the 16th. In the meantime the Crutchley and Berkey cruiser task forces sortied from Seeadler Harbor and took up covering stations off shore. Early on 16 May the slow LSTs moved to Tanahmerah Bay to be in position for a night run to Wakde.

Allied air forces had been preparing for the Wakde and Biak operations for almost three weeks. As early as 28 April large strikes were directed at Biak and at Wakde, Sawar and Sarmi by V Army Air Force B–24s, B–25s and A–20s. Next day B–25s returned to bomb and strafe, and that night B–24 snoopers, operating from Markham Valley bases, raided Wakde in coöperation with a naval bombardment of coastal targets by Admiral Berkey's TF 75. Weather then slowed the pressure on Wakde-Sarmi until 13 May. In the meantime, Liberators from the XIII Army Air Force based in the Admiralties kept Biak under almost daily attack. From 13 May through the 16th, V A.A.F. heavy and medium bombers dropped a heavy tonnage of bombs on Wakde and Sawar. On the

17th—D-day at Wakde—three groups of heavy bombers hit Biak. Other air elements flying from Darwin systematically worked over Japanese air bases in the Vogelkop Peninsula. These attacks on and around Wakde, and on airfields within supporting distance, eliminated enemy air interference during the assault phase.

At dark 16 May the attack force departed Hollandia in three echelons, roughly parallel. In a run of only 120 miles it was un-detected by the Japanese.

Lieutenant General Tagami, commander in the Wakde-Sarmi area, after sending part of his forces to relieve Hollandia on 24 April, had created a "Right Sector Force" responsible for Wakde Island and for coast defense from near Toem to the Maffin air-strip. Between 2000 and 2500 troops, of which 800 were on Wakde, defended this thirteen-mile stretch. Tagami also com-manded a "Left Sector Force" around Sarmi, and a "Central Sec-tor Force" in the middle, which did not get into the fight for some time. Altogether he had about 11,000 men under his com-mand. Only about half of them were trained combat troops, and all were taken completely by surprise.

At 0600 May 17, by Zone minus 10 time, it was still dark. There was a bright moon in its last quarter, obscured at times by passing tropical showers. A brisk naval bombardment announced the ar-rival of Eastern Attack Force, informing all Japanese garrisons from Sarmi to Wakde that their time had come to die for the Emperor. The Crutchley group (H.M.A.S. *Australia, Shropshire, Warramunga* and *Arunta;* U.S.S. *Mullany* and *Ammen*) pounded mainland targets at Sawar and Sarmi; the Berkey ships (*Phoenix, Boise* and *Nashville*) poured salvos of six-inch shells into Wakde, in the hope of neutralizing any guns that might interfere with the landings. Captain Richard F. Stout's ten destroyers moved close in shore to pound targets between Toem and Maffin Bay. For fifty minutes the naval bombardment continued, encouraged by ex-plosions and large fires. At 0655, a quarter hour after sunrise, gun-fire lifted for five minutes so that cruiser float planes could mark the western end of Beach Yellow with smoke bombs. Then two rocket-equipped LCIs drenched the land behind the beach with salvos of 4.5-inch rockets. Close air support for the landing force was on call basis, with fighter plane C.A.P. and a squadron of medium bombers from Hollandia orbiting over the objective. A–20s of the V Army Air Force put their main effort on Wakde, softening it up for next day's landings. No Japanese aircraft appeared and no Allied planes were lost; no enemy activity was observed ashore, except a little rifle fire.[5] The mainland beachhead was secured on schedule in an orderly fashion.

Attention of the commanders was now directed to the capture of Wakde Island, the bombardment of which commenced as soon as the first boat waves were ashore on Beach Yellow.

Under cover of shell and rocket fire, a detachment of mortar and machine gunners was landed on Insoemanai, the small island nestling inshore of Wakde, at 1100 May 17. They found the island unoccupied by Japanese, and before dark their weapons were adding to the bombardment of Wakde. By noon the landing force artillery, sited on the mainland about a mile east of Arara, began a systematic shelling of Wakde. The fire support cruisers then hauled off shore, lest the Japanese Navy decide to interfere, but destroyers continued to fire. This continued all the afternoon. Finally the Japanese garrison was needled into action. During the afternoon of 17 May, they began to bite back with machine-gun bursts and mortar fire directed at American positions on Insoemanai.

American land-based artillery continued to keep Wakde under intermittent fire throughout the night. No details for the landing had been worked out beforehand, since they would depend upon developments at Toem. In the afternoon of the 17th, Captain Bern Anderson was alerted by voice radio to direct the landing waves to the beach the following day, details to come later. Captain Noble's dispatch assault order, which he issued early next morning, was probably the shortest and most succinct of the entire war.

The only practicable landing beach at Wakde, 600 yards of coral sand, extended south from the jetty in the southwestern

[5] CTG 77.2 Action Report of 5 June; Advon 5 Liaison Officer Report of 19 May.

bight. For the boat waves to have a straight run for this beach, they had to take a course around and inside of Insoemanai. The landing force, consisting of the 1st Battalion 163rd Infantry, was to land in six waves at five-minute intervals beginning at 0900. Two medium tanks, boated in LCMs, would bring up the rear and complete the assault movement.

At 0830 May 18 *Wilkes* and *Roe* commenced their scheduled fifteen-minute bombardment while the gunners on Insoemanai poured a rain of heavy machine-gun fire on the Wakde shore that flanked the boat lane. The control vessel, *SC–703*, took station off the reef northwest of Insoemanai. In the meantime landing craft were embarking troops on the beaches near Toem, forming up for their two-mile journey. So far, no hitches and no hint of unpleasant things to come.

At about 0850, two rocket LCIs, leading the first boat wave, rounded the control vessel, headed toward the beach, and began laying a rocket barrage on the beach itself and around the jetty. A third LCI took care of the southern shore of Wakde Island, which flanked the boat lane. To the well-disciplined defenders this was the signal for action. The shoreline flanking the boat lane erupted. Here the Japanese had emplaced machine guns, some in gun turrets borrowed from damaged aircraft, and all cleverly camouflaged and protected. And for the next half hour the scene between Insoemanai and Wakde did justice to what Hollywood seems to think a modern battle should look like. The high point came as the first boat wave rounded the control vessel at 0853 and began its run for the beach. The boats then became the target for concentrated fire. Geysers from mortar shells popped up all around and splashes from machine-gun bursts ruffled the otherwise smooth water in the bight. But the boat crews were not caught napping and their own machine guns chattered back. The three LCIs, as soon as they had discharged their rockets, ranged themselves between the boat lane and Wakde Island, about 150 yards clear of the fringing reef. Without pause they kept the enemy machine-gun positions under heavy fire with every automatic weapon they could bring to bear. *SC–703*, a target for enemy fire when no better one seemed to offer, joined the action with her three-inch and 20-mm guns whenever the range was clear. Close-in fire from the LCIs served to draw off a large part of the Japanese venom which otherwise would have been directed at the boats.

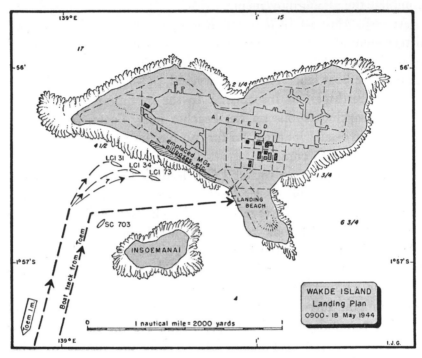

LCI–34 and *LCI–73* drew the bulk of enemy fire and lost three killed and eleven wounded — 20 per cent of their two crews; their continuing action under such circumstances was very commendable.

The first boat wave reached the beach at 0903, three minutes late. At five-minute intervals, five more waves of LCVPs ran the gantlet. All made it in good order. Troops could crouch low behind the armor plates, but the crews had to sweat it out in the open. In one boat every crew member was wounded and in another 68 shell fragments and slugs were later counted. Yet the landing on the whole went off as planned and remarkably close to schedule. Company A, 542nd Engineer Boat and Shore Regiment, richly deserved the praise that it received for this performance.

By 0930 all troops had landed and action shifted ashore. The defense was skillfully organized and directed and, as in the case of other small island actions in the Pacific, courageous to the point of fanaticism.

Even while possession of the beach itself was being hotly contested, four LSTs carrying aviation engineers arrived and began unloading under sniper fire. But the critical moment had passed. The troops were ashore and determined to stay, and it would be but a matter of time before they would finish their job and be withdrawn to make way for the engineer and aviation units, who would rebuild and operate Wakde as a new field in the Allied air network.

About two and a half days were required to mop up, foxhole by foxhole and bunker by bunker. The final count was 759 Japanese killed and four prisoners; the rest lay buried in coral caves. American casualties were 40 dead and 107 wounded.

The Kumamba Islands, lying 10 miles north of the Sarmi Peninsula, were occupied 19 May, with no opposition and only one casualty — a native chieftain who was wounded. Search radars with their operators were promptly installed.

Wakde was now securely in Allied hands. By noon 21 May, the Army engineers had made the airstrip operational. It had to be extended to both shores in order to accommodate heavy bombers, and the whole island was converted into a parking area. Wakde, like Roi in the Marshalls, had become an immovable "flattop," and on 27 May naval Liberators based there made the first air reconnaissance of southern Mindanao since early 1942. For the next few months Wakde was a key airfield in the Southwest Pacific offensive, supporting two heavy bomber groups, two fighter groups, a B–25 reconnaissance squadron and part of a Navy PB4Y squadron. As new bases were taken along the road to the Philippines, Wakde's importance declined, and by December 1944 it had been reduced to the lowly status of an emergency field.

*   *   *

On the mainland, the securing of a beachhead behind Beach Yellow was only a beginning. General Krueger, believing that a passive defense of that section of New Guinea was not feasible with 10,000 Japanese troops in the vicinity, decided that the landing force, already being reinforced, should take the offensive, capture the Maffin and Sawar airstrips, and clear the enemy from the Sarmi region. To this idea the Japanese objected vigorously. In a mountainous terrain overlooking Maffin Bay, they dug in. We shall leave it to the Army History to describe in detail the hot and dirty jungle fighting that took place in this vicinity for more than three months. From 17 May through the first of September Allied casualties were about 400 dead and 1500 wounded; and in the same time almost 4000 Japanese dead were counted. The rest withdrew toward Sarmi and were still there at the end of the war.

Indirectly, this campaign contributed to the ability of all armed forces to meet the close schedules demanded in the near future. Lifting troops from Wakde instead of Hollandia, as in the three next operations, saved many days' steaming for the assault shipping. Combat units of the Alamo Force were staged forward to Wakde and Toem, and many fought their first fight in the Trier Mountains. Destroyers and patrol craft, eager for live targets to sharpen up bombardment training, were always welcomed by the soldiers ashore. So this little island and the mainland opposite served as useful steppingstones on the road to the Philippines.

CHAPTER VIII

Biak[1]

27 May–1 June 1944

1. Biak-Bosnik

BIAK, as we have seen, was on the timetable for the tenth day following Wakde. The Hurricane Task Force, as the ground elements were designated, was commanded by Major General Horace H. Fuller USA of the 41st Division, while Rear Admiral Fechteler handled the naval elements and the amphibious aspects. This turned out to be the most interesting operation in Dutch New Guinea, because for the first time in any Pacific advance since November 1943 the Japanese Navy intervened.

The Schouten Islands lie across the mouth of Geelvink Bay. The natives, about 25,000 in number, have been described as "a rather iikeable race, well built and pleasantly lazy. They have abandoned piracy and like to sit all day to watch the waves break upon the coast. They work best in large groups, where two out of three can sit and offer technical advice on how to lift an axe or carry a bucket of water." [2] Naturally these children of nature failed to appreciate such energetic taskmasters as the Japanese; but, being as prudent as they were virtuous, they kept out of the fighting

[1] Action Reports of ships and commands involved, especially CTF 77 (Rear Adm. Fechteler) on the Biak Operation, 10 June 1944; Capt. Bern Anderson "Capture and Occupation of Bosnik Area Biak Island," 12 June 1944; Gen. Krueger's Report of the Wakde-Biak Operation, 25 Feb. 1945; R. R. Smith *The Approach to the Philippines;* "Amphibian Engineer Operations"; Craven and Cate *Army Air Forces in World War II,* Vol. IV; McCartney *The Jungleers; History of the Second Engineer Special Brigade.*
[2] Southwest Pacific Area Terrain Study No. 61, "Area Study of Northwestern Netherlands New Guinea and Geelvink Bay," p. 37.

until it was clear that the Japanese were beaten — when they took delight in the enticement of half-starved fugitives into their clutches by promises of rice, and then delivered them to the Americans.

Biak is the largest of the Schoutens. About 45 miles long and 20 wide, it is covered with low, flat-topped hills supporting a thick jungle growth. Most of the coast is fringed with coral reef, there are no natural harbors, and the hundred-fathom curve generally lies less than a mile off shore. Bosnik, on the southeast coast opposite the Padaido Islands, was the administrative center of the Schouten Islands, and for harbor facilities had two stone jetties built across the reef to deep water. For nine miles along the south shore, from a point about three miles east of Bosnik to just west of Mokmer village, a coral cliff rises about 200 feet to a flat escarpment. For the most part the cliff starts 500 yards or more inland, but it touches the coast near the village of Parai, leaving just room enough for the motor road. A mile west of Mokmer the cliff swings north, leaving a flat coastal plain on which the Japanese had constructed three airstrips within a space of six miles: the Mokmer, the Borokoe, and the Sorido.

Reports of the landing at Tarawa had reached the VII 'Phib planners long since, and they were understandably skeptical about risking a landing, even with amphtracs, over a coral reef of such irregular and uncertain surface as photographs showed along the shore near the airstrips. Army planners, with the lessons of Hollandia fresh in mind, sought firm ground behind the beaches for dispersal and maneuver, and Bosnik was finally selected as the least of all evils. It was not backed by swamps, the jetties appeared to be usable, and the reef was at least no worse than anywhere else.

Intelligence showed a heavy concentration of dual-purpose guns around Mokmer airstrip. Bosnik, a Japanese supply base, was also well protected with antiaircraft defenses, and the existence of several coast defense guns was suspected. To Admiral Fechteler and his planners this meant a heavy shore bombardment before the landings.

The coral reef fronting the beach at Bosnik ruled out the use of

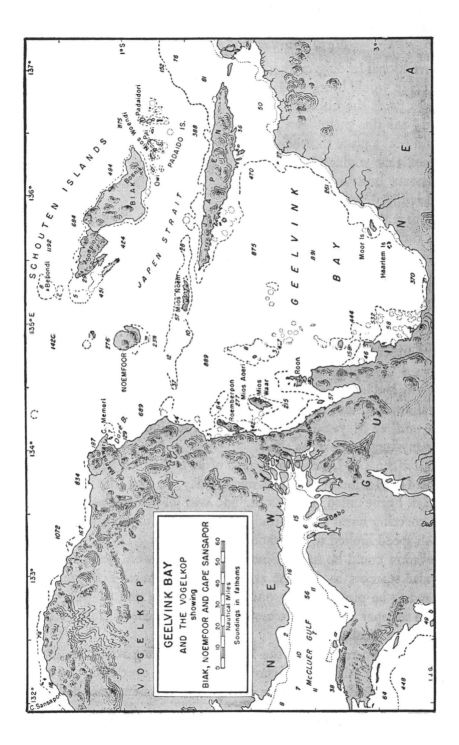

GEELVINK BAY
AND THE VOGELKOP
showing
BIAK, NOEMFOOR AND CAPE SANSAPOR

Nautical Miles
0 10 20 30 40 50 60
Soundings in fathoms

SCHOUTEN ISLANDS

VOGELKOP

NOEMFOOR

JAPEN STRAIT

GEELVINK BAY

McCLUER GULF

NEW GUINEA

C.Sansapor

Bebondi

Bosnik

Soepiori

Sorido

BIAK

PADAIDO IS.

Owi

Padaidori

Woendi

Mios Pai

Mios Noem

Moor Is

Haarlem Is

Roembepon

Mios Aoeri

Mios Waar

Roon

C. Memari

Manokwari

Dore B.

Babo

I.J.G.

conventional landing craft for assault waves; so it was planned that six LSTs would bring up 63 LVTs and 25 dukws for the first four waves, with the bulk of the troops to follow in 15 LCIs which could use the jetties. And, since it was uncertain whether LSTs could find a place to beach, Admiral Fechteler and General Fuller agreed that engineering equipment must be landed promptly to construct beaching points. This equipment, together with tanks and artillery, was loaded in eight LCTs to be towed by the LSTs, and, as it were, shoved ashore on the reef opposite Beach Green 1. But the planning was so hasty and knowledge of reef conditions so incomplete that Admiral Fechteler felt obliged to warn his forces to be alert for radical changes and to "execute them with speed and accuracy." [3]

The LVTs were manned by troops of the 542nd Engineer Boat and Shore Regiment; the dukws by an Army motor transport company attached to the ESBs. The dukw drivers, all Negroes, were given a vital place in this amphibious operation. None of these vehicles had been trained to float out of LSTs, or to operate under naval control, and not many of them nor any LSTs were available until 22 May. So the rehearsal, held at Hollandia on the 23rd, was anything but a dress affair.

After the 41st Division and most of its equipment had been embarked at Humboldt Bay on Z minus 2 day, 25 May, the Hurricane Attack Force sailed that evening and was joined next morning by the covering naval vessels, under Admirals Crutchley and Berkey. With speed limited to 8.5 knots by LSTs towing LCTs, no effort at evasion could be made. Since the Japanese were known to fly regular searches as far east as Hollandia, Admiral Fechteler expected to be picked up by one of these planes, and he was; [4] but as the snooper was not detected the Admiral believed that he had attained tactical surprise.

While preparations for the landing were being rushed at Hollandia, Allied Air Forces were busy working over Biak and the Japanese airfields farther west. XIII A.A.F. bombers from the Ad-

[3] CTF 77 Op Plan 5-44, Annex A.   [4] *Inter. Jap. Off.* II 287.

miralties joined those of the V A.A.F. from Nadzab on 17 May, making 99 B–24s that hit Biak. Every day but one until Z-day, one or the other air force made a bomber strike. For three days A–20s from Hollandia struck airfields and enemy barges at Biak, while Liberators based at Darwin pounded air bases on the Vogelkop on alternate days to those of the A–20 strikes. Fighter cover for the landing forces at Biak was provided by elements of the V A.A.F. based at Wakde.

Allied estimates of Japanese troops on Biak were universally optimistic, varying from a vague "not heavily held" up to 2000.[5] Actually on 27 May there were nearly 10,000 soldiers on the island, almost as many as the attackers; about 40 per cent were combat trained, but the rest, used as auxiliary infantry, were no mean fighters. The core of the defense was the 222nd Regiment, crack troops and veterans of the China campaign. The regimental commander, Colonel Naoyuki Kuzume, also had overall charge of island defense. He had a well-balanced force, with light tanks, field and antiaircraft artillery, aviation engineers, a naval guard unit, and a recently organized naval special base force of 1500 men under Rear Admiral Sadatoshi Senda.

As soon as they knew about the Hollandia landings, the Japanese commanders in Davao and Manokwari, and on Biak itself, felt sure that Biak was on the Allied timetable. But they did not expect the assault to come so soon, and they were discouraged by the vacillation of Imperial Headquarters. Since 1943 Biak had been considered an important link in the perimeter defense line, but on 9 May the war lords astounded their underlings by announcing that the defense line would henceforth be pulled back to Sorong and Halmahera, leaving Biak as another outpost to be defended to the last man.[6] Subsequently, as we shall see, Imperial Headquarters changed its mind, but at the time of the landings Colonel Kuzume was prepared to make the best of a hopeless situation. Expecting the Allies to land near the Mokmer airstrip, he concentrated his defenses

[5] Adm. Kinkaid Op Plan 6A–44, Annex A; CTF 77 Op Plan 5–44, Annex G.
[6] Smith *The Approach to the Philippines* pp. 232–33. Apparently they had been discouraged by the casualties to Convoy "Bamboo."

around it. On the beach were four 4.7-inch DP guns and one 6-inch coast defense gun. On a coral terrace behind the field and on a spur ridge behind Mokmer village, positions commanding the entire area, he emplaced field and antiaircraft guns, automatic weapons and mortars. Limestone caves about 1200 yards north of the western end of Mokmer airstrip were the key to his defenses. The naval headquarters were located in these "West Caves," as we called them; they were big enough to shelter a thousand men. On the main ridge north of Mokmer village was another series of caves. A third pocket of resistance, also provided with caves and fortified with pillboxes, lay in a series of knifelike forested ridges west of the Parai defile.

Although Colonel Kuzume had been warned, his troops were not prepared for the landing when it came. He chose to remain on the defensive, wisely concentrating his defense on terrain that would enable him to interdict his enemy's use of the Biak airfields for the longest possible time. He conducted a skillful defense that denied these fields to the Allied air forces for nearly a month.

2. Z-day at Bosnik, 27 May

The attack force arrived off Bosnik about fifteen minutes ahead of schedule on 27 May. When satisfied at 0629 that everyone was in his proper position, Admiral Fechteler ordered "Execute landing plan." This signal set off the 45-minute pre-landing bombardment, which extended from the westernmost airstrip at Sorido to well east of Bosnik. *Phoenix, Boise* and *Nashville* lobbed one thousand rounds of six-inch shell into positions around the three airfields, while destroyers took on targets near the landing beaches.

Two minutes after the cruisers started firing, a fast-moving motor boat was spotted inshore near Mokmer airfield. Destroyer *Hutchins* (Commander C. B. Laning) was ordered to take it under fire. When close inshore and firing, her foremast was hit by a 4.7-inch shell. It failed to explode but continued through the radar room and made a four-foot hole topside, wounding three men. *Hutchins* retired at high speed to determine the extent of dam-

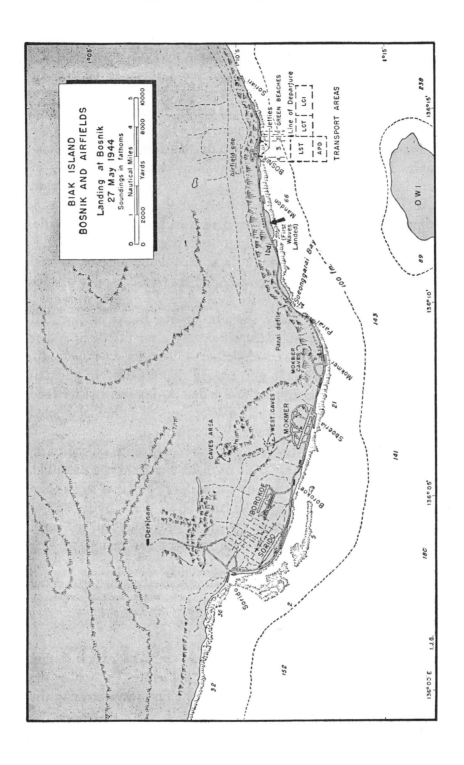

BIAK ISLAND
BOSNIK AND AIRFIELDS

Landing at Bosnik
27 May 1944
Soundings in fathoms

Nautical Miles
0   1   2   3   4   5

Yards
0   2000   4000   6000   8000   10000

TRANSPORT AREAS

GREEN BEACHES
Line of Departure

Jetties

1   2   3

LST   LCT   LCI
APD

BOSNIK

Mandon (First Waves Landed)

Ibdi

Soronggarai Bay

Parai defile

Parai

Mokmer

MOKMER CAVES

Sboeria

MOKMER

WEST CAVES

CAVES AREA

Borokoe

L'BOROKOE

SORIDO

Sorido

Derhinam

OWI

Soljan

Solo

89

238

32

152

180

141

143

21

2

5

100 fm.

36 fm.

1°05'   1°15'

136°00' E   136°05'   136°10'   136°15'

I.J.G.

age. Destroyer *Bache* was then ordered inshore to silence the Japanese battery, which returned her fire but missed. At 1300, essential repairs completed, *Hutchins* closed the beach again. "Fired 32 three-gun salvos into the area where we believed our friend, the 4.7 battery, to be. He did not return this fire," reported Commander Laning. All this was pretty small change in the way of shore bombardment and counterfire, but it was a lot more than Seventh Fleet fire support ships had been used to for many months, and presaged a much livelier operation than Hollandia or Wakde. The offending battery turned out to be a naval dual-purpose 4.7-inch outfit sited on high ground behind Mokmer airstrip. Several days' attention from destroyers and bombers was required to silence it for good.

For the air part in Z-day support, twelve B–24s of the XIII A.A.F. bombed the Bosnik defenses shortly after first light and at 0700 25 more bombed the beach defenses. Between 1103 and 1150, 77 B–24s bombed targets in and around the airfields.[7] In addition to these heavy bomber attacks, B–25s and A–20s were maintained over the objective for call strikes. Weather conditions prevented fighter cover from arriving on station until 1100.

The weather on 27 May was partly overcast with a dead calm, which was succeeded about 0700 by light airs from the east. The aërial and naval bombardment created a heavy cloud of smoke and dust, which hung heavy over the land. Stone jetties and all other landmarks were soon obscured by smoke and dust, and the small radar sets on the control SCs were not sensitive enough to pick them up.

We shall relate the events of the Bosnik landing in some detail because they did not go "according to plan," like most of those preceding; and because they proved that the VII 'Phib could change and improvise if it had to.

The LSTs, with amphtracs and dukws embarked, took station about 500 yards seaward of the line of departure. Launching the LVTs was well timed and coördinated, the first wave crossing the

[7] *Army Air Forces in World War II,* IV 634.

line of departure only three minutes late. Visibility fell to 500 yards as a heavy pall of smoke and dust slowly drifted over the water. At the line of departure, rocket-armed *LCI–31* and *LCI–34* took station, one on each flank of the leading wave, to accompany it to the beach and lay a last-minute rocket barrage. Commander Dwight H. Day in *LCI–73* had the not small task of finding suitable beaching points for LCIs and LCTs after the first wave had landed. When about 500 yards past the line of departure, the LCI on the left flank became the target of heavy machine-gun and mortar fire from the shore. Rocket fire promptly silenced it, and by 0719 the first wave had landed. The second and third waves of LVTs were then roaring in toward shore, and the fourth and fifth, consisting of dukws, were waved on to follow.

So far, so good; but Commander Day reported that he was unable to locate the jetties, and that the initial waves were landing at a poor spot with steep to backing. Captain Anderson now realized that a serious error had been made in the landing point, and that, if the LSTs were to be unloaded, the error must be corrected. He directed destroyer *Kalk*, which was standing by near his control vessel, to locate the jetties accurately with her radar. She did so, reporting that they were about two miles to the east of where the initial waves were landing! Anderson then directed *Kalk* to lead the sixth wave of LCPRs to the proper place, and ordered the LCIs to tag along.

What had happened was this. While the LSTs were launching, and amphtracs and dukws were slowly slogging shoreward, the entire formation had drifted westward in a 2- to 3-knot current; and this had gone unperceived because of the smoke and dust. The first wave actually landed in a mangrove swamp about 3000 yards west of Beach Green 4.[8] As Admiral Fechteler reported, "The formation and disposition of the assault regiment had been badly disrupted. . . . However, it was able to reorganize quickly, without interference from the enemy."

---

[8] Even if there had been no smoke, little could have been done to keep LVTs straight as they could just about hold their own against a 3-knot current.

It was almost 0730 when the sixth boat wave was held up at the line of departure, and another 20 minutes elapsed before the jetties were located and the shift eastward commenced. Visibility improved as the smoke-and-dust cloud drifted slowly westward. *Hobby* fired a white phosphorus shell to mark the inner end of the east jetty, and at 0807 she was directed to fire about 350 rounds of 40-mm inshore of the jetties to cover the approach of the LCPRs. These touched down between 0810 and 0815, and reported no opposition. Captain Anderson then sent the LCIs in to the jetties, which fortunately were found to be in good condition. The rest of the landing was then carried out as originally planned. LCTs found a suitable beaching point, and some were unloaded at the eastern jetty as soon as the LCIs were clear. During the morning Captain Scruggs of the LST transport unit ascertained that the west jetty could easily accommodate LSTs, and four LSTs were so beached, while the other three were unloaded in the stream by landing craft. By the time unloading knocked off at 1715 Z-day, some 12,000 troops, 12 tanks, 28 artillery pieces, 500 vehicles and 2400 tons of supplies had been unloaded, greatly exceeding all expectations. Only 300 tons of miscellaneous supplies remained in the LSTs when they departed.

Conditions ashore also turned out to be better than expected. Even though the first four waves landed at the wrong place, they all landed at the same place. This put ashore intact the 2nd Battalion 186th Infantry, which by 0730 was pushing through the mangroves to the main coastal road. Two companies of the 3rd Battalion 186th Infantry landed from the last wave of dukws about 800 yards to the east,[9] but the rest of the troops, including the whole 162nd Regiment, landed on the proper beaches.

At 0740 Colonel Newman, commanding the 186th Infantry, with more than half his regiment ashore at the wrong spot, suggested that his regiment exchange missions with the 162nd Infantry; for

[9] "Amphibian Engineer Operations" V 76–77, using ESB sources only, says all waves after the 1st did a "by the right flank" and landed troops on the correct beaches. This is only partly correct for the fifth wave, and that did not reach the right place.

Colonel Newman's regiment was supposed to secure the beach-head, while the 162nd drove rapidly west to capture the Mokmer airstrip. But General Fuller did not wish to change the plan of maneuver and ordered the 186th Infantry to continue its original mission. This forced the two regiments to pass through each other in reaching their assigned positions. Fortunately, at that time the Japanese had hardly awakened and the maneuver was completed with a minimum of confusion. By noon the 186th Infantry had secured the initial beachhead line.

The shore party, Colonel Benjamin C. Fowlkes's 542nd Engineer Boat and Shore Regiment, promptly went to work preparing exits, dumps and a road net around Bosnik, and making repairs in the terrain. By this time the engineers were used to picking up after the Navy; the more successful and prolonged the naval bombardment, the more work for them. They placed two pontoon sections on the reef near the east jetty to be used as beaching points. By the after-noon everything was under control and LSTs were rapidly dis-charging. The organization of supply points, control of vehicular traffic, and unloading of shipping at the Bosnik beaches was carried out with less confusion and congestion than in any other operation so far in New Guinea. And on 30 May a naval demolition unit blasted a five-foot-deep channel off Beach Green 1 for the use of LCMs and LCVPs.

At 1100 on Z-day four Japanese fighter planes appeared over the airstrips but disappeared after making a few halfhearted passes. In the late afternoon two fighter-bombers flew over the cliff behind Bosnik at low level and dove on beached LSTs at the western jetty. Three small bombs, dropped from such a low level that they struck before becoming fully armed, hit *LST–456* but failed to explode; two of them were picked up by sailors and flung over the side. A few minutes later four twin-engined planes came in together, low and down-sun. As they cleared the edge of the cliff they were brought under intense antiaircraft fire from ashore and afloat. Two burst into flames and crashed; one, badly hit and smoking, flew off close inshore, and the fourth burst into flames as it passed destroyer

Sampson, Admiral Fechteler's headquarters ship. The Japanese pilot made a deliberate effort to suicide-crash *Sampson;* but antiaircraft fire clipped off part of his wing and the plane passed over the bridge and struck the water 400 yards beyond. Its wing tip hit the water about 20 yards from *SC–699* and the plane catapulted into the subchaser, which in a few seconds became engulfed in flame and smoke. With the aid of tug *Sonoma* the fires were soon under control and within a short time extinguished. One man died of his burns, another was missing and eight more were wounded in this freak crash.

At 1800 May 27, Admiral Fechteler departed Biak with the LST echelon, leaving the rocket LCIs and two destroyers to provide gunfire support for the troops. The advance of the 162nd Infantry that afternoon was held up for a time at the coastal defile by a few well-placed Japanese, but tanks and rocket LCIs cleared them out, and by dark the troops, well pleased with their progress, dug in around the village of Parai. As usual in these virtually unopposed landings, the worst was yet to come.

3. *The Drive for the Airfields*

General MacArthur had counted on using bombers from Biak airfields to strike Palau and Yap in support of the Saipan landing on 15 June. But by Saipan D-Day the Japanese were still denying these airfields to him.

Early in the morning of 28 May the 162nd Infantry continued its drive for Mokmer field, and for a time made good progress. *LCI–34,* when steaming along shore abreast of the troops, in order to fire rockets in their support, was herself taken under fire at 0850 by an enemy shore battery. As the first few shots straddled her, she turned up flank speed and "hollered for help." Destroyers *Stockton* and *Reid* answered her call. *Stockton* opened fire at 0922 and almost at once drew accurate return fire from the battery behind Mokmer airstrip that had shown its teeth the day before. She received a

4.7-inch hit on the starboard side forward four feet above the water-line, which killed one man and injured another. The hole was about four feet in diameter, and the explosion did a good deal of internal damage. The enemy battery continued to fire accurately for a few minutes and was silenced by *Reid*, but not permanently; it later shot down an A–20, and at 1629 opened up again on *Reid*.

Although enemy air activity was still negligible, the situation ashore rapidly grew worse on 28 May. Elements of the 162nd Infantry, whose attack was canalized along the narrow coastal strip, reached a road junction west of Mokmer by 0930, but were pinned down there by machine-gun and mortar fire. Japanese defenses, now rapidly building up in the thick vegetation, coral caves, and crevices of the cliffs and high ground, placed increasing pressure on this regiment and in the afternoon forced it to withdraw to its lines of the previous day. *Wilkes* and *Nicholson* alternated during the night delivering harassing fire into Japanese positions near Mokmer village. But the Japanese had already moved into ridges at the Parai defile, cutting road communications of the 162nd Infantry, against which they opened a heavy counter-attack at 0850 May 29.

By noon it was apparent that the Biak airfields could not be taken until the Japanese were cleared out of the high ground dominating them and the coastal strip. Dense vegetation, cave cover and the nearness of American troops to the targets made it impossible for artillery and naval gunfire to root out the enemy. The 162nd RCT was hemmed in on three sides, and any movement brought it under fire from well concealed, dominating positions. There was only one way out, by sea. All amphibian vehicles and landing craft were pressed into service to withdraw the 162nd —a maneuver rarely employed in Pacific Ocean operations. The evacuation was well performed during the afternoon of 29 May under cover of artillery, air support and naval gunfire. By nightfall new positions were set up about 500 yards east of the defile.

After this setback a new plan had to be worked out. General Fuller now wished to attack along the ridge back of Bosnik, but needed more troops. Alamo Force headquarters arranged for two battalions of the 163rd RCT then at Wakde to be lifted up to Biak immediately by LCIs. So for two days the 162nd rested and waited. Antiaircraft units destined for the defense of the Biak airstrips were arriving in each LST echelon. General Fuller had them all emplaced for immediate action within the beachhead. Altogether they made an exceedingly heavy concentration of antiaircraft weapons, so that enemy planes attempting to fly over the beachhead ran into practically a solid sheet of fire.

At 1300 May 31 arrived 16 LCIs carrying the reinforcement battalions from Wakde. These were landed and the LCIs departed at 1530. Destroyers *Wilkes, Kalk* and *Gillespie* were now assigned to Captain Anderson for gunfire support. *Gillespie* brought a fighter-director team, one of several organized by the V A.A.F. and specially trained to operate from combat information centers on board destroyers. Any fighter planes coming into the area checked in with the fighter-director, who was then in position to vector them out to bogeys, just as in a carrier task force.

The 186th Infantry on 1 June began advancing westward along the inland plateau while the 162nd pushed along the coast. But it was not until the 7th that Mokmer airstrip was captured, and for another week the Japanese with mortars and light artillery in the caves were able to thwart the engineers' efforts to get to work putting the strip in order.

On 2 June Owi and Mios Woendi Islands off Bosnik were occupied. The Army Engineers constructed an excellent airstrip on Owi which was ready 17 June, while Mios Woendi was developed into a motor torpedo boat, seaplane and amphibious repair base.

As May turned into June, all reports indicated that the Japanese Navy was at last about to show its hand. Over a year had elapsed since the Seventh Fleet had sighted any Japanese warship bigger than an armed barge, so these reports created considerable perturbation. Intelligence summaries from Seventh Fleet headquarters indicated great naval activity in the vicinity of Tawi Tawi, Davao and Halmahera, and the staging of carrier-type planes to within striking distance of Biak. On 2 June a heavy air raid brought confirmation.

CHAPTER IX

The Japanese Reaction to Biak[1]

(Operation "KON")

27 May–13 June 1944

1. Decisions and Air Strikes

MAY the 27th, date of the Allied landing at Biak, happened to be the 39th anniversary of the Battle of Tsushima, an event dear to the Japanese Navy. In that decisive naval action of the Russo-Japanese War, Admiral Rozhdestvenski's fleet had been almost completely destroyed by Admiral Togo's.

This anniversary found the Japanese Fleet assembling for another decisive battle which it hoped to fight somewhere near Palau or the western Carolines. Admiral Toyoda's plan for this operation, designated A-Go, had been issued three weeks before; and Admiral Ozawa's Mobile Fleet had promptly moved from Lingga Roads near Singapore to Tawi Tawi. Yet, as we have seen, Army section of Imperial Headquarters, discouraged by MacArthur's capture of Hollandia and the losses of Convoy "Bamboo," on 9 May had ordered Biak to be left to its fate. In the land-based aircraft deployment plan for Operation A-Go, issued 18 May, the 23rd Air Flotilla (Rear Admiral Yoshioka Ito), whose headquarters were at Sorong,

---

[1] R. R. Smith *Approach to the Philippines* chap. xv has a full, detailed account of this operation, which he kindly let us use in advance of publication. Principal Japanese sources are Japanese Monograph No. 87; No. 90; No. 91 (851–97); "A-Go Operation Log"; "The KON Operation for the Reinforcement of Biak," *Inter. Jap. Off.* II 450–54. Allied sources: Action Reports of ships and commands concerned, especially Rear Adm. Crutchley RN "Report of Proceedings 2–12 June Combined TFs 74, 75 – Biak Area" 21 June 1944; Capt. Anderson's Action Reports; *Army Air Forces in World War II*, IV.

and which then comprised only 18 planes, was to repel any Allied attack on Biak that might develop. Obviously, Biak was still looked upon by the Japanese Army command as a position to be abandoned to a last-man defense, like so many other island outposts.

Yet when the Allies did land on Biak 27 May, the Japanese Navy reacted so promptly to defend it as to suggest that the fortuitous connection with the Tsushima anniversary compelled it to insist on change of plan. The Navy section of Imperial Headquarters made the decision. Its first action, 28 May, was to order Admiral Ito's 23rd Air Flotilla to be strengthened by 50 fighter planes from Japan via the Philippines, plus 20 fighter planes and 20 bombers from the Marianas. On the 31st it ordered 20 bombers, 8 reconnaissance planes and 48 fighters from the Carolines to Sorong and Halmahera.[2] And on 29 May Combined Fleet staff hurriedly drew up a plan for the relief of Biak. This was the operation designated "KON."

The KON plan was to transport 2500 troops of the 2nd Amphibious Brigade from Mindanao to Biak in warships, since only one transport, a Japanese LST, was available. Rear Admiral Naomasa Sakonju in heavy cruiser *Aoba* was given the command. He had light cruiser *Kinu* and destroyers *Shikinami*, *Uranami* and *Shigure* to lift the troops, and battleship *Fuso*, heavy cruisers *Myoko* and *Haguro* and five destroyers as screen. They were to embark the troops at Zamboanga 31 May, and land them on Biak 3 June. The 23rd Air Flotilla would provide advance neutralizing strikes on the Allied ships off Biak, and the small Southwest Area Fleet would transport reinforcements from Manokwari to Biak by barge.

Obviously the high strategists at Imperial Headquarters had experienced a sudden change of heart about Biak. They realized that the three airfields there were essential for the air components in Operation A-Go, and Colonel Kuzume let them know that he could not hope to hold out without prompt assistance.

---

[2] Smith *Approach to the Philippines* p. 350; other figures given in Japanese Monograph No. 91.

The approach of reinforcements to Biak was heralded by the most severe air attack that the Seventh Fleet had experienced in 1944. On 30 May, as we have seen, Admiral Ito had only 18 planes at his immediate disposal. But the 166 planes ordered in from the Marianas and elsewhere began to reach Sorong in sufficient numbers 1 June to enable him to launch a big strike against Allied shipping at Biak the very next day.

An echelon of eight LSTs arrived off Bosnik from Hollandia on 2 June, and by 1630 four of them had completed discharging. Five minutes later a formation of planes, large for that area, was observed through the broken clouds over the island. The LSTs at the beach were alerted and preparing to retract. At 1640 these Japanese planes commenced diving and strafing the LSTs still at the beach. No Allied fighter planes were present — they were grounded at Wakde and Hollandia by weather; but an intense volume of antiaircraft fire, from shore and ship batteries, was maintained throughout the attack. For an hour and five minutes enemy planes were in the air, going for various ships singly and in pairs. In this aërial battle, pressed home vigorously and concentrated on shipping, the enemy lost 12 of his 54 planes and inflicted only slight damage, a near-miss on *LST–467*.[3]

2. *First Reinforcement Attempt, 31 May–4 June*

The three destroyers of the KON transport unit (escorted by Admiral Sakonju in *Aoba*) fueled at Tarakan, embarked 1700 troops at Zamboanga 31 May, and continued to Davao where they rendezvoused with *Myoko*, *Haguro* and three more destroyers. This part of the force departed shortly before midnight 2 June. The other 800 troops of the amphibious brigade were embarked at Zamboanga in a "detached force" consisting of minelayers *Itsukushima* and *Tsugaru* and *Transport No. 127* (a Japanese LST);

[3] Capt. Anderson Action Report; 23rd Airflot War Diary, WDC 160264, N.A. 12546.

subchaser escort was provided for the run to Biak. Battleship *Fuso* and two destroyers took a more northerly and evasive course. On the morning of 3 June, Sakonju's force sighted a periscope; later its owner was overheard sending a contact report; and before noon the entire group was sighted and shadowed by one of Commodore Combs's Seventh Fleet Liberators flying from Wakde.[4]

Having hoped to surprise the Allies at Biak, the Japanese were upset at being sighted so early and so far from their destination.[5] The loss of surprise and the possibility of encountering strong naval forces at Biak, including a reported aircraft carrier which was not there, caused Admiral Toyoda to suspend the entire operation at 2025 June 3. *Fuso, Myoko, Haguro,* and destroyers *Asagumo* and *Kazagumo* returned to Davao, at the entrance to which the last-named was sunk by United States submarine *Hake* (Commander John C. Broach). *Aoba, Kinu* and six destroyers, together with the detached force, proceeded (heckled by V A.A.F. bombers) to Sorong, where they disembarked troops on the evening of 4 June.

Off Bosnik on 3 June rode destroyers *Reid, Mustin* and *Russell,* eight LCTs, three rocket LCIs, and one LCI with demolition parties embarked. These were subjected to a second air assault by the reinforced 23rd Air Flotilla, consisting of 32 Zekes and 9 Navy bombers, with which 10 Army planes from the Fourth Air Army at Samate coöperated.[6]

Shortly before 1100, the destroyers' radar screens showed bogeys approaching from the northwest. In a series of very determined attacks between 1105 and 1132 these planes dive-bombed and strafed the beach and the shipping. Commander Samuel A. Mc-Cornock, skipper of *Reid,* which was in the channel between Owi Island and Bosnik when bogeys first appeared, rang up emergency flank speed and prepared to maneuver radically in the impending

---

[4] *Inter. Jap. Off.* II 452; Seventh Fleet War Diary; Japanese Monograph No. 87 p. 11.

[5] Japanese Monograph No. 87 p. 9. On the afternoon of 3 June, destroyer *Hokaze,* torpedo boat *Kiji,* and a subchaser, engaged in reinforcing Manokwari, were attacked by V A.A.F. planes near that place; *Hokaze* was slightly damaged by a near-miss.

[6] Same p. 12.

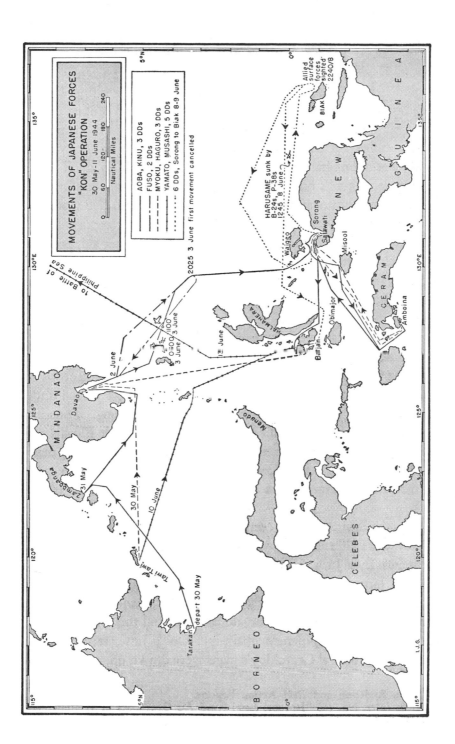

MOVEMENTS OF JAPANESE FORCES
"KON" OPERATION
30 May-11 June 1944

Nautical Miles
0   60   120   180   240

——————— AOBA, KINU, 3 DDs
— — — — FUSO, 2 DDs
— · — · — MYOKU, HAGURO, 3 DDs
— — — — YAMATO, MUSASHI, 5 DDs
· · · · · · · · 6 DDs, Sorong to Biak 8-9 June

2025 3 June first movement cancelled

to Battle of
Philippine Sea

Allied surface
forces
sighted
2240/8

HARUSAME sunk by
B-24s, P-38s
1245, 8 June

BIAK

Sorong
Salawati
Waigeo
Misool

NEW   GUINEA

CERAM

Amboina

Obimajor

Batjan

HALMAHERA

12 June

0600, 1100
3 June   3 June

2 June

MINDANAO
Davao

Zamboanga
31 May

30 May

10 June

Menado

CELEBES

Tawi Tawi

BORNEO

Tarakan depart 30 May

I.J.G.

attack. *Reid* was making 30 knots when about 14 enemy planes singled her out for a series of dive-bombing and strafing attacks, making very low and steep dives out of the sun and broken clouds. Zigzagging at 30 knots or better in the three-mile-wide channel off Bosnik called for seamanship of high order. *Reid* fought off the planes for about half an hour before she was able to duck into a passing rain squall; hit by numerous bullets from the strafing, and by shrapnel from near-misses, she lost one killed and five wounded. But, except for two radars put out of commission temporarily, the damage was superficial. For that, she could thank her skipper's excellent ship handling. Destroyer *Mustin*, standing by in the gunfire support area off Mokmer, also was attacked, but suffered neither damage nor casualties; *LCT–248* had two men wounded.[7] At 1125 friendly fighter cover which had been delayed by weather arrived over Biak and drove off the remaining enemy planes.

Japanese records reveal that 11 of the 41 planes taking part were lost. But the Fourth Air Army at Menado was being reinforced by some 70 planes from the Marianas, and these too were placed under the operational control of Rear Admiral Ito at Sorong.[8] Thus in a matter of a few days the air strength of the 23rd Air Flotilla was built up from 16 to some 200 aircraft. Fortunately for us, many of the Japanese pilots came down with malaria, but all who could fly threw their planes at the Allied troops and ships on and around Biak.

The two cruiser groups commanded by Admirals Crutchley and Berkey were alternately covering Biak from positions northeast of the island. By 2 June Admiral Kinkaid and his staff were convinced that the Japanese Navy was about to move that way. He recalled Crutchley to Humboldt Bay to refuel and replenish, placed both cruiser groups under his command, and ordered this combined task force to meet the Japanese challenge. On 3 June, replenishment completed, Admiral Crutchley's plans were drawn up, and in a con-

[7] Capt. Anderson and *Reid* Action Reports.
[8] USSBS *Inter.* No. 360 "Japanese Land-Based Air Operations in Western New Guinea" p. 4.

ference that afternoon at Hollandia he went over the details of his proposed deployment. He also arranged with Commander Morton K. Fleming, in tender *Orca* at Hollandia, to provide three Catalinas for night search to a radius of 120–130 miles from his force while it was at sea.

Kinkaid, with reports of the enemy force sighted by Commodore Combs's PB4Ys in hand, ordered Crutchley to sortie from Hollandia in time to reach a position about 25 miles north of the eastern end of Biak by 1715 June 4. There he was to endeavor to destroy inferior forces attempting to reinforce Biak, or to retire before superior forces, or, in case no Japanese were encountered during the night of 4–5 June, to retire toward Hollandia next day and repeat the movement. The combined Crutchley force departed Hollandia at 2345 and headed for the initial position at 16 knots. It comprised cruisers *Australia*, *Phoenix*, *Boise*, *Nashville*, and 14 destroyers, of which two were Australian.

Early in the morning of 4 June, Captain Anderson at Biak was informed by Commander Seventh Fleet of Admiral Crutchley's instructions, and ordered to keep all United States vessels then off Bosnik out of Crutchley's way and also out of the expected battle, unless expressly invited in by the task force commander. *Reid*, *Mustin*, *Russell* and several landing craft were still present at Biak. The destroyers patrolled waters between Owi and Japen Islands during the night; landing craft were instructed to remain within the protective arc of shore batteries off Bosnik. General Fuller, also alerted, conferred with Captain Anderson and shifted his shore batteries during the day, in order to cover the sea approaches to Bosnik and resist an enemy naval bombardment. General Whitehead alerted his bombers at Wakde to strike the Japanese force when sighted.

The situation was ominously similar to that at Guadalcanal just before the Battle of Savo Island — where, it will be remembered, Admiral Crutchley had been O.T.C. But the Japanese Navy had lost the daring and tactical edge that it had possessed in 1942, and the outcome was very different.

About noon 4 June, a Japanese reconnaissance plane sighted Crutchley's force about 120 miles east of Biak, and the 23rd Air Flotilla promptly dispatched a strike of 28 fighters and 6 bombers against it. Shortly before 1730, as Crutchley was closing Biak, bogeys were picked up 50 miles to the westward and closing. Combat air patrol provided by the V Army Air Force left about 1720 in order to land on Wakde before dark. Now the cruiser and destroyer sailors had reason to regret rather bitterly that no carriers were with them, for carriers could provide C.A.P. around the clock. Admiral Crutchley immediately ordered his force into an antiaircraft defense formation and turned up 25 knots. Ten minutes later the formation was attacked by enemy planes diving out of the sun. *Nashville* was slightly damaged by a near-miss which exploded under water about ten feet to starboard, aft.

The combined task force reached its assigned covering position at 1900. Kinkaid had advised Crutchley that if the Japanese attempted to land troops that night the probable place would be Wardo, a bight on the west coast of Biak. So Crutchley decided to make a sweep of the south and west coasts of the island. When radar plot in *Reid* indicated that he was heading through the channel between Owi and Biak in darkness, Captain Anderson warned him by TBS that the shore batteries were alert for a surface attack. He answered that General Fuller should be informed of his intentions. *Reid* had trouble raising the beach, but finally got word through as the cruisers were passing Bosnik. Fortunately, since his troops were itching for a chance to fire on Japanese ships, General Fuller recognized *Australia's* silhouette in the bright moonlight.

After sweeping the coast as far as Wardo, Crutchley reversed course and returned to his position northeast of Biak. Four Japanese planes sighted his force passing through the Owi-Biak channel about 0115 June 5, and made a low-level torpedo attack from ahead. At least three torpedoes were dropped, but none found its target. That evening, two Japanese bombers attacked Wakde Island, crowded with about a hundred Allied planes parked wing-and-wing. The damage was very heavy, and as a result the air force at Wakde was almost useless during the next few days.[9]

During the past few days the three American destroyers off Biak had been able to provide so little support to the troops ashore, and yet were so threatened by the increased scale of enemy air attacks, that Admiral Fechteler, with General Fuller's consent, ordered *Reid* and *Mustin* to withdraw to Hollandia at noon 5 June. *Russell* remained as fighter-director during the day and then escorted an echelon of LSTs that had unloaded. Now only two small mine-sweepers and eight LCTs remained at Biak.

Thus ended the first phase of Operation KON. The Japanese main purpose had been thwarted, but all on the other side expected another attempt; nor were they disappointed.

3. Battle off Biak, 8–9 June

Combined Fleet staff quickly planned a second attempt to reinforce Biak. Satisfied by plane reconnaissance that there were no American carriers in those waters, it ordered destroyers *Shikinami*, *Uranami* and *Shigure* to embark 600 troops at Sorong. Escorted by destroyers *Harusame*, *Shiratsuyu* and *Samidare*, each towing one large landing barge, and covered by cruisers *Aoba* and *Kinu*, this transport unit would land the troops at Biak during the night of 8–9 June. On the morning of 7 June *Aoba* and *Kinu* made rendezvous with the six named destroyers north of Misool Island, west of the New Guinea bird's mouth, and there Rear Admiral Sakonju shifted his flag to destroyer *Shikinami*. The cruisers proceeded to Ambon for replenishment, after which they were instructed to return to Salawati Island, just off the western end of the Vogelkop, and stand by for developments. Sakonju's force then steamed to Sorong to embark troops, and at midnight 7 June departed for Biak. Daylight fighter cover for the movement was provided by the 23rd Air Flotilla.

---

[9] *Army Air Forces in World War II*, IV 638, where no figures are given and the raid is slighted. I have reason to believe that about two thirds of the planes on the island were either destroyed or damaged.

While these Japanese preparations and movements were under way, Admiral Crutchley's cruiser force maintained its nightly prowl, retiring toward Hollandia during the morning hours and at noon reversing course toward Biak, to be at the initial covering position by sundown; but on the evening of the 7th, when by exception he was refueling at Hollandia, he received dispatch orders from Kinkaid to be off Korim Bay, on the northeast coast of Biak, by 2200 June 8. His force now comprised heavy cruiser *Australia* (*Shropshire* being in Australia for repairs), light cruisers *Phoenix* and *Boise*, and 14 destroyers.[10] One hour after receiving this order Crutchley's force sailed from Humboldt Bay.

On 8 June Wakde Island, still patching-up from the 5 June raid, could put only a few reconnaissance planes in the air; but ten B–25s from Lake Sentani, escorted by long-range P–38s, put the finger on Admiral Sakonju. At 1245 they located his six destroyers northwest of Manokwari, made a low-level bombing and strafing attack, sank destroyer *Harusame*, holed *Shiratsuyu*, and inflicted minor damage on *Shikinami* and *Samidare*. After rescuing *Harusame's* crew, the remaining five destroyers resumed their run toward Biak. Before they got there, at 1900, Sakonju received a report that Japanese aircraft had sighted an enemy task force steaming west at high speed in his direction. At 2340, according to his time (which was 15 or 20 minutes faster than ours), one of the screening destroyers sighted Admiral Crutchley's task force. Sakonju was no Tanaka.[11] He promptly decided to retire. But he was not to retire in peace.

The sighting reported to him at 1900 had been made by a Betty at 1440, when Crutchley's force was about 120 miles east of Korim Bay. The British Admiral, with no fighter cover owing to the shortage of planes at Wakde, could do nothing about it and the Betty escaped.[12] Expecting an air strike in consequence, Crutchley made

[10] Adm. Crutchley's Report p. 6. *Nashville* was too damaged to participate.
[11] See Vol. V for Rear Adm. Tanaka's exploits around Guadalcanal.
[12] Destroyer *Gillespie*, fighter-director at Biak, overheard Crutchley's request and diverted fighter planes en route to Biak to get the snooper, but before they arrived the Betty had disappeared. Admiral Crutchley's Narrative pp. 6, 7.

an evasive change of course for forty miles before resuming his run toward Korim Bay at 2000, expecting to arrive at 2200. The moon, two days past full, rose at 2023, but the sky was overcast with passing showers. As the cruisers approached Korim Bay bogeys began to appear on their radar screens; one closed to within three miles and was taken under fire. The Admiral, having received no intelligence of Sakonju's whereabouts, decided to make a sweep parallel to the coast of Biak, detaching destroyer *Mullany* to take a close look at Korim Bay.

Shortly after 2200 a PB4Y night search plane reported to Crutchley that five unidentified ships were about 60 miles NW by W of his force, making 12 knots in his direction. The Admiral recalled *Mullany* to his formation and set a course to intercept. At 2320 *Boise* reported a surface radar contact bearing 290° distant 13 miles. Crutchley ordered his force to deploy for battle on a northerly course. Desdiv 42, then three miles ahead of the cruisers, was ordered to take station on their port quarter; but if Commander Albert E. Jarrell heard the order, he did the equivalent of Lord Nelson's putting his blind eye to the telescope. For Jarrell, in *Fletcher*, had the radar contact too and was already working up speed to 30 knots to close. Admiral Sakonju's destroyer group sighted the Allied force at almost the same moment that they saw him, cast off the barges it was towing, turned northerly to fire torpedoes and then northwesterly to retire. It was a bitter disappointment to Admiral Crutchley that they declined action.

Commander Jarrell, observing the enemy destroyers' turn, reported his opinion at 2329 that they had fired torpedoes. Two minutes later Admiral Crutchley ordered all his destroyers to pursue the enemy. Desdiv 42 (*Fletcher, Jenkins, Radford* and *La Vallette*) was already hot on the chase. Desdiv 47 (*Hutchins, Daly, Beale, Bache*), Captain Kenmore M. McManes, was about 3000 yards to the eastward, and Desdiv 48 (*Abner Read, Ammen, Mullany, Trathen*), Commander John B. McLean, about the same distance astern of Desdiv 42. H.M.A.S. *Arunta* and *Warramunga* were coming up from the rear of the cruisers. By 2340 the contact was definitely identified as three destroyers in one column, two destroyers in another column on their starboard hand, all making about 32 knots.[13] Jarrell's report about the torpedoes was confirmed at 2340 when *Boise* reported a torpedo passing her stern. Crutchley

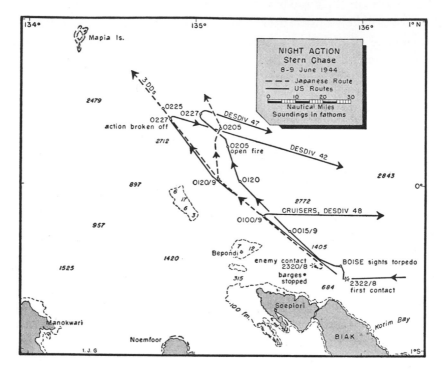

turned the now screenless cruisers and combed the wakes successfully.

"A stern chase is a long chase." That old maxim of sailing-ship days still holds good. At 2343 the pursuing destroyers passed several troop-laden barges which had been cast off by the Japanese destroyers and took them under fire in passing. The Americans were now working up to 35 knots and settling down for a slow decrease of the range. The cruisers followed, making 29 knots, their best speed in these warm waters. *Fletcher*, leading the van, had closed

[13] They had been towing barges at 15 knots when discovered, and it took them some time to build up flank speed after casting off.

the range to 17,000 yards by 0018 June 9, and promptly opened fire with her bow guns. Commander Jarrell had little expectation of hitting at that range but hoped he might force the enemy to zigzag and lose distance. Japanese destroyers in the rear replied, and from then on through the remainder of the chase there were intermittent exchanges of gunfire between the two groups.

By 0045 Admiral Crutchley was satisfied that there were no other enemy forces supporting the destroyers and, since Desdivs 42 and 47 were closest to the enemy, giving him a margin of eight ships to five, there was nothing to be gained by pushing the cruisers at high speed. So at 0048 he ordered Captain McManes to continue the pursuit with the two American destroyer divisions until 0230, or break off earlier at his discretion, and then return at high speed to a rendezvous within range of shore-based fighter cover. At 0100 the cruisers turned eastward at 15 knots with Desdiv 48 screening. *Arunta* and *Warramunga* were ordered to search for the cast off enemy barges.

The chase was rapidly leading the destroyers into an area previously announced to Allied air forces as one where they were at liberty to bomb anything afloat. Crutchley sent a warning message to all friendly aircraft, and to shore headquarters, advising them of the situation, but he felt anxious about the possibility of error by aircraft or submarine. That is why he placed a time limit on the chase.

At 0020 Commander Jarrell assured Captain McManes that he had a good chance of catching the Japanese, especially if they turned left toward Manokwari. The ranges at the time were 17,000 yards for Desdiv 42 and 24,000 yards for Desdiv 47. For the next hour it was a matter of slowly closing range, *Fletcher* exchanging shots with the fleeing Japanese destroyers. By 0125, with only an hour left before he was ordered to turn back, Jarrell tried to trick the enemy into maneuvering. Assuming that Sakonju was not aware of Desdiv 47's being in the chase, he turned his column to port in order to unmask the batteries of his four destroyers and ordered the whole division to open fire, hoping that the sudden volume of fire might cause the enemy to change course to starboard, thus giving McManes a chance to get into the fight. The northern Japanese column of two destroyers took the bait and deviated about 50° to starboard. Jarrell's heavy fire also provoked the enemy to fire torpedoes; at 0144 a torpedo track passed *Fletcher*.[14]

The success of Jarrell's foxy maneuver enabled Desdiv 47 to close range on the northern couple of destroyers to 15,000 yards, and at 0205 McManes opened fire. Six minutes later an explosion was observed on *Shiratsuyu*, the only ship on either side to be hit during this action; she dropped back about 1000 yards but soon picked up speed. At 0227 the range was down to 10,000 yards, but for several minutes the Japanese had been holding their own, and Crutchley's deadline had arrived. The destroyer commanders broke off action and steamed to their rendezvous with the Admiral at 31 knots. During the two-hour stern chase, about 1300 rounds had been exchanged. Besides the hit on *Shiratsuyu*, *Shikinami* and *Samidare* were slightly damaged by near misses; but *Fletcher*, which had received the bulk of enemy attention, was not even scratched.

A few soldiers may have landed at Korim Bay from barges cast off by the Japanese destroyers, but most of the troops were taken back to Sorong. *Shiratsuyu* and *Samidare* of the screening unit went direct to Batjan, where they joined cruisers *Myoko* and *Haguro*. *Shikinami*, *Uranami* and *Shigure* returned to Sorong, disembarked troops, and joined cruisers *Aoba* and *Kinu* at Salawati, after which all ships went to Batjan, arriving 10 June.

Sakonju's second reinforcement attempt had been thwarted. Ito still had about 150 planes with sick and ill-trained pilots in his beefed-up 23rd Air Flotilla; but before they had had time to recover, their planes were recalled to help the Mobile Fleet in Operation A-Go.

[14] Comdesdiv 42 Action Report.

4. A-Go Cancels KON, *Biak Secured,* 10–22 June

After the failure of this second phase of Operation KON, Admiral Ozawa, commanding the Mobile Fleet already committed to Operation A-Go, was even more eager to reinforce and hold Biak. Admiral Toyoda, agreeing, on 10 June ordered the 18-inch-gunned battleships *Yamato* and *Musashi*, light cruiser *Noshiro* and six destroyers to be detached from the Mobile Fleet and attached to the KON Force. These ships, under the command of Vice Admiral Ugaki in *Yamato*, departed Tawi Tawi at 1600 June 10 and arrived at Batjan on 11 June. On the same day two more destroyers were added. Forces assigned to this operation were now organized as follows: —

Attack Division, Vice Admiral Matome Ugaki

Battleships	YAMATO, MUSASHI
Heavy Cruisers	MYOKO, HAGURO
Light Cruiser	NOSHIRO
Destroyers	SHIMAKAZE, OKINAMI, ASAGUMO

Transport Unit 1, Rear Admiral Naomasa Sakonju (Comcrudiv 16)

Cruisers	AOBA, KINU
Destroyers	SHIKINAMI, URANAMI, YAMAGUMO, NOWAKI

Transport Unit 2

Minelayers	ITSUKUSHIMA, TSUGARU

Transport No. 127; several subchasers, several freighters

By the evening of 11 June this greatly strengthened KON force had assembled at Batjan. The reinforcement run to Biak was scheduled for the 15th. Admiral Ugaki intended to land his troops at all costs, and at the same time to inflict a destructive bombardment on Allied positions at Biak and Owi. But by this time Admiral Toyoda had a new situation to worry about. Pacific Fleet carrier planes attacked Guam and Saipan on the 11th and again on the 12th. It was evident that Spruance was aiming at the Marianas, not Palau; the long-anticipated chance for a big naval battle was fast approaching. So, at 1830 June 12, Admiral Toyoda issued orders to start Operation A-Go at once. KON was "temporarily" suspended, never to be resumed. Admiral Ugaki hastened north with *Yamato, Musashi, Myoko, Haguro, Noshiro* and five destroyers to rendezvous with Ozawa in the Philippine Sea.[15]

At the same time Toyoda ordered the 23rd Air Flotilla to forward all naval aircraft then in New Guinea to Palau. But before its departure the flotilla got in a Parthian shot at Biak. On 12 June at 1036 four Japanese planes singled out *Kalk*, one of four destroyers that were about to finish escorting an LST echelon to Biak. She was working up to flank speed when a single plane dived on her out of the sun, and, although taken under fire during the dive, dropped a bomb which hit at the base of her torpedo tubes abaft the forward stack. The bomb exploded the air flasks of *Kalk's* torpedoes, blowing out the structure between the stacks and causing extensive damage on deck and in the forward engine and boiler rooms. Several fires were started but shortly brought under control; 4 officers and 26 men were killed or missing, 4 officers and 36 men wounded. PT boats rushed out from Mios Woendi and took wounded men ashore for treatment. *Kalk* had to be towed to Hollandia.[16] In the more than two weeks of repeated air attacks at and near Biak, she was the only seriously damaged Allied ship.

Admiral Toyoda's order to execute Operation A-Go sealed the fate of Japanese ground forces on Biak.

After the failure of Operation KON the Japanese made sporadic efforts to reinforce the Biak garrison by barges from Manokwari via Noemfoor. At most, about 1100 troops slipped through Allied patrols and reached the island. General Anami ordered Colonel Kuzume to prolong the defense as much as possible, and prolong it he did. Mokmer airfield was taken on 7 June, but enemy positions in the caves and high ground prevented engineers from trying to recondition it until the 13th, when they were driven off by enemy

---

[15] See below, chap. xiv.
[16] *Kalk* Action Report.

fire. Clearing out the caves was a slow, hard process. General Krueger, dissatisfied with the progress, relieved General Fuller by General Eichelberger on 15 June. Every Japanese strong point had to be blasted and burned out.[17] Not until the 20th could the engineers resume work on Mokmer airfield. The same day, Borokoe a.1d Sorido airstrips were captured. On 22 June the first fighters began to operate from Mokmer.

Colonel Kuzume's defense had denied the airfields to the Allies for nearly a month. Realizing the hopelessness of his position, this brave and resourceful officer caused his regimental colors to be burned during the night of 21–22 June. Whether he then took his own life or was killed in action is not known, but his death marked the end of a well-directed and stubborn defense.

The capture of this island cost Allied ground forces 438 killed or missing and 2361 wounded.[18] In addition to battle casualties, there was a large incidence of disease within the Hurricane Task Force. Some 3500 cases were diagnosed as "fever, undetermined origin," but at least a thousand of them were due to an epidemic of scrub typhus which broke out on Owi Island and spread to Biak. Stringent control measures finally conquered this virulent infestation. Naval casualties in the capture of Biak were 22 killed, 14 missing, and 68 wounded.

MacArthur's prompt and vigorous invasion of Biak proved to be a serious embarrassment to the enemy on the eve of the Battle of the Philippine Sea. That alone made the operation worth while; but, in addition, Biak became an important Allied air base for the subsequent liberation of the Philippines.

[17] Details will be found in R. R. Smith *Approach to the Philippines* and in W. F. McCartney *The Jungleers.*
[18] Gen. Krueger Report.

CHAPTER X

Noemfoor and Sansapor

2 July–3 September 1944

1. Noemfoor Island,[1] 2 July–31 August

EARLY in June 1944, when Biak was proving difficult, General MacArthur's planners were searching for airfield sites farther west and looking for a foothold on the Vogelkop peninsula. About midway between Biak and Manokwari lies the almost circular island of Noemfoor, about eleven miles in diameter. Undeveloped before the war, it had been visited by trading vessels about twice a year to pick up copra and ironwood. The natives, similar to those on Biak and numbering about 5000, lived in scattered villages along the coast. Noemfoor is surrounded by a coral reef penetrated by a few small boat channels; harbors or protected anchorages do not exist. Like Biak, this island has a coral base and rises in jungle-covered hills and ridges up to 700 feet.

Exactly when the Japanese occupied Noemfoor we do not know; nor does it much matter, since they showed no interest in developing it until the New Operational Policy of September 1943 made it a link in their defensive perimeter. The natives, unappreciative of their "liberation" from "Western imperialism," and appalled at the prospect of work, concealed themselves in the hills. So the Japanese imported some 3000 Indonesians from Surabaya

---

[1] Action Reports of commands and ships taking part, especially that of CTF 77 (Rear Adm. Fechteler); ms. "Command History U.S. Naval Forces in the Southwest Pacific Area" in Div. of Naval History, Washington; Gen. Krueger's Reports of the Noemfoor and Sansapor operations; R. R. Smith *Approach to the Philippines* chaps. xvii, xviii; Craven and Cate *Army Air Forces in World War II* Vol. IV.

and other cities in Java to build the airfields. Underfed and over-worked, these wretched people died like flies of disease and starvation; only 403 survivors, almost skeletons, were alive when the Allies secured the island.

Three airfields were completed by mid-1944: Kamiri and Kornasoren on the north shore, and Namber on the southwestern side of the island. These were what made Noemfoor the next Allied prize. They could be quickly put in shape for use by Allied air forces, they would help to consolidate the Biak base by providing outlying fighter and satellite fields, and they were well placed for supporting future operations on the Vogelkop.

On 5 June General Krueger was warned by General MacArthur that it might be necessary to capture Noemfoor. On the 14th the Supreme Commander directed his principal subordinates to prepare plans to seize the island only two weeks later, on 30 June. Admiral Fechteler and all hands in his command ship *Blue Ridge* had enjoyed but three days' liberty at Sydney when the order of 14 June cut short that pleasant interlude, at least for "Admiral Bill." On 17 June Admiral Kinkaid issued his operation order for the naval part of Noemfoor, and on the 19th Admiral Fechteler, having flown up to New Guinea, broke his flag in transport *Henry T. Allen* at Cape Sudest. In her he arrived at Cape Cretin on the 20th for active planning at Krueger's headquarters. A postponement of D-day to 2 July was approved by General MacArthur.

The landing force, called the "Cyclone Task Force," was built around the 168th Regiment, Brigadier General Edwin D. Patrick USA, reinforced by artillery, antiaircraft, tank, engineer and service units to 7100 troops. As this regiment was then trying to drive the Japanese out of Sarmi, the 6th Infantry Division had to be moved up to Wakde to relieve it. Captain Bern Anderson, informed by radio that he would be the landing control officer, received a copy of Fechteler's plan at Hollandia on 24 June, and next day went to Wakde with eight LSTs of the assault echelon, four destroyers and two of the four PCs. Admiral Fechteler arrived three days later. Planning Noemfoor was as hectic as its code name "Tabletennis" suggested; yet in execution it was probably the smoothest of all Southwest Pacific operations.

General Krueger, distrusting maps based on photographic reconnaissance, and without informing Admiral Fechteler, sent a party of Alamo scouts up to Noemfoor in PT boats on the night of 22–23 June to get firsthand information on the beaches off Kamiri. The scouts were promptly detected by the Japanese and forced to withdraw with little information except that the enemy was alerted.[2] Colonel Shimizu, the Japanese commander, decided from the place where they came ashore that an Allied landing would be made at Kamiri during the first week of July. He had only about 2000 troops to defend the island, and as they had been on short rations for some time, their morale was low. Concentrating his defenses at and around the airfield, he placed obstacles along the beach, including about 300 land mines improvised from bombs; but, being thoughtfully marked to protect Japanese troops, they caused Allied troops no trouble.

Since the landing was planned to take place at the center of enemy power on Noemfoor, Admiral Fechteler decided to give the place a good preliminary pounding by the Berkey and Crutchley cruiser groups (the latter now under command of Commodore John A. Collins RAN), with 14 extra destroyers.[3] Sustained attacks on Noemfoor by Allied Air Forces began 20 June. Between that date and 1 July, some 800 tons of bombs were dropped on the island, mostly around Kamiri airstrip. These attacks encountered slight antiaircraft fire and no air opposition, since on 13 June the rest of the Japanese aircraft under the 23rd Air Flotilla had been sent north again to contest the Americans at Saipan. By 1 July Japanese air power in the Vogelkop had completely evaporated. Nevertheless, the V A.A.F. provided the naval attack force with C.A.P. by day and night fighters between dusk and dawn. Finding no enemy aircraft to contend with, these planes strafed targets designated by the air controller before returning to base.[4]

[2] CTF 77 Action Report.
[3] CTF 77 War Diary. Commo. Collins relieved Rear Adm. Crutchley 13 June.
[4] *Army Air Forces in World War II* Vol. IV 656–58; CTF 77 Action Report;

The Naval Attack Force, mounted at Finschhafen and at Toem, near Wakde, moved to Noemfoor in three separate groups; 40 LCMs, 50-foot open landing craft manned by the 3rd ESB, made the 700-mile passage from Finschhafen in 12 days.[5] Five LCTs loaded with tanks, tractors and bulldozers left Toem 29 June under

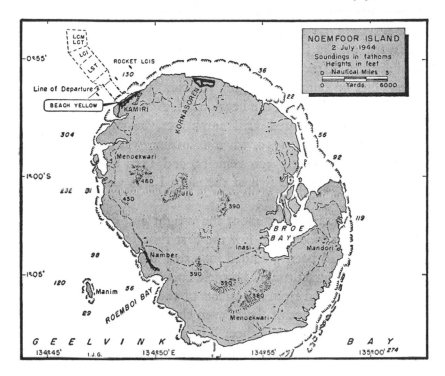

escort of three PCs and called at Mios Woendi for a short rest and to embark troops.

On D-day, 2 July, the sky was partly overcast, a very light south-easterly breeze was blowing, and the sea was smooth — ideal conditions for the landing. Everything went off on schedule. Naval bombardment began at first light; the only enemy reaction was antiaircraft fire, soon silenced, at spotting planes. The boat officers found the edge of the reef broken by coral heads and crevices but

A–20s were also on station at the objective for on-call missions and a Navy Catalina stood by for air-sea rescue work.
  [5] "Amphibian Engineer Operations" V 142–43.

reported that LCIs could beach there. This was important, for if it had not been feasible to beach LCIs the troops would have had to be ferried ashore in amphibian vehicles.[6]

Since dust and smoke kicked up by the bombardment reduced visibility to about 500 yards, the control vessels rigged floodlights pointing seaward, which made good markers for the approaching assault waves of LVTs, launched from the LSTs about 800 yards to seaward of the line of departure. Two battalions of troops landed abreast. After passing through the 400-yard-wide boat lane and crawling up onto the reef, the vehicles fanned out in order to cover a half-mile front on the beach itself. Accompanying the first wave were four armored ESB amphtracs, heavily armed with automatic weapons. By 1750, when unloading was belayed for the day, 7100 troops, nearly 500 vehicles, and 2250 tons of supplies had been discharged and five of the eight LSTs were completely unloaded.

There was no complaint about the weight and quality of naval bombardment at Noemfoor. For the first time in the Pacific war, the defenders had been pounded into that desirable state known to pugilists as "punch drunk." Japanese encountered around the airfield were so stunned from the effects of the bombardment that all the fight was taken out of them; even those in nearby caves were dazed and offered little resistance.[7] The first to be seen were about 40 Japanese who ran out of a cave in the coral terrace behind the airstrip, milled about aimlessly, showed neither fight nor desire to surrender, and were mowed down by rifle fire and machine guns from the armored amphtracs supporting the front-line troops. As they advanced, the troops mopped up every foxhole and cave. Beginning at the eastern end of the airstrip was a series of emplacements, dugouts, barbed-wire entanglements and prepared positions covering the reef and sea approaches, all the way to Kornasoren airfield. Most of these were already abandoned but each had to be checked.

[6] CTU 77.3.7 (Capt. Anderson) Action Report.
[7] Gen. Krueger Report on Noemfoor Operation.

The only effective enemy reaction was provided by a battery in the interior which dropped shells intermittently on the reef for about an hour, destroying two vehicles and killing one man before being silenced by naval gunfire.

A company of the 27th Engineers, aided by the 62nd Works Wing R.A.A.F., began reconditioning Kamiri airstrip early on D-day. General Patrick's chief engineer, Group Captain W. A. O. Hale RAAF, supervised the airfield work and he had Kamiri strip ready for planes on 6 July, when a squadron of Australian P–40s arrived and began operating.

General Patrick landed and assumed command ashore at 1025. Shortly afterward, he sent a message to Alamo headquarters reporting that Kamiri airstrip appeared to be ready to receive paratroops, and requesting that the 503rd Parachute Infantry (Lieutenant Colonel George M. Jones USA, already alerted at Hollandia) fly in to reinforce the Cyclone Task Force, for prisoners taken during the morning indicated that there were more Japanese on the island than had been expected — an error, as it turned out. This drop was the only mishap of the operation. On 3 July the 1st Battalion of the 503rd, 739 strong, was flown up from Hollandia to bail out over Kamiri airstrip. Several planes flew in too low, resulting in 72 casualties, many of them severe fracture cases. Next day the 3rd Battalion flew in and bailed out, with 56 casualties resulting. Nine per cent casualties were several times as much as the paratroops could afford to take, so it was arranged to have the 2nd Battalion ride into Noemfoor on LCIs.

Kornasoren airstrip was taken on 4 July and the beachhead extended about a mile to the south of Kamiri. Here the Japanese made their only real counterattack, were cut to pieces, and by 0630 July 5 it was all over. Next day a shore-to-shore movement from Beach Yellow to seize Namber airstrip was executed by the 2nd Battalion 158th RCT, in 20 LCMs. The troops quickly seized the airfield without opposition.

At the beginning of the naval bombardment on D-day, Colonel Shimizu planned a general withdrawal to Broe Bay on the eastern side of the island in the hope of being evacuated, but most of his troops fled to the hills. Those who resisted, broken into small parties, were cut off by Allied troops and destroyed. Colonel Shimizu himself, with some 200 men, was finally trapped in the southeastern part of the island by mid-August.

The Netherlands East Indies Civil Administration detachment with the landing force finally established contact with natives hiding in the interior, and they came out of their hiding places waving Dutch flags which they had concealed. Late in July the native chiefs of the island formally declared war on Japan, and the natives cheerfully assisted in the final mopping-up of the remnants of the Japanese garrison.

By 31 August, when the operation was officially terminated, the Cyclone Task Force had lost 66 killed or missing and 343 wounded. But it had accounted for 1900 Japanese, including 186 captured, together with 550 Formosans. And it had recovered 403 emaciated Javanese laborers.

2. Sansapor, 30 July–31 August

In his plans for returning to the Philippines, General MacArthur had always set his sights on an air base at the western end of the Vogelkop Peninsula. Sorong first appeared to be the most attractive spot, for several reasons: extensive Japanese developments, the presence of the Klamano oilfield about 30 miles to the southeast, and Waigeo Island 30 miles northwestward, suitable for an air and naval base. The Klamano oilfield had long figured in Allied plans as the first significant oil deposit in enemy hands that could be recaptured and exploited. As early as February 1943 the Joint Chiefs of Staff authorized preparations for restoring the crude oil facilities in the Dutch East Indies. Quantities of equipment had been stockpiled in California, and specialists were assembled for the project by early 1944. But the subsequent speed-up of the Pacific war made it evident that the Klamano field could not produce soon enough to be of any material assistance, and the project was canceled in July.[8]

In outlining to the J.C.S. on 8 May 1944 his plans for taking Wakde and Biak, the Supreme Commander set the target date of 1 August for seizing airfields on the Vogelkop. Once that peninsula was secured, he proposed to move into Halmahera on 15 September, when the Pacific Fleet was to seize the Palaus.

On 17 June submarine *S–47* (Lieutenant Lloyd V. Young) had sailed from the Admiralty Islands for Waigeo with a large scouting party composed of all manner of experts. But, since the study of new aërial photographs at headquarters revealed the lack of suitable airfield sites on that island, *S–47* was diverted to Sansapor and Mar. These villages lie about 55 miles northeast of Sorong and 15 miles west of the Cape of Good Hope, the northernmost point in New Guinea. The party landed 23 June, spent nearly a week examining the region, and returned a favorable report, on the strength of which the General canceled Sorong-Waigeo and ordered the seizure of Sansapor-Mar on 30 July.[9]

Good landing beaches existed near these villages, and a coastal plain with potential airfield sites swept back to the Tamrau Mountains. The region was heavily forested, but there were several places partially cleared and covered with second growth. At Sansapor village, 13 miles southwest of Mar, there was a Japanese barge-staging station manned by about one hundred troops. A few miles off Mar are the Mios Soe Islands, Middelburg and Amsterdam.

Admiral Fechteler and most of his planners were at sea taking part in the Noemfoor operation on 4 July when they received word that Operation "Globetrotter" was on the cards for the 30th. The Admiral had to hasten back to Hollandia to learn that "Globetrotter" meant Sansapor and Mar. The first planning conference at General Krueger's new headquarters on Humboldt Bay was held on 8 July. Representatives of the V A.A.F., the VII 'Phib, the Typhoon Task Force (6th Infantry Division, Major General

[8] R. R. Smith *Approach to the Philippines* pp. 425–28.
[9] Admiral Kinkaid's Op Plan 9–44.

Franklin C. Sibert USA), which was chosen to make the landing, and of the PT squadrons, were present. All agreed that the target date of 30 July could be met, and Admiral Fechteler's plan was ready on the 15th. The ships taking part were first given a short overhaul at Hollandia — the very first instance in the whole Dutch

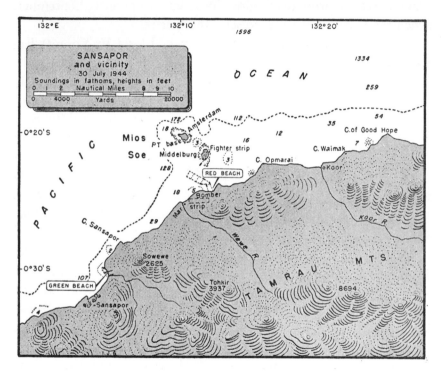

New Guinea campaign when these vessels enjoyed such a luxury. In the meantime, V A.A.F. bombers kept Japanese airfields on the Vogelkop neutralized, and on 27 July they staged a big raid of 80 B–24s, 45 B–25s and four squadrons of P–38s on the Halmahera airfields. Only token opposition was met in the air and from the ground. Next day the Amboina-Ceram region was raided, and B–25s searched for shipping in Halmahera and around the Vogelkop.[10]

At 2300 July 27 the expeditionary force, consisting of 11 de-

[10] *Army Air Forces in World War II* IV 666–67.

stroyers, 5 destroyer-transports, 19 LCIs, 8 LSTs, 4 PCs and a fleet tug, got under way from Toem and Wakde for the run to Sansapor. Two Army scouting parties brought in and out by PT boats reported still no enemy activity, so Admiral Fechteler hoped that complete tactical surprise could be obtained. Consequently he and General Sibert agreed that there should be no preliminary bombardment.

The landing, in six waves, was carried out within an hour, starting at 0700 July 30. No Japanese were seen or heard from. Amphtracs were used only in the secondary landings on Middelburg and Amsterdam Islands. All LSTs were unloaded by 1730 and on their way back to Wakde to pick up another load.

On 31 July a shore-to-shore movement was carried out from the mouth of the Wewe River near Mar to Beach Green at Cape Sansapor, where an unopposed landing was made and Sansapor village occupied. Cape Sansapor was used for an air warning radar, but the proposed PT base was shifted to Amsterdam Island.

Since airfield construction was the one object of securing Sansapor, Brigadier General E. W. Barnes of the XIII A.A.F. landed with the D-day echelon to select the sites. He chose Middelburg Island for the fighter strip, and on 17 August reported it ready for operation. A 6000-foot steel mat bomber strip constructed near Mar was ready to handle medium bombers on 3 September.

During August the 6th Division, with supporting ships and craft, actively patrolled the coast in both directions from Sansapor to hunt down scattered groups of Japanese. From captured documents it was learned that the Second Army had begun to evacuate Manokwari at the end of June, moving overland toward Sorong and southward along the coast toward Babo. Most of these troops concentrated at Windissi on Geelvink Bay, but some units up to battalion strength were intercepted and wiped out east of Sansapor. There was no enemy air reaction for nearly a month after the landing; on 27 August three Japanese planes made a night raid that caused little damage. On the 31st, when Operation "Globetrotter" officially ended, the total casualties in the Typhoon Task Force were 34 killed and 85 wounded. In addition, nine men had died from an epidemic of scrub typhus that had broken out among troops on the beachhead.

Sansapor was the final stop in New Guinea for General Mac-Arthur's long journey back to the Philippines; the next move, to Morotai in the Halmaheras, we shall have to postpone to a later volume. His rapid occupation of key positions, a push of nearly 1000 miles along the coast in less than four months, was made possible by sound planning and vigorous execution in which all hands and every branch of the armed services played their parts superlatively well.

3. *New Guinea Epilogue*

In the Southwest Pacific, General Douglas MacArthur was supreme commander in fact as well as in name. His dynamic personality and dramatic qualities presented to the world a picture somewhat different from the one seen by subordinates who translated his decisions and orders into action. They saw a thoroughly competent and businesslike officer who was open to suggestions; but always, after he had heard and considered them, made firm decisions. Without exception, every commander who served under General MacArthur, in whatever arm of the service and from whatever country, entertained a great respect for his military judgment and leadership. We have seen how smartly his operations were executed, on or very close to the target dates he set, with few of the snarls that are inevitable in military affairs.

A spot-by-spot advance toward the Philippines after breaking the Bismarcks Barrier would have brought his forces into direct conflict with the strongest concentration of Japanese troops in New Guinea. With the temporary loan of Pacific Fleet carriers, he was enabled to "leapfrog" this concentration into Hollandia, transforming a serious threat into a mere nuisance in his rear. Once established at Hollandia, MacArthur pushed his forces relentlessly to keep them rolling westward, his only limiting factor being the range of his land-based fighter planes to cover them.

The advance of 550 miles from Hollandia to Cape Sansapor required little more than three months, with three Japanese-developed air bases picked up on the way. Expert and flexible planning and a high order of teamwork between Army, Navy and air forces were necessary to show such results, and these MacArthur and his principal subordinates enjoyed.

The invasion of Biak alarmed the Japanese high command more than that of any other place in this theater; and a glance at the chart of the Pacific Ocean will show why. On 1 June 1944, the westernmost point held by Admiral Nimitz's forces was Eniwetok, 1000 miles east of Guam; but MacArthur's forces were on Biak, only 800 miles from Davao in the southern Philippines. The Central Pacific forces had made no important amphibious moves since February, and something new from that quarter was expected by Imperial Headquarters. But the big American carriers had gone all-out at Hollandia; could this mean that MacArthur's thrusts were actually the main Allied offensive? At any rate, he was getting close to Japan's main oil-line and rice-line, and to a position threatening the Philippines. These factors could not be ignored, and the abortive KON operation was hastily devised to meet them. Then, on 11 June, Japanese scout planes discovered the Pacific Fleet moving toward Saipan. That cleared the situation. Imperial Headquarters no longer had any doubt where the main threat lay. Japanese pressure was promptly removed from the Southwest Pacific and applied at the Marianas.

General MacArthur certainly deserved this respite after his well conceived and smartly executed moves — Aitape, Hollandia, Wakde, Biak, Noemfoor, Sansapor. We shall leave him consolidating his positions and preparing for his heart's desire, the Return to the Philippines, while we shift our attention to the great doings around the Marianas and in the broad reaches of the Philippine Sea.

PART III

The Marianas

(Operation "Forager")

East Longitude dates except for events in Europe, the United States and Hawaii. "King" Time (Zone minus 10).

CHAPTER XI

Preliminary Poundings and Final Plans

February–April 1944

1. *Ladrones-Marianas*

THE fifteen Marianas or Ladrone Islands stretch for some 425 miles in an arc, of which the 145th meridian east longitude is the chord. Starting with Farallon de Pajaros, 335 miles southeast of Iwo Jima, and ending with Guam, 250 miles north of the Carolines, this chain forms with the Bonins the upright bar of the big Micronesian "L." The four biggest islands, Saipan, Tinian, Rota and Guam, all at the southernmost end, are those with which we are concerned; for only they have any military or economic value.

Unhappily for their native race, the Chamorros, these four happen to lie athwart some of the principal sail and steamer routes from America to Manila, Canton, Shanghai and Japan.

Magellan sailed across the Pacific for 98 days without sighting a single inhabited island until, on 6 March 1521, he raised the hills of Rota. At Umtac Bay in Guam he obtained much needed food and water, but did not tarry as the natives threatened to make away with everything movable on board; his revenge was to name the group *Las Islas de los Ladrones*, the Isles of Thieves. Legaspi, en route to the Philippines in 1565, took formal possession for Spain; but over a century elapsed before Spain did anything about the Ladrones. By arousing the interest of Queen Maria Ana, Father Louis de Sanvitores obtained royal permission to convert the natives and to rename the islands *Las Marianas* after his patroness. Sailors, nevertheless, continue to call them the Ladrones to this day. For almost two centuries the Marianas slept. Only the annual call of the Acapulco-Manila galleon on her westward passage brought a little life to Agaña. Commodore Anson, on his scurvy-ridden voyage of 1742 around the world, found Tinian, though uninhabited, teeming with wild cattle, poultry and fruit that the Spaniards had provided or planted. He would fain have made it a British possession, but the government of George II was not interested and it remained for an American shipmaster, who had read the narrative of Anson's voyage, to try and practice what Anson had preached.

This was Captain Brown of the ship *Derby* of Salem. He and other shipmasters who were engaged in the fur and sandalwood trade between New England, the Northwest Coast, Hawaii and Canton wanted a provisioning port for the long Pacific crossing. Accordingly, they attempted to colonize Saipan and Aguijan with Hawaiians in order to cultivate the land and raise cattle. But they reckoned without the Spanish governor of the Marianas, who sent troops over from Agaña, destroyed the Americans' crops and buildings and enslaved the Hawaiians.[1]

In 1825 the Spanish government began to recolonize the larger islands with Filipinos. But there was enough of the old Chamorro leaven to make the people today very different from any one of the numerous races in the Philippines. Light brown in color, often of fine stature and physique, they are intelligent and ambitious, and the most faithful and loyal group of Pacific islanders over whom the American flag has ever flown.

Flown it had over Guam since 1 February 1899, when Commander Edward D. Taussig of U.S.S. *Bennington* took formal possession, for Guam had been ceded to the United States the previous December. Spain, having lost the Philippines, had no use for the Marianas, and the United States could have bought the rest cheap; but the McKinley administration felt that Guam was sufficient as a coaling station and outpost to the Philippines. Ger-

[1] P. J. Searles in *Guam Recorder* VII (1932) p. 476.

many then purchased the 14 remaining Marianas for the moderate sum of $4,500,000.

The tide of conquest now rolled eastward. Japan captured the German Marianas in World War I and was given a mandate over them by the League of Nations in 1920. And Japan, it must be admitted, did more to develop them in a quarter-century than Spain had done in three centuries. The South Sea Development Company continued the planting of sugar which Germany had started, and by 1930 they had become an important source of Japan's domestic supply. By the time the war broke, the Japanese in the Marianas outnumbered the natives more than two to one. American possession of Guam, always resented by the Japanese, was one of the first things they attended to, only two days after the Pearl Harbor attack.[2]

During its 43 years under American rule, Guam had been a good example of that "salutary neglect" which Edmund Burke regarded as the best colonial policy. Guam remained under the Navy Department, which appointed a succession of naval officers as governors. Much was accomplished for the health, education and general well being of the Chamorros, but no attempt was made to colonize the island or develop it industrially; and, although bigger than Japanese Saipan, it produced much less. A Guamanian might sail over to a Japanese-held island to earn money, but he found Japanese rule irksome and always returned home, if he could get away.

For there was always work to do on the three larger Japanese islands. Eleven-mile-long Rota, visible from Ritidian Point, Guam, produced enough sugar cane to feed two sugar refineries, complete with distilleries for manufacturing "Scotch whisky" and "port wine" from molasses; and to employ 764 Chamorros and 4800 Japanese and Koreans in 1935. During the war the Japanese constructed a small airstrip on the level northern part of the island.

Forty-one miles NNE of Rota is the little uninhabited island of Aguijan; from which it is less than five miles to Tinian. This

[2] See Vol. III of this History, pp. 184–86.

10½-mile-long island, third in area of the Marianas group, is the least mountainous; the highest elevation is only 690 feet above sea level. As one approaches Tinian from seaward it presents a pleasant picture of cane and cornfields, groves of hardwood and casuarina, pretty Japanese-style houses set in red-flowering trees, and cattle pastures on the hillsides. The civilian population of 18,000 in 1941 was almost entirely Japanese and Okinawan. There were two sugar mills at Tinian Town on Sunharon Bay, connected by a narrow-gauge railway with the canefields. During the war three airstrips were under construction and a good airdrome was completed on Ushi Point, overlooking Saipan Channel.

This three-mile-wide channel separates Tinian from Agingan Point, Saipan. The second of the Marianas in size, Saipan is 13 miles long, 2½ to 5 miles wide, with an area of 71 square miles, and rises to over 1500 feet on Mount Tapotchau. It, too, is a beautiful island, the lowlands a checkerboard of sugar cane and cornfields; for the soil is rich and the rainfall heavy. Garapan, with over 10,000 inhabitants, was the seat of Japanese administration in the Marianas. There were sugar mills both here and in the small town of Charan Kanoa, with a narrow-gauge railway to the canefields. Saipan also has a good harbor on the leeward side, Tanapag, which the Japanese had done much to improve. According to various accounts, the population before the war was between 23,000 and 28,000 of whom about 2500 were Chamorros and 1000 Koreans and Caroline Islanders; the rest, Japanese or Okinawan. The Aslito airfield on the southern end of Saipan, which the Japanese began to construct for "cultural purposes" at a time when military installations in the Mandates were forbidden by the League of Nations, was developed during the war into the most important airdrome between Japan and Truk.

The ten other Marianas, all north of Saipan and all but one steep volcanic cones, were largely uninhabited in 1944. Anatahan, 60 miles north of Saipan, supported a few dozen natives and served as a refuge for survivors of bombed convoys. Pagan, consisting of an active volcano joined by a fertile isthmus to an extinct one, had

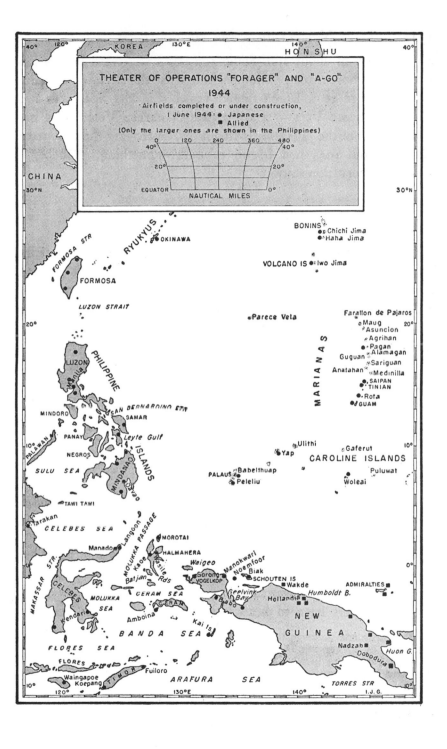

THEATER OF OPERATIONS "FORAGER" AND "A-GO".
1944
Airfields completed or under construction,
1 June 1944: ● Japanese
■ Allied
(Only the larger ones are shown in the Philippines)
NAUTICAL MILES

a population of about 200. Some 500 miles westward lies an isolated reef whose three pointed rocks against the skyline bear such a resemblance to a lateen-rigged vessel that the Spaniards had named it Parece Vela — "a sail appears." Parece Vela was a no-man's land, but the Japanese leveled it off, destroying the silhouette, and by June 1944 had begun to build something, probably a weather observation station.

2. *First Call, 23 February*

On 23 February 1944, only five days after the first great strike on Truk, planes from six of Vice Admiral Mitscher's carriers dropped the first bombs on the Marianas. Cincpac, anticipating the J.C.S. directive of 12 March, ordered this raid mainly to obtain photographic intelligence, since no American or Allied plane had flown over these islands since the fall of Guam.

The Marianas Striking Force was organized in two groups, TG 58.2 commanded by Rear Admiral Alfred E. Montgomery flying his flag in *Essex,* and TG 58.3 under Rear Admiral Frederick C. Sherman with flag in *Bunker Hill.* The former, which included Admiral Mitscher's flagship *Yorktown,* concentrated on Guam and Saipan while Sherman's group took care of Tinian and Rota.[3] They had made good about half the distance from their last fueling rendezvous when a Japanese plane sighted and reported them, and between 2000 February 22 and 0900 next morning, the task force was subjected to four air attacks, each lasting between one and four hours. Mitscher had no night fighters aloft to intercept, but owing to brisk maneuvering and the high quality of antiaircraft fire, not a single ship was hit.

Since carriers have to head into the wind to launch and re-

[3] *Enterprise* and *Saratoga* were not included as they were wanted elsewhere. The "Big E," cruiser *San Diego* and six destroyers, made two strikes on Jaluit 20 Feb. on their way back to Majuro from Truk, and then, with *Belleau Wood,* supported the occupation of Emirau 20 March (see this History, Vol. VI 423). *Saratoga* and 3 DDs joined H.M. carrier *Illustrious* and the British Eastern Fleet, Admiral Sir James Somerville RN, in raids on Sabang, Sumatra (19 Apr.) and Surabaya (17 May).

cover planes, Mitscher took his ships to the lee or west side of the Marianas and launched from a distance of about 100 miles, commencing at 0745 February 23. American ignorance of the Marianas at that time was so complete that the pilots could not even be briefed on where to find airfields; but find them they did, coming in under heavy cumulus clouds. According to Japanese records, no less than 168 enemy aircraft were destroyed, more than the aviators claimed! [4] In addition, two 4800-ton freighters and a few small craft were sunk by the carrier-based bombers. But the greatest damage to shipping was inflicted by coöperating submarines of the Pacific Fleet.

The plan, that had already been tried at Truk, of stationing submarines about the islands to shoot surface game flushed by aircraft, worked well in the Marianas. The alarm given on 22 February sent several ships right into the periscope sights of *Searaven, Sunfish, Tang, Apogon* and *Skipjack. Sunfish* (Lieutenant Commander E. E. Shelby) sank two *Marus* totaling 9400 tons, just before and after daybreak on the 23rd. *Tang* (Lieutenant Commander R. H. O'Kane) sank four, totaling 14,300 tons, in four days; and the total bag of shipping, including those sunk by carrier planes, came to about 45,000 tons.

Admiral Mitscher described this strike in his first report as "historic for courage and determination of purpose." In retrospect, the photographic intelligence obtained was even more important than the destruction wrought. New airfields under construction were discovered and some excellent obliques were taken of the shores where the Marines were destined to land in June.

Task Force 58 now took a short rest before undertaking the strike on the Palaus which we have already described,[5] and landbased air carried the ball during March.

It found a tough team to play against. The Japanese air forces

---

[4] Mitscher claimed 87 aircraft destroyed on the ground and 48 shot down. Capt. Ohmae informs me that 101 were destroyed on the ground (11 at Guam, 20 at Saipan, 70 at Tinian), and that, out of 74 planes that took the air, 67 (of which 47 were bombers) failed to return. The American losses were 5 fighters and 1 TBF.

[5] Above, chap. iv.

had abandoned the Bismarcks, but units in the Carolines had no intention of throwing in the sponge. Leakage of air strength to Rabaul was now at an end; Imperial Headquarters had decided that there was no sense in shifting planes to the Bismarcks to be shot down by Airsols. An American reconnaissance plane discovered in early March a new airstrip on Ponape, and suspicious activity on Puluwat, Woleai and Satawan. The Japanese still held airfields in Mili, Wotje and Maloelap in the Marshalls, but could not use them owing to preventive bombings by the VII Army Air Force and by Marine Corps planes based on Majuro.

Japanese air activity in the Carolines and Marianas could now be dealt with by land-based planes of three different air commands: General Kenney's V A.A.F., now based on Cape Gloucester and New Guinea; [6] Airsols of the South Pacific Force, based on Munda, Torokina and (by early May) on Green and Emirau Islands; and Vice Admiral John H. Hoover's Central Pacific command, including the VII A.A.F. and sundry Navy and Marine Corps squadrons based on Roi, Eniwetok, Makin, Tarawa and Abemama. The number of airfields in all three areas was now sufficient for coördinating attacks on the same target. Owing to the great distance, most of these attacks were made at night by heavy bombers.

Truk was the principal target. Thirteen B–24s based in the Gilberts and staged through Kwajalein dropped bombs on Dublon and Eten Islands in the early hours of 16 March. This meant a round trip of about 3500 miles. Airsols bombers from Bougainville attacked Truk by day 29 and 30 March; Kwajalein-based bombers attacked four nights running, 29 March to 1 April inclusive. Ponape, fortunately, was near enough to Eniwetok (362 miles) for fighters to escort the bombers. Here, on 26 March, the enemy managed to get interceptors aloft for the first time in six weeks, and for the last time too, as most of them were shot down.

[6] The XIII A.A.F., formerly a part of Airsols, was detached from it in April and moved up to the Manus and Los Negros fields in the Admiralties.

These are but samples of the constant hammering of by-passed Japanese air bases, which went on up to and through the Marianas campaign and which prevented any effective interference with Operation "Forager" from the south or east.

3. *Plans, Problems and Procedures*

The decision to place Saipan, Tinian, and Guam next on the program of conquest after the Marshalls, with target date 15 June, was not made by the Joint Chiefs of Staff, as we have seen, until 12 March 1944. It was high time for a decision. The Gilberts and Marshalls were already conquered and Hollandia was coming up soon. The Pacific Fleet had become immensely powerful in every type of combatant ship and auxiliary. It was ready to deal another hard blow to the Japanese Empire. And, although most of American ground forces were earmarked for England and Africa to launch the great invasion of Europe, there were three Marine and two Army divisions in the Pacific, ready to mount a major amphibious operation that summer.

The leading considerations that put the Marianas, rather than the Palaus or some other southwesterly target, into the strategic picture, have already been discussed. First, there was the Navy's desire to develop Guam and Saipan into advanced naval bases. Second, the Air Force wanted superfortress bases for bombing Japan.[7] In addition, American possession of the southern Marianas would leave the enemy guessing about the next move, and would in fact give the Allies a choice of moves: southwest to Palau; west to Leyte or Luzon; northwest to Formosa; or up the Bonins' ladder to Japan. Finally, Guam was an American possession, which we would like to recover promptly in order to end the misery of Japanese rule for our loyal fellow nationals. This may have had no direct influence on strategy, but it made the decision all the more acceptable

---

[7] The B-29 bases already in China, when first used against Japan in June 1944, had logistic and other difficulties which made them inadequate.

to the Navy and Marine Corps. Chamorros are great favorites in the United States Navy, in which many had served for years as stewards and mess attendants, winning friends by their willing service and happy personalities.

On 28 March Admiral Nimitz issued a directive [8] allotting the forces and ordering the definitive plans to be drawn up. Admiral Spruance, as Commander Fifth Fleet, assigned the tasks to each of the major forces involved and saw that they were properly co-ordinated with the rest of the Pacific Fleet. The major divisions were as follows: [9]

Under Admiral Nimitz

FIFTH FLEET, Admiral Raymond A. Spruance
RECONNAISSANCE AND PATROL SUBMARINES, Vice Admiral Charles
   A. Lockwood
SERVICE FORCE PACIFIC FLEET, Vice Admiral William L. Calhoun

Under Admiral Spruance

JOINT EXPEDITIONARY FORCE, Vice Admiral Richmond K. Turner
FAST CARRIER FORCES, Vice Admiral Marc A. Mitscher
FORWARD AREA CENTRAL PACIFIC (LAND-BASED AIRCRAFT), Vice
   Admiral John H. Hoover

Cincpac-Cincpoa staff had learned to plan for every possible contingency while the Joint Chiefs were making up their minds. For several weeks before the 12 March directive, Admiral Turner's staff at Hospital Point, Pearl Harbor, had been studying prewar charts of Saipan and Tinian, bearing the sporty code names of "Tattersalls" and "Tearaway," and of Guam, with the prosaic one of "Stevedore." Photographs taken in the February carrier-plane strike provided data on beaches, airfields and Japanese installations. Admiral Turner returned to Pearl Harbor from the Marshalls

[8] Cincpac letter of 28 Mar. 1944. Admiral Nimitz, who returned to Pearl from his Washington visit 29 March, left for Majuro 6 April to set up the Pacific Fleet support for the Hollandia operation, and there brought the J.C.S. Directive to Admiral Spruance's attention.
[9] See Appendices II and IV for complete task organizations.

about 21 March, held a staff conference and announced that "Tattersalls" would be the first objective. He chose Saipan because it had the best airfield in the Marianas, and lies 100 miles nearer Japan than Guam, which would be easier to capture after the smaller island. Admiral Turner personally drafted the concept, dated 4 April, on which the whole was based: "The objective is the capture of Saipan, Tinian and Guam, in order to secure control of sea communications through the Central Pacific for the support of further attacks on the Japanese."

This was to be Turner's fifth major amphibious operation.[10] Schooled by adversity at Guadalcanal and Tarawa, he was not spoiled by success in the Marshalls. He had learned more about this specialized brand of warfare than anyone else ever had, or probably ever would. Energetic and nervous, he was apt to be abrupt to junior officers who came to him with new suggestions; then think them over carefully, and incorporate these suggestions in his next draft plan. For Turner, with all his rugged personality and rough tongue, had a keen intellect and complete intellectual honesty.

As finally organized, Turner's Joint Expeditionary Force (Task Force 51) was divided into two attack forces, of which "Kelly" as usual took the one expected to strike first: —

JOINT EXPEDITIONARY FORCE (TF 51), Vice Admiral Richmond K. Turner. Expeditionary Troops, Lt. Gen. Holland M. Smith USMC

NORTHERN ATTACK FORCE, Saipan and Tinian (TF 52), Vice Admiral Turner Carrying V 'Phib Corps, General Holland Smith, comprising 2nd and 4th Marine Divisions, reinforced. Mounted in Hawaii and on the West Coast

SOUTHERN ATTACK FORCE, Guam (TF 53), Rear Admiral Richard L. Conolly Carrying III 'Phib Corps, Maj. Gen. Roy S. Geiger

[10] For the earlier ones (Guadalcanal, Central Solomons, Gilberts, and Marshalls) see Vols. V through VII of this History. For Turner's earlier career see V 14*n*. He was promoted Vice Admiral, belatedly it would seem, on 9 March 1944.

USMC, comprising 3rd Marine Division and 1st Provisional Marine Brigade. Mounted in Guadalcanal-Tulagi Area

FLOATING RESERVE (TG 51.1), Rear Admiral William H. P. Blandy Carrying 27th Division U.S. Army reinforced, Maj. Gen. Ralph Smith USA

All these moved up to the Marianas at the same time. There was also a General Reserve, the 77th Division U.S. Army, which was called upon in July to help capture Guam.

No operation on so vast a scale, with a final thousand-mile "hop," had ever before been planned, although Operation "Torch" — the North African affair of November 1942 — was a close approximation. Inherent difficulties peculiar to amphibious warfare[11] were enhanced by the distance of the Marianas from any Allied continental base, and by the operation's size. No fewer than 535 combatant ships and auxiliaries[12] carried four and a half reinforced divisions — 127,571 troops — of which over two thirds were Marines.[13] The destination lay 1017 miles' steaming from Eniwetok, the nearest advanced base, which was little more than an anchorage. And Saipan lay about 3500 miles from Pearl Harbor. Logistics problems alone would have condemned this operation as impossible in 1941, for the distance meant that the entire expeditionary force had to be afloat at the same time, and that the ships allotted could do nothing else for at least three months. There was little enough time to round up the ships, planes, men and supplies and to decide how every ship and unit was to be employed every day. For in an amphibious operation nothing can be left to chance, and nice timing is the essence of success.[14]

From the first, Admiral Turner set D-day for Saipan for 15 June, and that date was kept. "W-day" for the landing on Guam

---

[11] See Vol. VII pp. 87–8.
[12] Including the beaching craft. Turner Report on Capture of Marianas p. 4.
[13] There were 71,034 in the Northern Attack Force; 56,537 in Southern Attack Force, not including the 77th Division.
[14] See chap. xviii below for special problems of logistics planning.

was left undecided, to depend on the turn of events in Saipan, as also would the day when Tinian could be invaded.

While the Joint Expeditionary Force was at sea, the Pacific Fleet was being reorganized, partly because of its increased size, partly in consequence of Admiral Halsey and the South Pacific Force having attained all their objectives and being ready to "transfer business to a new location"; but mostly to accelerate the tempo of the Pacific war. The old South Pacific command was still maintained at Nouméa, which now became an important rear base, but Admiral Halsey was pulled out from under General MacArthur's command and placed for all purposes under Admiral Nimitz, with the title Commander Third Fleet, in the same echelon as Admiral Spruance. Under Vice Admiral Turner, commanding all the amphibious forces of the Pacific Fleet, were his own V Amphibious Force and, for the Marianas, the III Amphibious Force, Rear Admiral Wilkinson, and each amphibious *force* had a corresponding amphibious *corps* of ground troops.

To put it another way, this reorganization divided the Pacific Fleet into two teams, the first comprising Spruance's command and the second, Halsey's. One could plan and train while the other fought, reducing time between operations. Vice Admiral Mitscher's Fast Carrier Force, designated TF 58 when under Spruance's command and TF 38 when under Halsey's, operated almost continuously, together with most of the gunfire support ships. As Admiral Nimitz put it, "The team remains about the same, but the drivers change." This simple reorganization, together with new logistics devices, had the effect of keeping every fighting ship of the Pacific Fleet at sea and speeding up the momentum of the war.

At the same time that V 'Phib planners were working on Operation "Forager" at Pearl Harbor under the watchful eyes of Admiral Turner, the last stages of planning Operation "Overlord," the cross-channel invasion of Normandy, were going on in England under General Dwight D. Eisenhower USA. "Overlord" was a much larger amphibious operation than "Forager," but it must be remembered that the difficulties of amphibious warfare increase in proportion to the distance from base to target; and the two principal points at which the Marianas invasion was mounted — Hawaii and Guadalcanal — lay respectively 3500 and 2400 miles from the objective. To be sure, we had a forward base at Eniwetok only 1017 miles away, but Eniwetok had nothing to offer except a fine lagoon, beautiful beaches and a few coconuts; everything else had to be brought there. In Europe the Royal Navy shared the burden and the honors with that of the United States; but in the Marianas every combatant ship and all but three of the auxiliaries,[15] every soldier, sailor, aviator, and Marine, every piece of equipment and the vast bulk of the supplies, were American. Added together, "Overlord" in Europe and "Forager" in the Pacific made the greatest military effort ever put forth by the United States or any other nation at one time. It should be a matter of pride and congratulation to the American and British people that their united efforts made June of 1944 the greatest month yet in military and naval history; that simultaneously they were able to launch these two mighty overseas expeditions against their powerful enemies in the East and in the West.

The three southern Marianas involved new problems in amphibious warfare. So far, Allied forces in the Pacific had had to deal with three types of targets. In the South and Southwest Pacific they encountered large, rugged islands covered with dense jungle growth and inhabited, if at all, by natives who were friendly or indifferent. In the North Pacific were mountainous, uninhabited islands with intense cold and excessive precipitation. In the Central Pacific, so far, it had been a story of coral atolls composed of islets only a few hundred yards wide, whence it had been comparatively easy to blast the enemy, once we had learned how at Tarawa.

Saipan, Tinian and Guam, however, combined the disadvantages of all three, from an assailant's point of view, with some special defensive advantages of their own. The first two were thickly settled with people loyal to Japan. All three afforded the enemy

[15] Two Dutch merchant ships and a Norwegian whale factory used as a tanker.

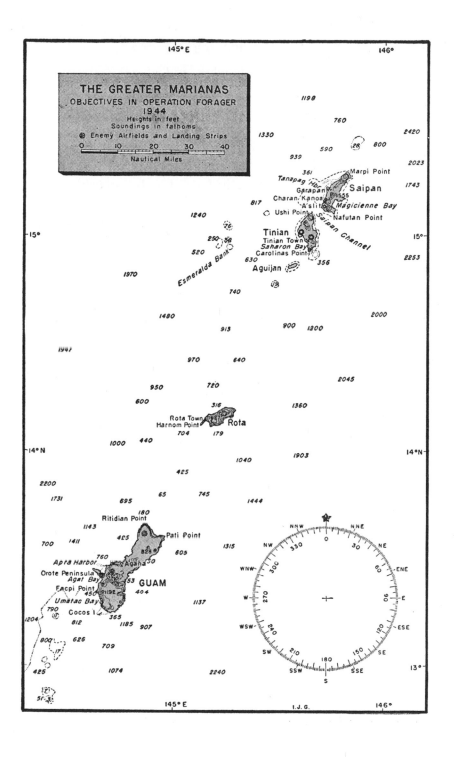

THE GREATER MARIANAS
OBJECTIVES IN OPERATION FORAGER
1944
Heights in feet
Soundings in fathoms
⊙ Enemy Airfields and Landing Strips

0   10   20   30   40
Nautical Miles

artillery sites to command the beaches, and plenty of coral-lime-stone caves for concealment.

It was so long since anyone on the Allied side had seen the southern Marianas, and information about the beaches and the Japanese defenses was so vitally needed, that special efforts were made to obtain good air-photo coverage. In view of the distances involved, this was remarkably well done. The best work, starting 18 April, was performed by the photographic wing of the Airsols command, composed of specially fitted Navy Liberators operating from Henderson Field, Guadalcanal.[16] First day out from Guadalcanal, the flying photographers made Eniwetok (1252 miles), rested there the second day, picked up fighter escort and left very early the third morning for Saipan (1017) or Guam (1035 miles). After performing their mission, they flew 940 (or if from Saipan 1040) miles to Los Negros field in the Admiralties. At the nearby naval base on Manus the photographs were developed that night, and flown to Guadalcanal on the fourth day and to Pearl Harbor on the fifth. Thus, prints from negatives taken 29 May were on board the ships of the Southern Attack Force when they sortied from Purvis Bay 4 June; prints of Saipan from negatives taken 1 June were finished in time for gunnery officers of the Northern Attack Force to study en route to the target.[17]

The usual escort of the photographic Liberators consisted of B–24s of the VII Army Air Force. These took care of intercepting Japanese planes and performed a little "token" bombing on their own. Beginning on 26 April, Squadron VD–4 of Admiral Hoover's command, stationed at Eniwetok, took part in these photo flights which, continuing through the first week of June, were especially useful for detecting enemy activities on Saipan.[18] The art of air photography had been so rapidly developed in the Pacific during

[16] First by Squadron VD–3 (Cdr. R. J. Stroh); relieved in May by Fleet Aircraft Photo Squadron 1 (Cdr. R. O. Greene) which included VD–1, and VMD–254 (Lt. Col. E. P. Pennebaker) of the Marine Air Arm.

[17] Turner Report, Narrative p. 4.

[18] Lts. Land and Van Wyen USNR "Air Operations in Marianas," ms. The first attack on Guam was 24 April.

the past six months that, in comparison with these photographs, those used in the Gilberts operation seemed amateur snapshots.[18] The Liberators came down low and took obliques of the shore, which provided views hardly different from what one would see from the deck of a fighting ship.

All relevant information derived from photographic and other sources was transferred to large-scale gridded charts of the islands, which were used by ships, ground troops and planes alike, eliminating the confusion that arose when Army and Navy used different maps.

While these three islands are big enough for a defense in depth, they are also provided with the same natural defenses as a coral atoll. Every beach on the leeward side suitable for a landing is protected by a drying or breaking reef; at Guam and Tinian a shelving scarp as at Tarawa or Kwajalein, at Saipan a coral barrier impassable by landing craft. Between the reef and beaches at Saipan stretches a long, shallow lagoon where the Japanese might be expected to plant underwater obstacles, and upon which their artillery would presumably be sighted. Without amphtracs, the LVTs that had enabled us to win through in the Gilberts and Marshalls, assaults on the Marianas would have been well-nigh hopeless.

A new combat element especially suited to cope with the peculiar hazards of reefs and lagoons was the Underwater Demolition Team (UDT).[20] These men were intensively trained for close reconnaissance of reefs and beaches, and for planting underwater explosives to demolish both natural and artificial obstacles. Both duties had to be performed by swimmers; amphibious warfare had gone down to the frog while rising to the eagle.

The first UDTs were organized early in 1943. Lieutenant Com-

---

[19] For earlier developments see Vol. VI 104 and VII index "photo reconnaissance."

[20] The following account is based on conversations with Capt. John P. Vetter, Cdr. Kauffman and Col. J. D. Kemp, a British Commando officer who was a close observer of their work at Saipan, and Mr. John T. Koehler, when he was Asst. Secretary of the Navy (Feb. 1949–Oct. 1951).

mander Draper L. Kauffman, then at the head of the Navy's bomb disposal school in Washington, opened a school for underwater demolitioners at Fort Pierce, Florida, which graduated its first class in July.

Among the many lessons learned at Tarawa was the need for close pre-landing reconnaissance of beaches and their approaches, since no photographic process yet invented could indicate depth of water. And it was desirable to have swimmers trained to place and detonate explosive charges in coral heads, to clear the way for landing craft. Admiral Turner, alert for new methods, sent to the West Coast for Lieutenant Commander J. T. Koehler USNR, who had been in Sicily, to organize a working team on Oahu. It was this team that went in at Roi-Namur,[21] with slight success because there were no underwater obstacles to report, and the "drone" (remote control) boats ran amok. The UDT school was moved to Kameole, and the lessons of Kwajalein were applied. The first of these was to cut out night reconnaissance, since the swimmers had to use their eyes in order to accomplish anything. But daylight reconnaissance meant fire support. Commander Kauffman, summoned from Fort Pierce, worked out details with Admiral Turner himself within two weeks of D-day. They decided to use LCIs armed with 40-mm guns to distract the enemy while the swimmers were performing.

Each member of the underwater team [22] had to be capable of a two-mile swim. His body was painted with black rings at 12-inch intervals, for taking shoal-water soundings. He had a fishline for measuring distances, and was equipped with a stylus and piece of waterproof plastic for taking wet notes. Besides making a close reef and beach reconnaissance before D-day, the underwater boys were supposed to clear out anti-boat mines and other obstacles; and, after the landing, to blast passages through the reef. The whole scheme sounded fantastic, but it worked.

[21] See Vol. VII of this History, p. 245.
[22] Total strength of a UDT was 16 officers and 80 enlisted men. It was divided into 4 operating platoons of 3 and 15 each, and a HQ platoon of 4 and 20.

4. *Japanese Preparations to Defend Saipan*

The Japanese on Saipan received little reinforcement after April 1944. When the American attack was delivered there were about 32,000 troops on the island, mostly belonging to the newly organized Thirty-First Army; but not all were fully armed and equipped, owing to the activities of United States submarines. And American mastery of the sea made it impossible to send last-minute aid to Saipan, even from Tinian or Pagan, where a mixed brigade lay immobilized. The military commander in Saipan, Lieutenant General Yoshitsugu Saito, was subordinate to the area commander, Lieutenant General Obata, who happened to be returning from an inspection trip to Palau at the time of the landings and got no farther than Guam. Both Saito and Obata were subordinate to Vice Admiral Chuichi Nagumo, now demoted from the fast carrier command to that of a small area fleet consisting of patrol craft, barges and ground troops. Nagumo's headquarters were on Saipan, but he did not presume to interfere with the military operations. Vice Admiral Takagi, the submarine commander, also was present. Full responsibility for the defense rested on Saito.

The Japanese military organization on Saipan, complicated from the American point of view, seems to have been adequate from theirs.[23] The two basic army units were General Saito's own 43rd Division and the 47th Independent Mixed Brigade (Colonel Oka), the original Saipan garrison. There were many odd companies and battalions, some composed entirely of survivors from submarine attacks on Japanese transports. *Sakito Maru*, carrying 4100 troops to Saipan, was sunk by U.S.S. *Trout* on 29 February; only 1680 of the men reached Saipan, without weapons or other gear; and they were sent on to Guam. A major unit, Colonel Ito's 118th Infantry Regiment, lost 858 officers and men out of 3463 in transit, and all its weapons and ammunition, when five ships out of a seven-ship

[23] Maj. Carl W. Hoffman *Saipan: the Beginning of the End*, with complete order of battle.

convoy bringing it to Saipan were sunk by United States submarines *Shark, Pintado* and *Pilotfish* on 4–6 June; this was the last convoy to reach Saipan, even in part, from Japan.[24] In addition to the 22,702 soldiers present, there were 6690 officers and men belonging to the Japanese Navy, including 800 of the famous Special Naval Landing Forces (sometimes called Japanese Marines) and a naval guard force of 400 men. Most of the aircraft maintenance crews and other air personnel had been flown south to the Vogelkop fields in May and early June to help the KON operation, and had sustained heavy losses. The survivors were ordered back to the Marianas on 11 June, but few had even reached the Palaus by D-day. The grand total of 31,629 military personnel on Saipan June 15 [25] was almost double that of our Intelligence estimate before the battle.

Aslito airfield on the coastal plain at the south end of Saipan dated from the 1930s; it had been greatly extended and improved during the war. A 4380-foot airstrip at Marpi Point, the northern end of the island, was under construction but usable only for emergency landings. The Japanese had also built a small runway, 140 by 3875 feet, at Charan Kanoa, on an almost north-south line crosswise to the prevailing wind, making so short a strip practically useless for anything bigger than a Piper Cub.

Japanese defense arrangements were incomplete, owing to the late start and the activities of United States submarines. General Saito served notice on Admiral Nagumo that, unless the Navy could give better protection to Saipan-bound convoys, no permanent defenses could be erected. So much construction material had been sunk, said he, that the soldiers could "do nothing but sit around with their arms folded."

Very well as an excuse; but the Americans found hundreds of

---

[24] See above, chap. ii; Interrogation of Maj. Kiyoshi Yoshida, in Cincpac-Cincpoa *Weekly Intelligence* I No. 6 (16 Aug. 1944) p. 34; "Saipan, the Japanese Defense," *O.N.I. Weekly* III No. 43 (25 Oct. 1945) pp. 3430–3434; *Inter. Jap. Off.* I 212.

[25] Latest estimate by Army historians. The count of Japanese dead and prisoners was 29,893. Final G–2 estimate 13 June was 15,000 to 17,600 (TF 56 Report on "Forager," Encl. D Annex F).

anti-boat mines not placed, bales of barbed wire not strung, tons of building material not used, and other evidence that the soldiers had not needed to "sit around." Saito's plan of defense, issued in late May, adopted the watchword, "Destroy the enemy on the beach." Field positions for attaining that desirable result were to be completed by 10 June, and "Thereafter we will rapidly construct permanent defensive positions in strategic places," especially to protect Aslito airfield. At various points on the coast, commanding all possible approaches, there were emplaced, at the time of the landings, eight Whitworth-Armstrong 6-inch guns, nine 140-mm, eight 120-mm dual-purpose, four 200-mm mortars, a few concrete blockhouses of the type familiar in the Marshall Islands, and a dozen or so concrete pillboxes. Many emplacements and trench systems for beach defense had just been begun; many guns had not yet been sited. After reading the official report on the defenses of Saipan, issued by the Marine Corps Engineers after the island was secured,[26] one must admit that a landing in October would have been at least thrice as costly and difficult as a landing in June. In view of its size and importance, Saipan was in a much less defensible state than Kwajalein or Tarawa. The reason is clear — until 1944 Japan had never thought she would have to defend it.

In view of all these deficiencies, General Saito's troops put up a commendable but completely futile fight. They lost the island and were almost completely annihilated in the process.

[26] Complete description in Engineer Exp. Troops (TF 56) *Report on Defensive Plan for Saipan* (July 1944).

CHAPTER XII

Approach and Bombardment

10 May–14 June 1944

Dates east of Kwajalein are West Longitude; all others, East Longitude.

1. *Rendezvous and Approach, 10 May–10 June*

THE movement plan by which units of the Joint Expeditionary Force proceeded to their common destination off Saipan was the work of Captain Leith and Commander Lewis of Admiral Turner's staff.[1] To keep the ships in manageable groups, provide fueling en route, avoid waters under enemy plane search, and allow time at Kwajalein and Eniwetok for the assault troops to stretch their legs and be transferred to the LSTs, required a nice calculation.

The three main subdivisions of the Joint Expeditionary Force, their assembly areas, and the dates of their respective arrivals, were as follows: —

NORTHERN ATTACK FORCE (TF 52), Admiral Turner, General H. M. Smith and 2nd and 4th Marine Divisions for Saipan. 37 transports, cargo ships and LSDs, plus tractor groups, assembled in Hawaiian Islands by 10 May. *Bombardment Group 1* (Oldendorf) went with this Force.

SOUTHERN ATTACK FORCE (TF 53), Admiral Conolly, General Geiger and III Amphibious Corps for Guam. Arrived Guadalcanal and Tulagi or Purvis Bay 10–18 May, as did *Bombardment*

[1] Com Fifth Fleet (Admiral Spruance) Op Plan Cen 10–44, May 12, 1944, Annex B.

Group 2 (Ainsworth), with fire support ships for both Saipan and Guam and *Minesweeper Group 2.*

FLOATING RESERVE (TG 51.1), Admiral Blandy, General Ralph Smith and 27th Infantry Division. In Hawaiian Islands by 10 May.

The Northern Attack Force held rehearsals at Maalaea Bay, Maui, and Kahoolawe Island between 14 and 20 May, after which the 27th Infantry used the same area and facilities. The Southern Attack Force held rehearsals on Cape Esperance, Guadalcanal, between 22 and 31 May.

A fatal accident marred the Maui rehearsal; an LCT in which Marines were sleeping was pitched overboard from the deck of *LST–485* by heavy seas, owing to insufficient lashing, and 19 men were lost. And at Pearl Harbor a few days later occurred a much more serious accident. In West Loch, in the midst of a cluster of LSTs that were loading mortar ammunition near the Naval Ammunition Depot, *LST–353* burst into flame and exploded with a roar that could be heard all over Oahu and far out to sea. This triggered off five other LSTs. Only by heroic firefighting, and towing clear of wooden ammunition barges by harbor tugs and other small craft, was a major disaster to the base, like the one at Halifax in World War I, averted. Six LSTs and 3 LCTs were lost and the casualties were heavy; 163 dead, 396 injured.[2] By quick staff work the lost beaching craft were replaced and the tractor groups left Pearl Harbor only a day late, which they made up en route. They entered Eniwetok Lagoon 7 June, took on board assault troops from the transports and, packed like sardine cans, departed the 9th.

The transports of Turner's Northern Attack Force, carrying the

---

[2] Lt. J. H. Timberlake USNR has kindly compiled these facts from the 2-volume Judge Advocate General's "Record of Court of Inquiry at Pearl Harbor, June 1944"; Admiral Turner's Report on "Forager," Encl. F pp. 203; and other sources. The Court and the Bureau of Ordnance agree that the initial explosion came from one or more 4.2-inch HE M–3 mortar shells going off while being loaded onto a truck on the elevator of *LST–353*. Why they exploded could not be ascertained, but it is suspected that the fuzes were defective. Admiral King, in reviewing the court proceedings, declared that this disaster was not an "Act of God"; that it was due to the failure of LST personnel to comply with safety precautions.

rest of the 2nd and 4th Marine Divisions with their vehicles and equipment, accompanied by two escort carrier divisions, departed Pearl Harbor in two sections 29–31 May and arrived Eniwetok 7 and 8 June.

The tractor groups of Admiral Conolly's Southern Attack Force sailed from Ironbottom Sound 31 May, and the transports on 4 June. Three battleships from Efate and nine more destroyers joined next day, and all rendezvoused at Kwajalein on the 8th. After refueling, they departed on the 12th, expecting to assault Guam a few days after Saipan. But the Guam landings were postponed to 21 July.

Blandy's reserve sailed from Pearl Harbor right after Turner, arrived Kwajalein 9 June and departed to make Saipan on the 17th. Garrison groups to relieve the assault troops arrived at Eniwetok between 14 and 21 June and there awaited orders.

Task Force 58, Mitscher's fast carriers, served as van to the entire force. They sortied from Majuro 6 June, fueled between sunset and dawn 9–10 June along a route beyond the possible limit of enemy search from Marcus and Truk. It was rightly calculated that the presence of carriers would attract enemy planes like flies to honey, and allow the main attack force to advance undetected.

A sortie from a coral lagoon is as handsome a naval spectacle as one can find anywhere. In a setting of sparkling blue water, the long reef stretching out of sight, lashed with dazzling white foam, islets covered with the tenderest green foliage and fringed by yellow sands, the battleships, cruisers and destroyers in their fantastic battle camouflage form a column that steams proudly through the pass at 15 knots. With much making and executing of long hoists of brightly colored signal flags, they deploy into a circular cruising formation. Transports are in the center; destroyers on the perimeter throw spray masthead high, commencing their anti-submarine patrol that will never cease as long as the force is at sea.

Steaming west from fifteen North, one-sixty East, with Saipan and Guam as objectives! Who could have guessed it a year earlier, when the Russells and Morobe marked our farthest advance, and even the outer filaments of the Micronesian web were still controlled by the enemy spider? For old Navy men and Marines, and the loyal Chamorros on board, and for any who had a feeling for history, there was a special emotion in the fact that we were on our way to recover the first territory wrested from us by a treacherous foe. This feeling was well expressed in Admiral Ainsworth's message to his bombardment group: —

"Today a large United States Naval Force of which your ship is a unit is on its way to take the Islands of Saipan and Tinian away from the Japs, and make them give up Guam to its rightful owners. . . . I promise you days and nights of hard fighting, as we must make the sea safe for our transports and pave the way for our Marines with plenty of shells and bombs. We are trained; we are ready; and we are going into close action. I have the utmost confidence in your ability to put the Japs where all the good ones are. . . ."

The invasion of Normandy, news of which was greeted with a roar of satisfaction when it was announced to the men of the Fifth Fleet by loud-speakers, occupied the public mind at home. Before many days were gone we hoped to give them something else to read about.

Expectation of a fleet action gave particular zest to this operation. Despite Mr. Kiralfy's assurances,[3] hopes were raised that this time the enemy would commit his capital ships. Officers cognizant of top-secret dispatches heard of Admiral Koga's "Z" plan for a fleet action, a copy of which had been captured at Hollandia. Admiral Koga was dead (though not shot down by an American plane as we then believed); but we hoped that his "Op plan" would go marching on.

By all indications it had. As the fleet advanced westward, reports flowed in from submarines at Tawi Tawi and coastwatchers in the Philippines that two Japanese task forces were on their way toward the Marianas. Admiral Toyoda, it appeared, was bent on putting his predecessor's plan into effect. It looked as if a second Battle of Midway were coming up.

[3] See chap. i above.

2. *Fast Carrier Air Strikes, 11–13 June*

Pre-assault air operations commenced as early as 3 June with a bombing strike on Palau from Southwest Pacific bases. Neutralization air strikes were launched 9 June against the Japanese airfields at Peleliu, Woleai, and Yap, while regular "interdiction" missions were flown against Truk, Puluwat and Satawan; all by the land-based Army Air Forces.[4] But from 11 June Admiral Mitscher's four fast carrier groups carried the ball. These, as then constituted, were in brief: —

TG 58.1 (Clark): HORNET, YORKTOWN, BELLEAU WOOD, BATAAN
TG 58.2 (Montgomery): BUNKER HILL, WASP, MONTEREY, CABOT
TG 58.3 (Reeves): ENTERPRISE, LEXINGTON, PRINCETON, SAN JACINTO
TG 58.4 (Harrill): ESSEX, LANGLEY, COWPENS [5]

The first enemy snoopers, encountered on the morning of 11 June, were shot down by combat air patrol. At 1300, when the formation had arrived at a point 200 miles east of Guam, the task force launched a deckload strike of 208 fighters and eight torpedo-bombers against that enemy base and airfields on Saipan and Tinian. These smothering tactics were intended to reduce the danger of enemy air attack during the following night, and to destroy as many planes and as much shipping as possible. The attack had been stepped up from daylight on the 12th to the afternoon of the 11th at Mitscher's urgent request, and the change paid off. Captain Ohmae believes that 36 Japanese planes were destroyed that day on the three islands.

At sunset 11 June, when the task force had reached lat. 13° N, long. 149° E, Admiral Clark's group continued toward Guam while the other three headed for Tinian and Saipan. Between 0315 and 0415 June 12, the northern groups were attacked by a formation of about ten Bettys from Truk, with the usual accompaniment

---

[4] Craven and Cate *Army Air Forces in World War II*, IV 687.
[5] Battleships, cruisers, and destroyers were fairly evenly distributed among the four groups at this time; the battle line had not yet been formed. See Appendix III for details.

of flares and float lights. No damage was inflicted and one plane was shot down.

Just ahead of the fighter sweep on 11 June, a convoy of 12 *Marus*, escorted by a torpedo boat, nine patrol craft and subchasers, departed Tanapag Harbor, Saipan, for Yokohama. At sea it was joined by 16 fishing vessels. About 160 miles NNW of Saipan on 12 June, it was spotted, struck twice by planes of Admiral Harrill's carrier group, and struck again next day. The convoy was devastated; the torpedo boat (*Otori*), three subchasers, ten *Marus* totaling over 30,000 tons, and an unspecified number of fishing vessels were sunk.[6]

Harrill's task group had also been conducting scheduled strikes on Saipan and Pagan, incidentally sinking naval auxiliary *Bokuyo Maru* (2726 tons), then under repair at Saipan, and damaging freighter *Keiyo Maru* (6441 tons) so that she had to be beached. Bombing attacks on Saipan and Tinian by planes of three out of the four carrier groups on 12 and 13 June reduced enemy air power on and near the target islands almost to zero; and one raid wiped out a sampan flotilla near Pagan, which might have been used to transfer soldiers from one island to another.

Admiral Clark's task group was engaged during 12 June in heavy bombing attacks on Orote Field, Guam. A *Hornet* search plane sighted a convoy of six or seven ships 134 miles west of Guam, but failed to get the report through in time for a strike mission to locate it.[7] During the night this convoy remained in about the same position, apparently intending to enter Apra Harbor when the American air strikes subsided, and got off almost scot-free. Clark's Hellcats caught up with the convoy next day and damaged a transport which was later sunk by carrier planes at Palau, but the convoy did land reinforcements at Guam.

[6] *Inter. Jap. Off.* I 489. The fishermen had been bound for Truk to catch fish for the garrison but were ordered home when it became clear they could never get through. The Kalischers' "Dark Angel of Anatahan," *Collier's* 26 Jan. 1952, describes the lurid experience of some of the survivors of the fishing vessels, who landed on Anatahan and held out there until November 1951.

[7] Japanese Monograph No. 116 corrects earlier sources. There was only one convoy, not two, as first reported by the carrier pilots.

On 13 June, two days before D-day, United States carrier-based planes were swarming all over the islands, looking for parked planes or targets of opportunity. Commander William I. Martin, pilot of an Avenger from *Enterprise*, sent to bomb antiaircraft installations near the Charan Kanoa airstrip on Saipan, had an amazing experience; his own story of it is one of the best personal narratives of the war.[8]

Immediately after he had pushed the bomb release at 3500-foot altitude, a burst from an antiaircraft gun shot down Martin's plane, right over the lagoon. He and his two crew members were tossed out at about 3000 feet, when the plane was making about 300 knots. The crewmen plummeted to their death. Martin could not get his parachute open, and, falling, he thought of his wife and two boys, and of a previous close call when he was flying from *Hornet* in the Battle of Santa Cruz. And he even found time to say to himself Psalm xxiii: —

> The Lord is my shepherd, I shall not want.
> He maketh me to lie down in green pastures,
> He leadeth me beside the still waters. . . .

Remembering a report of a bailed-out pilot at Guadalcanal who had survived without a parachute by straightening his body when he hit the water, Martin did just that; the parachute opened just in time to check his speed, and he entered shallow water at an angle with his toes pointed. The lagoon there being only four feet deep, he was surprised to find himself sitting on a soft sand bottom, unharmed except for a bruise on his hip. The plane splashed about 30 feet away, burning briskly, and pieces of its tail structure were still falling all around. He was less than 300 yards from the beach in a reef-encircled lagoon. The Japanese ashore started shooting at him with rifles. He ducked under to escape the bullets, towing his seat-sack with the still folded raft, and carrying the parachute under one arm. By "submarine navigation," coming up for air when necessary, he reached the reef. Finally the rifle fire fell off, but he saw two boats putting out in pursuit.

[8] *Enterprise* Action Report 3 July 1944.

Magicienne Bay and Aslito Field
Tinian in background

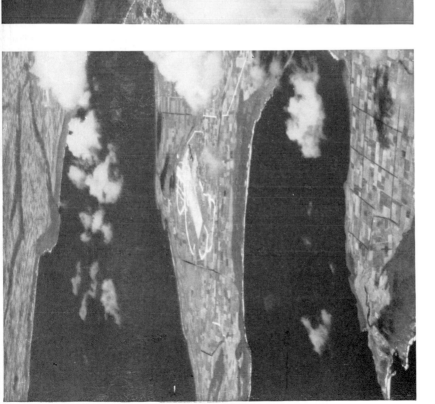

Charan Kanoa
Showing reef, lagoon and airstrip

Saipan and Tinian from the Air, 29 May 1944

Commander Robert H. Isely USN

Having reached the reef, Martin lay on its inner slope with nose and eyes only above water. He recognized the shoreline from the map which, as air coördinator, he had studied; he began to think he might survive, and made mental notes. Then he thought of the two crewmen, Williams and Hargrove, who had been with him since the summer of 1942. Knowing that they must have been killed, he indulged in a little quiet weeping.

Two bursts of 20-mm fire splashed nearby. So, gathering his gear, Martin made a run for it across the reef and plunged into the breakers off its seaward edge. The surf made a good screen from the enemy. He inflated his life jacket for support. The American air strike scheduled for that morning was just coming in, and with gratification he watched some of their bombs hit the targets. Now that the Japanese had other things to occupy their minds, he ventured to inflate his life raft, rigging the parachute and seat-pack as a sea anchor, filling the raft with water to reduce its visibility and windage. Drifting seaward, he reflected that if not soon rescued his next call would be the Philippines; but he did not despair, as he found food and water on the raft.

A Hellcat and an Avenger approached, and Martin used his mirror and marker-dye to attract their attention. The pilots saw him and he recognized them. Japanese soldiers ashore fired at the planes, but one of them returned and dropped an emergency kit near the raft. Fire support battleships far off shore commenced bombardment and their shells roared overhead. Now that he was seen, Martin decided to haul in his sea anchor and get beyond enemy gunfire range. With parachute rigged as sail, the raft made three knots and took him right into the fire support area. At 1130 two SOCs from *Indianapolis* landed near him and one of them carried him to the flagship. He was taken to the bridge to talk with Admiral Spruance, who thought his observations of the reef so valuable that he sent them out by dispatch. Martin had brought intelligence of the depth of water in the lagoon, the small number of coral heads, the absence of underwater obstacles, the length of the reef and the height of surf.

Martin was returned to his carrier by destroyer *MacDonough*, but first she had a bombardment mission to perform. The rescued aviator was able to direct her fire and had the satisfaction of seeing her knock out the antiaircraft gun that had shot him down.

This day — 13 June — was not without its tragedy too. A certain number of Avengers in *Lexington's* Air Group 16 were armed with rockets. Rocket-carrying planes had been employed against submarines by the Royal Air Force for a year or more, but in the Pacific Fleet this form of armament was still in the experimental stage. These rocket-armed Avengers, led by Lieutenant Commander Robert H. Isely, the squadron commander, made runs on Aslito Field, Saipan, in shallow glides, launching rockets at ranges of 1000 to 2000 yards. Isely's plane leading, and two more that followed, were hit by antiaircraft fire during the glides, Isely's and one other burst into flames and crashed, and the third was damaged. Two entire crews were killed. Isely was one of the most distinguished pilots in the Navy, having performed brilliantly in an escort carrier killer group in the Atlantic; and Lieutenant (jg) Paul Dana USNR, his radioman and tail gunner, also was one of the best. Their loss convinced the carrier air officers that rocket launchers, useless except at close range, were out of place on a vulnerable Avenger. And it was evident that Japanese antiaircraft fire had vastly improved during the past year.[9]

Carrier plane strikes continued 14 and 15 June in decreased tempo, because two of the carrier groups had to fuel and the other two went up north to hit the Volcano Islands.[10] It was symptomatic of the feeble enemy air strength in and around the Marianas that no more air attacks were directed at the fast carriers until the evening of D-day, the 15th. At dusk, when the Reeves and Montgomery task groups were recovering planes about 40 miles west of Saipan, bogeys were detected approaching from the direction of Guam. *San Jacinto's* combat air patrol, sent out to intercept, shot down seven of them and broke up this attack, but a

[9] *Lexington* Action Report, Report of ComAirGroup 16 (Cdr. E. M. Snowden).
[10] See chap. xiv below.

second developed at 1912, after sunset. Two night fighters attacked and dispersed the Japanese fighter cover, but about a dozen torpedo-bombers[11] kept on coming and delivered a torpedo attack on Reeves's group, concentrating on Admiral Mitscher's flagship *Lexington* and the "Big E." There were many close misses, but all "fish" were successfully dodged and most of the attacking planes were shot down.

3. Pre-landing Bombardments, 13–15 June

On the morning of 13 June (D minus 2 day) the seven new battleships under Admiral Lee's command, together with a number of destroyers, were detached from the fast carrier groups to deliver the first scheduled bombardment of Saipan and Tinian. Reports of land-based reconnaissance planes on 29 May had shown intense activity in the strengthening of the Saipan defenses. The fringe of the island was well provided with coast defense and antiaircraft guns, but very few blockhouses. Miles of new trenches had been dug.[12] Admiral Turner's fire support groups were not due to arrive until the 14th, hence the big ships of the carrier groups were given the assignment to start bombardment a day earlier.

Sad to relate, the bombardment of 13 June was a failure. These fast battleships simply did not know the technique. They had been too busy steaming around with carriers to practise bombardment, a type of firing that requires slow and patient adjustment on specific targets, differing widely from main battery fire in a naval engagement. Pilots of the battleships' spotter planes had not learned to distinguish targets. And the battlewagons were required to shoot from ranges between 10,000 and 16,000 yards because they were considered too valuable to risk in the unswept shoal area which

[11] These were in two groups, 3 Judys with 6 Zekes, and 10 Franceses with 5 Zekes, all from Yap. Eleven did not return.

[12] Reports of a new strong point near Chatcha village above Magicienne Bay perhaps induced Admiral Turner to give up a bold feature of his original operation plan, a night landing on that bay 14 June by a few companies of raiders, with the object of rushing up Mt. Tapotchau and gaining the summit to spot for the artillery.

extends about six miles to leeward of Saipan.[13] The result was that most of the 16-inch and 5-inch shells went completely wild, and the only targets destroyed were large, conspicuous, and of no military value, such as farmhouses and the Charan Kanoa sugar mill.[14] Actually 2432 high-capacity 16-inch and 12,544 five-inch shells were expended in all this sound and fury.[15] There was much truth in a humorous bluejacket's description of this bombardment as "a Navy-sponsored farm project that simultaneously plows the fields, prunes the trees, harvests the crops, and adds iron to the soil."

Next day, when shore bombardment was taken over by the "old" battleships which had practised at the Kahoolawe range, results were better. Admiral Oldendorf had at his disposal two battleships with eight 16-inch guns each (*Maryland* and *Colorado*); six armed with twelve 14-inch guns each (*Pennsylvania, Tennessee, California, New Mexico, Mississippi, Idaho*); six heavy cruisers with nine 8-inch each; five light cruisers with twelve or fifteen 6-inch each, and about 26 destroyers with 5-inch guns. The secondary batteries of the battleships also were to fire. Careful plans for the shoot had been drawn en route, at a conference between flag officers concerned and Oldendorf's and Ainsworth's staffs. For bombardment purposes, Saipan was divided into six sections. Specific land batteries and other definite targets were assigned to individual ships. Ample provision was made for spotting from the ships' own Seagulls and Kingfishers, and there was a plane patrol up from the escort carriers to direct call fire. Admiral Ainsworth's unit included *Williamson*, an old four-stack destroyer converted to a seaplane tender, so that cruisers would not have to interrupt bombardment to gas their own planes.[16]

[13] Cdr. R. S. Moore's six minesweepers swept this shelf during this bombardment, the only possible benefit of which was to protect them from the fire of coast defense guns.

[14] The tall stack of the sugar mill, however, survived intact, and although it made a convenient point of reference for American artillery it also provided a well-concealed post for a Japanese observer, who directed fire thence for many days undetected. Hoffman pp. 36–37, 80; H. M. Smith *Coral and Brass* (1949) p. 162.

[15] Cincpac Monthly Analysis June 1944 p. 34.

[16] Cdr. I. E. McMillian "Gunfire Support Lessons Learned in World War II," U. S. Naval Inst. *Proceedings* LXXIV (1948) pp. 979–90.

June the 14th opened overcast, with a waning moon shining through clouds as a faint blob, and a grayish-green dawn in the light of which the outlines of Saipan and Tinian became increasingly visible to the approaching bombardment groups. An easterly tradewind sprang up at dawn. Oldendorf's group swung around Marpi Point, the north cape of Saipan; Ainsworth's approached Saipan Channel from the northeast. At 0539 Ainsworth's group opened fire on the coastal battery of 6-inch guns on the cliffs of Nafutan Point. Flashes of return fire were seen a minute later. "The nerve of 'em!" a *Honolulu* bluejacket was heard to say. These shots were fired at the spotting plane, not at the ships, whose gunfire caused the Japanese artillerymen to retire to their dugouts. The range closed to 8000 yards, yet no reply to the ships; later *Pennsylvania* took this target in hand. Through Saipan Channel some of Oldendorf's ships could be seen hull-down, and in the channel itself Admiral Joy's *Wichita* with *New Orleans* and *St. Louis* were directing enfilading gunfire onto the beaches. The American firing was very deliberate, every shot timed, allowances strictly adhered to; for the ships were thousands of miles from ammunition depots.

There are few things prettier than a naval bombardment, provided one is on the sending not the receiving end and (as in this case) has lost all feeling of compassion for the human victims. Nearby ships belch great clouds of saffron smoke with a mighty roar. Distant ones are inaudible, but their flashes of gunfire leap out like the angry flick of a snake's tongue. Planes drop white phosphorus bombs which explode in clouds white as new-fallen snow, and throw out silver streamers which ignite canefields, whence clouds of yellowish sugar-cane smoke arise. Cape Nafutan, with green herbage atop steep cliffs, made a noble spectacle when "shorts" from *Pennsylvania's* main battery threw up columns of spray hundreds of feet high like those tossed up by breaking waves after a storm.

Admiral Oldendorf, in the meantime, had been "comin' round the mountain." While his bombardment group maneuvered in the darkness 12 miles north of Marpi Point, the shore battery there opened fire and dropped three 2-gun salvos very near the ships. And a well-camouflaged unit on Maniagassa Island off Tanapag harbor, made a few passes at battleship *Maryland* as she steamed by, two miles off shore. Even at that range its shots fell 1000 yards short. *Maryland* and *California* soon silenced this battery, which gave no further trouble.

The Tinian gunners were more enterprising than their fellows on Saipan. Shortly after the forenoon watch began on 14 June, a fire support unit was delivering a shoot on the shore near Tinian Town, when first one and then a second shore battery opened up. They straddled *Cleveland*, hit *California* (one killed, nine wounded) and destroyer *Braine* (3 killed, 15 wounded). Next day a battery on the north point of Tinian took *Tennessee* under fire and hit a 5-inch gun mount on the third salvo, killing 8 and wounding 26 men. All three ships made temporary repairs and continued to operate. Not until long after was it ascertained that these shots had come from 4.7-inch field artillery concealed in the mouth of a cave.

This D minus 1 bombardment completely ruptured the Japanese communications lines,[17] but it could have accomplished more. *Pennsylvania* pounded away at Nafutan Point for hours, and *Honolulu* threw more hardware that way on the 15th, without provoking a reply. After she had ceased fire and hauled off shore, *Montpelier*, her consort and rival, steamed close around the point only two or three miles distant. Nafutan gunners could not resist that. Suddenly they gave tongue; near-misses spouted geysers around the cruiser, *Montpelier* and her screening destroyers went to rapid fire, which in a few moments silenced the shore battery, and retired at flank speed. This brisk encounter was followed with intense interest by officers and seamen topside in *Honolulu*. Happily no ships were hit; but neither were three of the four Japanese guns.[18]

[17] Information obtained in 1952 from Capt. Tatsuji Nakamura, senior staff officer of naval base force.
[18] There is, however, something wrong with the statement in Engineer Exp. Troops *Report on Japanese Defensive Plan for Saipan* p. 3, to the effect that three of these guns "had not been fired" and that the fourth had only "fired 10 rounds

Any bombardment ship must take time and spend some ammunition "finding her way around." The fault at Saipan, one of planning rather than execution, was the failure to direct gunfire immediately to the rear and on the flanks of the beaches, where concealed machine-gun nests and mortars would be emplaced. The underwater demolition teams, swimming close to shore, before noon observed heavy flanking fire from Afetna Point and also reported that pillboxes and gun positions along the beaches, already noted in Intelligence reports, were still intact. In the prelanding bombardment of D-day those immediate threats to the landing force should have been destroyed, but they were not.

Lieutenant General Yoshitsugu Saito, the Japanese commander, regarded the 11 June bombing as a routine "hit and run" affair; but Imperial Headquarters at Tokyo took a different view. With their approval, Commander in Chief Combined Fleet ordered the Mobile Fleet to get under way for the decisive battle. After two more days' bombardment, Saito decided that a landing was imminent. At first he expected it to be at Magicienne Bay where the best beaches were, and no reefs; but on 14 June he inferred from the special attention that ships and planes were giving to Charan Kanoa that his enemy would land there. So he withdrew most of his troops and shifted his field artillery to new locations well back of the shore, and transferred his headquarters to a well-masked cave on Hill 500 overlooking the entire southern third of the island.[19]

4. *The Underwater Demolition Teams* [20]

During the bombardment of 14 June the UDTs (Underwater Demolition Teams), brought up in destroyer transports, carried

in the direction of Charan Kanoa." I myself saw two-gun salvos falling around *Montpelier*.

[19] Captured documents summarized in CTF 56 (Gen. H. M. Smith) Report on Marianas Operation 20 Oct. 1944, Enclosures A–D p. 570.

[20] Composition and tactical employment on this operation is described in Comcrudiv 9 (Rear Adm. Ainsworth) Op Plan 2–44, June 2, 1944, Annex D Appendix 2. Conversations with Col. J. D. Kemp, a British commando leader who observed these operations with great interest, and with Cdr. Kauffman.

out reconnaissance right under the arc of naval gunfire, which protected them from molestation. Two 96-man teams, one commanded by Lieutenant Richard F. Burke USNR and the other by Commander Draper Kauffman, shoved off from the APDs in four ramped landing craft, each holding 4 officers and 20 men, and arrived off the reefs opposite their respective beaches at daybreak, 14 June. Parallel to the reef and as close to it as possible they moored small buoys, at each of which two swimmers dropped off. One swam straight in to the beach, estimating the distance, while the other swam around on each side of him, taking soundings with his body or with 4-fathom mackerel lines. Landing craft picked up the swimmers and returned them on board ship to chart depths and reef data, which were promptly reported to Admiral Turner.

The particular object of this reconnaissance was to chart "paths" from the reef through the lagoon, so that the Marine Corps tanks might reach the beaches under their own power. This was done. Incidentally, the UDTs confirmed the findings of the miraculously preserved Commander Martin, for the small section of reef and lagoon that he had covered. No boat mines, jetting rails, horned scullys or similar monsters with which the Allies were then coping on the beaches of Normandy were present at Saipan. On the evening of D-day the teams came in again to perform their original function of demolition. This time each swimmer placed packs of tetratol to explode a new boat passage through the reef off Beach Red 2, and also to blast out ramps so that dukws could climb over the reef. At a cost of four men killed and five badly wounded by enemy rifle and mortar fire, these true amphibians procured information useful beyond all price. "Their skill, determination and courage," said Admiral Turner of them, "are deserving of the highest praise." [21] Not until they reported to the Admiral did he feel sure that the amphtracs, on which so much depended, could climb over the reef or that the Marine Corps tanks could make the beach.

In the small hours of 15 June the several transport and tractor

[21] Turner Report p. 32.

groups of the Northern Attack Force were making a nicely timed circuitous approach to the west coast of Saipan, passing Marpi Point well to the north, beyond possibility of observation from the shore. At sunrise the inhabitants of the island looked out on the greatest display of shipping ever beheld in the Marianas. Admiral Nagumo and General Saito may have been astonished, but they were not dismayed. They had every confidence in the ability of their ground troops to delay and harass the Yankee invasion until Admiral Ozawa and the Mobile Fleet, now hastening north from Tawi Tawi, could smash up this arrogant array of amphibious power. The enemy might take unconsidered atolls like Tarawa and Eniwetok; but Saipan — never!

CHAPTER XIII

Saipan[1]

15–21 June 1944

1. D-day Battle, 15 June

D–DAY rose over the Marianas in a golden sunrise under a clear
sky. In every direction, save where Saipan and Tinian arose
to take the morning, one saw "ships, fraught with the ministers and
instruments of cruel war." Vice Admiral Turner was on the bridge
of *Rocky Mount,* a command ship fitted with every device to communicate with ground, surface, and air forces. Lieutenant General
Holland M. Smith USMC was with him; Rear Admiral Harry Hill,
Turner's second in command, stood by in *Cambria.* A flight of 20
Avengers from a carrier passed high overhead with a sinister roar,
the low sun lighting up their wings as they tore past the waning
moon. It was as cool (83°) and lovely a daybreak as you could expect at sea in the tropics; one that grew into a bright, blue tradewind day, a perfect setting for the pageant of amphibious warfare
about to unroll.

While the transports floating the two assault regimental combat
teams of the 2nd and 4th Marine Divisions [2] steamed into their re-

[1] Besides the Turner, H. M. Smith, and other official reports, there are several
printed books on the assault and capture of Saipan. Of these, Major Carl W.
Hoffman USMC *Saipan: The Beginning of the End* (Historical Division HQ,
U.S. Marine Corps, 1950) is one of the best campaign histories of the Pacific war:
thorough, accurate, well written, and scrupulously fair to the other armed services
and to the enemy. General H. M. Smith gives his point of view in *Coral and Brass*
(1949). J. A. Isely and P. A. Crowl, *The U.S. Marines and Amphibious War*
(1951) devote chapter viii to an analysis of this operation; and a participant,
Robert Sherrod, has the most vivid account of the actual fighting in *On to Westward* (1945).

[2] The 2nd Marine Division (Maj. Gen. Thomas E. Watson) included the 2nd
(Col. Walter J. Stuart), 6th (Col. James P. Riseley), and 8th (Col. Clarence R.

spective areas several miles off the Charan Kanoa beaches, other transports of the Northern Attack Force, carrying troops due to land later in the day, staged a diversion off Mutcho Point, Garapan. Landing craft were lowered and filled as if they were about to land on the beaches inside Tanapag Harbor. General Saito was not much impressed by this ruse, being already convinced that the pay-off would come at Charan Kanoa; but he kept one regiment ready at Tanapag Harbor, just in case, and also continued to man his positions commanding Magicienne Bay. In due course the Marines afloat off Tanapag were reëmbarked, their boats were hoisted in, and the transports proceeded to the main area.

This brief diversion, together with the hit scored on *Tennessee* by a Tinian battery that morning, prompted Tokyo to put out a premature victory broadcast. Japanese forces had sunk a battleship, "probably the *New Jersey*," shot down 124 planes, and had driven the Americans back to their boats. Captain Matsushima, the Navy's spokesman, told the press that the enemy's "reckless approach" was just what Japan wanted; we had been "lured" to Saipan in accordance with the strategic principle of Sun Tzu, a Chinese sage, who had said, "Strike the enemy when he is impatiently jerking at the end of his tether." At the same time "Tokyo Rose" was amusing American soldiers and sailors with hot jazz and scraps of intelligence artfully suggesting that she knew all about Operation "Forager," coupled with the cheery assurance that each member of the Ex-

---

Wallace) Regiments, the 10th (artillery, Col. Raphael Griffin, with 4 battalions); a howitzer battalion, 2 battalions of the 18th Regiment (the shore party), a tank battalion, two amphibian tractor battalions, a motor transport, a service, and a medical battalion. Total, 21,746 officers and men.

The 4th Marine Division (Maj. Gen. Harry Schmidt) included the 23rd (Col. Louis R. Jones), 24th (Col. Franklin A. Hart), and 25th (Col. Merton J. Batchelder) Regiments; the 14th Regiment (artillery, Col. Louis G. DeHaven) with 4 battalions; a howitzer battalion; the 20th Regiment (artillery), Lt. Col. Nelson K. Brown; a tank battalion, an amphibian tractor battalion, and a motor transport, a service, and a medical battalion. Total, 21,618 officers and men. A Marine infantry regiment contains 3 battalions, each with 33 officers, 804 men, 2 Navy surgeons, and 40 Naval medical corpsmen; total, 879. The 1st Battalion, 29th Marine Regiment, with 1084 officers and men was sometimes attached to the 2nd, sometimes to the 4th Division. For a further breakdown of the battalions into companies, platoons and squads, see Isely and Crowl p. 341.

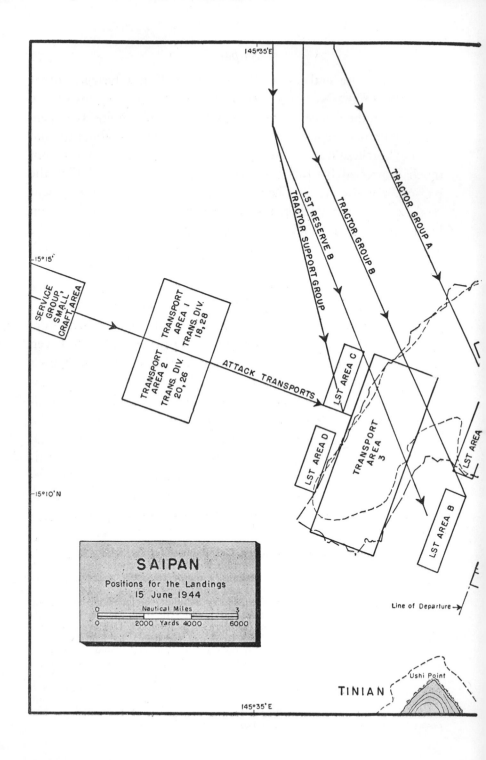

145°35'E

15°15'

SERVICE GROUP SMALL CRAFT AREA

TRANSPORT AREA 1 TRANS. DIV. 18, 28

TRANSPORT AREA 2 TRANS. DIV. 20, 26

ATTACK TRANSPORTS

LST RESERVE B TRACTOR SUPPORT GROUP

TRACTOR GROUP B

TRACTOR GROUP A

LST AREA C

LST AREA D

TRANSPORT AREA 3

LST AREA

LST AREA B

15°10'N

SAIPAN

Positions for the Landings
15 June 1944

Nautical Miles
0   3
0   2000   Yards 4000   6000

Line of Departure →

TINIAN

Ushi Point

145°35'E

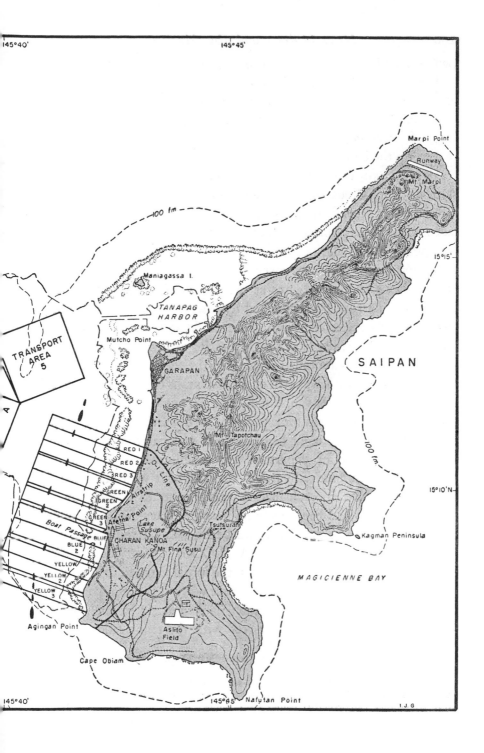

peditionary Force was doomed to early death and a watery grave.

The Marine assault battalions breakfasted at 0445, fifteen minutes after the two-hour naval bombardment had commenced. At 0630 began half an hour of air strikes.[3] At 0700, an hour before the landing craft were to jump off from the line of departure, naval gunfire picked up the ball again.

Already, at 0542, Admiral Turner had given the classic signal that starts an amphibious assault: "Land the Landing Force." Chaplains offered a last prayer and a blessing, over loud-speakers. Amphtracs laden with troops poured from the maws of the LSTs. From the big transports, other Marines crawled down landing nets into boats. Everyone knew where to assemble and what to do. Those who were curious enough to gaze at the shoreline through binoculars could see a narrow beach backed by sandy soil and low scrubby trees, with an occasional palm grove or flame tree blooming with vermillion flowers; the land rose in a series of low escarpments like steps, and Mount Tapotchau dominated the scene. It was not in the least like Tarawa or Kwajalein or the Solomons or Cape Gloucester; it might have been Hawaii, but for the Japanese-style houses.

These Saipan landings took place on a two-division front almost four miles long. The eight beaches were designated by colors and numbers. The line of departure was established 4000 yards off shore, and fifteen hundred yards to seaward of it were stationed 64 LSTs (8 to a beach), each loaded with amphtracs manned by assault troops who had been taken on board at Kwajalein or Eniwetok. Each wave of 12 amphtracs per beach was flanked on the way in by landing craft control boats (LCCs). Twenty-four "Elsie Item" gunboats (LCI–Gs) preceded the initial wave to deliver close fire support with 40-mm guns. The first wave was accompanied by 18 armored amphtracs, six on each flank and six in the center.[4] These climbed over the barrier reef with the troop-laden LVTs,

---

[3] Gen. H. M. Smith Report Enc. G (air officer's) p. 3. Some of the strikes were on Tinian.

[4] These were the LVT–A1s (or A4s – see Vol. VII p. 209) carrying no passengers but armed with a 37-mm cannon (or 75-mm howitzer) and 3 or more MGs; sometimes (incorrectly) called LVT tanks.

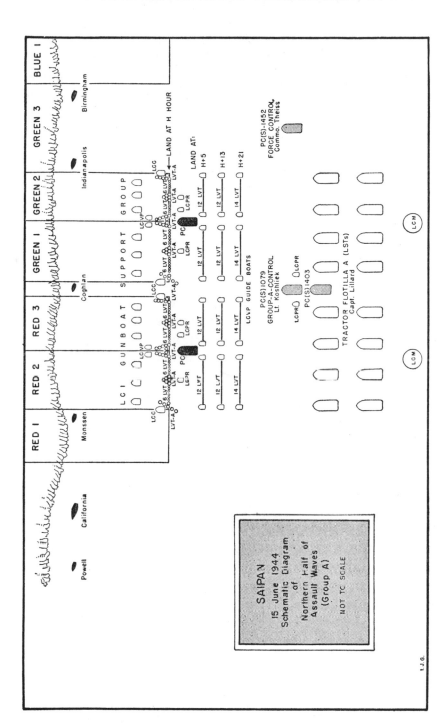

SAIPAN
15 June 1944
Schematic Diagram
of
Northern Half of
Assault Waves
(Group A)

NOT TO SCALE

splashed through the lagoon, and, if they survived the beach, rumbled inland looking for machine-gun nests. Between every pair of beaches a big patrol craft marked the boundary; and between Waves 1 and 2 there were ramped landing craft (LCPR) for salvage. Each LST, LCI, LCC and PC flew a large flag with a distinctive color combination representing the beach to which it was assigned — a white flag with two vertical green stripes for Beach Green 2, for instance — and these gay, fluttering banners with red, green, blue and yellow stripes gave the spectacle the deceptive appearance of a yachting regatta. *PCS–1452*, from which Commodore Theiss directed this great ship-to-shore movement, hoisted a No. 1 "meat-ball" pennant at each yardarm five minutes before H-hour, and "executed" at 0812. As the long waves of amphtracs, each trailing a plume of white spray, raced with their supporters toward the eight landing beaches, the fire-support battleships, cruisers and destroyers, anchored only 1250 yards off shore, delivered frontal and enfilading fire on the beach defenses. And as the amphtracs began crawling over the barrier reef, 72 planes from the escort carriers, including 12 Avengers armed with rockets, came down in vicious, hawklike swoops to strafe the beaches and the area just behind, the rockets making a sound like the crack of a gigantic whiplash.

At 0844 the initial wave hit Beach Red 2 and at once came under intense fire, but pressed resolutely on. Within eight minutes there were troops on every beach, and some were fighting their way across the Charan Kanoa airstrip. As the second wave came in, around 0857, amphtracs of the first were beginning to retract, passing through the second, third and fourth waves with expert helmsmanship.[5] Among these 600 and more LVTs and landing craft, tearing to and fro for a space of two hours, there was not a single serious collision, so well had the training center done its work.

[5] The writer's diary of messages received; report of Col. J. D. Kemp, British Army observer on board a control boat, to British Joint Staff Mission (Washington, 17 July 1944); reports of various transport commanders. The same amphtrac battalion that had fouled things up for the 4th Marine Division at Roi-Namur (Vol. VII p. 244) served here too, but this time it did a superlative job.

The initial landings, 15 June. Mount Tapotchau in background

Saipan

The Charan Kanoa beachhead, 25 June
Tinian in background

Marines fighting on Saipan

Saipan

Casualties were heavy among the LVTs, which had to cross the reef and the lagoon and strike inland; but the landing craft, which either discharged at the reef or took the boat passage, fared better. The nine ships of Transdivs 18 and 28 lost in all only 10 LCVPs and 4 LCMs. "Communications with the control vessels were uniformly excellent," owing to the advance preparation and training conducted by Lieutenant Harry Baker and other officers in the control group.[6]

On the left flank the 2nd Marine Division assault troops landed too far north. The 2nd Battalion 8th Regiment landed on the 3rd Battalion's Beach Green 1 instead of Green 2, making a dangerous congestion; and the two assault battalions of the 6th Regiment, scheduled for Beaches Red 2 and 3, landed on Red 1 and 2. The Marines declared (and the Navy denied) that this was due to mistakes of the naval officers in the guide boats; probably the main reason of the deflection was an instinctive avoidance of a heavy field of enemy fire. All four battalion commanders, including Lieutenant Colonels Henry P. Crowe and Raymond L. Murray of Tarawa fame, were wounded during the early hours of the battle.[7]

The preparatory naval bombardment also was a disappointment, judging from the number of enemy defenses it left intact.[8] The Japanese had reëstablished prepared artillery positions on both forward and reverse slopes of the saucer-like depression behind Mount Fina Susu on the edge of the Marines' O–1 (objective first day) line, and as far away as Tsutsuran overlooking Magicienne Bay. They had 75-mm and 105-mm field pieces well sited, artfully concealed, and with wall diagrams marking registration points on the reefs, beaches, roads and elsewhere. Obviously this was the

---

[6] Comtransdiv 18 (Capt. H. B. Knowles) Report of Saipan Operation p. 24.
[7] Hoffman p. 50. For "Jim" Crowe see Sherrod *On to Westward* p. 58.
[8] Gen. H. M. Smith Report, Enc. G, Air Officer's Report, p. 11. Admiral Turner, however, declared in his Report p. 27 that naval gunfire had done all that could be expected in the time allotted to it. "The spaces for deployment of enemy artillery were large; they had been carefully sited and registered, and . . . it is exceedingly difficult to discover the positions of field artillery and mortars, either from the air, ground or sea," when they use flashless powder. "It is a patient and lengthy process to search out and destroy these guns, particularly when they are firing from reverse slopes."

work of many days, not a last-minute improvisation. There were also mortars and machine-gun nests between the field artillery and the beaches; and pillboxes, camouflaged trenches and other strong points on Afetna and Agingan Points, from which some of the landing beaches could be enfiladed, intact after the naval and air bombardments. As the initial wave came in, artillery shell and mortar projectiles, some from Tinian, began to drop among the LVTs, the landing craft and the LSTs. There was machine-gun fire, too, from the Charan Kanoa sugar mill and elsewhere. But it was not until the fourth wave approached that the enemy began concentrating his fire on the beaches and on the reef. He then laid down such a barrage that the whole reef was curtained with spray, and many observers to seaward thought that the reef itself must have been mined. The most deadly and devastating fire came from the field artillery of Colonel Nakashima's 3rd Regiment, located 2½ miles from the beaches, almost on Magicienne Bay.

On the southernmost landing beaches (Yellow 1 and 2), conditions were bad. The 1st Battalion 25th Regiment, which had the bad luck to draw Yellow 2, was forced by heavy frontal and enfilading fire to debark at the water's edge; its LVTs hightailed out without bothering to unload ammunition, mortars or machine guns, and the battalion was pinned down for an hour while a pitiless fire raked it from Agingan Point. The 2nd Battalion, next to the north, was able to get 500 to 700 yards inland in its amphtracs, but most of the 2nd Battalion 23rd Regiment after landing on Beach Blue 2 was stopped in its tracks about 100 yards inland.

On the Red beaches at the north of the line, the 2nd and 3rd Battalions 6th Marine Regiment came under intense artillery and mortar fire, and the few amphtracs that succeeded in running this gantlet and locating a beach exit were stopped by rocky terrain and the swamp around Lake Susupe. A number of the armored amphtracs were neatly hit by enemy fire, and their exploding shells added to the discomfiture of the Marines. At 1000 Colonel James P. Riseley USMC, commanding the 6th Regiment, called on his reserve battalion, the 1st, to land. As it approached the beach an "abandoned" Japanese tank suddenly came to life and killed several key men. The 1st suffered 147 casualties out of a total strength of 880 that day, and more the next; and at the end of D plus 2 only two of the seven captains were left.[9]

Despite all hazards, about 700 LVTs carrying 8000 Marines got ashore in the first 20 minutes; and all day long, and after dark, landing craft were plying furiously between the transports and the beaches. Toward the end of the day an underwater demolition team swam in and blasted shelves off the southernmost beach, Yellow 3, to enable LSTs to beach as soon as Agingan Point was captured. Fortunately the reef at this point bends so near the shore, narrowing down the shallow lagoon, that it could be bridged by pontoon causeways. Some LSTs remained at the line of departure to refuel and repair LVTs and dukws.[10] Others were equipped to act as emergency hospitals until the regular hospital ships came in on the fourth day. Dukws rolled out of LSTs and LSDs, carrying the Marines' 75-mm field artillery, while LVTs boated their 105-mm guns. The transports which had earlier pretended to debark troops off Tanapag Harbor steamed south and discharged troops in their own landing craft; some of these went into the Blue beaches through the natural boat channel, others were transferred to LVTs outside.

The assault Marines were fighting from the moment they left the amphtracs; demands for water, ammunition and other items soon became insistent. Between Beaches Green 3 and Blue 1, where the boat passage came through the reef, there was a small pier to serve the sugar mill, whose chimney still rose over its ruins. As it was low tide at 0952, Lieutenant (jg) Walter D. Ellison USNR, in charge of the beach party on Blue 2, saw that the only way to get the water ashore from landing craft was on this pier, which so far had been avoided because it was under heavy enemy fire. With 20 bluejacket volunteers he manned the pier and for half an hour

[9] Robert Sherrod in *Marine Corps Gazette* Oct. 1944.
[10] LSTs distinguished by red flags maintained six fueling stations, 3 on either hand, for delivery of 100-octane gas (which the LVTs drank like dragons) from steel drums. *LST-224* Action Report 5 July 1944.

helped to get supplies ashore and inland. The Japanese then poured mortar shells into and around the pier, killing six and wounding ten of the volunteer party; but the Marines got their water.[11]

The big LCMs, preloaded with tanks, which had been brought up in LSDs *Lindenwald* and *Oak Hill,* made a particularly neat landing. They were to have come in through the boat passage to Beach Blue 1, but since the passage at times was interdicted by artillery and mortar fire from Afetna Point, the 2nd Division tanks were landed on the reef opposite Beach Green 1. Thanks to "paths" laid out by the UDTs, the tanks were able to churn through the lagoon at half tide shortly before noon; mortar shells were dropping all around, but out of 36 tanks, only one, which capsized, was lost. The 4th Division tanks were not so fortunate. Some suffered direct hits from enemy fire, some were drowned out in potholes, others bogged down in soft ground. Next day the tanks brought up in the transports were hoisted out into LCMs and went ashore under heavy fire.

To a superficial observer, the scene might have appeared completely mad, and the shouting and swearing over voice radio circuits at times did sound like bedlam let loose; but to anyone familiar with amphibious technique the landing was a magnificent demonstration of planned and courageous activity. Commodore Theiss and his control officers in the PCs and LCCs had the thing in hand every minute of the day.

Although the landings may be said to have gone "according to plan," in a more nearly literal sense than that stale expression generally connotes, nothing went according to plan after the troops were ashore. The principle behind the plan, the reason why the Marines landed on so long a front, was to seize a beachhead broad and deep enough to allow deployment. Depth would be obtained by the amphtracs' giving troops a mechanical lift inland, so that the élan of the first few assault waves might continue to the O–1 line. That line, in general, followed the 100-foot contour of the foothills about a mile behind the beach, but included the 295-foot Mount

[11] *Polaris,* Mar. 1945, p. 28.

Fina Susu. Subsequent waves were to mop up behind the first, dig in for the night, and next day capture the airfield, strike through to Magicienne Bay, and perhaps even capture Mount Tapotchau. In a few days' time Saipan would be "in the bag" and the assault on Guam could start.

But it did not work out that way. The O–1 line was not fully attained for three days, nor Saipan secured for three weeks. And the assault on Guam had to be delayed until 21 July.

The main reason for this miscarriage was the skill of the Japanese artillery and mortar fire, which prevented the amphtracs from carrying out their assignment, forcing most of them to disgorge their troops near the water's edge. Take for instance Afetna Point, which sticks out between Beaches Green 2 and 3. On 14 June "combined fires of *Birmingham* and *Indianapolis* throughout the morning failed to achieve destruction." Admiral Kingman then ordered *Tennessee, California* and *Birmingham* to concentrate on Afetna that afternoon, and two strafing-bombing strikes were placed on it as well. Again, on the morning of D-day, Afetna Point was blasted with 14-inch shells from *California,* 8-inch from *Louisville* and 6-inch from *Birmingham.* Nevertheless, the enemy poured a wicked enfilading fire on the beaches from Afetna Point, and the Marines had to take it with bayonet, hand grenade, and flame thrower.

After the Marines were ashore, naval counter-battery fire was handicapped by poor initial functioning of shore fire-control parties. The V 'Phib Corps, especially Major Joseph L. Stewart USMC, had given much thought to that important branch of amphibious warfare. In theory, every battalion of the landing force had a shore fire-control party led by professional gunners and including a naval liaison officer whose duty it was to keep in touch by radio with a designated gunfire ship, in order to obtain "call fire" when and where requested by the troops. These shore fire-control parties were better trained and organized than any before them. But their effectiveness depended on successful radio communication (and many of the SFCP radios were soaked getting ashore); on officers' moving about to observe fire (and the enemy pinned them down to the beach); and, finally, on ability of the party to survive (and casualties were heavy, especially among the naval liaison officers without whom they could not function). Consequently, during most of D-day, the most powerful naval fire support group ever seen in the Pacific was unable to help troops in a tough spot, because they were unable to make their wants known. The cruisers and battleships had air spotters in their own float planes, but the battle-field was so covered with dust and smoke that they could see very little.[12] However, the mistakes made at Saipan helped everything to go much better at Tinian and Guam.

The D-day objective set in the plan was not attained except at Mount Fina Susu, and at the extremities where the O–1 line touched the sea. The 2nd Division amphtracs advancing from the Red beaches were stopped by the swamp, by artillery and by grazing machine-gun fire. The 2nd Battalion 8th Regiment, as a penalty for landing on the wrong beach (Green 1), spent most of the day taking the right beach (Green 2) as well as Afetna Point and Green 3, which were wanted to command the boat passage through the reef. The enemy had not evacuated this area; numerous pill-boxes, supported by infantry trenches, were intact, and every hummock on the beach was a strong point.

On the southern half of the beaches the 4th Marine Division was having plenty of trouble. The unfortunate 1st Battalion of the 25th Regiment, pinned down on an enfiladed beach, observed a Japanese counterattack developing from Agingan Point around 0940. It called for help from air and naval gunfire, and both of them it obtained; the advancing Japanese were discouraged by strafing and bombing attacks and gunfire from *Tennessee*. But the battalion continued to lose men by accurate artillery fire delivered from high ground not half a mile inland. During the afternoon Colonel Merton J. Batchelder, the regimental commander, sent a part of the 3rd Battalion to help the 1st take Agingan Point. They there found

---

[12] I am indebted to Lt. Col. R. D. Heinl USMC for letters and articles on the subject of shore fire-control parties.

something new in Japanese tactics — "spider holes" not unlike those at Parry [13] with the additional refinement of a well-camouflaged lid over the hole. The point was taken on the afternoon of D-day with the aid of medium tanks which had just come ashore on Beach Blue 2. The 2nd Battalion, which landed on Beach Yellow 1, was carried by its LVTs about 500 yards to the narrow-gauge railway embankment. There they came under artillery fire, some of it from Nafutan Point, and mortar fire, which friendly planes disposed of. Up to this point the only protection that this battalion enjoyed came from the armored amphtracs of the Army's 708th Amphibian Tank Battalion.

The 23rd Marine Regiment (Colonel Louis R. Jones) which landed on the Green beaches opposite Charan Kanoa passed through that devastated town without much trouble and pushed almost to its sector of the O–1 line. It was balked, first, by an unexpected swamp extending south of Lake Susupe, and by Mount Fina Susu. That 295-foot hill, so conspicuous from seaward that it looks like an island detached from Saipan, had been chosen as an anchor of the O–1 line. The armored amphibians could not climb it, and the Japanese artillery was sighted on it. The 23rd Regiment's command post, set up in a depression between Beaches Blue 1 and 2, was under almost continuous fire from enemy mortars and field artillery. Colonel Jones decided that his forces on the O–1 line were too thin to withstand a night counterattack, and under cover of darkness withdrew the 2nd and 3rd Battalions to a position about 800 yards west.

By nightfall a little more than half the planned beachhead had been occupied, but there was a dangerous no-man's corridor between the 2nd and 4th Marine Divisions. The Marines' positions were good, but the enemy's were much better.

2. *Beachhead Secured, 15–17 June*

Already it was clear that the capture of Saipan would be no pushover but a long, tough job. About 20,000 assault troops had been

[13] See Vol. VII of this History, pp. 302–303.

landed, but several hundred were already dead and the total casualties were over two thousand.[14] As experience had shown that field hospitals could not be set up on a narrow beachhead, casualties were evacuated to the three LSTs designated as hospital ships, by a series of transfers — from field dressing stations to amphtracs at the beach, to landing craft at the reef, to LSTs off shore, and, when these were filled, to transports. In the moderate swell that prevailed on D-day and the next, this was a slow and painful process. During the first three days 1449 wounded were received in the LSTs and about 3600 (including many of the former group) in the transports. The first two hospital ships, *Solace* and *Bountiful*, reached Garapan Roads 18 June.[15]

At dusk the transports and tractor groups, with some of the fire support ships as escorts, could be seen from the shore to be pulling out. They were retiring only for the night, to escape possible submarine or air attack.[16] Admiral Turner ordered Admiral Oldendorf to stand by in flagship *Louisville* with four destroyers, to deliver night harassing and call fire.

Unhappy hours lay ahead for the Marines. As one of their officers admitted, "There is something definitely terrifying about the first night on a hostile beach. No matter what superiority you may boast in men and matériel, on that first night you're the underdog, and the enemy is in a position to make you pay through the nose." [17] As usual, the Japanese saw to it that nobody slept for more than a few minutes. A company or two of their infantry, driven from beach positions into the Lake Susupe swamp, counterattacked in small squads and got themselves wiped out. At 1712 *California*, which by this time had belatedly made contact with a shore fire-control party, threw 31 rounds of 5-inch shell into the midst of an

[14] Hoffman p. 69, who admits that this is a guess. Lt. Col. Heinl informs me that D-day casualties of 2nd Marine Division alone were 553 killed or missing, 1022 wounded.

[15] CTF 58 Report, Report of Corps Surgeon, p. 7.

[16] There was an air attack of about 4 Kates on TG 52.14 at 1840 but no hits were made.

[17] Statement by 2nd Lt. J. G. Lucas USMCR in Navy Dept. Release of 28 June 1944.

infantry movement east of Beach Red 2 and north of the beach-head, where a thousand or more Japanese were streaming down from the hills. But there were plenty left to keep the 6th Regiment very busy from 2200 on. At 0300 June 16, after a series of probes, the big effort was announced by a Japanese bugler; and with much screaming, brandishing of swords and waving of flags the enemy launched an attack that was supposed to drive the Marines into the sea. The battlefield was illuminated by star shell from three destroyers. As the Japanese fell others replaced them, and the fighting on this flank did not reach its climax until sunrise, at 0545. Five Marine Corps tanks then stopped the last attack, and the Japanese withdrew under a blanket of gunfire from destroyers *Phelps* and *Monssen* and cruiser *Louisville*. About 700 enemy dead were left on the field of battle.

Naval paratroops, who were supposed to support the Japanese soldiers on this northern flank, were delayed by the bad condition of the churned-up roads and arrived just in time to encounter soldiers retreating. Mistaken for enemies, they were fired upon, and for a short time there was a brisk little skirmish between the Japanese Army and Navy at this point.[18]

On the southern flank a strong attack, preceded by artillery and mortar preparation, was launched against the 25th Regiment which had come ashore on the Yellow beaches. The Japanese used civilians, including women and children, to mask their approach and create the impression that this was a civilian surrender; but the ruse was detected and the attack was broken up by 105-mm howitzers. The most dangerous counterattack was directed against the Marines' center. At 0530 about 200 Japanese rushed down the slot between the 2nd and 4th Division areas, for the Charan Kanoa pier. The 3rd Battalion 23rd Regiment destroyed almost the entire contingent, but not before it had taken temporary possession of the pier and damaged it badly.[19] This pier and the boat passage approaching it

[18] Information received in 1952 from Capt. Nakamura, a member of Admiral Nagumo's staff.
[19] Report of Force Beachmaster (Cdr. C. E. Anderson USNR), Enclosure B with CTG 52.2 Report; conversations with Capt. Knowles of Transdiv 18.

were key points, because the moderate sea which made up that night prevented LVTs from crossing the reef; hence all night landings had to be made through the boat passage, and even that could not be used within an hour and a half of low water. The range of tides at this point was only 18 inches to two feet, but even that makes a lot of difference to landing craft.

Dawn came none too soon for the Marines, but it found them still there. General Saito's last chance to "destroy the enemy at the beachhead" was gone. He was far from downhearted, though, since he had been assured that an irresistible fleet was about to bring him succor.

Admiral Turner seldom erred on the side of timing, but on this occasion he did. From flagship *Rocky Mount* the landings appeared to be going so smoothly and enemy resistance seemed to be so spotty that, estimating the capture of Saipan would take about a week, he advised Admiral Spruance before noon on D-day to set 18 June as W-day for the assault on Guam by the Southern Attack Force. Shortly after so doing,[20] Admiral Spruance received word from a submarine that a Japanese carrier force was heading in his direction from San Bernardino Strait; and at 0400 June 16 he received another submarine's contact report on a second Japanese force, steaming north off Surigao Strait.[21] Rightly assuming that a naval battle was imminent, Spruance during the morning watch of 16 June canceled the 18 June date for the Guam landings and went on board Turner's flagship for a conference with him and General Holland Smith. There some crucial decisions were made: —

1. To commit at once the reserve, the 27th Infantry Division, and to use the Guam Attack Force as a floating reserve for Saipan in case of need.

2. To detach certain cruisers and destroyers from the fire support ships to augment the fast carriers' screen.

---

[20] Fifth Fleet War Diary 15 June, "Upon the advice of CTF 51"; Cincpac *Monthly Analysis* June 1944 p. 53 says the decision was made at night.
[21] See chap. xiv below.

3. To continue unloading until dark 17 June, then send the transports to a safe position easterly until recalled.

4. To send the fire support battleships about 25 miles westward to cover Saipan against a possible evasion of the fast carriers by the Japanese Fleet.

5. To depend exclusively on the escort carriers for close air support to the troops.[22]

All day 16 June (D plus 1) the landing beaches and the entire beachhead were under artillery fire; many casualties were incurred and few supplies or equipment were landed until the afternoon. A pocket of serious resistance on Afetna Point was eliminated. By 1800 all the Marines' artillery except the 155-mm howitzers was ashore.[23] For the most part this day was employed in getting the rest of the two Marine divisions ashore, in consolidating and strengthening lines, and in mopping up; little ground was gained.

Shortly after noon Major General Ralph C. Smith USA, commanding the 27th Infantry Division whose transports were cruising well off shore, was ordered to prepare to land his 165th Regimental Combat Team and divisional artillery. They began coming ashore in their own landing craft at dusk, and the movement continued all night.

That night the Japanese counterattacked stubbornly. Only about 500 troops got into it, but General Saito committed 44 tanks, about half of what he had. The attack began at 0330 June 17 and lasted until 0700. Shore fire-control parties called for illumination from the ships standing by. They responded with enthusiasm and threw up so much star shell that the attack was delivered in conditions of high visibility that were of tremendous assistance to the 1st Battalion 6th Marines, who met the onslaught with bazooka fire from their shoulders, 37-mm gunfire, and hand grenades. As tanks were hit and set afire they silhouetted others coming out of the flickering shadows. Many tanks were "unbuttoned," a captain directing them from an open turret; some had infantry clinging to their handrails;

[22] Turner Report p. 6 and ff.   [23] Report 20 Oct. 1944 p. 6.

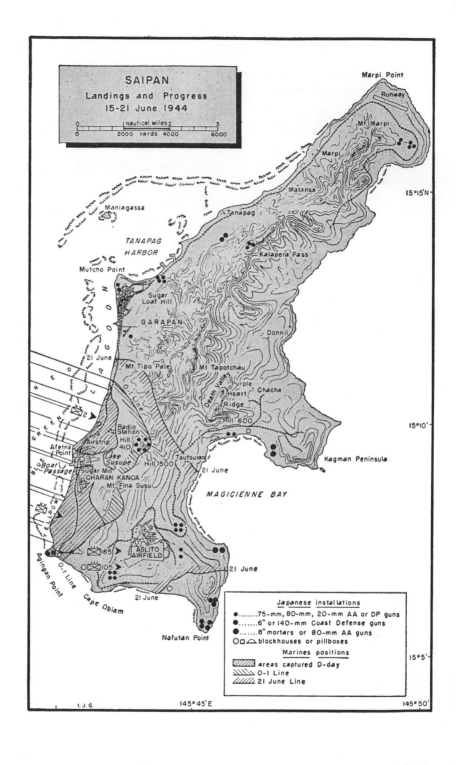

SAIPAN
Landings and Progress
15-21 June 1944

Nautical Miles
0 — 3
0   2000 yards 4000   6000

Marpi Point

Runway

Mt. Marpi

Marpi

Matansa

15°15'N

Maniagassa

Tanapag

TANAPAG
HARBOR

Kalapera Pass

Mutcho Point

Sugar
Loaf Hill

GARAPAN

Donnii

L
A
G
O
O
N

21 June

Mt. Tipo Pale

Mt. Tapotchau

Purple
Heart
Ridge

Chacha

Death Valley

Hill 600

15°10'

O
-
1

L
i
n
e

Radio
Station
Hill
410

Airstrip

Afetna
Point

Lake
Susupe

Tsutsuran

Hill 500

21 June

Kagman Peninsula

Boat
Passage

Sugar Mill

CHARAN KANOA

Mt. Fina Susu

MAGICIENNE BAY

G
R
E
E
N

B
L
U
E

Y
E
L
L
O
W

165

ASLITO
AIRFIELD

Agingan Point

O-1 Line

105

21 June

Cape Obiam

21 June

Nafutan Point

Japanese installations
●........75-mm, 80-mm, 20-mm AA or DP guns
●.......6" or 140-mm Coast Defense guns
●.......8" mortars or 80-mm AA guns
O☐△ blockhouses or pillboxes

Marines positions
▨ areas captured D-day
▨ O-1 Line
▨ 21 June Line

15°5'

I.J.G.

145°45'E

145°50'

some even carried buglers. As dawn broke the 8th Regiment's special weapons company, 75-mm guns on half-tracks, rolled up and gave the finishing touches to all but one. At 0700, when the one surviving tank was seen climbing a winding road, the Marines' naval liaison officer obtained prompt action from a destroyer, whose 5-inch fire took it apart. About 27 others were left burning on the field of battle.[24]

The most severe fighting occurred during the first two days ashore. Losses were particularly heavy among the artillery batteries — which had no room to maneuver, no time to camouflage, no way to escape the sharp eyes of Japanese observers. Yet this unorthodox commitment of so much artillery on so narrow a beachhead fully paid off in consolidating the beachhead and repelling counter-attacks.

Strikes were launched on the 16th from several fast carriers against airfields on Guam and Tinian, to prevent their being used in the expected naval battle. A number of Japanese planes were destroyed in the air and on the ground, but attempts to neutralize the airfields were not successful. Their antiaircraft protection was too good; a number of American planes were shot down.[25] Hard to kill was Ensign W. R. Mooney USNR of *San Jacinto*, who made a safe water landing with his riddled plane and got on board his life raft some 14 miles off shore. He spent nights hiding ashore on Guam, and days at sea hoping for rescue, but was not picked up until 3 July.[26]

By the morning of 17 June there was no doubt in anyone's mind, American or Japanese, that the Saipan beachhead was secured, but Saipan itself was far from being secured.

[24] Maj. James A. Donovan USMC "Saipan Tank Battle," *Marine Corps Gazette* Oct. 1944 p. 25. This was one of the few instances in the war when a powerful night tank attack was broken up by infantry. CTF 56 Report, Report of Naval Gunfire Officer Expeditionary Troops, p. 13; Hoffman pp. 87–90.

[25] Cdr. F. M. Snowden, commanding Air Group 16 in *Lexington*, in his Action Report of 6 July, and the C.O. of Air Group 2 in *Hornet*, in his Action Report of 29 June, make a vigorous plea for naval bombardment of airfields before sending in bombers.

[26] *San Jacinto* Action Report Part VI.

3. *Shore Advances and Counterattacks, 17–21 June*

Even before the Japanese tank attack had been liquidated, naval gunfire shoots, escort carrier strikes and field artillery fires were being prepared for a morning assault ordered by the commanding general. It speaks well for the training of the 2nd Marine Division that it jumped off for the attack in less than an hour after the finish of its night battle with the tanks. By the end of 17 June the beachhead north of Beach Green 3 had been more than doubled in area. General Holland Smith set up his command post in Charan Kanoa at 1530. Parts of the shores of Lake Susupe with its swamps were still in enemy hands, but south of that point good progress was made by the newly committed reserve, the 165th RCT (Colonel G. W. Kelley USA), which was the best regiment of the 27th Division. By 1400 the 2nd Battalion 165th had reached the southwest corner of Aslito airfield, while the 1st was fighting to obtain control of a ridge between that corner and Cape Obian. North of the airfield the 24th Marine Regiment captured a commanding height.

Abundant naval gunfire support continued to be furnished, and shore fire-control parties functioned better as casualties were replaced. Still, the system was cumbrous. Requests for bombardment from a naval officer ashore could be made only twice daily unless there was an emergency, and every such request had to be cleared through Admiral Turner and assigned to a ship that had enough ammunition and was not otherwise employed — a process that sometimes required hours. Naturally the Marines preferred to use their own artillery whenever possible; and they blessed "Howlin' Mad" Smith for insisting on its being landed at the first possible moment. The most effective aid given by the Navy to the Marines at this phase of the assault was night illumination with star shell, of which there was seldom enough; and deep support, which meant deliberate, well-spotted fire on Japanese installations behind the zone of combat.

Fortunately the Marines had embarked in the escort carriers an appreciable number of their own "Grasshoppers" (Stinson Sentinels, OY–1) for artillery spot. Just before dark 17 June, the first of these landed on the Charan Kanoa strip, which they continued to use until there was room on Isely Field.

That evening the Japanese Base Air Force made a bid to carry out its orders to effect a 33 per cent attrition of American forces before the "decisive naval battle." Five Jill torpedo-bombers and one Irving took off from Truk, attacked a twenty-transport convoy east of Saipan at 1750, and claimed to have "sunk one transport and left one destroyer listing heavily." What they encountered was Captain G. B. Carter's tractor group of the Southern Attack Force, still standing by in expectation of invading Guam. In a brisk battle of three minutes, three planes were shot down, but a torpedo hit *LCI–468*, killing fifteen men and wounding three. She was taken in tow but had to be scuttled before reaching port. A second raid, mounted at Yap, consisted of 31 Zekes, 17 Judys and 2 Franceses. This formation passed high over Admiral Ainsworth's fire support group without attacking, and attempted to bomb the vessels that were unloading off Charan Kanoa. No large ship suffered; *LST–84* was set afire by a bomb but later salvaged. After turning back, this same formation encountered and at dusk attacked the escort carrier groups that were maneuvering off shore. *Gambier Bay* and *Coral Sea* took near-misses and *Fanshaw Bay* received a hit that penetrated the after elevator and exploded at hangar-deck level, killing eleven men and starting fires that were soon brought under control. She had to return to Eniwetok for repairs. In the fading twilight there was a good deal of mistaken identification and unnecessary damage. Most of the 46 Wildcats sent out to intercept missed the enemy bombers altogether, and two Wildcats returning to *White Plains* were first fired on by "friendly" antiaircraft, then attacked by four "friendly" planes. None were shot down but one was so damaged that it made a faulty landing, as a result of which six planes were knocked overboard, or had to be jettisoned.[27] The Japanese aviators,

[27] Pacific Air Operations Monthly Analysis June 1944 p. 9; Comcardiv 24 (Rear Adm. F. B. Stump) Action Report 1 July. There was a 4-plane attack on the CVEs, which did no damage, shortly after sunrise 19 June; and the same day 2

imagining that they had sunk three or four fast carriers of Task Force 58, were greatly encouraged and tried again next day.

Although shore parties for handling supplies had been carefully trained by the Marines for this operation, surf on the reef and the unexpectedly early commitment of the reserve fouled things up. The 27th Division came ashore on beaches not yet adequately cleared; their food, water and ammunition had to be rushed ashore onto any vacant spot available. On two occasions most of the shore party was ordered to the front to help repel an attack.[28] Fortunately the famous "Squeaky" Anderson, to whom such situations were a challenge, was senior beachmaster. Few but he could have brought order out of that chaos.

By 18 June, when the 105th RCT of the 27th Division was ready to land and the beaches next Agingan Point had been prepared for LSTs by bulldozers and the UDTs, the troops were transferred from transports to LSTs which beached.[29] The UDTs also blasted a passage through the reef opposite Beach Red 2, which greatly relieved the congestion in the natural boat passage.

Now that he had lost hope of driving his enemy into the sea, General Saito made such dispositions of his fighting men as to take full advantage of the rugged terrain and limestone cliffs of Saipan. The garrison of Aslito airfield withdrew to Nafutan Point, a maneuver that made sense only on the supposition that reinforcements were expected to land there from Tinian and mount a counterattack. The main body withdrew to a line running roughly from Garapan town over the summit of Mount Tapotchau and through Chacha village to the eastern shore. Enough troops were left facing the Marines to make two small and unsuccessful counterattacks on the night of 17–18 June.

Rapid progress was made on 18 June. With the 2nd Marine Division acting as pivot, the 4th swept across the island to the

large flight of planes from Yap and Palau, in search of the same carriers, encountered an oiler group off Saipan and damaged *Neshanic* and *Saranac*. See chap. xviii.

[28] CTG 52.2 (Rear Adm. Hill) Action Report p. 70.
[29] Transdiv 7 Action Report p. 9, and Annex on beachmaster. This report gives high praise to the work here performed by the beach party from *J. F. Bell*. They spent 11 days on the beach with no relief, working 18 hours a day.

southern shore of Magicienne Bay and the 165th RCT took Aslito airfield unopposed. The runways were not badly damaged. Seabees soon began repairing it and on 22 June the field, renamed Isely after the aviator who had lost his life attacking it a week earlier, began to receive Army P-47s of the 19th Fighter Squadron, catapulted from *Manila Bay* and *Natoma Bay*. Within four hours they delivered a rocket strike on Tinian. Two days later the 73rd Fighter Squadron of "Black Widows" (night-fighting P-61s) and the rest of the 19th Fighter Squadron came ashore.[30] Four months later, B-29s were flying bombing missions from Isely Field against Japan.

On the night of 18–19 June the enemy made an attempt at amphibious counterattack, moving 13 loaded barges south from Tanapag Harbor along the shore. They were detected and promptly sunk by "Elsie Item" gunboats and amphtracs.

With the exception of some of the LSTs, the entire American transport force was kept at sea east of Saipan on 18 June, and most of it for two days longer until the Battle of the Philippine Sea was won. At General Holland Smith's urgent request, some of the assault shipping was allowed to return and resume unloading on the 19th.

Congestion was bad on the Blue beaches, which received the most attention from enemy shells. The PC control boat for that sector now became very busy guiding LSTs through the dredged and enlarged boat passage to the newly-laid pontoon causeway. There were not enough vehicles to take matériel inland as fast as it was landed. Dukws, driven by Negroes of the United States Army, did all they could; but the V 'Phib's ambition to pull off one amphibious operation where supplies were not piled up on the beach for days was not fulfilled at Saipan.

On 19 June, elements of the 27th Division had pushed over and behind Aslito airfield to the eastern coast, isolating the enemy forces at Cape Nafutan. General Holland Smith at 1000 June 20 formally took over command of ground forces from Vice Admiral Turner.

---

[30] This brought the number of P-47s on Isely Field up to 73. Craven and Cate *Army Air Forces in World War II* IV 690–1; Robert Sherrod *History of Marine Corps Aviation in World War II* p. 252.

That day the 4th Marine Division overran the plateau north of the airfield, and established a line extending from a few thousand yards north of Beach Red 1 through the village of Tsutsuran to Magicienne Bay, including the important Hill 500. That former command post of General Saito was taken by a methodical and well-executed attack.

On the 21st Turner's flagship *Rocky Mount* and the rest of the transports and fire support ships returned to the waters off Charan Kanoa, unloading was resumed with increasing tempo, and, now that adequate logistic support was assured, the attack was pushed with greater force.

4. PHELPS'S *Adventures, 16–21 June* [31]

Of all the fire support ships under Admirals Oldendorf and Ainsworth, the one that had the most adventures was destroyer *Phelps*, Lieutenant Commander David L. Martineau. One of the 1800-ton *Porter* class whose 5-inch guns could not be trained on high-flying aircraft, she was assigned to the night harassing gunfire group that supported the Marines on their first few nights ashore. After repeated efforts to communicate with a naval liaison officer ashore, *Phelps* finally did so at 0420 June 16 and shot up a position where the enemy was troublesome. All day June 17 she did anti-submarine patrol east of Saipan Channel. The following night she provided illumination for the takeoff of PBM float planes ordered up from Eniwetok to conduct night searches in the hope of sighting the Japanese fleet. That job finished, at 0036 June 18, *Phelps* illuminated the shore for other ships, and when daylight rendered star shell unnecessary she was ordered to shell an area near Garapan. Standing in toward the beach, she observed several LCI gunboats drawn up in a lunette, firing toward the shore with their 40-mm guns. They were breaking up an attempted counterattack on the

[31] *Phelps* Action Report 29 June 1944; conversations with her C.O. and with the British naval observer Cdr. Harry Hopkins RN who was on board. This episode is the basis of a story assigned to the same time and place, with similar circumstances, in Herman Wouk *The Caine Mutiny* pp. 273–74; but the novelist's account of the C.O. of another ship showing the white feather when the destroyer was fired on is pure fiction, according to Capt. Martineau's letter to me, 23 July 1952.

beaches by Japanese troop-laden barges. Thirteen of the barges were destroyed, and the rest turned back. At 0540, when 4800 yards off Mutcho Point, *Phelps* was taken under accurate fire by a Japanese shore battery. Within a few seconds she was hit by a shell which burst in the executive officer's cabin. "Guns" at once reported he had the shore battery in his sights and was ready to open fire. Martineau gave the word. Just before it was executed, the ship received another hit near No. 2 stack which knocked out a fireroom and wounded 18 men, one of whom subsequently died. Clarence Hencey, Water Tender 1st Class, suffering from steam burns and shrapnel wounds, in a fireroom filled with steam and smoke, directed his men so that both boilers were secured after one had been pierced, and the game little ship continued firing as she closed the range. The enemy battery was silenced and *Phelps* was ordered by Admiral Hill to clear out. Martineau, nevertheless, sought and obtained permission to close range and stand by in case the battery reopened, but it did not. *Phelps* lost pressure and went dead in the water for a few minutes.

At 0912, relieved of her fire support duties by destroyer *Shaw*, *Phelps* closed the battle-damage repair ship *Phaon*, a converted LST of the Mobile Service Base which had anchored in the transport area off Charan Kanoa. Observing that *Phaon*'s position was an excellent one from which *Phelps* might deliver fire support to the Marines, if she could moor so as to bring her full broadside to bear, Commander Martineau made a "Chinese landing," bow to stern and stern to bow. In that odd situation she was in a position to fire, and did so frequently during the next two days while undergoing repairs. At one moment on the night of 19–20 June, *Phelps* was firing on the shore from her two forward mounts and simultaneously loading ammunition from an LCVP over the stern, while a repair party from *Phaon* performed a welding job on her deck amidships.

After completing repairs and casting off, *Phelps* continued fire support as requested from the shore. At 2100 June 20, Japanese snipers set off an ammunition dump near the beach. It continued to burn and explode all night, although salvage vessel *Preserver* sent a firefighting unit ashore to get it under control. The Japanese attempted to profit by the confusion to launch another amphibious counterattack from Tanapag Harbor in barges. These were armed with 40-mm guns whose bullets whistled over *Phelps's* bridge as she stood in to break it up; one burst grazed a bluejacket close enough to rip up his pants. The destroyer spotted her searchlight on a barge at a range of one mile, and sank it with a 5-inch salvo; two other destroyers joined in and, although it is not certain that all barges were sunk, the counterattack fizzled out.

Next morning at 0910 *Phelps* was sent to reconnoiter the beaches near Garapan for signs of enemy landing craft. Martineau reported many floating targets left in Tanapag Harbor and along shore, and requested permission, which was promptly granted, to take them under fire. The forenoon watch was spent in beating up sundry small steamers and barges, and firing on a blockhouse. At 1614, while maneuvering to go alongside an ammunition-carrying LST in order to replenish, *Phelps* fouled her port propeller on a sea-plane wire mooring line, and while moored to the seaward side of the LST she was taken under fire by a shore battery. *Phelps* naturally could not risk shooting across the decks of the LST, heaped up as they were with ammunition and drums of aviation gasoline. Shrapnel burst overhead and close aboard, but destroyer *Cassin Young* managed to silence the battery while *Phelps* was doing an emergency break-away (with one screw working) to unmask her guns. Replenishment completed, *Phelps* anchored, and salvage vessel *Preserver* came alongside to clear her propeller. It was *Preserver's* first underwater assignment. Her diver squad plunged in and "with eagerness and loving care" completed the job shortly before midnight, using cutting gear and underwater lights. The light had to be doused for a time because a low-flying enemy plane was around.

After fueling and transferring some of her ammunition,[32] *Phelps* was assigned to the escort of a transport division returning to Pearl Harbor, and steamed the 3700 miles without refueling.

[32] *Phelps* had expended 2021 rounds of 5-inch 38, including star shell, 480 rounds 20-mm and 1469 rounds 40-mm during her seven days off Saipan.

CHAPTER XIV

Battle of the Philippine Sea,[1] Preliminaries

3 May–18 June 1944

1. Operation A-Go, 3 May–13 June

THE "New Operational Policy" of Imperial Headquarters, adopted September 1943, provided that the entire battle strength of the Japanese Fleet be thrown against the United States Pacific Fleet, whenever and wherever it appeared, in order to destroy it "with one blow."

[1] Sometimes called the "first" Battle of the Philippine Sea, but there was only one; the great action of 25 Oct. 1944, improperly called the "second" Battle of the Philippine Sea, is the Battle for Leyte Gulf. This June 1944 action has not yet been the subject of an exhaustive War College Analysis. The wartime analyses, good as possible with very slender knowledge of the Japanese sources, are the Cincpac Monthly Analysis for June 1944, with charts; Commander Air Force Pacific Fleet "Analysis of Pacific Air Operations, Marianas Operations 11–30 June 1944," Cominch Secret Information Bulletin No. 20, "Battle Experience, Supporting Operations for the Capture of the Marianas," Dec. 1944. Principal U.S. sources are Commander Fifth Fleet (Admiral Spruance), Initial (13 July) and Final (30 August) Action Reports and War Diaries; CTF 58 (Vice Admiral Mitscher) Action Report, 11 Sept. 1944; and Action Reports of each carrier group and ship involved, and the Aircraft Action Reports of each squadron. Cdr. R. M. Smeeton RN "Battle of the Philippine Sea," by a young British naval air observer in *Lexington*, written immediately after the battle, presents an interesting point of view.

The principal Japanese sources are A-Go Operation Records of Various Participating Units, WDC 161,517; Supply Forces and Subdiv. No. 51, WDC 161,640; 601st and 652nd Naval Air Groups, WDC 161,642, National Archives 12,261; Cruiser *Tone* Action Report and War Diary, WDC 160,144, National Archives 11,841; *Kumano* War Diary, WDC 160,162, National Archives 11,975; Tabular Records of Movements of Japanese Warships, CVs, WDC 160,677, National Archives 11,792; BBs, WDC 160,624, N.A. 11,791; CAs, WDC 160,623, N.A. 11,784; CLs, WDC 161,407, N.A. 11,789; Japanese Monographs Nos. 90 (851–60) "A-Go Operation" and 91; USSBS Interrogations in *Inter. Jap. Off.* and *Camp. Pac. War.*

Mr. Roger Pineau made a special visit to Tokyo in 1952 to obtain additional material, and Capt. Ohmae has been assiduous in answering questions and interpreting Japanese documents.

An important reorganization of the Japanese Fleet was effected on 1 March 1944 in recognition of the fact that aircraft carriers had replaced battleships as the most important ships in the Navy. A new designation, First Mobile Fleet (*Dai Ichi Kido Kantai*),[2] was adopted to include practically every ship in the Combined Fleet that was not a submarine or in one of the area organizations. Mobile Fleet command was given to Vice Admiral Jisaburo Ozawa, who already commanded the carriers and their screening destroyers. This had the desired effect of placing the battleships and heavy cruisers under a carrier admiral's tactical command. The same thing had been done in the United States Navy almost two years earlier.[3]

Admiral Shimada, chief of the Naval General Staff, in a policy-making order dated 3 May 1944 to Commander in Chief Combined Fleet, announced that "surprise operations will be carried out insofar as is possible and the enemy's spirit for attack will be broken. . . . The waters for the decisive battle will be as near the stand-by area of our Mobile Fleet as is possible." [4]

This last observation was not so naïve as it sounds. Fuel shortage, for which United States submarines were largely responsible, had severely limited the striking range of the Japanese Navy. Early in the war the Japanese thought they had a bonanza in the oilfields of Tarakan and Balikpapan, because the Borneo petroleum was pure enough to be piped into fuel bunkers without processing. But the unprocessed Borneo petroleum contained highly volatile elements which greatly increased fire hazard on board ship, as well as impurities which fouled boilers. Consequently, an order was issued that Borneo petroleum must be processed at the Tarakan, Balikpapan or Palembang refineries before being issued to the fleet. From these ports it was a short haul for tankers, but the Mobile Fleet

[2] Sometimes translated "First Task Fleet." As a further complication, 1st Mobile Fleet (*Kantai*) became 1st Mobile Force (*Butai*) for a tactical operation like the "A-Go," when ships not ordinarily part of the fleet were assigned to it. I have consistently called it Mobile Fleet in this volume.

[3] Letter of the Secretary of the Navy 18 July 1942, by virtue of which, for instance, Mitscher commanded TF 58 although batdiv commanders senior to him were in the task force.

[4] Imp. Gen. Hq. Navy Section Directive No. 373, Annex in Vol. III, trans. by Military Hist. Div., Military Intelligence Sec., General Staff FEC.

could not get enough processed fuel to give battle as far away as the Marianas.

By May 1944 Imperial Headquarters realized that the great moment for a decisive naval battle was fast approaching. On 3 May, by virtue of a directive from the Chief of the Naval General Staff, the new Commander in Chief Combined Fleet, Admiral Soemu Toyoda, issued the general order for Operation A-Go. He designated the Palaus and the Western Carolines (Yap and Woleai) as the two "decisive battle areas" where naval and air strength would be concentrated. If the Pacific Fleet, instead of thrusting into one of these, should appear off the Marianas, it must be assaulted there by land-based air forces only, and "lured" south into waters where the Japanese could best handle it, "and a decisive battle with full strength will be opened at a favorable opportunity. The enemy task force will be attacked and destroyed for the most part in a day assault." The order continues, "As soon as the enemy is damaged, he will be pursued," and subjected to ceaseless air, surface and submarine attacks. "Complete success is anticipated." [5]

The leading concept of the A-Go plan was to tempt the Pacific Fleet into waters south of the Woleai-Yap-Palau line. Toyoda and Ozawa wished to meet it there for two very good reasons: the Mobile Fleet in early May did not have enough fuel to fight at any greater distance from its base, and the insular airfields to the west and south would afford Japanese land-based aircraft golden opportunities for sinking enemy ships.

As soon as the basic A-Go plan was released, senior staff officers of each fleet flew to Saipan, where they received copies from Vice Admiral Kusaka, chief of staff to Admiral Toyoda. They there discussed what should be done if the United States Navy proved so unaccommodating as to aim at the Marianas. To Captain Ohmae, who raised this point, Admiral Kusaka replied that

[5] The order was designated Combined Fleet Ultra Secret Operation Order No. 76. We fished this copy up from the wreck of cruiser *Nachi*. (ATIS Trans. No. 30, VIII 169–70). Admiral Toyoda followed his op order by an ultra-secret dispatch, 4 May, to all commanding officers, announcing his appointment as C. in C. Combined Fleet.

the fuel situation ruled out the Marianas as a decisive battle area until the latter half of 1944. If the Americans attacked Saipan, it must be defended by General Saito's ground troops, who were confident they could beat the enemy at the beachhead. Ships must be harassed by the Japanese Navy's land-based air arm, which Kusaka believed to be capable of sending many units of the Pacific Fleet to the bottom.

Nevertheless, the higher authorities must have been uneasy about these overconfident assumptions, because in early May, realizing they were "on a spot," they rescinded the order that all fuel must be processed, and allowed the Fleet to refuel with crude Tarakan petroleum. This decision enabled the shuttle tankers during May to top off every ship at Tawi Tawi, and fill up the fleet oilers as well. Thus the possible radius of fleet operations stretched, and by early June the Japanese Navy felt able to give battle near the Marianas, should they turn out to be the American objective.

Wherever battle was joined, Vice Admiral Jisaburo Ozawa would be in tactical command. At the age of 57 Ozawa was one of the ablest admirals in the Imperial Navy; a man with a scientific brain and a flair for trying new expedients, as well as a seaman's innate sense of what can be accomplished with ships. Although not himself an aviator, he was a strategist, and it was he who had initiated the offensive use of aircraft carriers. At the beginning of the Pacific war Rear Admiral Ozawa commanded the arm of the "octopus" that strangled Indonesia and Malaya.[6] In November 1942 he relieved Admiral Nagumo in command of the Third Fleet, the famous carrier force. That command he still retained, and since 1 March 1944 he had also been Commander in Chief First Mobile Fleet, which comprised at least 90 per cent of the Combined Fleet, the surface part of the Imperial Japanese Navy. Altogether, Ozawa was a worthy antagonist to Mitscher.

By 11 May the major part of the Mobile Fleet, including Ozawa's

---

[6] Note the frequent references to him in Vol. III of this History, in the first edition of which I failed to give him due credit, by assigning forces commanded by him (pp. 334–35) to Admiral Kurita.

Commander in Chief Combined Fleet
Admiral Soemu Toyoda

Commander Mobile Fleet

Admiral Jisaburo Ozawa

own Cardiv 1 (*Taiho, Shokaku, Zuikaku*) lay in Lingga Roads south of Singapore, where it had been training for over two months. It departed in two groups on 11 and 12 May for Tawi Tawi. The other part of the Mobile Fleet, Rear Admiral Joshima's Cardiv 2 (*Junyo, Hiyo, Ryuho*) and Rear Admiral Obayashi's Cardiv 3 (*Chitose, Chiyoda, Zuiho*), which had been training new air groups in the western part of Japan, sailed from the Inland Sea on the 11th, accompanied by battleship *Musashi*. After calling at Okinawa on the 12th to fuel destroyers, this force proceeded to the anchorage at Tawi Tawi and arrived 16 May.

Tawi Tawi is the westernmost island of the Sulu Archipelago that stretches from Zamboanga Peninsula, Mindanao, to the north-eastern cape of Borneo. The anchorage there occupies a central position on the main convoy route from Makassar Strait to Manila, Formosa and Japan, and is equally well placed for a fleet sortie to the north, east or southeast. Only 180 miles from Tarakan, it could obtain quick deliveries of unprocessed petroleum. But Tawi Tawi had two major disadvantages: lack of an airfield to help train the green carrier air groups, and ready access for prowling submarines.

Seventh Fleet Intelligence got a hint of what was coming up from a copy of Admiral Koga's earlier Z plan captured at Hollandia. Admiral Kinkaid's operation plan of 11 May stated, "A powerful striking force is believed to be gathering in the northern Celebes Sea, using anchorages in the vicinity of Tawi Tawi. It is believed that the assembly of this force will be completed by 15 May." [7] His estimate of its composition and strength was very nearly correct. As yet, he could only guess what Admiral Toyoda had in mind; but he asked Admiral Christie, submarine commander at Fremantle, to make a "spot check" of Tawi Tawi. *Bonefish* (Commander Thomas W. Hogan), then patrolling the northwest coast of Mindanao, was promptly diverted to Sibutu Passage. En route, on a dark, moonless night (14 May), Hogan sighted a convoy of three tankers and three destroyers, one of which, *Inazuma*, he sank. And

[7] Admiral Kinkaid's Op Plan 6 A–44, Annex A.

at noon 15 May, just as he was entering Sibutu passage, he spotted a Japanese carrier, three battleships, a cruiser and destroyer screen steaming toward Tawi Tawi. *Bonefish's* periscope was sighted but she escaped and Hogan made his important contact report soon after dark. Next morning he had a good periscope look into Tawi Tawi. Admiral Christie ordered him to prowl around and procure more information, which he did to the best of his ability; but a submarine could not see the inner anchorage through a periscope. *Ray* sighted capital ships in Davao Gulf on the 14th. On 25 May an unnamed observer on Tawi Tawi, presumably a Filipino coastwatcher, got a message through with almost the correct count of the Mobile Fleet — 6 carriers, 10 battleships and heavy cruisers, 40 other warships and fleet auxiliaries.

Ozawa now had under his command the new carrier *Taiho*, largest afloat except U.S.S. *Saratoga; Zuikaku* and *Shokaku* (veterans of Pearl Harbor, the Coral Sea and the Eastern Solomons); Cardivs 2 and 3, comprising 6 flattops; *Yamato* and *Musashi*, monstrous twins of the battle line; 4 older battleships; 11 of the famous heavy cruisers that had fought so well early in the war; some 30 destroyers with their squadron flagships light cruisers *Yahagi* and *Noshiro;* and 8 to 10 tankers.

Admiral Toyoda, with as yet no intelligence of the Pacific Fleet's next target, on 20 May issued the order, "Prepare for Operation A-Go." This simply meant that all plans were completed. Ozawa speeded up training, not without interruption. *Puffer* (Lieutenant Commander Frank G. Selby), which had relieved *Bonefish*, fired a spread of torpedoes at carrier *Chitose* off Tawi Tawi on 22 May and made two hits, but the torpedoes must have been duds, as *Chitose* sustained no damage. Two days later *Gurnard*, returning to base after breaking up the "Bamboo" convoy,[8] sank *Tatekawa Maru*, one of the fleet tankers.

An integral and essential part of the Japanese forces that were to deal the decisive blow to American hopes in the Pacific was the Base Air Force or First Air Fleet, as the Japanese called their land-

[8] See chaps. ii and ix of this volume.

based naval aircraft. Deployment started 23 May, to be completed on the 26th. By early June, according to our best Japanese authority,[9] 540 aircraft had been distributed among the crucial airfields, from north to south, as follows: Chichi Jima, 4; Saipan, 35; Tinian, 67; Guam, 70; Truk, 67; Yap, 40; Palaus, 134; Davao, 25; Cebu, 40; Kaoe and Wasile (Halmahera), 42; Sorong and Babo (Vogelkop), 16. Note how heavily weighted this deployment is to the southward, where the Pacific Fleet was expected, and that only 172 planes were stationed in the Marianas, where Nimitz intended to strike. The A-Go plan provided that Base Air Force must destroy "at least one third of the enemy task force carrier units . . . prior to the decisive battle." And there were other air groups in Japan that could be staged south via the Bonin Islands, and still others in the Dutch East Indies that might be moved north. Admiral Ozawa was assured that he could count on at least 500 land-based planes being ready to assist him, wherever the enemy might appear.

The reader will observe the great dependence of the Japanese on land-based air power throughout this campaign, and he will see how miserably their hopes were disappointed.

Another duty of the Base Air Force was what the Japanese called a *teishin* reconnaissance of the enemy advanced bases. The word, which may be translated "daring," suggested that the pilots would face extraordinary danger, and the best pilots were thus employed. One of them, flying 27 May from Truk via Buin (the supposedly inoperational field in Southern Bougainville) to Tulagi, had a good look at Admiral Conolly's Southern Attack Force. Two made the 1000-mile flight from Truk to Nauru, where they split tacks; one flew to Majuro and the other to Kwajalein. Between them they sighted most of Fast Carrier Forces Pacific Fleet, together with a large number of transports, tenders and planes on the Kwajalein airfields. Another *teishin* pilot reconnoitered Majuro 5 June, re-

[9] Capt. Ohmae's list furnished 3 Nov. 1951, compiled "from every available document and interrogation of the officers concerned." The C. in C. of the Base Air Force in the Marianas was Vice Adm. Kakuta; headquarters on Tinian.

porting an impressively large carrier fleet anchored in the lagoon.

All this, and American diversionary air raids on Marcus and Wake Islands on 20 and 24 May, failed to give Imperial Headquarters the hint that their enemy would attack the Marianas. More significant in their eyes was the landing of General MacArthur's forces on Biak Island, on the 27th. This landing confirmed their hope and expectation that the Pacific Fleet would steam right into the jaws of land-based air power. Biak airfields were so important in the A-Go plan that something had to be done quickly. We have already described, in Chapter IX, how over a hundred planes were flown into Sorong and other bases to support Biak, leaving only 172 in the Marianas; and how Operation KON was improvised for the relief and reinforcement of that island.

Briefly to recapitulate the story of this futile operation, whose effect was to weaken the forces available for A-Go, the first attempt was called off on 3 June. Two days later submarine *Puffer*, still prowling around Tawi Tawi, sank two tankers, *Takasaki* and *Ashizuri*; and on 6 and 7 June submarine *Harder* reduced Ozawa's fleet by two destroyers, *Minazuki* and *Hayanami*. On the night of 8 June destroyer *Tanikaze* got a sound contact on *Harder* and bore down on her at high speed, in company with a second destroyer. Commander Dealey spotted them by radar, sonar and periscope, let go a full salvo, and sank *Tanikaze*.

Admirals Toyoda and Ozawa began to feel that, no matter where Nimitz intended to strike, Tawi Tawi was getting too hot for the Mobile Fleet.

In the meantime the second attempt to relieve Biak, by troop-carrying destroyers, was under way and also under observation. On 8 June General Kenney's fliers attacked and sank destroyer *Harusame*, and Admiral Crutchley's task force chased away the other five. Nevertheless, on the 9th Admiral Ozawa radioed Commander in Chief Combined Fleet that Japan could not afford to lose the island with its valuable airfields; that reinforcements "might draw the American Fleet into the anticipated zone of decisive battle and enable us to launch A-Go." Toyoda appreciated the force of these arguments. On 10 June he added his two biggest battle-wagons, a light cruiser and six destroyers, to the twice-baffled KON group. Vice Admiral Matome Ugaki, who flew his flag in *Yamato*, took command of this strengthened force. But, before it could make a fresh start for Biak, Toyoda heard of the 11 June American carrier strike on Saipan. Deciding that his enemy was moving into the Marianas, Toyoda "suspended temporarily" Operation KON on 12 June, and ordered Ugaki's force to steam northeast immediately to rendezvous with Ozawa in the Philippine Sea.

Now everything began to move toward the Philippine Sea and the Marianas. Ozawa shoved off from Tawi Tawi on 13 June. Submarine *Redfin* observed the move and reported it to Pearl Harbor. She did not, however, observe an accident that cast a deep gloom over the Mobile Fleet. A Jill torpedo-bomber, flown by an inexpert pilot, made a crash landing on the deck of flagship *Taiho*, collided with another bomber, burst into flames; and before the fire was put out two Zekes, two Judys and two Jills had been consumed. To the Japanese mind this was something more than the loss of six valuable planes; coming so shortly after the sortie, it was considered an evil omen. Mobile Fleet, having already lost three tankers and four destroyers, steamed northward and fueled at the entrance to Guimaras Straits between Negros and Panay, on 15 June.

At 0855 Admiral Toyoda, from his flagship in the Inland Sea, sent out the following message to all his flag and commanding officers: —

On the morning of the 15th a strong enemy force began landing operations in the Saipan-Tinian area. The Combined Fleet will attack the enemy in the Marianas area and annihilate the invasion force. Activate A-Go Operation for decisive battle.[10]

[10] Message File of 601st Air Group, WDC 161,642, N.A. 12,261.

2. *The Japanese Submarine Offensive, 14 May–4 July* [11]

In the submarine aspects of Operation A-Go, the Japanese followed the same futile tactics of advance scouting and patrol lines that they had tried in the Gilberts and Marshalls. At least 25 RO-boats and I-boats were employed in one way or another during the Marianas campaign. They gleaned no valuable information; they failed to sink or even to damage a single United States ship; [12] and 17 of them were sunk by United States destroyers, destroyer escorts, or planes.

Because of fuel shortage, headquarters of the Japanese Sixth or Submarine Fleet (Vice Admiral Takeo Takagi) were shifted in the spring of 1944 from Truk to Saipan, where no repair facilities were to be had. The main deployment in preparation for A-Go began on 14 May. But, as the Japanese submariners' post mortem ruefully remarked, "It's easy enough to plan a skillful deployment of submarines, but very difficult to make it effective."

We may first dispose of the supply mission, to which two RO-boats and two 1600- to 2000-tonners were initially assigned. *I–184* went all the way from Kure to Jaluit in the Marshalls with food and medicaments. *RO–41* and *I–5* performed the same service for Kusaie and Ponape in the Carolines, and *RO–15* made a similar round trip from Truk to Wewak, the heavily garrisoned place on the New Guinea coast that General MacArthur had leapfrogged. Each of these missions was completed, but only two of the boats got home.

Readers of this History may wonder why so little has been said about anti-submarine operations of the United States Navy in the Pacific. The principal reason is that we have little to tell. Japanese submarines were always far less numerous and much less enter-

[11] U.S. Naval Technical Mission to Japan, *Ships and Related Targets, Jap. Sub. Operations* (Index No. S–17), is the principal Japanese source; U.S. Action Reports on the other side.

[12] They claimed a "*Wasp*-class carrier" and an "*Iowa*-class battleship" sunk off Rota and Saipan respectively on 19 June; but our forces were not even aware that they were being shot at. *Japanese Sub. Operations* pp. 32, 46, 73.

prising than the German U-boats. According to prewar doctrine, they were used mainly to attack warships or as scouts for the fleet, not to attack convoys or merchant vessels. And, although the United States anti-submarine training facilities at San Diego and Nouméa were ample, the demand for anti-submarine vessels and weapons in the Atlantic was so great, until the tables were turned on the U-boats late in 1943, that only a few of the new destroyer escorts equipped with ahead-thrown weapons ("hedgehog" or "mousetrap") [13] had reached the Pacific Fleet before mid-1944.

When they did, the South Pacific became a happy hunting ground. The destroyers and destroyer escorts' biggest bags were made at the expense of supply submarines en route to Bougainville, and submarines of the scouting line. This latter group, known to the Japanese during its brief existence as the "NA" line, was set up about 20 May with seven RO-boats, along a NE–SW bearing, starting at a point about 120 miles northeast of the Admiralties. In this disposition one sees the same wishful strategic thinking evident in the A-Go plan as a whole. Since Nimitz had sent his fast carrier reinforcements for the Hollandia operation through that area, it was assumed he would do so again; Imperial Headquarters hoped that he would, counted on his doing it, and sent the pick of the Japanese submarine force to intercept him.

Submarines carrying supplies to the Japanese still in Bougainville were the first to encounter United States ships within a month of Saipan D-day.

On 16 May 1944 Destroyer Division 94 (Commander L. K. Reynolds), consisting of *Haggard*, *Franks*, *Hailey* and *Johnston*, was moving northwesterly up from the Solomons. About two and a half hours before midnight, they were steaming in scouting line some 125 miles E by N of Green Island. *Haggard* (Commander D. A. Harris) made a sonar contact on her starboard bow at a range of 2800 yards. It was 1600-ton *I-176*. *Franks* (Commander N. A. Lidstone) was ordered to assist, *Hailey* (Commander P. H. Brady) and *Johnston* (Commander E. E. Evans) to stand by. Five

[13] See Vol. I of this History, pp. 211–12.

separate attacks were made with full depth-charge patterns, and between the last two a heavy underwater ripple explosion was heard. The destroyers continued their search until the following evening without regaining contact, but they recovered souvenirs of Japanese origin from a diesel-oil slick that extended over seven miles of ocean. The attack was assessed only as a "probable," [14] but it is now certain that *I–176* was sunk.

May of 1944 was a merry month indeed for submarine hunters. Three days after Desdiv 94 scored, there began a series of exploits by destroyer escort *England* (Lieutenant Commander W. B. Pendleton) that are unparalleled in anti-submarine warfare in any ocean. Although but one of a group, *England* delivered the death blow to six submarines within a period of twelve days. Newly built, named after an ensign of the naval reserve killed in the Pearl Harbor attack, she had had about ten weeks' sea experience and was awaiting routine convoy duty at Purvis Bay, on 18 May, when she received a fruitful assignment. Admiral Halsey ordered her to join destroyer escorts *Raby* (Lieutenant Commander James Scott) and *George* (Lieutenant Commander J. E. Page USNR) in a foray against the Bougainville supply line.

That afternoon the three destroyer escorts, with Commander Hamilton Hains in *George* as O.T.C.,[15] departed Purvis Bay and headed for lat. 5° 10′ S. 158° 10′ E to prevent fresh supplies from reaching the by-passed Japanese garrison at Buin. At 1335 May 19, half an hour before their scheduled time of arrival, the three ships were steaming over a calm sea on scouting lines two miles apart: *Raby* on the port hand, *George* in the center and *England* to starboard. *England* had a sound contact about a mile away, steamed over the spot to make sure it was a submarine, and delivered five hedgehog attacks. Two hits were obtained from the second salvo, and three from the fifth. A minute later there occurred a violent

---

[14] *U.S. Fleet A/S Bulletin* July 1944 pp. 32–33.
[15] Hains was ComCortdiv 39, senior to ComCortdiv 40 (Cdr. C. A. Thorwall) in *England*. Our sources for the following exploits are the Action Reports of these commanders, *U.S. Fleet A/S Bulletin*, Aug. 1944, and the original "ship's history" of *England*.

underwater explosion astern, of such intensity as to lift *England's* fantail out of the water and to knock seamen flat throughout the ship. Many on board thought they had been torpedoed, but it soon appeared that a submarine had exploded very close aboard. A long oil-slick appeared, followed by mattresses, furniture and other debris. A school of sharks took care of any human remains that were spewed up from 2100-ton *I–16*, first victim of *England's* skill and enterprise.

After standing by until morning in the hope of collecting further evidence, and observing oil still coming from the same spot in the 950-fathom deep, the three destroyer escorts proceeded northwesterly, outside the Bismarcks. On 22 May they disposed of *RO–106*, which happened to be the northern anchor of the Japanese NA line. All three DEs picked up sound echoes from a surfaced target distant seven miles at about 0350. Turning up flank speed, they moved in to box the target, which, briefly illuminated by *George's* searchlight before it dove, was seen to be a submarine. *George* made the first run, without result; then *England*, who had the contact too, piled in with hedgehog. In two minutes' time, *RO–106* blew up, leaving only splintered planking and an oil-slick to heave up and down on the ground swell.

RO–104 was moving up to the NA line on 23 May, when the same team caught her in full daylight. After *Raby* and *George* had made runs and missed, the submarine started hightailing out. Commander Hains (still O.T.C.) called on *England*, and by the end of her second run, at 0834, Lieutenant Commander Pendleton could hang up a third scalp.

Moving due south, this tough little task group did not have to wait long for a fourth fight. *RO–116*, another of the NA group, was caught by *George's* radar in the darkness before dawn of 24 May. The boat submerged when four miles distant. *England* established sound contact with a very wiggly and evasive object, which her fathometer showed to be 168 feet below the surface. A full salvo of hedgehog tore the unfortunate boat apart. There was a loud rumbling noise, and debris fairly bounced to the sur-

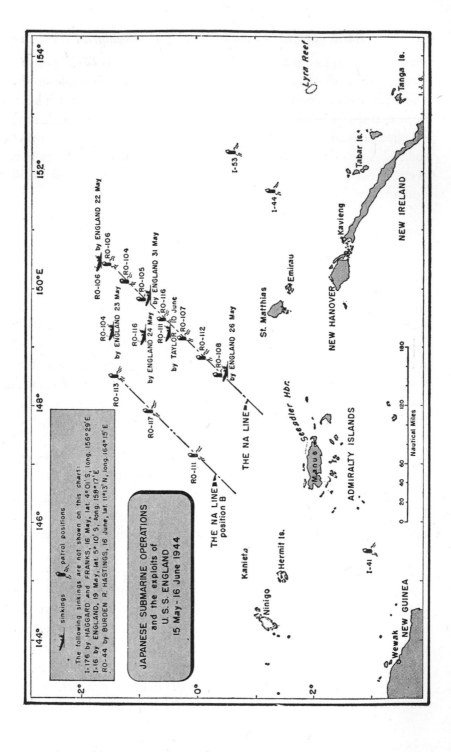

JAPANESE SUBMARINE OPERATIONS
and the exploits of
U. S. S. ENGLAND
15 May - 16 June 1944

The following sinkings are not shown on this chart:
I-176 by HAGGARD and FRANKS, 16 May, lat. 4°.01'S, long. 156°29'E.
I-16 by ENGLAND, 19 May, lat. 5°.10'S, long. 158°17'E.
RO-44 by BURDEN R HASTINGS, 16 June, lat. 11°13'N, long. 164°15'E.

sinkings   patrol positions

THE NA LINE
position B

THE NA LINE

RO-111

RO-117

RO-113

RO-104

by ENGLAND 23 May

RO-116

RO-106   by ENGLAND 22 May
RO-106
RO-104
RO-105
by ENGLAND 31 May
RO-116
RO-111
RO-107
by TAYLOR, 16 June
by ENGLAND 24 May

RO-112
RO-108
by ENGLAND 26 May

Kaniets

Ninigo

Hermit Is.

I-41

Wewak

NEW GUINEA

ADMIRALITY ISLANDS

Manus

Seeadler Hbr.

St. Matthias

Emirau

NEW HANOVER

Kavieng

NEW IRELAND

Tabar Is.

Tanga Is.

I. J. G.

Lyra Reef

I-53

I-44

Nautical Miles
0   20   40   60   120   180

2°

0°

2°

144°   146°   148°   150°E   152°   154°

face. Some of it, recovered after daylight, could be identified as wood from a chronometer box or sextant, indicating a bull's-eye hit on the conning tower.

Next day, 25 May, Commander Hains received orders by radio to refuel and to load more hedgehog at Seeadler Harbor, while a killer group built around escort carrier *Hoggatt Bay* (Captain William V. Saunders) took over the hunt.[16] En route, an hour before midnight of the 26th, all three DEs made a radar contact eight miles distant. The O.T.C. gave *Raby* the first chance, as it was becoming a little embarrassing to have one ship make all the kills; but *Raby* lost contact and *England* would not be denied. She picked up *Raby's* quarry, fired a full hedgehog salvo at 2323, and caught *RO-108* some 250 feet below the surface. Four or five explosions and the unmistakable rumble of a lethal hit were heard. Five down!

After standing by until daylight to recover evidence, Commander Hains resumed course for Seeadler Harbor. There he met a fourth destroyer escort, *Spangler*, which had brought up an extra supply of hedgehog from Purvis Bay. After distributing these valuable missiles, *Spangler* joined *England*, *Raby* and *George*. The four returned to their prolific hunting grounds, and there made rendezvous at noon 29 May with Captain Saunders's killer group. As the combined forces were steaming cautiously northward in the late hours of 30 May, destroyer *Hazelwood* made a sound contact on *RO-105*. As she was busy protecting *Hoggatt Bay*, she requested two of the DEs to take over, with destroyer *McCord* acting as contact keeper. The O.T.C., again wishing to give his other ships a break, ordered *England* to stand clear while *Raby* and *George* hunted. The Japanese skipper after eluding them for several hours, indiscreetly surfaced his boat between *Raby* and *George* and turned on a searchlight to locate his pursuers. This was too much for Commander Thorwall on board *England*, now

---

[16] This TG 30.4, comprising *Hoggatt Bay*, DDs *Hazelwood*, *Hoel*, *McCord* and *Heermann*, had moved up to the area just after Hains's group, and had been operating to the west of them.

O.T.C. for her and *Spangler*. Back they raced toward the position of the telltale pencil of light. By 0500 May 31 they were in communication with *Raby*, *George* and Commander Hains, who directed each ship to maintain sound contact but not to attack before daylight. As soon as day broke, *George*, *Raby* and *Spangler* in succession were given a chance, but all missed. Finally *England* had to be called upon. At 0735 her hedgehog salvo detonated about nine seconds after hitting the water, a tremendous explosion followed, and *RO–105* was no more.[17]

"God damn it, how do you do it?" signaled the O.T.C. a few minutes later. To which Commander Thorwall blandly replied, "Personnel and equipment worked with the smoothness of well-oiled clockwork. As a result of our efforts, Recording Angel working overtime checking in Nip submariners joining Honorable Ancestors." And from far-off Washington Admiral King signaled, "There'll always be an *England* in the United States Navy!"[18]

After making six kills in twelve days, the hunter-killer group returned to Seeadler Harbor and another, organized around *Hoggatt Bay* with four destroyers[19] of Desdiv 41 (Captain A. D. Chandler), took up the hunt. On 10 June an escort carrier plane sighted a telltale oil-slick of *RO–111* eight miles west of the hunter-killer disposition. Destroyer *Taylor* (Commander N. J. Frank), which had done some good hunting in the Solomons, was sent to investigate. Obtaining sound contact, she dropped two depth-charge patterns

[17] Summary of *England's* six sinkings: (1) *I–16*, May 19, lat. 5°10′ S, long. 158°10′ E; (2) *RO–106*, May 22, lat. 1°40′ N, long. 150°31′ E; (3) *RO–104*, May 23, lat. 1°26′ N, long. 149°20′ E; (4) *RO–116*, May 24, lat. 0°53′ N, long. 149°14′ E; (5) *RO–108*, May 26, lat. 0°32′ S, long. 149°56′ E; (6) *RO–105*, May 31, lat. 0°47′ N, long. 149°56′ E. In the official record the other ships mentioned, and *McCord*, are credited with a share in the sixth kill; but there is no evidence that they made any hits.

[18] Other than this, no particular attention was paid to *England's* extraordinary exploit. In contrast, when the Second Escort Group (H.M.S. *Starling* and four other sloops) entered the Mersey in Feb. 1944 after sinking six U-boats in 19 days, they were cheered all the way up the stream; were met at the dock by the C.O. and crew of H.M.S. *King George V* and "masses of Wrens"; and were boarded by the First Lord of the Admiralty, who made a "rousing speech" of welcome. D. E. G. Wemyss *Walker's Groups in the Western Approaches* (1948) pp. 125–26. Much credit for *England's* success is due to her "exec," Lt. J. A. Williamson USNR.

[19] *Taylor, Nicholas, O'Bannon, Hopewell.*

in the morning of 11 June, regained contact at the unusual range of 3400 yards at 1541, and, after stopping all engines to facilitate sound-tracking, saw *RO–111* surface, dead ahead, a mile and a quarter away. Turning to port to unmask her batteries, *Taylor* commenced firing with everything she had, and in three minutes' time made ten 5-inch and innumerable 40-mm hits. *RO–111*, not relishing this attention, crash-dived. A shallow pattern of depth charges was dropped over the place, and at 1558 a very heavy underwater explosion, followed by an enormous bubble 10 feet high and 30 feet in diameter, signaled that the RO-boat was breaking up.[20] Since there was no concrete evidence of a kill, the hard-boiled assessment board of the Tenth Fleet awarded *Taylor* only a "probable," but from Japanese records it is certain that she had sent *RO–111* down for keeps.[21]

In the Marshalls, less heavily patrolled than the more southerly waters through which the Pacific Fleet was expected to pass, the Japanese lost two more submarines. *RO–44*, departing Saipan 23 May, patrolled about 100 miles northeast of Eniwetok and made close-up periscope observations of the atoll on 10 and 13 June, after most of the United States ships had departed. In the early hours of the 16th, when proceeding toward Bikini, this boat was sunk by destroyer escort *Burden R. Hastings* (Lieutenant Commander E. B. Fay USNR).[22] *RO–42*, also on patrol off Eniwetok, on 10 June was sunk by destroyer escort *Bangust*.[23] *I–10*, a 2400-tonner with a disassembled plane stowed in cylinders on deck, assembled and launched it to reconnoiter Majuro on 12 June. Since the American expeditionary force had departed six days earlier, the aviator saw nothing important, and his plane, crashing on landing, had to be abandoned.

On 14–16 June Admiral Takagi, the submarine fleet commander

[20] *U.S. Fleet A/S Bulletin* Sept. 1944 pp. 28–29. The position was lat. 0°26′ N, long. 149°16′ E.
[21] *German, Japanese and Italian Submarine Losses* p. 23, and JANAC p. 12, incorrectly list the victim of this attack as *I–5*.
[22] *U.S. Fleet A/S Bulletin* Aug. 1944 p. 26.
[23] *G. J. and I. Sub. Losses* p. 24 and JANAC p. 12 are incorrect in stating that the victim of *Bangust's* attack was *RO–111*.

in Saipan, got in touch with *I–10*, *I–185* and *I–5*, and ordered them to deploy on a line east of Saipan in the hope that they could help in the planned attrition of the Fifth Fleet. The assignment proved fatal to all three boats. *I–185* was sunk by destroyers *Newcomb* and *Chandler* on 22 June. *I–5* disappeared before the end of the month, but we have been unable to ascertain what plane or ship was responsible. *I–10* had the ill fortune to encounter destroyer escort *Riddle* (Lieutenant Commander Roland H. Cramer USNR) and destroyer *David W. Taylor* (Commander William H. Johnsen). They were screening six oilers and escort carrier *Breton*, standing by off Saipan to fuel ships and replenish planes. At 1702 July 4, *Riddle* made a sound contact less than a mile distant. *Breton*, the tankers and one destroyer turned away, leaving *Riddle* and *Taylor* to deal with *I–10*. After a hunt lasting an hour and a half and the delivery of six hedgehog or depth-charge attacks, undersea explosions were heard and debris bearing Japanese characters came to the surface.[24]

I–184, returning from Jaluit, ran afoul of the anti-submarine air patrol put up by escort carrier *Suwannee* on 19 June, day of the "turkey shoot." One of her Avengers, piloted by Ensign Guy E. Sabin USNR, caught this boat — and sank it. *RO–36*, after reporting the weather and the situation near Saipan on 13 June, was spotted and depth-charged out of existence by destroyer *Melvin*. The same destroyer, with the help of *Wadleigh*, caught *RO–114*, freshly sent out from Japan to Saipan, on the 16th; and next day *RO–117*, which followed her, was detected and sunk by a Liberator of VB–109 from Eniwetok.

Thus, 17 of the 25 or more Japanese submarines that were deployed as part of Operation A–Go, and for supply of by-passed garrisons, were lost.[25]

The exploits of *England* and her friends had an important bearing on the success of the Marianas operation, for the Japanese sub-

---

[24] Same, and *Japanese Submarine Operations* p. 61.
[25] This score, which Capt. Ohmae and Mr. Pineau have spent much effort to establish, is the best we can do with existing records.

marines that they sank might otherwise have been moved north to harass the Fifth Fleet. Task Force 58, when engaged in the Battle of the Philippine Sea, was not interfered with by a single submarine. A few attempted to jab at the amphibious forces around Saipan, but with notable ill success.

3. *"Forward to Decisive Victory," 12–15 June*

On the eve of the famous Battle of Tsushima, Admiral Togo had thus addressed his fleet: "The fate of the Empire rests on this one battle. Every man is expected to do his utmost." Thirty-nine years later Admiral Toyoda repeated the message at 0900 June 15, just five minutes after his order activating A-Go and directing the Fleet to "attack the enemy in the Marianas area." Admiral Ozawa transmitted Togo's fighting words to every ship in the Mobile Fleet, as it sortied from Guimaras anchorage.

The Mobile Fleet, now cognizant of its mission, steamed through the Visayan Sea toward San Bernardino Strait and threaded that narrow passage between Samar and Luzon. At 1835 June 15, as the Fleet debouched into the Philippine Sea, it was spotted by submarine *Flying Fish*, and reported. Throughout that night it steamed eastward to the scheduled rendezvous with Ugaki's battleship detachment coming up east of the Philippines. The former KON Force, which had departed Batjan anchorage on the morning of 13 June, was joined by the First Supply Force at 1000 June 16, at lat. 11° N, long. 130° E. These four oilers and escorting destroyers had had a rocky passage from Davao. Just after midnight 14 June, destroyer *Shiratsuyu*, dodging a nonexistent torpedo reported heading her way, tried to cross the bows of *Seiyo Maru*. The oiler rammed and sank the destroyer, cutting off her fantail before the depth charges could be set safe, and the resulting explosions killed over a hundred of her crew.

Ugaki's force fueled promptly and at 1650 June 16 made rendezvous with Ozawa's. First Supply Force proceeded to fuel

Ozawa, a process that was not completed until 2000 June 17, when the Mobile Fleet was at about lat. 12°15′ N, long. 132°45′ E. The tankers waited nearby to rendezvous with the Second Supply Force (two oilers escorted by two destroyers) which had departed Guimaras at 1800 June 15, in the wake of Ozawa. All six tankers then proceeded to a stand-by point at lat. 14°40′ N, long. 134°20′ E.

By the evening of 17 June Ozawa had received fairly accurate intelligence of the general make-up and disposition of American naval forces near the Marianas. He knew that two carrier groups had attacked Chichi and Iwo Jima on 15 and 16 June, while the other two fueled; that landings on Saipan had started 15 June; that the amphibious forces had escort carriers for close support, which would enable them to dispense with the fast carriers; and that troops were coming up for a later landing on Guam. In addition, he suspected that Admiral Spruance had learned of the Japanese concentration in the Philippine Sea, and guessed that he would remain on the strategic defensive, covering Saipan, instead of aggressively seeking battle with the Japanese carriers.[26] He hoped, however, that a part of the American carrier force would be diverted to attack Yap and Palau around 18 June. Later in the evening of the 17th, Ozawa heard from Tokyo that one enemy carrier group was thought to be off Guam, that exact movements of the others were unknown, and that Spruance might be preparing to give battle on the morrow. So, when the 18th of June was only eight minutes old, Admiral Ozawa addressed a final exhortation to every ship under his command: —

I humbly relay the message which has been received from the Emperor through the Chief of Staff, Imperial General Headquarters, Naval Section:

"This operation has immense bearing on the fate of the Empire. It is

[26] Admiral Ozawa informed us in 1952 that he already knew from captured documents that Mitscher commanded TF 58, and also, by intelligence obtained from captured U.S. aviators, that Spruance was now in command; he inferred from Spruance's "known caution" that he would not take his ships more than 100 miles west of the Marianas.

On bridge of *Lexington*

Lieutenant Commander Ralph Weymouth reports to Vice Admiral Mitscher and Commander William J. Widhelm (back to camera)

Vice Admiral Marc A. Mitscher USN

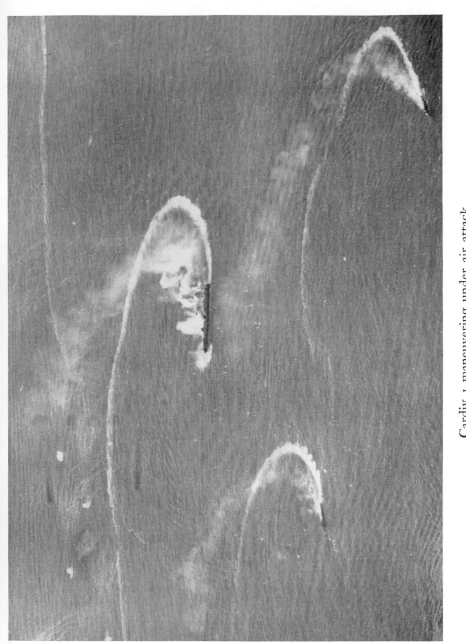

Cardiv 1 maneuvering under air attack
The large carrier is *Zuikaku*

Part of the Mobile Fleet during Battle of 20 June

hoped that the forces will exert their utmost and achieve as magnificent results as in the Battle of Tsushima." [27]

Postponing the question of what Spruance knew about Ozawa's movements, we may make a tabular comparison of the two fleets that were approaching battle:

	Carriers	Light Carriers	Battle-ships	Heavy Cruisers	Light Cruisers	Destroyers
Japanese	5	4	5	11	2	28
United States	7	8	7	8	13	69

The disparity in aircraft strength was even greater: —

	Fighters	Dive-bombers	Torpedo-bombers	Total CVs	Float Planes [28]	Grand Total
Japanese [29]	222	113	95	430	43	473
United States [30]	475	232	184	891	65	956

From this bald summary it is clear that Ozawa was inferior to Mitscher in every naval category except heavy cruisers. Yet Ozawa possessed three tactical advantages that made him confident of victory. First, he intended to, and did, give battle within range of the Japanese land-based planes at Guam, Rota and Yap, while Mitscher was forced to engage without any such assistance. Second, the Japanese carrier planes, owing to lack of armor and self-sealing fuel tanks, had greater range than the American. Ozawa could search out to 560 miles, Mitscher only to 325 or 350; Japanese planes could profitably attack at 300 miles, ours not much beyond 200, although they had to fly farther on 20 June. And, third, if the easterly tradewind held, Ozawa would have the lee gauge, enabling him to approach his enemy while launching and recovering planes.

Search was vital. The Japanese had learned that from their failure at Midway to put a finger on the American carriers in time.

[27] Message File of 601st Air Group (WDC 161,642).

[28] On battleships and cruisers.

[29] Figures as of dawn 19 June, provided by Capt. Ohmae, who was then Admiral Ozawa's senior staff officer. Mobile Fleet had already lost 11 CV and 2 float planes since start of A-Go. Of the 222 VF, 71 were fighter-bombers. See task organization in Appendix III, sec. 2.

[30] Comairpac "Aircraft Availability Report" 24 June 1944, which has figures as of 13 June.

Their searches, conducted largely by the float planes carried by their battleships and cruisers, were both far-ranging and flexible. We shall have occasion to observe how much more successful Ozawa was in this aspect of carrier war than Mitscher.

But if Ozawa offered battle with more confidence than facts (let alone results) seem to warrant, he did so largely because of his dependence on land-based air assistance. He counted on the use of two big airfields and several small strips in the Marianas for his carrier planes, and a very important "assist" from planes already based on Saipan and Guam. If Spruance stayed close enough to the islands so that Japanese carrier planes could strike his ships, then fly to Guam to refuel and rearm, their military value would obviously be increased. If several hundred land-based planes could coöperate with Ozawa, American plane superiority might be more than canceled. The A-Go plan, as we have seen, called for 500 planes to be at Yap, Guam, Tinian and the Palaus, ready to coöperate with Ozawa. Other planes, including the Hachiman Group of 48 Bettys and 48 Jills at Yokosuka, were readied to fly south if wanted.[31] These land-based air forces, according to plan, were to pounce on Mitscher's carriers and Turner's amphibious forces and subject them to at least 33 per cent attrition before any fleet action occurred. Up to June 18, they had done nothing to help Ozawa while suffering heavy attrition themselves, and damage to their Marianas airfields. But, as Admiral Kakuta in his messages had consistently minimized this damage and blown up American losses, Admiral Ozawa still, on 18 June, imagined he could count on heavy assistance from Guam. He even broke radio silence on the night of 18–19 June to inform Kakuta where Task Force 58 could be found,[32] and to arrange for coördinated attacks next day which

[31] Report prepared for this History by Capt. Masataka Nagaishi, former C.O. of Hachiman Group. Only 32 Bettys and 18 Jills of this group reached Iwo Jima 18 June, and only 13 and 8 were left when it was withdrawn to Japan 10 July. The Japanese post mortem, "Impressions and Battle Lessons (Air) in the A Operation" (*Camp. Pac. War* p. 263), says: "It was planned that . . . we would chiefly use shore-based aviators. The Army section of Imperial Headquarters in Tokyo was so confident of the ability of their ground troops plus land-based air to defend the Marianas, that even after the invasion they assured the Emperor that the Americans would be repelled."   [32] *Inter. Jap. Off.* I 10–11.

Kakuta was completely unable to deliver. For (to anticipate a bit) Japanese air strength at Guam was in fact but a fraction of what it should have been, and that fraction was destroyed by the planes of Task Force 58 on the morning of 19 June before it could attack the United States ships. So this essential part of the A-Go plan completely miscarried.

One other factor, that defies numerical evaluation, was the poor training of the Japanese carrier aviators. In the United States Navy at that time every naval aviator had two years' training and over 300 hours' flying time before he was considered fit to fly from a carrier. Most of the air groups under Mitscher were veterans of many strikes. But the air groups of Ozawa's best carrier division had had only six months' training when they left Tawi Tawi; those of Cardiv 3, only three months; and those of Cardiv 2, only two months. Very few planes were equipped with radar, and their crews were not properly trained in its use. Moreover, the month spent at Tawi Tawi before the sortie was lost, because the Fleet was immobile most of the time to save fuel and avoid prowling submarines. Consequently the air squadrons, as the Japanese post mortem said, "loafed there for a month, decreasing the efficiency of their training." [33]

Ozawa, in a sense, "wore three caps" — he was commander of the Mobile Fleet, tactical commander of all carriers, and of the senior carrier division. These functions on the American side were split among Admiral Spruance, Vice Admiral Mitscher, and Rear Admiral Reeves. Spruance hardly needs introduction to readers of this History.[34] Victor at Midway, subsequently chief of staff to Admiral Nimitz and deputy Cincpac, Commander Fifth Fleet in the Gilberts and Marshalls operations, Spruance was tried by experience and unspoiled by victory. Modest and retiring by nature, he had a healthy prejudice against publicity in any form; he shut up like a clam in the presence of news correspondents, who were apt to find him "colorless." Power of decision and coolness in action were perhaps Spruance's leading characteristics. He envied

[33] *Camp. Pac. War* p. 264.   [34] Biographical sketch in Vol. IV 82*n*.

no one, rivaled no man, won the respect of almost everyone with whom he came in contact, and went ahead in his quiet way, winning victories for his country.

Vice Admiral Mitscher,[35] too, was a simple, unassuming gentleman with a soft voice and quiet manners. He, too, was averse to personal glorification and would have avoided publicity if he could, but that was impossible. His slight, wiry figure (he weighed only 135 pounds) and leathery, wizened face, usually seen under a long-visored lobsterman's cap, "made copy" in spite of himself. A pioneer of naval aviation, Mitscher had, as it were, grown up with the flattop. Since March 1944 he had commanded the fast carrier forces of the Pacific Fleet. He gained devotion and admiration, partly by an exceptional performance of duty, and partly by a very unusual thoughtfulness and consideration for the officers and men under him. Rescue operations were for him as important as battle operations; preservation of his sailors' lives as important as risking their lives to attain victory. This quality of compassionate consideration, as well as an innate respect for the dignity of man, made him one of the most beloved officers in our naval history.

Mitscher was in tactical command throughout the Battle of the Philippine Sea; but the major decisions had to be made, or concurred in, by Admiral Spruance.

[35] Marc A. Mitscher, b. Wisconsin 1887, Annapolis '10; at the "wooden end" of the class in which "Savvy" Cooke graduated second, he served in several battleships and destroyers until 1915, when he learned to fly on board *North Carolina*, one of the first ships to carry a plane, and there won his wings. After further flight training at Pensacola and service in *Huntington* during World War I, he became successively C.O. of N.A.S. Rockaway, Long Island, and of N.A.S. Miami. In May 1919 he piloted NC-1, one of the three seaplanes that attempted a transatlantic flight from Newfoundland to England. He had various aviation duties until 1926, when he helped fit out *Saratoga* and served in her for three years. "Exec." of *Langley*, 1929; three years' duty in Buaer; chief of staff to Commander Aircraft, Base Force; Compatwing One, 1938; helped fit out and assumed command of *Hornet* in Oct. 1941, and in her took part in the Halsey-Doolittle raid on Tokyo and the Battle of Midway. Compatwing 2, July-Dec. 1942, when he became Commander Fleet Air Wing at Nouméa, and, in April 1943, Comairsols. Commander Fleet Air West Coast, Aug. 1943; Vice Admiral and Commander Fast Carrier Forces Pacific Fleet 21 March 1944, and as such directed the fast carriers in the Marshalls campaign, and the February strikes on Truk and Saipan. In March this force became TF 58, command of which he held until 27 May 1945, leading the spectacular carrier strikes in the Philippines, Iwo Jima, and Okinawa campaigns. Deputy C.N.O. for Air, July 1945; Cinclant with rank of Admiral July 1946; died while on active duty Feb. 1947.

Of the four task group commanders under Mitscher, the senior was Rear Admiral "Black Jack" Reeves.[36] Since the age of 48, when he had won his wings, Reeves had been in naval aviation. A stern, steady, dependable officer, he could always be counted on to get the most out of his men. Slightly junior to him but of longer aviation experience was Rear Admiral Montgomery,[37] who had commanded almost every air station in the Navy, as well as *Ranger;* and, after taking charge of an escort carrier division, had been transferred to the fast carrier forces early in 1944. The other two task group commanders will be introduced shortly.

4. *Strikes on Iwo and Chichi Jima, 15–17 June*

The first intimation received by Admiral Spruance that Ozawa might be coming out to fight was submarine *Redfin's* report of his sortie from Tawi Tawi on 13 June. Since a quick calculation showed that the Mobile Fleet could not be in a position to engage

[36] John W. Reeves, b. New Jersey 1888, Annapolis '11, served in battleships and a destroyer until 1916, when he helped fit out *Sampson* and served in her through most of World War I in the Queenstown command; "exec." of *Maury* Sept. 1918, flag sec. to Commander Naval Forces E. Mediterranean 1919–20. Helped fit out *Concord* and served as her engineer officer 1923–26, C.O. *Worden;* matériel division, office of CNO, for two years. C.O. *Parrott* 1928; Navy Dept. duty in 1931–33, when he helped fit out *New Orleans* and became her First Lieutenant. Won his wings at Pensacola, 1936; "exec." of *Langley,* exec. and C.O. Fleet Air Base Pearl Harbor, 1937–39. Helped fit out *Wasp* in 1939 and served as her C.O. to May 1942, when promoted Rear Admiral. Commanded Alaskan sector NW Sea Frontier 1942–43, then given command of a carrier division. Commander Western Carolines Sub Area, Sept. 1944–Jan. 1945; head of NATS to 1948, when he became chief of naval air training at Pensacola. Retired 1 May 1950, with rank of Admiral.

[37] Alfred E. Montgomery, b. Omaha 1891, Annapolis '12, first served in *West Virginia* and became a submariner in 1915. Commanded *R–20,* 1918–20. In 1922 qualified as naval aviator and became "exec." of several tender-based observation plane squadrons in succession. C.O. Torpedo and Bombron 1, 1924–25; assembly and repair officer and "exec." N.A.S. San Diego, 1925–28. Senior air officer, *Langley,* 1928; squadron commander in *Saratoga,* 1929; C.O., N.A.S. Seattle, 1930–32; staff aviation officer in *Chicago,* 1932; C.O., N.A.S. Anacostia, 1934; staff plans and operations officer in *Saratoga* and "exec." *Ranger,* 1936, and became her C.O., 1940; chief of staff to Comairlantfleet 1941; commandant Naval Air Training Center, Corpus Christi, 1942–43; Rear Admiral from 29 May 1942. Comcardiv 12, Aug. 1943, with flag in *Essex,* and of Cardiv 3, March 1944, with flag in *Bunker Hill;* he distinguished himself in the raids on Kwajalein, Saipan and Palau. After the Marianas campaign he commanded TG 38.1 in the Battle of Leyte Gulf; became Commander Fleet Air, West Coast, Jan. 1945; Commander Fifth Fleet, Aug. 1946; C.O., N.O.B. Bermuda, 1949; retired 30 June 1951; died 15 Dec. 1961.

him before the 17th, Spruance coolly refrained from interfering with the tasks assigned to the carriers for the next four days. The most important were scheduled strikes on Iwo and Chichi Jima.

These raids on two little-known islands, respectively 635 miles NNW and 755 N by W of Saipan, were highly profitable. Their airfields (on one of which the American flag was raised the following March), important staging points between Japan and Micronesia, were full of planes earmarked to harass Turner's amphibious forces off Saipan.

For the strikes, Task Groups 58.1 (*Hornet, Yorktown, Belleau Wood, Bataan*) and 58.4 (*Essex, Langley, Cowpens*) were relieved from stand-by duties on the night of 14 June and sent north under the tactical command of Rear Admiral Clark.[38] "Jocko" Clark, as this Oklahoman has been called since Naval Academy days, is part Cherokee Indian and part Southern Methodist, but all fighter. A picturesque and lovable character who looked (and dressed) more like a western desperado than a naval officer, he used rough and explosive language but knew his business thoroughly and had more than a fair share of energy and dogged determination. A specialist in naval air, promoted to flag rank at the age of 50, he had just relieved Rear Admiral Frederick C. Sherman in command of TG 58.1, Rear Admiral W. K. Harrill,[39] a newcomer in

[38] Joseph J. Clark, b. Oklahoma 1893, Annapolis '18; served in World War I and qualified as naval aviator in 1925. Senior aviation officer of *Mississippi;* "exec." of N.A.S. Anacostia, 1928; C.O. *Lexington's* fighter squadron, 1931; aeronautical member of Board of Inspection and Survey, 1933; air officer of *Lexington* and *Yorktown,* 1940–42. Fitted out *Suwannee* and commanded her in Operation "Torch." Fitted out new *Yorktown* and commanded her until promoted Rear Admiral 31 Jan. 1944. Flying his flag in *Hornet* until the end of the war, he then became Asst. C.N.O. for Air till Nov. 1948. Later commanded carrier divisions, naval air bases, and 1942 Seventh Fleet. Ret. Dec. 1953 as Admiral.

[39] William K. Harrill, b. Knoxville, Tenn., 1892; Annapolis, '14. During World War I, assistant communications officer in *Pennsylvania* and staff duty with Commander Mine Force Atlantic Fleet in laying North Sea barrage. Completed flight training 1921, served as aircraft squadron commander and in other capacities in *Langley* and *Saratoga.* Aide to Asst. Sec. Nav. for Aeronautics, 1927. "Exec." and C.O. Anacostia Air Station, 1932–35; assistant naval attaché for air in London Embassy, 1937. At outbreak of war C.O. of *Ranger,* and for two years had charge of the carrier replacement squadrons of the Pacific Fleet. After June 1944 he commanded Fleet Air West Coast at Alameda, Calif., and took particular interest in the logistics of naval aviation. Retired 30 June 1951.

the fast carrier groups, had recently relieved Rear Admiral S. P. Ginder, who had worn himself and his subordinates ragged during recent operations. Harrill fought this group well through the Marianas "Turkey Shoot" but came down with appendicitis 28 June and was then relieved by Rear Admiral Wilder D. Baker.

During the night of 14–15 June, while pushing north at 25 knots, Clark received word from Spruance to limit his strikes to a single day, the 16th, and to rendezvous with the rest of Task Force 58 on the 18th near Saipan in order to engage the Japanese Fleet. "Jocko," however, was not to be balked. He decided to "beat the gun" and start strikes on the afternoon of the 15th, in order to get in two days' worth after all. With Harrill he arranged to launch a fighter sweep against Iwo at 1430, followed by deckload strikes against Iwo, Chichi and the intermediate Haha Jima half an hour later. The weather was squally, a strong force 6 breeze was blowing from the S by E,[40] and the two principal targets were distant 135 and 142 miles respectively from the launching point.

A few hours before they reached that point, the anti-submarine and "anti-snoop" [41] patrols picked up a 1900-ton freighter, *Tatsutagawa Maru*. They gave her what bombs they had and summoned to the spot destroyers *Boyd* and *Charrette*, which sank her and recovered the unusual number of 112 survivors.

The deckload strike encountered interception over Iwo, shot down an estimated 20 Zekes (actually 10) and destroyed 7 planes on the ground, at a loss of two planes and pilots. At Chichi Jima no planes were encountered airborne, but antiaircraft fire destroyed one of ours. Three small freighters were left burning in the harbor, 21 seaplanes were destroyed and a hangar was burned.[42]

That night, as the task groups retired to the ESE, the sea made up very rough, with such heavy swells that the prospect for launching next day looked slim. Daybreak brought a succession of

[40] *Yorktown* Action Report.
[41] In Guadalcanal days U.S. carrier movements were always "snooped" by Japanese planes; C.A.P. never seemed able to keep them out of visual distance. Thereafter an "anti-snoop" screen was thrown out ahead of the carriers to catch search planes.
[42] Figures checked by Capt. Ohmae from Japanese sources.

heavy squalls, and so much evidence of a typhoon that weather-wise "Jocko" canceled the scheduled morning strike on Chichi and concentrated on Iwo in the afternoon, when he was rewarded by the wind's falling to force 4, although it was a pesky breeze for carriers, veering and backing as it did through the western quadrant. The Japanese, expecting no attack in such foul weather, had sent out no air patrol, and their planes were nicely lined up on the airfield at 1330 when 54 carrier planes struck. Only one was shot down by antiaircraft and a total of 63 Japanese planes destroyed on the ground was claimed.[43]

Plane recovery was very difficult in the heavy seas and rain squalls, on wet, pitching decks, but it was effected with only one crash, and that by a battle-damaged plane. Clark watched every plane land on *Hornet* and occasionally did a little "back-seat driving" himself. Recovery completed by 1710, the carriers refueled their destroyer screen on a southwesterly course. Task Group 58.1 then turned south toward its rendezvous with Admiral Mitscher. Harrill's *Essex* group, en route to a fueling rendezvous east of the Marianas, took time out at 0800 June 17 to launch a 35-plane strike on Pagan, where the Japanese had a small runway. No planes were found, but a number of buildings were damaged. That afternoon, destroyers *Converse* and *Dyson* picked up twelve survivors of the Saipan-Yokohama convoy broken up on 12–13 June, while *Conner* rescued the skipper and 17 crew members of freighter *Shinjiku Maru* which *Hornet's* planes had sunk on the 13th.

The fueling of TG 58.4 was called off by an urgent order from Admiral Spruance to rendezvous with him and the rest of TF 58 next day.

5. Feeling Each Other Out, 15–18 June

During these anxious days of mid-June, the problem most on Admiral Spruance's mind was the location and disposition of the Japanese fleet. An enormous initial advantage in a carrier battle

[43] The check-up in Japanese sources reports none so destroyed, but this is incredible; in view of the pilots' reports, at least 30 must have been hit.

is won by the side that finds the other first. Through Admiral Nimitz, Spruance on 15 June requested General MacArthur to extend air searches of his Liberators from Wakde and Los Negros (Admiralties), to the maximum distance of 1200 miles. These searches, in connection with those from Mitscher's carriers, should have covered the Japanese approach to within 600 miles of Saipan; but they did not. Ozawa had planned his approach so as to elude American land-based searches;[44] Spruance's only intelligence of enemy movements before 18 June came from submarines.

Submarine warfare is as chancy as any other aspect of naval warfare, perhaps more so; but there was little room left for chance in the excellent dispositions made by Admiral Lockwood before Operation "Forager."[45] Their scouting functions were admirably performed. *Flying Fish* observed Ozawa's main body debouching from San Bernardino Strait at 1835 June 15, and one hour later, at 1945, *Seahorse* sighted Ugaki's battleship force coming north, at a position about 200 miles ESE of Surigao Strait.[46] *Seahorse* gave chase; but with one engine not working she was soon left far behind, and Japanese radio stations succeeded in jamming her radio so that she was unable to transmit a contact report until 0400 June 16. These two reports, so close together in time yet so distant on the chart, proved that two separate enemy forces were approaching. This materially altered Admiral Spruance's estimate of the situation and caused him, on the morning of 16 June, to postpone the invasion of Guam, which he had set for the 18th.

Submarine *Cavalla*, on her way to relieve *Flying Fish* off San Bernardino, added another piece to the picture at 0510 June 17, reporting a group of two large oilers and three destroyers at lat. 13°29′ N, long. 130°45′ E, on course 120°. This was the Second Supply Force, which had followed Ozawa from Guimaras. Immediately on receipt of this message, Admiral Lockwood, from

[44] He did actually pass through one of the PB4Y search sectors, but on a day when it was not fully covered, owing to bad weather. Cincpac Monthly Analysis June 1944 p. 77.

[45] For Lockwood's order see above, chap. ii.

[46] Com. Fifth Fleet War Diary, 15 and 16 June. See chart "Battle of the Philippine Sea, I" for these positions.

Pearl Harbor, ordered *Cavalla* to change course and follow the convoy's track, figuring out that a fueling group should lead her to the enemy fleet. *Cavalla* was unable, for lack of speed, to carry out this assignment; and it was lucky she could not, because she ran into a first-rate target, as we shall see.

Obviously the Japanese Mobile Fleet was looking for a fight. As the word spread through Task Force 58 and the Expeditionary Force (it was not supposed to but it did), everyone was jubilant. With "Pete" Mitscher as O.T.C., "Ching" Lee handling the battle line, and Spruance in overall command, a complete clean-up was anticipated.

Admiral Spruance's first reaction to the submarine contacts, as we have seen, was to postpone the invasion of Guam. Next, during the forenoon watch 16 June, he went on board Admiral Turner's flagship *Rocky Mount* off Saipan for a conference. Both Admirals agreed that a sea battle was imminent, and made dispositions accordingly. They agreed to detach 5 heavy and 3 light cruisers and 21 destroyers from Turner's fire-support groups to augment Task Force 58, leaving 7 battleships, 3 cruisers and 5 destroyers to protect the Saipan beachhead from a possible flank attack by the Japanese. Admiral Hoover at Eniwetok was ordered to send over six of his radar-equipped PBMs next day, to make night searches out to 600 miles from Saipan roadstead.[47] Rendezvous for TF 58 — Clark's and Harrill's groups, which were then

[47] Spruance did not then ask for more because tender *Ballard*, already ordered to Saipan, could not handle more, but tender *Pocomoke* arrived Saipan 18 June and was ready for business next morning, and the rest of Squadron VP-16 followed from Eniwetok. These PBMs had a very unhappy time at Saipan. They had to operate from the open roadstead off Garapan, where the water was frequently rough. Within two hours of the arrival of the first five, on the evening of 17 June, they and their tender *Ballard* were attacked by an enemy dive-bomber, and in the mêlée one PBM taxied out to sea and was temporarily lost. The other four took off shortly before midnight; and it was one of them that made the important contact hereinafter described. One PBM on dawn patrol 19 June, attacked by four Hellcats which evidently mistook her for a Japanese Mavis, was severely damaged and one of her crew was killed. One was sunk off Saipan by the clumsy attempts of a fuel barge to come alongside in a heavy ground swell, contrary to orders. A third was shot down by destroyers of TF 58, searching for survivors from the night landings of 20 June, because her IFF did not show, and the entire crew of 11 was lost. The Mark-3 IFF then in use was very unstable, nor was the calibration consistent throughout the Fleet.

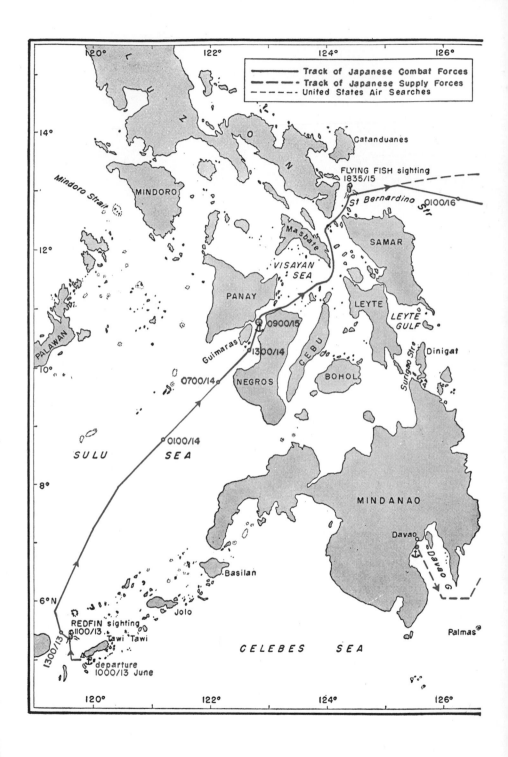

Track of Japanese Combat Forces
Track of Japanese Supply Forces
United States Air Searches

14°

Catanduanes

FLYING FISH sighting
1835/15

Mindoro Strait

MINDORO

St Bernardino Str. 0100/16

Masbate

12°

SAMAR

VISAYAN
SEA

PANAY

LEYTE

0900/15

LEYTE
GULF

1300/14

Guimaras

CEBU

Dinigat

10°

0700/14

NEGROS

BOHOL

Surigao Str.

PALAWAN

0100/14

SULU   SEA

8°

MINDANAO

Davao

Davao G.

Basilan

6°N

Jolo

Palmas

REDFIN sighting
1100/13

Tawi Tawi

CELEBES   SEA

1300/13

departure
1000/13 June

120°   122°   124°   126°

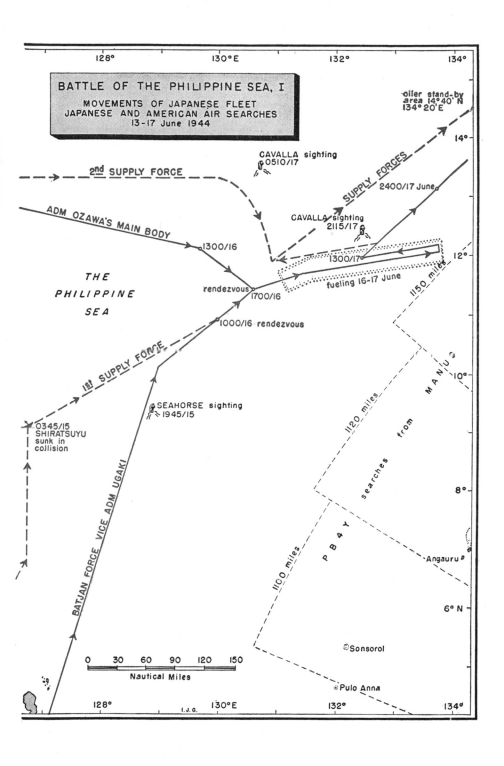

BATTLE OF THE PHILIPPINE SEA, I
MOVEMENTS OF JAPANESE FLEET
JAPANESE AND AMERICAN AIR SEARCHES
13-17 June 1944

oiler stand-by
area 14°40' N
134°20'E

14°

2nd SUPPLY FORCE

CAVALLA sighting
0510/17

SUPPLY FORCES

2400/17 June

ADM OZAWA'S MAIN BODY

1300/16

CAVALLA sighting
2115/17

1300/17

THE
PHILIPPINE
SEA

rendezvous

1700/16

fueling 16-17 June

12°

1150 miles

1000/16 rendezvous

1st SUPPLY FORCE

SEAHORSE sighting
1945/15

10°

MANUS

0345/15
SHIRATSUYU
sunk in
collision

1120 miles

searches from

8°

PB4Y

1150 miles

Angauru

BATJAN FORCE VICE ADM UGAKI

6° N

1100 miles

0   30   60   90   120 150

Nautical Miles

Sonsorol

128°   130°E   132°   134°

Pulo Anna

128°   130°E   132°   134°

I.J.G.

completing their strikes on the "Jimas," and Reeves's and Montgomery's groups, which had been operating west of Saipan — was set for 1800 June 18 at a point about 180 miles due west of Tinian. Montgomery and Reeves fueled from an oiler group on the 16th, west of the Marianas.

When the conference was over and the important decisions made, Admiral Spruance in *Indianapolis*, with reinforcements from the Expeditionary Force, steamed out to join the carriers. At 1415 June 17 Commander Fifth Fleet issued his battle plan: —

> Our air will first knock out enemy carriers, then will attack enemy battleships and cruisers to slow or disable them. Battle line will destroy enemy fleet either by fleet action if the enemy elects to fight or by sinking slowed or crippled ships if enemy retreats. Action against the enemy must be pushed vigorously by all hands to ensure complete destruction of his fleet. Destroyers running short of fuel may be returned to Saipan if necessary for refueling.

A little later, in reply to an inquiry from Mitscher, Spruance sent the following message to him and to Lee: —

> Desire you proceed at your discretion selecting dispositions and movements best calculated to meet the enemy under most advantageous conditions. I shall issue general directives when necessary and leave details to you and Admiral Lee.[48]

Late that evening (the 17th) a second contact by submarine *Cavalla* showed that the Japanese were still coming. At 2115 she sighted "fifteen or more large combatant ships" making 19 or 20 knots on a due east course at lat. 12°23′ N, long. 132°26′ E.[49] That was a part of Ozawa's Mobile Fleet. This interesting information was received on board *Lexington* about 0345 June 18.[50] Darkness prevented *Cavalla* from seeing the whole fleet, and by dawn, for want of speed, she had lost contact.

To sum up these contact reports: the one from *Flying Fish* off San Bernardino Strait, and almost simultaneously from *Seahorse* east of Mindanao, proved that there were at least two Japanese

---

[48] Cincpac Monthly Analysis June 1944 p. 80.
[49] This contact is plotted on chart "Battle of the Philippine Sea, I."
[50] CTF 58 Action Report p. 46.

forces at sea. *Cavalla's* second contact did nothing to dispel the idea that there might be more than one Japanese force, as had so often been the situation in the past.

The two top commanders reacted differently and characteristically to these contact reports. To Admiral Spruance the significant thing was the number reported by *Cavalla* — 15 ships. Since he already knew from Intelligence that Ozawa had, or was supposed to have, at least 40 combatant ships, this report suggested that a part of the enemy force was outside of the American search area and had not been seen. Ozawa, cognizant of Spruance's movements, might be planning to flank him and break up the landing at Saipan. Admiral Mitscher's reaction was very different. He figured out that if TF 58 steered west, a night surface action could be had, with a daylight bomber strike to follow. Of the battle line commander, Vice Admiral Lee, he inquired: "Do you desire night engagement? It may be we can make air contact late this afternoon and attack tonight. Otherwise we should retire to the eastward tonight." But Lee threw cold water on this proposal. He replied very emphatically, "Do not (repeat, *not*) believe we should seek night engagement. Possible advantages of radar more than offset by difficulties of communications and lack of training in fleet tactics at night. Would press pursuit of damaged or fleeing enemy, however, at any time." [51]

Admiral Lee's reaction requires explanation. He flew his flag in battleship *Washington*, which almost alone had won the decisive action off Guadalcanal on 14 November 1942. Nobody who knew Lee can for a moment doubt his competency or his courage. He knew more about radar theory and practice than any flag officer in the Navy. All his battleships were equipped with Mark-8 radar, and had carefully established their pattern of gunfire for that installation. His battleships had repeatedly proved their ability to straddle a fast-moving target on the first salvo at 35,000 yards. He had heard about the Japanese 18-inch-gunned battleships and was confident that his own 16-inch-gunned ships of the *Iowa* class were

[51] CTF 58 Action Report p. 47. This occurred on the morning of 18 June.

capable of beating them. En route from Majuro to Eniwetok, Lee had exercised the battle line and its screen continuously for three days before joining Task Force 58. From his reply to Mitscher's query, ". . . difficulties of communications and lack of fleet tactics at night," and in view of his vivid experience of Japanese night-fighting technique, especially with torpedoes, I conclude that he was loath to risk canceling his gunfire superiority by the chances of night action. And, on the overall strategic picture, Lee doubtless saw eye-to-eye with Spruance. He was not a carrier admiral.[52]

Whatever their motives may have been, both the desire of Lee and the decision of Spruance to play the battle-line cards close to their chests were correct. The carriers were going to need the antiaircraft fire of Lee's battle line.

Not one American search plane on 18 June sighted a Japanese ship. But the dawn search missions from the American carriers within one hour (0755 to 0850) encountered three planes searching ahead of the Japanese fleet.[53] These interceptions of enemy search planes could have helped the task force staff to plot the enemy's movements; but for reasons unknown to this writer little attention seems to have been paid to them.

The afternoon search from the American carriers, launched at 1330 and covering the sector from NW to S, 325 miles out, found neither plane nor ship; it missed Ozawa by about 60 miles. As the weather was clear and the search thorough, Admiral Spruance was satisfied that the enemy fleet had not reached a position within 400 miles of Saipan.

On the Japanese side, land-based searches from Guam, Yap and Palau should have located Mitscher's carriers and passed the word to Ozawa.[54] Apparently he received no information whatsoever

[52] Admiral Lee made no Action Report. The above is my own conclusion after consulting all surviving members of Lee's staff who were available.

[53] These had been launched from Ozawa's carriers at 0600 when at lat. 13°54' N, long. 134°12' E.

[54] An early morning reconnaissance by 9 Bettys out of Yap on the 18th missed the fast carriers but located one of the escort carrier groups SE of Saipan. A raiding unit of 11 Zekes and 6 Franceses from Yap and 38 Zekes and one Judy from

from the Base Air Force on which he laid so great dependence, but he obtained excellent results from his own carrier-plane searches as he steamed in a northeasterly direction, right into the wind, which made launching and recovery easy.

On the afternoon of the 18th, as a result of a seven-plane search mission launched from his own carrier division at noon, Ozawa obtained a really hot contact. The pilot of Plane No. 15, flying the "dog-leg" at the limit of his 420-mile easterly flight, at 1514 reported "enemy force including an unknown number of carriers" at lat. 14°50′ N, long. 142°15′ E. Later he amplified his report to "several carriers, two battleships and an unknown number of other ships." Plane No. 17, searching the next sector south of No. 15, shortly before 1600 sighted and reported "unknown number of carriers, ten plus other ships," in lat. 14°12′ N, long. 141°55′ E.[55]

Each search plane had sighted TF 58 after the rendezvous. The disposition covered so much ocean that the first pilot saw the northern edge of it, and the second, the southern, some 40 miles apart.

At 1530, after receiving Plane No. 15's report, Ozawa made an important decision. He ordered battle disposition to be formed and course changed from 60° (NE by E) to 200° (SSW). He had found the enemy and he intended to maintain a 400-mile gap in order to benefit by the longer range of his planes and choose his own time to fight. At 1540, when he was about 360 miles bearing 266° from the position given by Plane No. 15, the change of course was executed.

At 1610, one minute after Plane No. 17's message was received, Ozawa issued Mobile Fleet Signal Operation Order No. 16 as follows: —

1. At around 1500 enemy task forces believed to be, one, 350 miles bearing about 220° from Iwo Jima, and the other, 160 miles west of Saipan.

2. Mobile Fleet will retire temporarily, after which it will proceed

Palau was then organized to attack this group. It did not find the carriers, but ran into one of the oiler groups (TG 50.17) SE of Saipan, and attacked it at 1645. See chap. xviii below for this fight.

[55] These contacts are plotted on Chart II.

north and tomorrow morning contact and destroy the enemy to the north, after which it will attack and destroy the enemy to the northeast.[56]

The "350 miles from Iwo" contact, which works out at lat. 20°30′ N, long. 137°30′ E, was a complete phony; a garbled transmission from a land-based search plane, via Tokyo, as Ozawa learned shortly. The other, "160 miles west of Saipan," was flag staff's interpretation of the sighting reports by Planes 15 and 17. At the time of Plane 17's good contact, the center of Task Force 58 was about 200 miles west of Saipan.

Plane No. 17, at 1710, elaborated as follows: "The enemy consists of two small groups: (1) two carriers of *Saratoga* class and ten to fifteen destroyers; (2) two regular carriers and ten or more other ships; ships' course of advance is east." [57]

During the following hour Ozawa learned by radio from Tokyo, which had received a corrected report from another land-based plane, that the northern sighting "350 miles 220° from Iwo Jima" was a phantom. Accordingly, at 1817 he issued another operation order (No. 19) announcing that the "enemy west of the chain of islands" (as reported by Planes 15 and 17) would be his one target on the morrow, and giving the position where his ships should assume battle disposition.

In relating these contacts we have run ahead of an important event, the canceled strike by Cardiv 3. Rear Admiral Obayashi, commanding this van carrier division (*Chitose, Chiyoda, Zuiho*), remembered the evil results of delay at the battles of Santa Cruz and the Eastern Solomons. He decided, on his own initiative, to launch a strike against the enemy sighted by Plane No. 15. Launching began at 1637 from a position which, for reasons not altogether clear to this writer, lay a good 50 miles N by W of the force flagship. When only a few planes from *Chiyoda* out of the 67 scheduled for this strike were in the air, Obayashi received Ozawa's

[56] Sighting reports and order from Cardiv 1 Message Log (WDC 161,642, N.A. 12,261) Pineau trans.

[57] 601st Air Group Detailed Battle Report (same no.).

Operation Order No. 16 (issued at 1610) and, assuming that it overrode his independent action, canceled the strike. Since, according to Ozawa's battle plan, all carrier planes launched after 1600 must land on Guam, and no word had been received that the Guam airfields were usable, the staff was relieved when this strike was called off; but many junior officers who did not grasp the complete tactical picture deplored the cancellation. Obayashi's attack would have been a surprise, coming out of the setting sun before Mitscher even knew that the Japanese carriers were within range. With luck the bombers might have hit an American ship or two, as *Princeton* would be hit on 25 October. Probably few planes would have survived, but the sacrifice might well have been worth while.[58]

Obayashi now trailed the main body on a southwesterly course after recovering planes of the aborted strike, and so continued until 1900 when Ozawa changed fleet course to SE (140°), speed 16 knots.

Ozawa's intention for the night of 18–19 June was to keep his main body about 400 miles, and his van about 300 miles, from Task Force 58, outside its presumed striking range. That had been anticipated in the A-Go operation plan, in which "stress will be laid on day attacks with large forces operating beyond the range of enemy planes." Excellent strategy, to profit by the two factors in which his force enjoyed superiority, the greater range of his planes and the presence of Japanese airfields on Guam and Rota where they might rearm and refuel, and whence land-based planes were supposed to fly in to help him attack the American carriers.[59] An-

---

[58] Information from Capt. Ohmae 24 March 1952. In a Japanese post mortem on this battle, *Camp. Pac. War* pp. 265–66, the feeling is expressed that Ozawa lost a wonderful opportunity for a surprise attack; but all Japanese officers consulted by us, from Admiral Toyoda down, believe that the cancellation was wise because the strength of the attack next day would have been weakened. The Japanese were unwilling to entertain the consideration that the complete failure of their attack on the 19th proves that any opportunity on the 18th should have been seized.

[59] Transfer of carrier planes to nearby airfields after a strike was Mobile Fleet doctrine. Ozawa on 19 June issued no orders to his planes so to land; it was left to the option of air squadron commanders to do so if they thought it advisable.

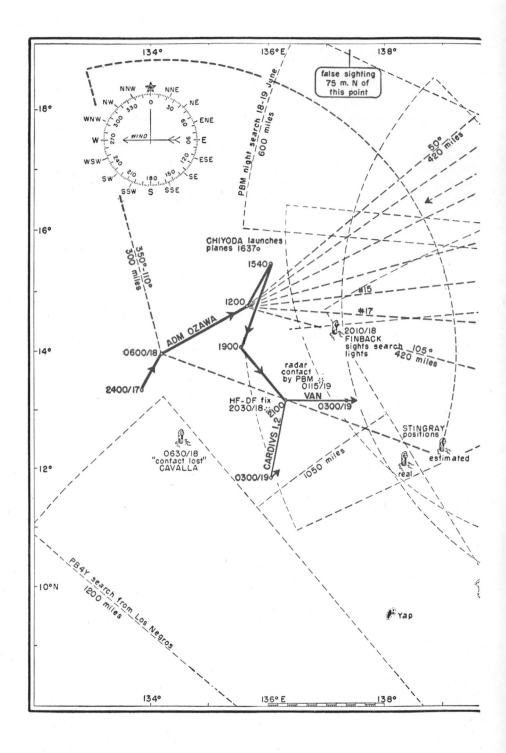

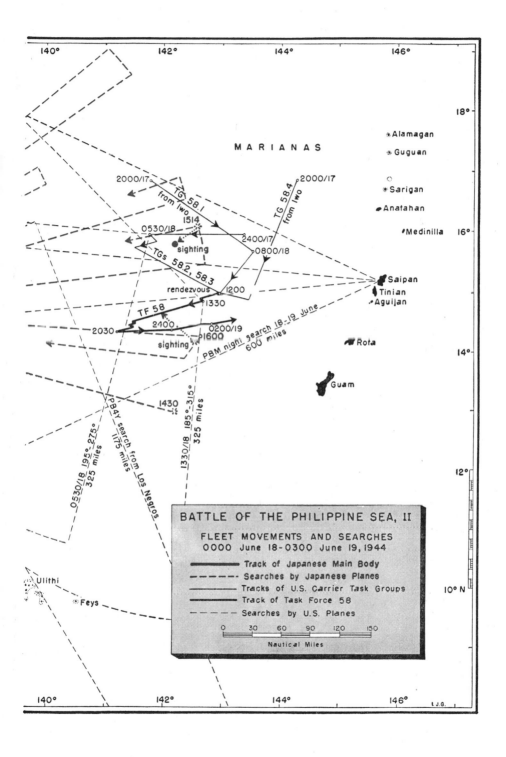

140°   142°   144°   146°

18°

M A R I A N A S

⊛Alamagan

⊛Guguan

○ Sarigan

⊛Sarigan

Anatahan

Medinilla 16°

2000/17   TG 58.1   TG 58.4   2000/17
from Iwo   from Iwo

1514

0530/18   2400/17

sighting   0800/18

TGs 58.2, 58.3

rendezvous 1200   Saipan
                Tinian
     1330   Aguijan

TF 58

2030   2100   0200/19
        1600
sighting   PBM night search 18-19 June
            600 miles

Rota 14°

Guam

1430

PB4Y search from Los Negros 1175 miles

1330/18 185°- 315° 325 miles

0530/18 195°- 275° 325 miles

12°

BATTLE OF THE PHILIPPINE SEA, II

FLEET MOVEMENTS AND SEARCHES
0000 June 18-0300 June 19,1944

—————— Track of Japanese Main Body
— — — — Searches by Japanese Planes
———————— Tracks of U.S. Carrier Task Groups
━━━━━━ Track of Task Force 58
— — — — Searches by U.S. Planes

0   30   60   90   120   150
Nautical Miles

Ulithi

Feys

10° N

140°   142°   144°   146°   t.J.G.

ticipating that his search planes would be able to track the American carriers, he planned to hit them next morning with "utmost strength" at a range of about 300 miles; and the course he followed that night enabled him to do just that. He had not the remotest intention of making an "end run" to attack the amphibious forces off Saipan. He was "firmly resolved" to make 19 June "the day of the decisive battle." [60] But his enemies could not read Ozawa's mind.

At 2100 June 18, the Mobile Fleet split courses to carry out this plan. Ozawa's main body, consisting of his own carrier division (*Taiho, Shokaku, Zuikaku*) and Rear Admiral Joshima's Cardiv 2 (*Junyo, Hiyo, Ryuho*), changed course to 190° (S by W) while Kurita's van (including Cardiv 3) [61] headed due east. At 0300 June 19, all turned northeasterly to course 50° and increased speed to 20 knots, in order to assume their assigned positions. By 0415 battle disposition was complete, and everything was set to hurl over 300 Japanese planes at the United States task force, still ignorant of Ozawa's position.

Now let us return to the American side. All four carrier groups were within sight of each other on the morning of 18 June, and the rendezvous was actually made at noon. Mitscher placed the three strongest carrier groups, 58.1, 58.3, 58.2, twelve miles apart on a north–south line perpendicular to the general wind direction. Thus any one task group could conduct flight operations without interfering with the others. He caused Lee's battle line to be formed in advance, to avoid the delay and confusion attendant on pulling ships out of four separate carrier screens during action; and he stationed it to leeward, on the enemy side, 15 miles west of flagship *Lexington*. The weakest carrier group, Harrill's TG 58.4, he

---

Ozawa preferred to get all his planes back on board the carriers; he valued the Guam-Rota fields chiefly for the land-based air forces they were supposed to have.

[60] Japanese Monograph No. 90 pp. 65–66, and my own conversation with Admiral Ozawa.

[61] Admiral Kurita in heavy cruiser *Atago* was in command of the van; Obayashi of the carrier division only.

placed about twelve miles north of the battle line to furnish it with air protection.[62]

To sum up, TF 58 was now organized thus: —

TG 58.1, Admiral Clark. *Hornet, Yorktown, Belleau Wood, Bataan,* 3 heavy cruisers, 1 antiaircraft light cruiser, 14 destroyers.

TG 58.3, Admiral Reeves. *Enterprise, Lexington* (force flagship), *San Jacinto, Princeton,* 1 heavy and 4 light cruisers (1 antiaircraft), 13 destroyers.

TG 58.2, Admiral Montgomery. *Bunker Hill, Wasp, Monterey, Cabot,* 3 light cruisers (1 antiaircraft), 12 destroyers.

TG 58.7, Admiral Lee. Seven battleships, 4 heavy cruisers, 14 destroyers.

TG 58.4, Admiral Harrill. *Essex, Langley, Cowpens,* 4 light cruisers (1 antiaircraft), 14 destroyers.

United States submarines continued to be watchful and enterprising. At 2010 June 18, at lat. 14°19′ N, long. 137°05′ E, *Finback* sighted two searchlights shooting up over the horizon.[63] These could only have come from Kurita's van, then about 70 miles distant. *Finback's* report, for reasons unexplained, did not reach Admiral Spruance until 0150 June 19,[64] after he had made one of the crucial decisions of the battle.

On the 18th, before the rendezvous, Commander Fifth Fleet advised both Mitscher and Lee: —

Task Force 58 must cover Saipan and our forces engaged in that operation.

He believed that the main enemy attack would develop from the west, but that diversions might come from either flank. His strategy, therefore, would be to advance westward during daylight and re-

---

[62] *Mobile* Action Report 25 June 1944 pp. 8–9. The relation between the various task groups was not rigid, but they were ordered to keep always within voice radio distance (30–35 miles) of *Lexington.* See chart of standard disposition in next chapter.

[63] *Finback* Patrol Report. The Japanese post mortem complains bitterly of the want of security in Ozawa's fleet in contrast to the one that attacked Pearl Harbor. Cardiv 3 carriers must have turned on searchlights to help recover late planes.

[64] Com Fifth Fleet Action Report p. 7.

tire eastward at night, "so as to reduce the possibility of enemy passing us in darkness." TF 58 must remain within support distance of Saipan "until information of enemy requires other action." He agreed with Lee that it would be undesirable to tangle with the enemy at night, because the chances inherent in night fighting would neutralize American superiority. "But earliest possible strike on enemy carriers is necessary."

At noon 18 June, when the rendezvous was completed, TF 58 shaped a southwesterly course. All planes were recalled at dusk, 1829, and the task force, when not engaged in recovery, headed into the setting sun so that any low-flying torpedo-bombers would show up clearly.[65] That was exactly when Obayashi's bombers would have struck, if he had not recalled them. At 2030 June 18, when darkness had fallen, the American Fleet reversed course to 80° (E by N) in accordance with Spruance's strategy. Since noon it had made good only about 115 miles on course WSW (245°), owing to the necessity of turning into the east wind every time search planes were launched or recovered.

Between 2030 and midnight Spruance received intelligence which might, and in the opinion of Mitscher should, have caused him to double back and seek action forthwith. The first was a dispatch from Admiral Nimitz giving the result of high-frequency direction-finder bearings on the enemy force.[66] Ozawa had broken radio silence to ensure maximum coöperation from his land-based planes at Guam and elsewhere. This enabled American HF/DF stations to locate him near lat. 13° N, long. 136° E, at 2023. Actually he was not more than 40 miles from that position; about 300 miles WSW of the spot where the American Fleet, at 2030, reversed course.

At 2200, when Spruance received this report,[67] he was increasing

[65] CTF 58 Action Report p. 48; time from *Lexington's* track.
[66] HF/DF stations had been established in the Aleutians, at Pearl Harbor, and elsewhere. These measured the directions of incoming enemy radio transmissions, and bearings from two or more stations could thus fix a transmitter's position, often within 100 miles.
[67] Com Fifth Fleet Action Report, but CTF 58 Report says it was received at 2245.

his distance from the enemy and by morning would be in no position to strike him. For the optimum launching distance at that time for a plane strike of mixed bombers and fighters was between 150 and 200 miles; the maximum distance considered possible, if the planes were to return, was 300 miles.

Mitscher did not overlook the possibility that another Japanese force might be sneaking up on Saipan from the southwest, but he believed that enough capital ships and escort carriers of the Expeditionary Force had been left around the island to protect our forces there. Accordingly, at 2325 he proposed to Spruance by voice radio that he reverse course again to due west at 0130, which he calculated would put the carriers in an ideal position for launching an air strike against the enemy at daybreak June 19.

For an hour Spruance discussed this proposal with his staff. Half an hour after midnight he rejected it. One factor in his decision was this: about an hour earlier his communications watch had intercepted and placed in his hands a dispatch from Admiral Lockwood (at Pearl Harbor) to submarine *Stingray*, stating that he had been unable to read one of her messages owing to radio jamming. Actually it was only a routine report, and the enemy was not jamming.[68] Spruance's staff, cognizant of *Stingray's* patrol area, estimated her position then to be lat. 12°20′ N, long. 139° E.[69] This was about 175 miles ESE of the HF/DF fix on Ozawa. Spruance, entertaining the possibility that *Stingray's* unreceived message was a contact on the enemy fleet, which in that event would be much nearer his forces than the HF/DF fix indicated, decided to continue his easterly course during the night. At 0038 June 19 he so informed Mitscher: —

Change proposed does not appear advisable. Believe indications given by *Stingray* more accurate than that determined by direction-finder. If that is so continuation as at present seems preferable. End run by other carrier groups remains possibility and must not be overlooked.[70]

[68] The trouble seems to have been a fire that broke out in the submarine's superstructure. "Here we are looking for the Jap fleet and we're looking like a Christmas tree," noted *Stingray's* commander in her log.

[69] Cincpac Monthly Analysis June 1944 p. 78. But *Stingray* was actually at that time at a different position (see chart "Battle of the Philippine Sea, II").

[70] Cincpac Monthly Analysis June 1944 p. 81.

Note this "end run," which figures so largely in discussions of the battle.[71] Admiral Spruance was as eager to close with the enemy as anyone, but at the same time he was deeply impressed with the sacredness of his assigned mission. "We were at the start of a very large and important amphibious operation and we could not gamble and place it in jeopardy. The way Togo waited at Tsushima for the Russian Fleet to come to him has always been in my mind. We had somewhat the same basic situation."[72] Moreover, Spruance had in his hands a translated Japanese document sent to him by MacArthur: a manual of enemy carrier doctrine, it seems, in which Japanese carrier force commanders were recommended to feint in the center, engaging their enemy's undivided attention, while sending detachments around his flanks to execute a pincer movement.[73] That is exactly what the Japanese had done at Coral Sea and in the battles around Guadalcanal, and what they had attempted to do at Midway, where Spruance defeated them by destroying their carrier-force center before the flanks could close. Knowing how tenaciously the Japanese clung to their strategic concepts — and they would try this one again at Leyte Gulf — Spruance had good reason to expect an "end run." He had to take into account the possibility that the transmission picked up by HF/DF might be from an enemy ship located off the main course with intent to deceive, and that *Stingray* had detected a Japanese force trying to sneak around his southern flank to get at Saipan. Moreover, the translated Japanese document suggested that a similar movement might be made on the American northern flank by another enemy force coming down from Okinawa or Japan.

Spruance's estimate was clearly wrong; and it is singular that he should have placed greater value on remote inferences from the

[71] To readers not familiar with American football it may be explained that an end run is a run by the player carrying the ball around the end rather than into the center of the opponent's line; thus it is equivalent to a fast flanking movement in military tactics.

[72] Letter to the writer, 20 Jan. 1952.

[73] Conversations in 1945 and 1952 with Rear Adm. C. J. Moore, Admiral Spruance's chief of staff at the time of the battle. The document in question may well have been Admiral Koga's "Z" plan, which planned that strategy to meet a similar case.

Stingray business than on HF/DF. He is not to be blamed for assuming that the Japanese would divide their forces. But no reinforcements were coming south from Japan, and Ozawa had no intention of trying an end run. That rugged Japanese sea dog was carefully selecting a position from which he could inflict maximum damage by a straight-from-shoulder punch, with all his strength behind it. The situation was almost the reverse of that on another bright June morning two years earlier, when the Battle of Midway was coming up. Ozawa knew where Spruance was, and had made every preparation to strike the first blow, but Spruance as yet had no certain intelligence of Ozawa's position and movements. He was as much in the dark as Admiral Nagumo had been in the early morning of 4 June 1942, when Spruance and Fletcher had learned his position from a patrolling Catalina.[74]

At 0150 June 19, after making the decision to continue eastward, Spruance received *Finback's* report of searchlights well northeast of the HF/DF fix. But it seemed strange for a force to turn on searchlights when seeking the enemy; could not this be another ruse? The Admiral saw no reason to reconsider, and TF 58 continued eastward. He did not know that, at 0115 June 19, one of the Garapan-based PBMs, searching 600 miles out of Saipan on the W to WSW sector, had made a very significant radar contact. The PBM's screen registered 40 fighting ships, disposed in two groups, and the position was only 75 miles NE of the HF/DF fix. Old "Huff-Duff" had made no mistake! This report, if received promptly, might well have caused Admiral Spruance to reconsider; for he knew from Intelligence sources how many ships Ozawa had, and the PBM's report accounted for nearly that number.[75] His staff could have figured out that at 0200 the two Fleets were a little more than 300 miles apart, which meant that if Spruance had then doubled back, and Ozawa had kept coming, Mitscher would have been within easy striking radius by daybreak.

[74] See Vol. IV of this History p. 107.
[75] It actually sighted only Kurita's van, but the total reported was so close to that of the Mobile Fleet that Fifth Fleet staff might well have concluded that the PBM had sighted the whole of it.

But the PBM's message did not reach Spruance for seven and a half hours. According to a story current at the time, the crew member who should have reeled out the trailing radio antenna for long-distance transmission forgot to do so; and the pilot, Lieutenant H. F. Arle usnr, receiving no "Roger" for his transmissions, hastened back to base and filed his message there. Another version has the message received and logged on board tender *Pocomoke*, but not passed to the Admiral. Both stories make excellent cautionary tales, but after investigation I believe neither to be correct. There was no failure on board the PBM; its radio equipment was thoroughly checked immediately after its landing and the crew interrogated, but nothing wrong could be found. The PBM squadron commander concluded that atmospheric conditions at the time had made the area west of Saipan blind for radio.[76] It was just another communications failure; nobody's fault.

After the war was over Admiral Spruance said, "It would have been much more satisfactory if, instead of waiting in a covering position, I could have steamed to the westward in search of the Japanese fleet." Only the possibility of being decoyed by one enemy detachment while another "made an end run around our flank and hit our amphibious shipping at Saipan," prevented him from so doing.[77] The implication is that if he had promptly received the PBM report he might have honored Mitscher's suggestion; but I rather think he would not have done so since, for aught he could tell, the Japanese admiral might detach carriers for an "end run" during the several hours that would elapse between a reverse of course and a daylight contact.

Be that as it may, Admiral Spruance need not have regretted

[76] At least one plane of another command operating from a distant base heard the PBM endeavoring to make her contact report but did not open up and offer to relay it; the message was received also by tender *Casco* at Eniwetok, but she did nothing about it. Letters of Cdr. W. J. Scarpino, Lt. Cdr. D. T. Felix usnr, and Lt. Cdr. Arle, Jan. 1952. It is true that the trailing antenna was not completely extended, but continuous wave messages such as this were customarily transmitted without using the antenna; and, although *Pocomoke's* radio log was never checked, I doubt that the message was received. See also W. L. Worden "Bronxville Flyer Found Jap Fleet," *New York Sun* 29 June 1944.
[77] Walter Karig *Battle Report* IV 252.

an opportunity lost since (as I hope to demonstrate) it was better for Task Force 58 to let the enemy strike the first blow. Not that the Admiral wanted it that way; it merely happened that way.

At 0100 June 19 the American task force was snooped by an enemy plane, probably from Guam, which dropped a flare and escaped.[78] An hour later *Enterprise*, whose air group specialized in night flying, sent 15 radar-equipped TBFs to search the W–WSW sector out to 325 miles. The planes, launched a little after 0200 from about lat. 14°30′ N, long. 143° E, flew 100 miles W by S (255°) to a rendezvous point, from which they fanned out on individual five-degree sectors for 225 miles more, between 240° and 270°. If Spruance had continued west at 2030 June 18, this search would almost certainly have found the enemy; as it happened, the search terminated 40 to 50 miles short of Kurita's van. The regular dawn search of 0530 June 19, launched from Task Force 58 at lat. 14°40′ N, long. 143°40′ E, was equally unproductive.[79]

These negative results from searches, whether carrier-based, Admiralties-based or tender-based, were exasperating. Even Spruance was irritated. That morning he sent a dispatch by message drop to Admiral Hill off Saipan, "Get additional patrol planes as soon as you can handle them and increase night search to 700 miles."

At 0520 another enemy snooper appeared, and escaped; and shortly before 0600 an American plane shot one down only 37 miles SSW of the carrier disposition. Obviously the enemy was on our heels. Something was bound to happen pretty soon.

[78] *Yorktown* Action Report.
[79] *Enterprise* Air Group Action Report 3 July 1944; searches plotted on chart "Battle of the Philippine Sea, III."

CHAPTER XV

Battle of the Philippine Sea,
the Action

19–20 June

1. *"The Great Marianas Turkey Shoot," 19 June*[1]

a. Guam-Rota Phase, 0530–1000

JUNE the 19th, memorable like other days of June in naval annals, broke warm and fair around 0430, with a last-quarter moon in the sky. At a little before six the sun rose over the blue ocean, kindling the carriers' topsides to pure gold for a brief moment. Night clouds soon dissolved, and by the forenoon watch it was clear that we would enjoy a pellucid tradewind day; sea all azure with argent high lights, clouds so few as to afford no cover for pouncing aviators. Wind remained in the eastern quadrant, varying from ENE to ESE, with a strength of 9 to 12 knots, force 3 to 4. Ceiling and visibility were unlimited; from *Lexington's* high superstructure one could see 40 miles all around.[2] Atmospheric conditions were of the rare sort that created vapor trails, long white streamers flowing back from the wing tips of aircraft. This worked entirely to the benefit of the Americans, as it rendered

[1] Cdr. Paul D. Buie of VF–16 in *Lexington,* who liked to compare the downing of enemy planes with shooting wild turkey, was responsible for the name.
[2] It is strange what inconsistent weather data one finds in U.S. Action Reports and logs. *Lexington,* for instance, gives wind at SE, force 3–4, all day; *Yorktown,* 100° to 110° and 8–10 knots (force 3); *Indianapolis,* 60° to 80°, force 4. The only data they agree upon is the air temperature, 83° to 85° F, with an erratic 94° in *Indianapolis.*

the Japanese planes unusually easy to spot, and interceptions could be made without difficulty.[3]

Not one man of the 98,618 embarked in Task Force 58 knew where the enemy fleet lay, but all expected action presently. The usual tenseness that precedes a battle was enhanced by a feeling akin to exasperation over the failure of air search to discover the Japanese. Aggressive action had become so normal to the American bluejacket and aviator that many were asking why so beautiful and powerful a fleet as this should wait for the enemy to appear, rather than drive westward to destroy him.[4]

Task Force 58 steered E by N until 0530, when it turned NE, directly into the wind; Task Groups 58.1 (Clark), 58.3 (Reeves) and 58.2 (Montgomery) were in a north-south line of bearing, their centers 12 to 15 miles apart. West of the flag group, and about the same distance, steamed TG 58.7, Lee's battle line, with TG 58.4 (Harrill) within signal distance to the north. Each carrier group occupied a circle four miles in diameter, the carriers well spaced for safe maneuvering; and the entire disposition covered an ocean area roughly 25 by 35 miles.

At 0530, when *Lexington* had reached lat. 14°40′ N, long. 143°40′ E, about 115 miles W by S of Tinian and 90 miles NW by W of Rota, dawn search, combat air and anti-submarine patrols were launched. Spruance changed course to WSW at 0619, hoping to close the enemy to profitable striking distance. But he could not hold that course long. At 0706, 0741, 0800 and 0830 the carriers had to head into the wind to launch planes, so that by 1023 the disposition was only a few miles farther west than it had been at daybreak.

Spruance suggested to Mitscher that, if the morning search found no enemy ships, a neutralization strike on Guam and Rota would be in order. Mitscher replied that he could not hope to do any good there for want of proper bombs, but that he would keep Guam under fighter-plane surveillance. Montgomery added a

---

[3] Lt. (jg) C. A. Dunn of *Monterey*, paper prepared for the writer.
[4] Lt. (jg) Robert J. Mead of *Bunker Hill*, paper prepared for the writer.

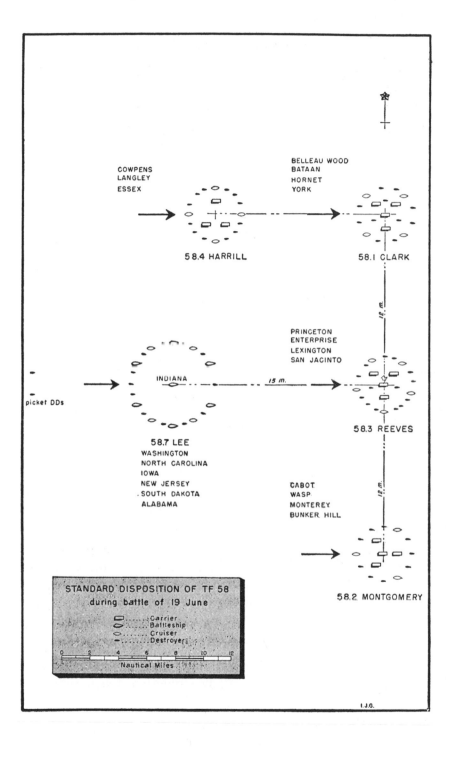

COWPENS
LANGLEY
ESSEX

BELLEAU WOOD
BATAAN
HORNET
YORK

58.4 HARRILL

58.1 CLARK

12 m.

PRINCETON
ENTERPRISE
LEXINGTON
SAN JACINTO

INDIANA   15 m.

picket DDs

58.7 LEE
WASHINGTON
NORTH CAROLINA
IOWA
NEW JERSEY
SOUTH DAKOTA
ALABAMA

58.3 REEVES

CABOT
WASP
MONTEREY
BUNKER HILL

12 m.

58.2 MONTGOMERY

STANDARD DISPOSITION OF TF 58
during battle of 19 June

▢ ...... Carrier
⬭ ...... Battleship
◯ ...... Cruiser
- ...... Destroyer

0   2   4   6   8   10   12
Nautical Miles

I.J.G.

pungent message to Mitscher, really intended for Spruance's ears: "I consider that maximum effort of this force should be directed toward enemy force at sea; minor strikes should not be diverted to support the Guam-Saipan area. If necessary to continue divided effort, recommend detachment of sufficient force for this purpose." [5] Since Ozawa was expected to send planes into Guam to refuel and again attack the American carriers, attention to that island could hardly have been called a diversion; but all flattop skippers were burning to attack ships and hated to send planes in the contrary direction. This time Spruance was certainly right, for his attacks on Guam early that morning spoiled Ozawa's plan for land-based coöperation.

As early as 0530 bogeys appeared on radar screens in the direction of Guam; a Hellcat from *Monterey* tallyhoed two Judys in that direction and destroyed one, and about half an hour later a Val was shot down by destroyers of the battle line. The first phase of the action was on.

Since the landings on Saipan, the Japanese had made desperate efforts to increase their air strength on the neighboring islands, already decimated by the American carrier strikes of 11–18 June. In this they had very slight success. None of those moved southwest to protect Biak ever got back in time. "Jocko" Clark's strikes on Iwo Jima disposed of many intended reinforcements. Others were held back by bad weather. No effort was made to rob Yap or the Palaus to benefit the Marianas, because up to the last minute the Japanese expected Mitscher to divert some of his carriers to strike one of those islands. Admiral Kakuta, from his headquarters on Tinian, ordered all operational planes at Truk — only 19 in number, including 15 Zekes — to be moved to Guam by the early morning of the 19th. They came up promptly, just in time to escape a 56-plane bombing attack on Truk by United States Army Liberators from Los Negros and Kwajalein.[6] This last-minute reinforcement brought the operational air strength at Guam only up

[5] CTG 58.2 Action Report p. 10.
[6] Craven and Cate *Army Air Forces in World War II* IV 687.

to about 50 planes of all types,[7] as compared with the 500 called for by the A-Go operation plan. But 50 planes from a land base, if used intelligently, can do a lot of damage to ships.

Admiral Mitscher, however, was correct in expecting the major attack from Japanese carriers, whose location he did not yet know. He was, as he expressed it, "in the unfortunate position of having to fight a defensive battle close on the lee side of enemy land bases to which carrier planes could be shuttled, and on the windward side of enemy carriers." His only consolation for being on the receiving end was the very large number of fighter planes — over 450 — at his disposal for interception.

American carrier commanders deserve the highest credit for the system they had worked out for deploying fighter planes to meet successive enemy attacks. The responsibility of Lieutenant Joseph R. Eggert USNR, task force fighter-director in *Lexington*, was colossal. He had to see that enough Hellcats were vectored out to intercept each enemy raid and that an adequate reserve was kept to handle later raids. This he did by keeping in voice-radio touch with the other four group fighter-directors,[8] sometimes shifting fighters from one to the other. The carriers had to steam constantly to windward so that planes could be launched or recovered at any moment. Each task group fighter-director exercised a general control over his own group, but allotted intercepting planes to the fighter-directors of individual ships, who controlled these planes until their missions were accomplished. This intricate system was instituted at a time when Fifth Fleet was in process of substituting a new very-high-frequency radio gear for the old ARC–5, and on 19 June no one group had the same equipment, and only two fighter-director channels were common to all. Yet the channels, though badly crowded, met every exigency.[9] All day long fighter

[7] Capt. Ohmae's estimate; there were 30 more that needed repairs.
[8] These fighter-directors were as follows: TG 58.1, Lt. C. D. Ridgway USNR; TG 58.2, Lt. R. F. Myers USNR; TG 58.3, Lt. J. H. Trousdale USNR; TG 58.4, Lt. Cdr. F. L. Winston USNR; TG 58.7, Lt. E. F. Kendall USNR.
[9] One attempt to vector out bombers already airborne to attack the enemy ships did not reach them because all channels were jammed (TG 58.3 Action Report); but the Japanese carriers were so distant that these planes would probably have run out of gas and ditched without accomplishing anything.

interceptions were directed promptly and intelligently; enough planes were provided to meet each raid as it came in and almost invariably they were properly stacked to give them initial altitude advantage over a very high-flying enemy. "Coördination between the fighter-directors and fighters was well-nigh perfect, and interceptions were made like clockwork." [10]

The performance of air-search radars (SC and SR) in the carriers also was excellent. They registered bogeys up to 150 miles away, and at any altitude. The Japanese tried to foul American radar screens with "window" suspended from parachutes, but most radar operators by that time were too expert to be fooled by so simple a device.

This day's battle opened at first light, around 0550, when a bomb-carrying Zeke, one of five or six scouting from Guam, took the picket destroyers of Lee's battle line by surprise. It glided out of a low cloud while everyone was engrossed in tracking a remote bogey, dropped a small bomb at *Stockham*, missed, and was shot down by *Yarnall*.[11]

For half an hour nothing more happened. Then, about 0630, a division of combat air patrol from *Belleau Wood* was sent to investigate a bogey over Guam, 100 miles distant, that had appeared on various radar screens. Upon arriving over the island at 0720 these Hellcats found themselves in a hornet's nest of Japanese planes taking off from Orote Field. They hallooed for help, which was furnished by another team from *Belleau Wood* and by 8 to 12 Hellcats each from *Cabot, Yorktown* and *Hornet*. But by the time these arrived over Guam the targets had disappeared; some had been shot down, others had landed and concealed themselves in well-camouflaged revetments off Orote Field. "It was apparent by this time," wrote Mitscher, "that we were probably due for a working-over by both land-based and carrier-based planes." It behooved him to deal with the former before the latter appeared.

---

[10] *Hornet* Action Report, Enclosure D p. 3 (with War Diary).

[11] *Stockham* and *Yarnall* Action Reports; the source of the raid is my assumption, but it definitely did not come from the carriers.

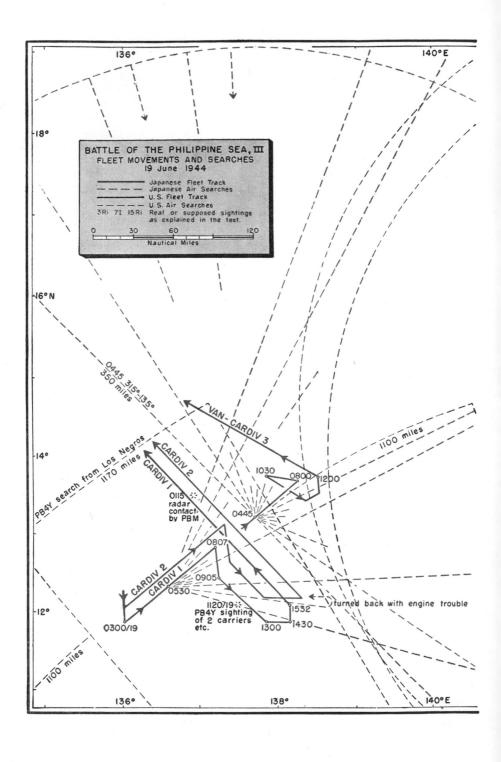

BATTLE OF THE PHILIPPINE SEA, III
FLEET MOVEMENTS AND SEARCHES
19 June 1944

Japanese Fleet Track
Japanese Air Searches
U.S. Fleet Track
U.S. Air Searches
3Ri 7I 15Ri Real or supposed sightings
as explained in the text.

0   30   60   120
Nautical Miles

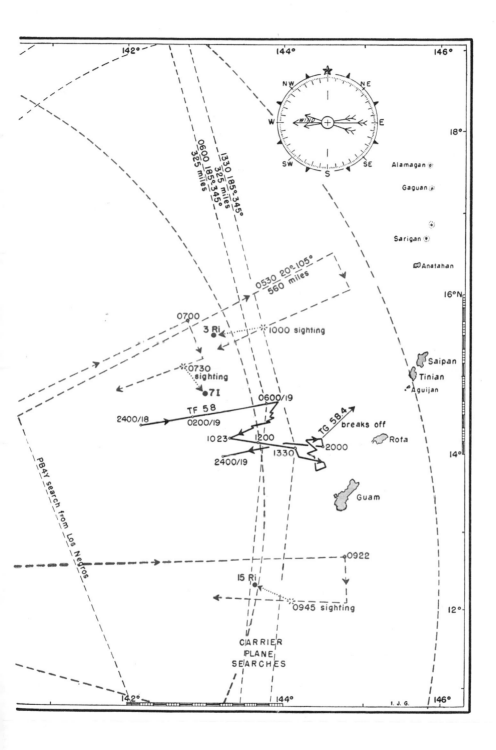

At 0807 a group of bogeys was detected 81 miles to the southwest, heading toward Guam. These were either the planes from Truk being rushed in as reinforcements, or an otherwise unrecorded reinforcement group from Yap; they certainly did not come from the Japanese carriers. Three of the task groups were ordered to launch 12 Hellcats each to intercept, the fighters already over Guam were vectored out at 0824, and for about an hour there was almost constant air fighting near and over Guam.[12] In this phase of the battle 33 Hellcats accounted for 30 Zekes or Hamps and 5 bombers, most of them belonging to the group approaching from the SW, but some freshly airborne from Orote Field. Nevertheless, planes were still taking off from Guam at the end of the fight and more were seen on the ground. Admiral Kakuta was doing his best to coöperate with Ozawa, and he did — toward almost total destruction.

At one minute before ten o'clock, when task force radar picked up flocks of bogeys 150 miles to the west, this phase of the action was over. Mitscher gave all his fighters over Guam a "Hey, Rube!"[13] and at 1023 the entire task force turned into the wind, a full team of fighters was launched, and flight decks were cleared of all bombers, which were instructed to orbit to the east on call.

b. Ozawa's Four Massive Raids, 1000–1450

Between 0300 and 0400 June 19 Ozawa formed his battle disposition. It was shaped something like a long-handled hammer with a hook at the handle. The head consisted of Admiral Kurita's van, in which Obayashi's Cardiv 3 furnished the air power. *Chitose, Zuiho* and *Chiyoda* steamed abreast, 10 kilometers apart, screened

[12] *Mobile* Action Report p. 9. See *Bunker Hill* VF–8 Action Report (Lt. Cdr. E. S. McCuskey) for a vivid account of a fight between his squadron and a number of Zekes and Hamps, whose pilots he said were the most skillful he had yet encountered.

[13] "Come back over the ship." This old circus cry was adopted by the first *Lexington* after her fight on 21 Feb. 1942 (Vol. III p. 267), because a second Japanese bomber raid came in when all but two of the ship's fighters were chasing the first raid back to Rabaul.

by four of the five battleships, nine heavy cruisers and eight destroyers. One hundred miles to the rear came Ozawa's own Cardiv 1, *Taiho*, *Shokaku* and *Zuikaku*, screened by one light and two heavy cruisers and seven destroyers. The "hook" was formed by Admiral Joshima's Cardiv 2, *Junyo*, *Hiyo* and *Ryuho*, screened by

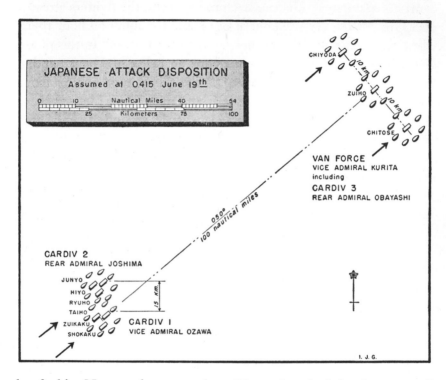

battleship *Nagato*, heavy cruiser *Mogami* and eight destroyers.[14] There were good reasons for this disposition, unknown to American carrier doctrine. It allowed best use of the cruiser and battleship float planes for search, and placed the three smaller converted carriers with a powerful antiaircraft screen where they would absorb any counterattack and protect the six larger carriers. If Spruance had followed Mitscher's advice and steered west the night before, and attacked in the early morning on the PBM contact,

[14] Capt. Ohmae, quoting 1st Mobile Fleet Battle Report, Combined Fleet Order No. 77, Annex. The diagram in *Camp. Pac. War* p. 270 is not correct.

the American bombers would almost certainly have engaged the Japanese van, and the outcome of the battle under such conditions is anyone's guess. Actually, this disposition served Ozawa very ill, because it denied his big carriers a proper anti-submarine screen, leaving them open to the attentions of U.S.S. *Albacore* and *Cavalla*.

At 0445, an hour and a half before sunrise, Ozawa commenced launching search planes.[15] The first flight, consisting of 16 Jake float planes from Kurita's battleships and cruisers, reached the outer limit of its search at 0700. One of these planes, on its return leg at 0730, sighted parts of Harrill's and Lee's task groups. This the Japanese called the "7 I" contact.[16] A second search of 13 Kates and a Jake from the van, launched at 0515 from approximately the same position, sighted only destroyers — probably Lee's picket line — and 7 of the 14 failed to return; they encountered Mitscher's dawn search and were shot down, mostly by planes from *Langley*. Ozawa's initial raid, which we shall call Raid 1, was directed toward the contact marked by the "7 I" point, and so fell into the embraces of TF 58 interceptors. A third search of 13 planes of which 3 failed to return, made an important contact which we shall deal with in due course.

Raid I consisted of 16 Zeke fighters, 45 Zekes carrying bombs, and 8 torpedo-carrying Jills, launched around 0830 from Obayashi's van carriers.[17] They were picked up by radar in Lee's battle line at 1000 when over 150 miles distant. At 1010 Admiral Mitscher ordered TF 58 to prepare to launch every available fighter plane. At 1019 he gave the "execute."[18] At 1023, when Raid I had closed to 110 miles from *Lexington*, the entire disposition swung into the

---

[15] Japanese Monograph No. 90 p. 41; sunrise at that position was 0622 (K).

[16] See chart "Battle of the Philippine Sea, III." Ten of the 16 Jakes failed to return.

[17] Launching times and compositions of Japanese raids 19 June are compiled from 1st Mobile Force Action Report and 653rd Air Group Action Report, WDC 161,517, and from other Japanese sources searched for us by Capt. Ohmae.

[18] According to *Wasp's* Action Report, the TF 58 disposition was then out of line. Taking TG 58.3 (*Lexington*, flag) as center, TG 58.1 bore 90°, 12–15 miles distant; probably it had worked out eastward when launching strikes on Guam. TG 58.2 (*Bunker Hill*, flag) bore 160°, 12–15 miles. TG 58.4 lay in the opposite direction, 340° and same distance; TG 58.7 (battle line) bore 260°, 12–15 miles.

wind for flight operations; and every ship that had not already done so went to General Quarters. "Stay on course into the wind!" signaled Mitscher. Launching commenced at 1023, when Raid I had closed to 72 miles. The Japanese planes now orbited at 20,000 feet altitude and regrouped before making their attack. This ten to fifteen minutes' grace was a boon to TF 58. It enabled flight decks to be cleared of bombers in order to facilitate the arming, servicing and launching of fighters on a rotating schedule; it gave the Hellcats time to be properly stacked for a good interception. At 1036 Mitscher signaled his ships to expect repeated attacks, and ordered, "Keep fighters available to repel these attacks, landing planes as necessary." [19]

At that moment the first Japanese raid, 64 planes strong, had closed to 60 miles from *Lexington*, which had not yet completed launching. Hellcats of combat air patrol, stacked from 17,000 to 23,000 feet, gave the tallyho just as Mitscher's message came across. A fierce mêlée ensued. Twenty-four of the enemy planes in close formation at 18,000 feet, with 16 more fighters above and astern, were tackled by 11 Hellcats from *Essex*, led by Lieutenant Commander C. W. Brewer.

The narrative of the ensuing fight, by the victors, is one of the best accounts we have of the skillful interceptions made on that mad morning. Brewer, selecting the leader of the formation for his first target, opened fire from a distance of 800 feet, and the Japanese plane exploded. Passing through the bomber's flaming debris, Brewer pulled up and shot at another; large chunks of it flew off, and the plane fell flaming into the sea. He then pushed over to catch up with a Zeke, which he slaughtered by hitting the wingroots. Next, the flight commander noticed a Zeke diving on him, got on its tail and fired successive bursts, after each of which the Zeke maneuvered violently, half rolled, "then after staying on his back briefly pulled through sharply, followed by barrel rolls and wingovers." Brewer stayed with him, hitting his fuselage, wings and cockpit, until the Zeke caught fire and went down in a tight spiral.

[19] *Princeton* War Diary. TG 58.2 alone got 50 F6Fs airborne.

Ensign R. E. Fowler, Brewer's wingman, downed the Zeke's wingman, two other Zekes and a Hamp fighter plane. Lieutenant (jg)
G. R. Carr USNR, who led the second division of four Hellcats,
helped Brewer bracket the enemy formation for the first overhead
runs. The first bomber that he fired at exploded immediately; Carr
had to fly through the debris before he could pull into a wingover,
at the top of which he got a second bomber for a "sitting duck
high-side." It burst into flames and "entered a graveyard spiral
from which it never recovered." Carr now discovered a Hamp on
his tail, pushed over into a perpendicular dive with air speed meter
indicating 430 knots, did an aileron roll to starboard, shook off the
Hamp, and his own wingman too. After climbing back to a good
fighting altitude, Carr found himself alone, with a Japanese bomber
coming in fast; he got a short burst into its engine and wingroots
and the bomber exploded. Pulling up, he saw two more bombers
ahead and some 2000 feet up, on a parallel course. Making a stern
run on one of them, he gave it a burst and "saw something leave the
plane which may have been the pilot," but did not take time to
make certain as he was skidding to the left to get on the tail of the
second. He got in a long burst which set this one afire. Carr did a
split-S to catch the bomber on the way down, but it exploded before he could get it back in his sights. By the time he had regained
altitude, no more enemy planes were visible; so he started back to
Essex, counting the plane splashes and oil-slicks on the water, "but
stopped at 17."

Brewer reported after his return that the enemy planes seemed to
have no formulated defense tactics. The bombers mostly scattered,
rendering themselves vulnerable, and the fighters did not appear to
cover them, but went into individual quick, sharp acrobatic man-
euvers — zooms and sideslips, skids, half-rolls, barrel rolls followed
by wingovers — to escape the Hellcats.[20]

[20] VF–15 Action Report prepared by Lt. R. McReynolds USNR in TG 58.4
Aircraft Action Report 13 July 1944 II. Brewer identified the bombers as Judys.
According to Japanese records, Raid I consisted of 16 Zeke fighters, 45 Zeke fighter-
bombers and 8 Jills. Judy was a new type, not unlike the Zeke in general appearance, of which U.S. Intelligence had very few photos. It seems probable that
the U.S. pilots mistook the Zeke fighter-bombers for Judys.

Forty-two out of the 69 Japanese planes in Raid I failed to return; and at least 25 were shot down in this interception. Brewer's VF–15 from *Essex* did not do it all; he himself credits with expert assistance eight Hellcats from *Cowpens*, who arrived at the tallyho; twelve more from *Bunker Hill*, several from *Princeton*; doubtless others from *Lexington* and *Enterprise* helped. Some of these, vectored out at 23,000-foot altitude, kept right on when they observed Brewer's fight going on well below them, thinking that another Japanese formation lay beyond; but a division from *Bunker Hill*, led by Lieutenant Commander R. W. Hoel usnr, peeled off and got into Brewer's brawl. Hoel himself shot down two Zekes and a bomber. During the latter encounter a Zeke got on his tail and fired some effective bursts before being chased away by his wingman. Hoel made his way back to *Bunker Hill* but was forced to bail out when his stick jammed all the way forward and the Hellcat was forced into an inverted power spin; he was picked up by a destroyer.[21] Every other plane that made this remarkable interception returned intact. The fight took place at such high altitude that the picket destroyers of the battle line, many miles distant, could see planes "falling like plums."

The remaining planes of Raid I, about 40 in number, eluded the F6Fs and continued toward their targets; but other Hellcats came out to meet them and about 16 more were destroyed.[22] A few planes, singly or in small groups, attacked picket destroyers *Yarnall* and *Stockham* west of the battle line; the "cans" gave a very good account of themselves and escaped without a scratch. Three or four bombers broke through to the battle line itself. Admiral Lee had formed this task group in a circular disposition, excellent for repelling air attack. *Indiana* as guide was in the center, the other six battleships and four heavy cruisers, interspersed with destroyers, were on a circle of six miles' diameter, all making 22 knots on course E by S. At 1049 a bomber scored a direct hit — the only one of the

21 *Bunker Hill* CVG–8 and CVF–8 Aircraft Action Reports.
22 Totaling 42 destroyed according to Japanese records (8 VF, 32 VB, 2 VT) but some of these must have been victims to TG 58.7 AA fire.

day's battle — on *South Dakota*. The explosion killed 27 men and wounded 23, but failed to impair the fighting or steaming efficiency of that veteran battlewagon.[23] Another made a very near miss on *Minneapolis*. Not one plane of this first raid got through to the carriers, although some were sighted from their flight decks. At 1057 flagship *Lexington* got the word that Raid I had been completely broken up.

Raid II, a really big one comprising 53 Judy bombers, 27 Jill torpedo-bombers and 48 Zeke fighters, was launched from Ozawa's own carrier division beginning at 0856.[24] One of the pilots, a warrant officer named Sakio Komatsu, right after his take-off sighted the track of a torpedo headed for *Taiho* from U.S.S. *Albacore* and crash-dived the "fish" at the cost of his plane and his life, without saving the carrier. Eight more planes developed engine trouble shortly and had to turn back. The other 119 planes, on their way, made the mistake of flying over Admiral Kurita's van, whose trigger-happy antiaircraft gunners gave them a few bursts and succeeded in splashing two and damaging eight more, which had to turn back. The rest stayed in one group. They were detected by radar at 1107, distant 115 miles.[25] This group — "about 50," according to the radar screen, but actually twice as many — was met 60 miles out from *Lexington* by a reception committee of "urgently scrambled" Hellcats which really did raise hell with them. Commander David McCampbell, leading a dozen Hellcats from *Essex*, gave the tallyho at 1139. He attacked one Judy halfway back, on the left flank of the tight Japanese formation. It blew up

[23] *South Dakota* Action Report and Rear Adm. Hanson's War Diary say that this bomber was shot down. The people in *Alabama*, however, observed that both it and another that missed got away. A third dive-bomber which scored two near misses on *Wichita* was shot down near *North Carolina*.

[24] Composition from Battle Report 601st Air Group, Capt. Ohmae trans.; position, lat. 12°39' N, long. 136°58' E. There were also two Jill "contact planes," sent out ahead to locate targets, bringing the total up to 130.

[25] *Lexington* Action Report; *Essex* Air Group 15 Action Report says 160 miles, which seems incredible. At this same time a reconnaissance plane from *Taiho* had dropped 15 bundles of "window" — radar-reflecting material — 40 miles NE of the American carriers, to draw attention from the attack planes approaching from the WSW. This ruse was nicely timed, and successful to the extent that it drew off a group of C.A.P. fighters of TG 58.1.

in his face, so he was unable to duck under this winged phalanx — ordinarily the safe side — to get at the other flank, and had to cross overhead, feeling as if every rear gunner was firing at him personally. Having made the right flank safely, he knocked down two more Judys, exploded the Japanese leader's wingman and worked onto the leader's tail, firing until it burned furiously and spiraled downward. In the meantime McCampbell's wingman, Ensign R. E. Foltz USNR, got two more Judys. Hellcats from other carriers were doing equally well; the total Japanese planes who "failed to return to their carriers" were 32 Zeke fighters, 23 Jill torpedo-bombers and 42 Judy dive-bombers. About 70 of these were shot down in this interception.[26] Aviators winging their way home reported a 12-mile expanse of oil-slicks studded with flotsam and burning debris.

At 1145 it was reported that about 20 planes of Raid II had broken through the air defense and were closing. Picket destroyer *Stockham* (Commander E. P. Holmes), then about 10 miles to leeward of the battle line center, spent twenty minutes "fighting off numerous attacks from all directions," but no damage resulted. "The battleships, cruisers and destroyers ahead put up a tremendous barrage which, together with the burning planes all around the horizon, created a most awesome spectacle."

Yorktown, with 36 fighters already airborne, sent 16 more to intercept; but, just as this group of Hellcats closed, most of the Japanese planes still flying were driven off by the gunfire of the battle line. *Alabama* "discouraged" two torpedo-bombers that had begun a run on Japan's favorite target, *South Dakota*. Two others made for *Indiana*, and one crashed into her at the waterline, but its torpedo did not explode. *Alabama* herself barely escaped two bombs. *Iowa*, too, was attacked by a torpedo-bomber. This antiaircraft action lasted from 1150 to a few minutes after noon.

Six Judys which had eluded both interception and the battle line attacked Montgomery's carrier task group at noon. Four of them

[26] Compare the slaughter of the old Devastators at Midway, Vol. IV p. 121.

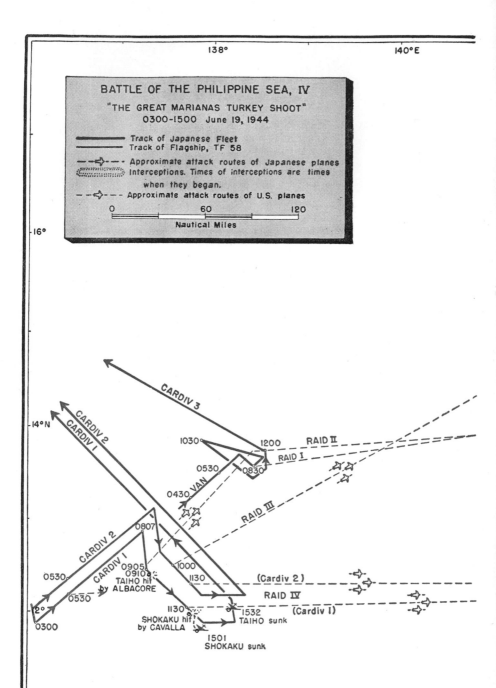

BATTLE OF THE PHILIPPINE SEA, IV
"THE GREAT MARIANAS TURKEY SHOOT"
0300-1500 June 19, 1944

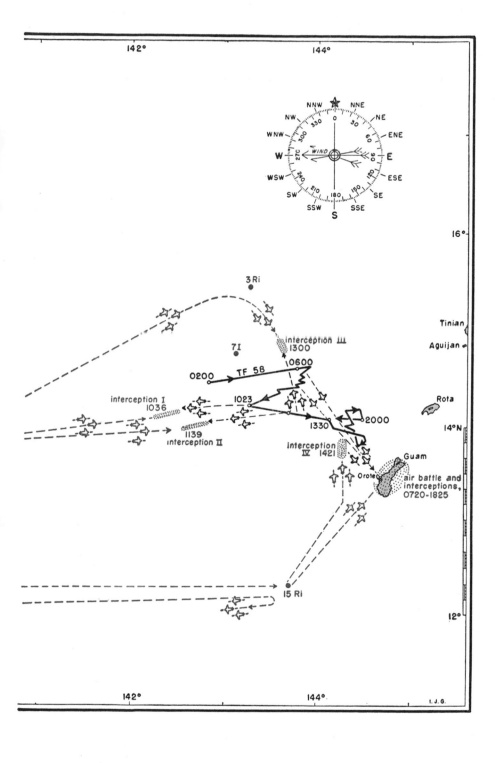

142°   144°

16°

3 Ri

Tinian
Aguijan

interception III
1300

71

0600

0200   TF 58

interception I
1036   1023

Rota

1330   2000

14°N

1139
interception II

interception
IV   1421

Guam
air battle and
interceptions,
0720-1825

Orote

15 Ri

12°

142°   144°

I. J. G.

went for *Wasp*. And although no hits were made, a bomb that burst overhead killed one man and wounded 12, and left *Wasp's* flight deck covered with bits of phosphorus that ignited when stepped on. Two Judys dove on *Bunker Hill;* each made a near-miss. Fragments of a bomb which burst in the water alongside killed three men and wounded 73, holed a plane elevator, knocked out the hangar-deck gasoline system temporarily, and started several fires which were promptly quenched. Both these Judys splashed after dropping their bombs and two more were shot down by the screen. Of the two survivors one landed on Rota and the other on Guam.

A small group of Jills also eluded the battle line and attacked Reeves's task group, north of Montgomery's. A torpedo exploded in the wake of *Enterprise* at 1157, and exactly at noon two torpedo-bombers making a shallow glide on *Princeton* were disposed of by her antiaircraft fire. A third attacked *Princeton* at 1202. Antiair craft fire from flagship *Lexington* and the intended victim exploded the plane and *Princeton* had to change course quick and hard to avoid the flaming wreckage.

Of the 128 planes launched in this second raid, 97 never returned.

Raid III, consisting of 47 aircraft (15 Zekes, 25 Zekes with bombs, 7 Jills), launched from Cardiv 2 between 1000 and 1015, came in from the north. Mitscher guessed that these planes had detoured to avoid the heavy antiaircraft fire of the battle line, but the real reason was more complicated. Ozawa's third dawn search of eleven Judys from *Shokaku* and two seaplanes from *Mogami*, launched at 0530 from lat. 12°20′ N, long. 136°35′ E, and supposed to search 560 miles out, had reported:

(1) at 0945, three carriers and other ships at lat. 12°22′ N, long. 143°43′ E. This was designated the "15 Ri" contact.

(2) At 1000, three carriers with other ships at lat. 15°33′ N, long. 143°15′ E. This was designated the "3 Ri" contact.

The position reported for the "15 Ri" contact was a mistake, due to uncorrected compass deviation in the search planes; but the second, the "3 Ri" contact, on the northern edge of Task Force 58, was correct.[27] Now the pilots of Raid III, originally ordered to the earlier "7 I" contact, were diverted shortly after take-off to position "3 Ri." The larger number, however, failed to receive the order to change targets and, unable to find anything at "7 I," returned to their carriers without a fight. The smaller group of about 20 planes got the word and headed for "3 Ri." En route they sighted two battleships but continued in search of the carriers. Not finding anything at the designated point, they turned back at 1255 to attack the battleships. Their approach had already been detected, when they were 99 miles due north, by radar in "Jocko" Clark's task group. At 1300, just as the Japanese planes sighted their first carriers — Clark's or perhaps Harrill's — they were intercepted, some 50 miles out, by 40 Hellcats from *Hornet, Yorktown* and other ships; there would have been more, but a flight of F6Fs had been diverted westward to a radar contact which turned out to be merely a heavy cloud.[28] Seven of the Japanese planes were shot down. A few broke through, made a fruitless attack on Harrill's task group at 1320; and escaped.[29] That was the end of Raid III, which could consider itself lucky; 40 out of the 47 returned to their carriers.

Several American carriers were now able to secure from General Quarters, and set condition of readiness "One-Easy." But that did not last long. During this lull in the battle, Mitscher launched a search mission. None of these planes sighted the Japanese fleet, and some failed to return.[30]

Between 1100 and 1130 Admiral Ozawa launched Raid IV, 82 planes strong, from *Junyo, Hiyo, Ryuho* and *Zuikaku.* It consisted of 30 fighters, 9 Judys, 27 Vals, 10 Zeke fighter-bombers and 6 Jills. They were ordered to attack the phantom enemy reported to be at "15 Ri" in lat. 12°22' N. Finding nothing there, a group from

---

[27] Consult chart "Battle of the Philippine Sea, IV" for the sighting positions.
[28] *Yorktown* Action Report.
[29] *Cowpens* and *Essex* Action Reports. One bomb, dropped by a Zeke, missed *Essex* by about 100 ft.
[30] CTG 58.2 Action Report. They shot down 3 more Japanese search planes.

Cardiv 2 headed for Rota but were diverted thence by sighting Montgomery's carrier group, whose radar picked them up 45 miles out. Six of them bore in under the C.A.P. when the carriers were busy recovering planes and started a glide from 6000 feet. An alert Marine lookout in cruiser *Mobile* sighted the first Judy and alerted his ship, which opened fire at 1423, just as the bombs dropped. *Wasp* avoided them by a sharp turn to port, and the bombs exploded harmlessly in the water. Three more dive-bombers then appeared out of the clouds, one making for *Wasp* and two for *Bunker Hill*. There were no casualties and only minor damage from this attack; and not more than one Judy escaped. And, at some point in this raid, the 18-plane group from *Zuikaku* tangled with Hellcats and lost half its number.

In the meantime the largest group in Raid IV, 20 Zekes, 27 Vals and 2 Jills from Cardiv 2, after failing to find anything at "15 Ri," headed for Guam. At 1449, when fairly near the island and jettisoning their bombs, they were picked up on TF 58 radar screens and the last C.A.P. of the day, 12 Hellcats from *Cowpens*, was vectored out to intercept.[31] The C.A.P. leader, Commander Gaylord B. Brown, tallyhoed "Forty enemy planes circling Orote Field at Angels 3, some with wheels down." Most opportunely he was joined by seven more Hellcats from *Essex* led by Commander McCampbell, and eight from *Hornet* led by Lieutenant William K. Blair USNR. These last had been in the air since 1130, and McCampbell's had been launched at 1423 to make a "precautionary fighter sweep" over Rota and Guam, a precaution well taken. Between them, these 27 F6Fs shot down 30 out of the 49 Japanese planes trying to land. Two of *Hornet's* Hellcats, one a night fighter piloted by Lieutenant Reiserer, broke into the landing circle of a string of Vals and knocked down five without damage to themselves.[32] The 19 Japanese planes which managed to land on Orote Field were so badly damaged as to be beyond repair.

Except for a few tail-end Charlies who did themselves proud,

[31] *Cowpens* and *Essex* Action Reports.
[32] *Hornet* Action Report 1 July 1944, Air Action of VF–2 for 19 June pp. 139–40.

this was the end of Raid IV. In all, including the final fight over Guam, 73 of the 82 were either shot down or rendered useless. Ozawa could no longer keep up his "every hour on the hour" schedule. He had shot his bolt. Over half the planes he had brought to the scene of battle had been disposed of; some by antiaircraft fire from the United States ships, but most of them by the intrepid Hellcat interceptors.

A unique rôle in this great air battle was played by the Japanese air coördinator. Mitscher's flag communicators got on his circuit early and Lieutenant (jg) Charles A. Sims USNR stood by to translate his orders to the Japanese aircraft into English. Someone proposed to vector out the air patrol to shoot him down, but wiser counsels prevailed; and this Japanese officer continued throughout the action to furnish Commander Task Force 58 with specific information of when and where strikes were coming in. After the slaughter was over, "Coördinator Joe" signed off and started for home. "Shall we get him now?" asked an eager officer. "No indeed!" said Admiral Mitscher. "He did us too much good!" [33] So little Joe flew home, proud of having done his duty to his Emperor, and followed by the blessings of American fighter-directors.

c. Mop-up on Guam, 1449–1845 [34]

Guam and Rota had not been neglected during the interception of the four big carrier raids. Spruance had seen to it that both islands were constantly patrolled by a few Hellcats from *Lexington* to prevent the enemy from launching a land-based strike.

At 1040 *Hornet* sent a group of 17 Helldivers and 7 Avengers, escorted by 12 Hellcats, to bomb Orote Field. They encountered no enemy planes airborne. Around 1300 Lieutenant Commander Ralph Weymouth, flight leader of *Lexington's* SBDs, which had been circling for over two hours to keep out of the way, on his own initiative took his formation over Orote Field where 20 to 30

[33] Story from Rear Adm. Arleigh A. Burke.
[34] The chronology of this phase is very difficult to establish; I have simply done my best from the various and often contradictory reports.

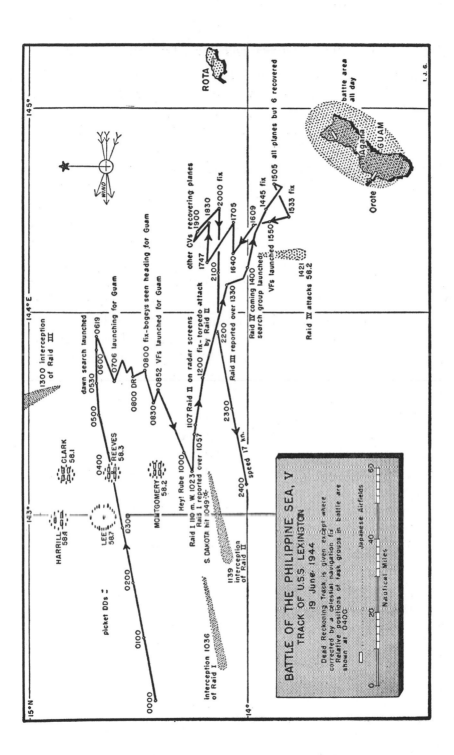

BATTLE OF THE PHILIPPINE SEA, V
TRACK OF U.S.S. LEXINGTON
19 June 1944

Dead Reckoning track is given except where corrected by a celestial navigation fix
Relative positions of task groups in battle area shown at 0400.

Japanese planes were grounded, and dropped armor-piercing thousand-pound bombs, which were not very destructive to airfields.[35]

At Admiral Montgomery's suggestion, the rest of the bombers, which had been sloughed off by the carriers since 1100 in order to clear flight decks for the Hellcats, were now ordered to work over the Guam airfields; 12 Hellcats from *Bunker Hill*, told off to escort them, paid special attention to planes parked off the runways. Eleven Helldivers from *Essex* delivered another bombing strike on Orote shortly before 1400. The Guam airfields were temporarily put out of business, so that most of the enemy carrier planes seeking refuge later in the day crashed; a few landed on the emergency clearing at the north end of the island.[36] At 1449, when Gaylord Brown and McCampbell chased a large contingent of Raid IV into Guam and shot down all but 19, the pendulum of battle definitely swung back from blue water to the islands. A fighter sweep from *Yorktown* patrolled Guam until sundown, when it was relieved by planes from *Hornet* and *Essex*.[37]

On these fell the honor of fighting the last fight on this eventful day. Four Hellcats, led by Lieutenant Commander Brewer, who had distinguished himself in the morning's interception, were patrolling over Orote Field when they saw a Jill coming in low. As the F6Fs flew down to pounce on her, they were jumped by an estimated four times their number of Zekes.[38] The American pilots managed to cut down the odds, but not before Brewer and Lieutenant (jg) J. L. Bruce, and Brewer's wingman, Ensign Thomas

[35] *Hornet* and *Lexington* Aircraft Action Reports. One of these SBDs, crippled by antiaircraft fire, made a water landing. The crew was rescued by two SOCs from *Montpelier,* which, unable to rise with the extra load, had to await rescue by a destroyer.

[36] Nucleus of the later B-29 field.

[37] CTG 58.2 Action Report, TG 58.4 Aircraft Action Reports, *Enterprise* VB-10 Action Report. Her VT-10 Action Report tells of enemy planes circling Guam, searching for a spot to land, and one pilot bailing out before being fired upon.

[38] *Essex* radar picked up a bogey estimated as 10-15 planes bearing 205° on course 25° distant 115 miles at 1748, and said bogey "did not close task force but headed for Guam." They were a remnant of Raid IV.

Tarr, USNR, had been shot down and killed. Darkness ended this fight, around 1845.[39]

The impression made on the receiving end may be gathered from a Japanese diary later captured on Guam. "The enemy, circling overhead, bombed our airfield the whole day long. When evening came our carrier bombers [Raid IV] returned, but the airfield had been destroyed by the enemy and they . . . had to crash. . . . I was unable to watch dry-eyed. The 'tragedy of war' was never so real."[40]

But the cost of interdicting Guam was relatively high: six Hellcats and one bomber, with their crews, were missing. Four out of the seven had presumably been shot down by antiaircraft fire, which at Orote Peninsula was the most intense experienced by American carrier planes up to that time.[41]

Three hundred American carrier planes, all but five of them Hellcats, had been engaged in the interceptions, and an additional number, including the bombers, in the fight over Guam. Only 23 had been shot down and 6 lost operationally. The net casualties, after rescues, were 20 pilots and 7 aircrewmen killed, together with 4 officers and 27 enlisted men in the three ships hit or near-missed. Seldom have the casualties been so one-sided. The Japanese had thrown 373 planes into their raids and searches. Only 130 returned. In addition, they had lost about 50 Guam-based planes, and others went down in the carriers sunk, or were lost by crashes and splashes, bringing their total losses on 19 June to about 315.[42]

By the time darkness fell, the air over Guam — and over the task force too — was clear of enemy planes. The "Great Marianas Turkey Shoot" was over.

This was the greatest carrier battle of the war. The forces engaged were three to four times those in preceding actions like Mid-

[39] *Essex* Air Action Reports, Air Group 15.
[40] Quoted in Maj. O. R. Lodge's Marine Corps monograph on Guam chap. v.
[41] *Yorktown* Action Report, Enclosure C (comments by Cdr. J. M. Peters, Air Group 1) p. 53.
[42] See chap. xvi §4, below, for table and discussion.

way, and victory was so complete that the Japanese could never again engage on such a scale. From any point of view, the "Great Marianas Turkey Shoot" of 19 June was a glorious and wonderful battle. For over eight hours, 1023 to 1845, there was continuous and fierce action in the air, directed by and supported by action on board ship. The brainwork of the combat information centers in tracking Japanese raids, and of fighter-directors in arranging interceptions; the energy of deck crews in rapid-fire launching, recovery and servicing of planes; the accuracy of battle line antiaircraft gunners — all contributed. But above all the skill, initiative, and intrepid courage of the young aviators made this day one of the high points in the history of the American spirit.[43]

2. *The Submarines' Contribution,*[44] *19 June*

On 15 June Admiral Lockwood at Pearl Harbor laid out an imaginary square in the Philippine Sea through which he believed the Japanese Fleet must pass, and sent submarines *Albacore, Finback, Bang* and *Stingray* to patrol 30-mile radii around its four corners. Three days later, as a result of the contacts and the HF/DF fix that we have already discussed, the Admiral ordered the four corners moved south 100 miles, which proved to be just right. Sightings of Japanese planes gave the hint that Ozawa's carriers were not far away; and, sure enough, at 0816 June 19 Ozawa's own division ran afoul of *Albacore* (Commander J. W. Blanchard) patrolling the southwest corner of the new square. Blanchard submerged his boat to avoid being snooped by an enemy plane; and when cruising at periscope depth, around lat. 12°20′ N, long.

[43] Limitations of space and inadequacy of records have prevented me from relating the interceptions, which were the crux of the battle, in greater detail. The magnificent exploits of Brewer, McCuskey and McCampbell were typical rather than exceptional, and the total score was divided almost equally by all air groups involved.

[44] War patrol reports of the submarines named; Theodore Roscoe *Submarine Operations* (1949) pp. 381–83, and Cdr. E. L. Beach *Submarine!* (1952) ch. xiv. Consult chart "Battle of the Philippine Sea, IV" for positions.

137° E, sighted a large carrier, a cruiser and the tops of several other ships, seven miles away bearing 70 degrees on the port bow. Battle stations were taken and speed was built up. Soon a second carrier appeared! This was the brand-new, 33,000-ton, 850-foot *Taiho*. As befitted the newest and biggest carrier in the Japanese Navy, she was flying the eight-rayed, single-banded flag of Admiral Ozawa. For Commander Blanchard she was just another flattop, which he selected as target because she was in an easier position to attack than the one first sighted.

Albacore had a nice setup at 9000 yards for a right-angle shot, with distance to the track 2300,[45] when a destroyer showed signs of getting in the way. Blanchard therefore closed to range 5300 and track distance 1950 yards. A quick look around with the periscope at 0904 revealed the other carrier, two cruisers, two destroyers, and numerous airborne planes. *Albacore* retracted periscope and got everything set to give the Emperor's proudest ship a salvo of six torpedoes. It looked as easy as pigeon shooting. But, all of a sudden, Lady Luck seemed to desert her. The torpedo data computer refused to show the light indicating "correct solution." Someone, somehow, had fed into it the wrong data, so the intelligent machine refused to come up with an answer. There was no time to recheck. The carrier was making 27 knots and her relative bearing was changing rapidly; soon she would open range, and a pursuing torpedo is not hard to evade. So, rather than miss out altogether, Blanchard upped periscope and fired a spread of six torpedoes, by "seaman's eye," at 0909½.

Ninety seconds later the boat "went to deep submergence with three destroyers heading her way," noted Blanchard. His crew had only 27 seconds more to wait for the sound and sensation of one of their torpedoes exploding. A second, too, might have hit, but for Sakio Komatsu's remarkable feat of exploding it by the well-directed suicide dive of his bomber plane.

[45] The carrier was then 9000 yards distant from *Albacore,* but since she was approaching the submarine the torpedo track would be only 2300 yards to point of contact. In other words, track distance was the short leg of a right-angled triangle, carrier's track the long leg, and range the hypotenuse.

Taibo had just completed launching 42 planes, her share in Raid II (second big contribution to the Turkey Shoot), when *Albacore's* torpedo struck her starboard side near the forward gasoline tanks. It jammed the forward plane elevator, whose pit filled up with gasoline, water and fuel oil; but no fires broke out, speed fell off by only one knot, flight deck remained clear, and the captain had every expectation that his crew would promptly put this "minor damage" to rights.

Albacore in the meantime was being depth-charged, apparently at random; the Japanese destroyers' subchasing technique was very poor. In the early afternoon she surfaced to continue her patrol. Ozawa's fleet had passed on, and *Taibo* with it. Discounting the infliction of lethal damage, and mortified at the foul-up in the computer, Blanchard made such a modest report that his attack was assessed at Pearl Harbor as having inflicted only "probable damage." It was many months before the cheering truth came out.

Admiral Ozawa did not take the torpedoing of his flagship very seriously. He still "radiated confidence and satisfaction." [46] *Taibo* was much better built than the carriers sunk at Midway; one torpedo hit, surely, couldn't hurt her much. Damage control and emergency repairs would certainly make her taut and shipshape in short order. It seemed significant that not a single American plane had appeared over the Japanese fleet.

Cavalla, still believing she was stern-chasing her former contact of 17 June, almost bumped into Ozawa's Cardiv 1, on a southeasterly course and about 60 miles beyond *Albacore's* point of attack. Lieutenant Commander Kossler raised his periscope at 1152. "The picture was too good to be true!" he recorded. "A large carrier with two cruisers ahead on the port bow and a destroyer about 1000 yards on the port beam!" [47] *Shokaku,* for it was she, was recovering planes. *Cavalla* approached undetected, although Kossler took three periscope sights on the way, with destroyer *Urakaze* abeam all the time.

[46] Letter from Capt. Ohmae, Ozawa's senior staff officer, in 1952.
[47] *Cavalla's* "declassified" Action Report 3 Aug. 1944.

He waited to make sure the flattop was not "friendly." At the last look, "there was the Rising Sun, big as hell! The exec. and gunnery officer saw it too. This destroyer hadn't sighted us as we headed in. I put the periscope up. We were at 1000 yards. I got ready to fire six torpedoes in such a way that if our dope was good at least four would hit. After the fourth I looked over at the destroyer and it was still on my neck. I fired the fifth and sixth on the way down. I know the first three hit." [48]

They did. The time was about 1220. *Shokaku* fell out of the formation, *Urakaze* standing by. Ruptured gasoline tanks started fires which damage control dealt with promptly, but deadly fumes continued to seep through the ship.

In the meantime *Cavalla* was fighting, or rather dodging, for her life. During the next three hours, Kossler counted 106 depth charges, half of them fairly close. Shortly after 1500 Kossler began to hear explosions and prolonged, monstrous rumblings. These were the death rattles of *Shokaku*. A bomb magazine had exploded, and the big carrier literally fell apart. [49]

Taiho shortly followed her down. The single torpedo hit from *Albacore* had ruptured one or more of her gasoline tanks. As she steamed to windward at 26 knots, a green damage-control officer ordered every ventilating duct to be operated full blast through a wide-open ship, trusting that the draft would blow the fumes away. The effect, on the contrary, was to distribute deadly vapor throughout the ship; not only the vapor from aviation gas but the volatile fumes from the crude Tarakan petroleum that she was using as fuel. Bungling efforts to pump free gasoline overboard added to the danger, until *Taiho* became little better than a gigantic supercharged cylinder awaiting ignition. At 1532 came a terrific explosion which heaved up the armored flight deck into something resembling a miniature mountain range, blew out the sides of the

[48] Kossler's story as told to Robert Sherrod 2 July 1944, in the latter's *On to Westward* p. 118.

[49] Nav. Tech. Jap. *Ship and Related Targets* Index No. S–06–03 pp. 8, 21. Nine planes went down with *Shokaku*. She was the fifth carrier which had taken part in the Pearl Harbor raid to be sunk.

hangar, blasted holes in the bottom, and killed everyone in the engine spaces. The ship at once began to settle. A cruiser and a couple of destroyers were ordered to close. A lifeboat ferried admiral, staff, flag, and Emperor's portrait to destroyer *Wakatsuki*, whence they were transferred to cruiser *Haguro*, arriving about 1706. At that time *Taiho* was swathed in flames; no destroyer could approach near enough for efficient rescue, and only about 500 of the crew of 2150 were saved. Ozawa's staff had hardly resumed duties in the new flagship when they heard and felt a shock like a torpedo explosion. That was the end of *Taiho*. She lurched to port, capsized, and plunged by the stern into a 2500-fathom deep.[50]

3. *Moving Westward, 2000 June 19–0500 June 20*

Through most of the daylight of 19 June, Task Force 58 had been making easting. A few westerly jogs were made in the early morning, but from 1023, when the first big flocks of bogeys had begun to appear on radar screens, launchings and recoveries were so frequent that the course made good was E by S. At 1431 Rota Island was sighted from *Yorktown*, bearing due east 40 miles distant, and two minutes later the *Princeton* lookouts made out Guam 37 miles away, bearing SE by S.[51] At 1500, when Admiral Spruance gave the order to start west again in pursuit of the enemy, *Lexington* was only 20 miles off the northwest point of Guam.

Admiral Mitscher now detached Harrill's group (TG 58.4), which had less fuel than the others, to oil up next day,[52] and in the meantime to keep Guam and Rota pounded down. In that assignment it was very industrious and successful. At about 0230 June 20 four night fighters were launched, two for each island. Those over Guam found the Tiyan airstrip near Agaña lighted up and promptly

[50] Same, pp. 23–24. She took 13 planes with her.
[51] At 1500 *Alabama* saw it too, bearing 145°, distant 52 miles; *South Dakota*, however, reported it only 38 miles distant.
[52] TG 58.4 fueled along a course W of and 70 to 132 miles distant from Saipan between 0700 and 1400 June 20, from TG 50.17. (See Task Organization, Appendix III.)

strafed it, causing the lights to go out. At 0410 they came on again and Japanese planes began taking off. The Hellcats, who were waiting for that, shot down three out of the four that rose. At dawn, Harrill sent fighter sweeps over both islands; Rota appeared to be completely dead but 30 to 40 grounded planes at Orote Field were strafed. According to Japanese records, TG 58.4 raised the Guam-based score to 18 planes shot down in the air and 52 destroyed on the ground. A dawn sweep on the 21st encountered no airborne opposition and little antiaircraft fire.

So much for Harrill's group. The other three had to zigzag northward for almost five hours to recover all planes. Finally, at 2000 June 19, Task Force 58 shaped a due west course for the night. Rota, whose jagged silhouette showed up bold and clear against the eastern sky, bore 35 miles due east. Admiral Mitscher ordered 23 knots to be bent on, in the hope of closing the enemy during the night. Faster than that he dared not steam on account of fuel consumption, for both he and Spruance were eagerly expecting a fight next day. Admiral Lee was ordered to operate his battle line 25 miles in advance of *Lexington*, and the relative positions of the three carrier task groups remained constant throughout the night.

That clear starlit night, 19–20 June, was one of enthusiasm and busy activity on board the American carriers. The "Turkey Shoot" was discussed in all its phases. Some 400 pilots had tales to tell of gloriously successful interceptions out in the blue, of slaughter over Guam, of chasing formations of Japanese fliers right into our antiaircraft fire. It was agreed by all hands that the enemy had lost his air cunning; that we were now dealing with greenhorns led by a few old hands capable of startling acrobatics but ignorant of air tactics. "It was the opinion of all the fighter pilots with whom I talked," wrote Ensign Charles D. Farmer USNR of *Enterprise*,[53] "that the Japanese attack was not a good one. Many of their fighter pilots were content to stay out of the action entirely. The dive-bombers and torpedo planes were loath to keep their de-

[53] Paper prepared for the writer.

fensive formations, and separated, thus losing all chance of a coördinated attack." The American pilots, somewhat calmed down from their excitement by a modest issue of two bottles of beer apiece, had to sit up late to tell their stories to Combat Air Intelligence, who then put in the rest of the night calculating the day's bag. As another air battle was expected on the morrow, deck crews were up all night servicing, testing, fueling and arming the Hellcats, which had certainly earned their names. There was a general feeling of hilarity over the day's doings; but no gaiety, for some 40 pilots and crewmen had not returned,[54] and anyone could predict that some who had been behind the guns in the turkey shoot would not survive another day.

After sundown, just as Scorpio was rising, the writer heard the good news on the bridge of cruiser *Honolulu,* one of the bombardment ships off Saipan, and recorded it as follows: —

"News comes from Mitscher that, although he could not find the enemy carrier force, they found him; and between what his antiaircraft shot down, and what his fighters shot down, they lost today about 300 planes."

In the course of the evening Admiral Spruance sent the following message to Admiral Mitscher: —

Desire to attack enemy tomorrow if we know his position with sufficient accuracy. If our patrol planes give us required information tonight no searches should be necessary. If not, we must continue searches tomorrow to ensure adequate protection of Saipan. Point Option[55] should be advanced to the westward as much as air operations permit.

The 23- to 24-knot speed of Task Force 58 should have closed range that night, for Ozawa was making only 18.[56] But the Japanese had a head start; Ozawa turned NW at 1808, two hours before the Americans turned W. And, as Mitscher could only guess at the enemy's course and distance, it naturally happened that he did not shape the shortest course for interception. A morning search over

---

[54] So many of these were subsequently recovered that the net loss was 18 pilots and 6 aircrewmen in action, 1 and 1 operationally. CTF 58 Action Report p. 14.
[55] For explanation of this carrier term see Vol. IV p. 130
[56] *Camp. Pac. War* p. 266.

a 120-degree sector, launched at 0530 June 20 from lat. 13°42′ N, long. 141°05′ E, went out 325 miles but fell just 75 miles short of the spot where Ozawa's ships were milling around, preparing to fuel. At the earnest request of his air operations officer, Gus Widhelm, who suspected that the Japanese had hightailed for home, Mitscher at noon sent a volunteer group of Hellcats led by Commander E. M. Snowden, armed with belly tanks and bombs, on bearing 340 degrees, 475 miles out. This stab completely missed its mark.[57] Ozawa was now careful to keep radio silence, so "Huff-Duff" could not fix him; he was well beyond the range of the Manus-based Liberators, and he had the good luck to escape Admiral Lockwood's patrolling submarines and the PBMs from Saipan.

"If we know his position with sufficient accuracy," Spruance had said. That was the rub. The great weakness of United States carriers, here as at Coral Sea and Midway, was search. It seems incredible that subsequent to the PBM contact on Ozawa at 0115 June 19 — delivered at 0915 — it was not until 1600 June 20 that Mitscher had any useful intelligence of his enemy from search planes. The PBMs missed him, the carrier planes missed him, all but one of the Liberators missed him; and that sighting, made at 1120 on the 19th,[58] merely confirmed the submarine contacts. Counting the Liberator's report, Mitscher could put his finger on Ozawa only thrice, the other two times being *Albacore's* hit on *Taiho* at 0910 and *Cavalla's* on *Shokaku* at 1215 June 19. After that, silence. He never knew of Ozawa's change of course in midafternoon; he could only guess that the Japanese would retire northwesterly. But why were only routine morning and afternoon searches made from the carriers? Mitscher had 24 night-fighting Hellcats, with belly tanks mounted, distributed through his task force; they could have covered every possible sector that night, out to at least 400 miles. He had the radar-equipped TBFs which had searched in the small hours of the 19th;

[57] *Enterprise* Action Report; *Bunker Hill* War Diary; information from Cdr. Weymouth. The pilots mistook Parece Vela for enemy ships and gave it the benefit of their bombs.
[58] This PB4Y, belonging to Manus-based Bombron 101 (Cdr. J. A. Miller), sighted *Shokaku*, *Zuikaku*, 2 CAs and 5 DDs at lat. 12°03′ N, long. 137°30′ E. See Chart No. III.

he had others which could have made extended daylight searches with belly tanks. Yet not one search mission was sent out on the night of 19–20 June to find an enemy fleet which he expected to engage as early as possible next day, and the one thin stab that he sent out at noon 20 June happened to be in the wrong direction.[59]

Probably the consideration that any plane launching in a downwind chase would lose the launching carrier at least 40 miles' distance had great weight with Admiral Mitscher. According to the best recollection of his chief of staff, the Admiral did ask for a night search from Reeves's task group, but Reeves replied at 2030 June 19 that the planes were unable to take off owing to engine trouble. Mitscher apparently decided that the PBMs searching from Garapan Roads could do the job, and at 2130 ordered no searches to be launched before dawn.[60]

I believe that there were two basic reasons for the few and far between night searches. The first was Admiral Mitscher's commendable tenderness for his aviators. He loathed the thought of a lonely searcher shot or forced down in a vast expanse of ocean with no hope of rescue. And he believed that every able-bodied pilot in Task Force 58 was dog-tired after the "Turkey Shoot," although the night fighters and the Avenger pilots, who had not been used extensively, were eager to go. The second reason was a sort of mental block regarding night fighters on the part of certain carrier group commanders. Clark and Reeves used them, but the others did not, and Mitscher did not much care for them. In some of the seven carriers that carried night-fighter detachments, they were considered a nuisance, especially by the overworked deck crews who needed a little "sack time."

Whatever the cause, not a single plane was sent out to locate the enemy on this crucial night of 19–20 June. If Ozawa had been found that night, or even in the morning watch of June 20, his carriers could have been subjected to an all-out strike by daylight, with no problem of night recovery. The nearer units of the Mobile

[59] See chart "Battle of the Philippine Sea, V."
[60] Letter of Rear Adm. Arleigh Burke, 1 July 1952. Cf. Cdr. James S. Gray's article on night fighters in U. S. Naval Inst. *Proceedings* LXXIV (1948) p. 850.

Fleet were within 325 miles of TF 58 at midnight 19 June, and again from about 0900 to 1200 June 20.

On board the Japanese carriers during the first night watch following the "Turkey Shoot" the atmosphere was far from merry, although until daylight nobody knew the extent of the disaster to their air groups. Few planes had returned, to be sure, but perhaps they had landed safe on Guam and Rota. Admiral Ozawa and staff knew less of the score than anyone. The Japanese Navy had such confidence in the sturdiness of *Taiho* that no preparations had been made for a relief flagship; the Admiral's staff was packed into a cabin under the bridge of *Haguro*, to which he had transferred his flag on the evening of 19 June, and the heavy cruiser's communications were such that it was very difficult to get in touch with other carrier divisions. *Haguro* straggled during the night and at daybreak *Zuikaku*, the one remaining flattop of Cardiv 1, was not in sight. Nor did Tokyo learn the score until the 20th.

Thus, Admiral Ozawa saw no reason to throw in the sponge. He had lost two big carriers, but knew nothing of his heavy plane losses. At 1820, from *Haguro*, he issued the order "All forces will proceed north." He had decided to fuel on the 20th and to renew his offensive the same or the following day, with the aid of those now vanished planes based on Guam. Nor was the atmosphere in Cardivs 2 and 3 one of defeat. Heavy losses do not depress the Japanese as they do most other people — so glorious are the rewards for dead warriors; and the aviators who had survived the "Turkey Shoot" brought in stories of sinking at least four American carriers, of having seen six flattops covered with black smoke, of an astronomical destruction of "Grummans," as they called the Hellcats. The official Tokyo broadcast even claimed eleven carriers and numerous other ships sunk!

"How were your plans changed as a result of the first day's battles?" asked Admiral Ofstie of Admiral Ozawa after the war was over. "No changes in basic plan," he replied, "but a necessitated change in Japanese movements."

4. *The Air Battle of 20 June*

a. The Approach

June 20 dawned clear and fair, with a golden sunrise. In the course of the day, weak remnants of a cold front brought increased cloudiness and showers. Across Task Force 58 the wind blew due east most of the day, dropping to 10–12 knots' velocity at 0900 and to very light variables at night. In this American sector of the Philippine Sea, as we might call it, the sea remained calm with a gentle ground swell; temperature of both air and water was about 85° Fahrenheit. The glass held so steady, at around 29.85, that altimeter settings for the planes could be forecast with accuracy.[61] Over on the Japanese side of the sea the wind was more often southeasterly than easterly.

Admiral Ozawa did not neglect search. At 0530 nine float planes went out from the van cruisers over a wide sector.[62] They found nothing, and three failed to return. At 0645 Obayashi sent six planes to search the sector from 50° to 10°. One of these, at 0713, reported two American carrier planes. Admiral Kurita, in communicating this to Ozawa after a good lapse of time and receiving some land-based plane contacts via Tokyo, advised a quick retirement to Japan; but Ozawa evaluated the contacts as false (which some of them were) and persisted in his plan to refuel that day and attack the next. Subsequently he admitted that he should have delegated tactical command to Kurita until he could move to a suitably equipped flagship; if he had done so, Kurita would have hightailed out promptly and there would have been no battle on 20 June. Finally, at 1300, *Chitose* and *Zuiho* sent three torpedo planes searching the sector between 100° and 130°. One of these at 1715 sighted a portion of Task Force 58 and so reported. But that was too late to help Ozawa.

[61] *San Jacinto* Action Report 1 July 1944, Part V, has the best meteorological data on the whole battle.
[62] See Chart "Battle of the Philippine Sea, VI." At 1435 *Zuikaku* sent two planes on a 140-mile search between 86° and 106°. This is not shown on chart.

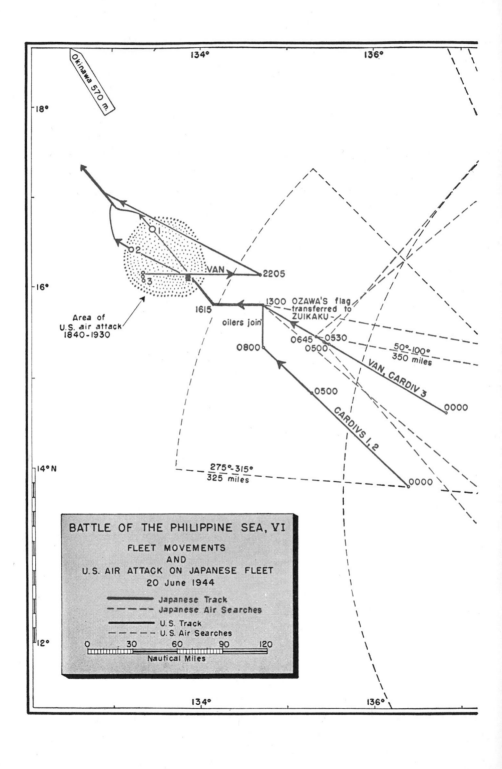

Okinawa 570 m.

VAN

2205

1615

1300 OZAWA'S flag
transferred to
ZUIKAKU

Area of
U.S. air attack
1840-1930

oilers join

0645 0530
0800 0500

50°-100°
350 miles

VAN, CARDIV 3

0500

0000

CARDIVS 1, 2

275°-315°
325 miles

0000

BATTLE OF THE PHILIPPINE SEA, VI

FLEET MOVEMENTS
AND
U.S. AIR ATTACK ON JAPANESE FLEET
20 June 1944

————————— Japanese Track
– – – – – – – Japanese Air Searches

————————— U.S. Track
– – – – – – – U.S. Air Searches

| 0 | 30 | 60 | 90 | 120 |

Nautical Miles

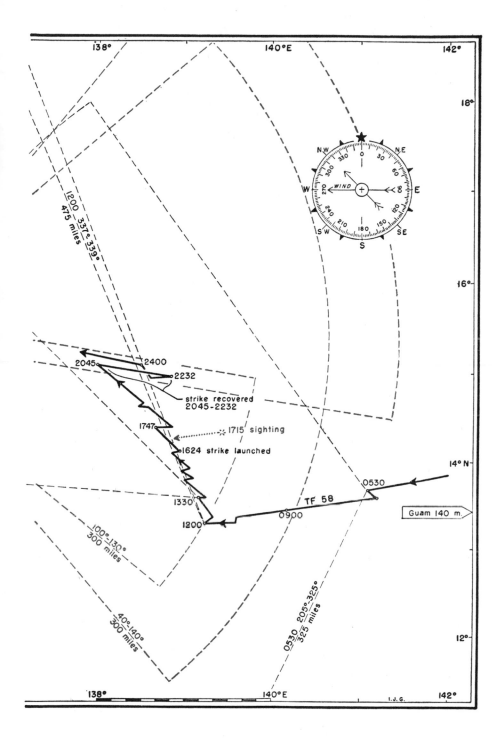

With Commander Mobile Fleet and his staff practically incommunicado, there was great confusion about making rendezvous with the two oiler groups at lat. 15°20′ N, long. 134°40′ E, as had previously been ordered. The tankers were there and ready to deliver fuel by 0920, but many of the combatant ships were not, because (as Ozawa's staff navigator explained) *Taiho* had been used as a sort of focal point for navigation and *Taiho* had gone down. For hours ships milled around the rendezvous point, flag hoists being made and lowered frequently, light signals blinking, and officers coming as near to making nasty remarks over voice radio as Japanese decorum permitted. Many officers were exceedingly nervous lest enemy planes attack while the disposition was in confusion or fueling. Ozawa did not feel ready to give the fueling order until 1230, and, before it could be carried out, more rumors came in that enemy forces were closing, and the order was canceled. Not a single ship in the Mobile Fleet took in fuel that day.

In the meantime, Task Force 58 was closing distance; and if Mitscher had sent out a fair-sized search during the forenoon watch it would almost certainly have caught Ozawa in this confused situation.

At 1300 Admiral Ozawa's flag was transferred to *Zuikaku*.[63] With improved communications the Admiral learned the bitter truth: that the day before his carriers had lost some 330 planes, leaving but an even hundred operational.[64] Yet the only change that the tough old sailor made in his plan was to postpone his next strike until the 21st. Word came from Vice Admiral Kakuta, the land-based air commander at Tinian, that a good number of Japanese carrier planes had landed on Rota and Guam;[65] true enough, but

[63] Her position at that time was lat. 15°45′ N, long. 134°42′ E.
[64] Plus 27 float planes. The breakdown, as given in 1st Mobile Fleet Action Report (WDC 161,517), is as follows: —

	Total
Cardiv 1: 17 VF, 7 VT, 3 VB, 5 recce	32
Cardiv 2: 38 VF, 8 VT	46
Cardiv 3: 13 VF, 9 VT	22
	100

Twenty-eight of the Zekes were equipped as light bombers.
[65] Ozawa's Interrogation p. 4.

they were all shot up. And Ozawa assumed that Kakuta's air strength by this time had been augmented by planes staged in from Iwo, Yap and Truk, all ready to help him tear and rend Mitscher. No word had come from Toyoda to deny him a second attempt, so the plan held — strike tomorrow with everything he had.

As hour after hour passed without any sign of their enemy, the Japanese began to hope that he had had enough. First evidence that a stern chase was on came at 1615 when cruiser *Atago* reported she had intercepted American plane radio messages indicating that the Japanese had been sighted. Ozawa at 1645 ordered fueling attempts to be called off, altered the disposition's course from W to NW, and bent on 24 knots.

Atago was right. Task Force 58 had finally pulled up sufficiently so that its afternoon 325-mile search, launched at 1330, reached the enemy.[66] The contact was made at 1540 by an *Enterprise* Avenger piloted by Lieutenant R. S. Nelson USNR, first carrier pilot in all these days of searching and fighting to sight a Japanese combatant ship.

b. Twilight Air Battle, 1840–1900 [67]

Admiral Mitscher received the intimation that Lieutenant Nelson had seen something, somewhere — nobody could make out what, the message was so garbled — at 1542. A quick decision was wanted, for time was running out; the sun would set by 1900.

He alerted the task force promptly, and at 1553 informed Spruance that he expected to make an all-out strike, even though recovery must take place after dark. At 1557 Mitscher received

[66] Before it did so, Spruance notified Mitscher that he wished to continue pursuit the following night if there were any indications that it might be profitable, and inquired into his fuel situation. Mitscher replied that some destroyers would be very low by next day, but he proposed to continue the pursuit relentlessly with such ships as had fuel. CTF 58 Action Report p. 50.

[67] This action was so swift that the American aviators made very confusing identifications of the Japanese ships they attacked, and the available Japanese reports give very few details, except of the results. I therefore do not feel that I have made really firm conclusions on who hit what; the story that follows is a close estimate of what actually happened.

Nelson's definite contact report, that the Japanese Fleet, spread out in three groups, was heading west at slow speed, apparently fueling.[68] Eight minutes later, at 1605, Nelson corrected his first report [69] and gave the Japanese position as lat. 14°30′ N, long. 134°30′ E. This placed the nearest enemy group over 275 miles from Task Force 58, which had now reached lat. 14° N, long. 139° E, about 370 miles west of Rota. It was the corrected report that *Atago* overheard.

The danger inherent in this decision, and the reasons why it was made, cannot be better stated than in Admiral Mitscher's own words: —

Taking advantage of this opportunity to destroy the Japanese fleet was going to cost us a great deal in planes and pilots because we were launching at the maximum range of our aircraft at such a time that it would be necessary to recover them after dark. This meant that all carriers would be recovering daylight-trained air groups at night, with consequent loss of some pilots who were not familiar with night landings and who would be fatigued at the end of an extremely hazardous and long mission. Night landings after an attack are slow at best. There are always stragglers who have had to fight their way out of the enemy disposition, whose planes are damaged, or who get lost. It was estimated that it would require about four hours to recover planes, during which time the Carrier Task Groups would have to steam upwind or on an easterly course. This course would take us away from the position of the enemy at a high rate. It was realized also that this was a single-shot venture, for planes which were sent out on this late afternoon strike would probably not all be operational for a morning strike. Consequently, Commander Fifth Fleet was informed that the carriers were firing their bolt.[70]

A little pep talk from Mitscher ending, "Give 'em hell, boys; wish I were with you," the word "Man Aircraft!" at 1610, and the

[68] Times here as in CTF 58 Action Report p. 57. Cincpac Monthly Analysis June 1944 p. 87 states definite report of enemy position received at 1548. Message file of TF 58 shows a message at 1512 to the effect that "birdmen" had found "something big," and that speed of 23 knots was ordered. Who or what made this probably erroneous sighting I am unable to discover.

[69] Lt. (jg) J. S. Moore checked his flight leader's navigation and found a 60-mile error in longitude.

[70] CTF 58 Action Report p. 57.

pilots ran across the deck as they never had before; chart boards under their arms, pistols at their hips, oxygen masks dangling from their helmets. At 1621 Task Force 58 turned into the wind, completed launching in the phenomenal time of ten minutes, and was back on its course at 1636. A full deckload was in the air — 85 fighters, 77 dive-bombers, 54 torpedo-bombers — from the six big carriers present (*Hornet, Yorktown, Bunker Hill, Wasp, Enterprise, Lexington*) and five of the six light carriers (*Belleau Wood, Bataan, Monterey, Cabot, San Jacinto*).[71] All Hellcats and Helldivers carried belly tanks for extra gasoline. A second deckload was alerted, but Mitscher decided to save that for next day.

At 1825, Japanese pilots sighted Mitscher's fliers; and they first sighted the enemy at 1840 after flying 275 to 300 miles at 130 to 140 knots.[72] Nature had provided a romantic setting which, in other circumstances, would have made the Japanese sailors feel very sentimental. The lower limb of the setting sun was just touching the horizon; the thinnest golden sliver of a new moon was setting, and about half the sky was covered with brilliantly colored clouds at altitudes between 3000 and 10,000 feet, which favored the attackers. Surface visibility remained excellent during the gathering dusk. The American planes were so near the end of their tether that there was no time to organize coördinated attacks. Fortunately for them, Ozawa had not yet reformed his battle disposition to receive air attack; the van no longer interposed between the larger carriers and the American line of approach.

Six oilers protected by as many destroyers made up the first group of enemy ships encountered; these had been left astern when Ozawa turned up speed. The seven Japanese carriers were disposed as before in three main groups, the approximate position of flagship *Zuikaku* being lat. 16°20′ N, long. 133°30′ E.[73] Kurita's van,

---

[71] *Princeton* would have launched a deckload in the second strike.

[72] Data from *Yorktown* Action Report; Cincpac Analysis p. 88 says the flights were 300–330 miles. *Bunker Hill* Action Report says her planes flew 315 miles to targets, and that *Bunker Hill's* position at launching was lat. 13°50′ N, long. 139°10′ E.

[73] According to Capt. Ohmae, who was on board, *Zuikaku's* position at 1800 was lat. 16°17′ N, long. 133°43′ E, course 320° at 24 knots. The position for the action given in CTF 58 Action Report, Enclosure B, p. 28, is clearly inaccurate.

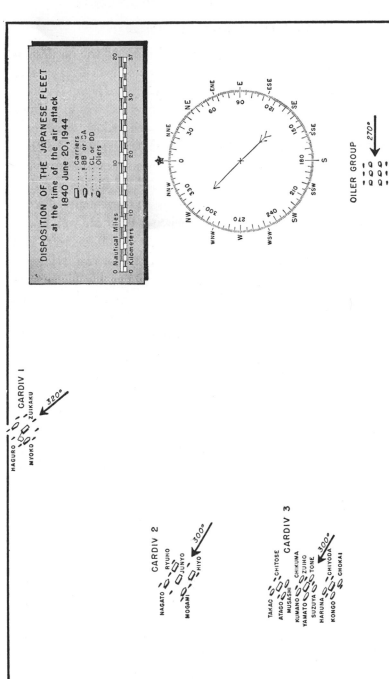

DISPOSITION OF THE JAPANESE FLEET
at the time of the air attack
1840 June 20, 1944

⬟ ... Carriers
⬭ ... ⚓ BB or CA
⬭ ... CL or DD
⬭ ... Oilers

0 Nautical Miles   10   20
0 Kilometers   10   20   30   37

NNW N NNE
NW   NE
        30   60
WNW   ENE
W   0   90   E
            120
WSW   ESE
SW   210   SE
    240
        180   150
    SSW S SSE

CARDIV 1
ZUIKAKU
320°
MYOKO
HAGURO

CARDIV 2
RYUHO
NAGATO
JUNYO 300°
MOGAMI HIYO

CARDIV 3
CHITOSE
TAKAO CHIKUMA
ATAGO ZUIHO
MUSASHI
KUMANO TONE
YAMATO 300°
SUZUYA CHIYODA
HARUNA CHOKAI
KONGO

OILER GROUP
270°

I.J.G.

including *Chitose, Zuiho* and *Chiyoda,* and most of the battleships and heavy cruisers, were on a north-south line of bearing about 38 miles W by N of the oilers. Cardiv 2 (*Junyo, Hiyo, Ryuho*), screened by *Nagato, Mogami* and eight destroyers, was in a single disposition about 8 miles north of the van; both groups were making best speed on course 300° (NW by W). Flagship *Zuikaku,* screened by two heavy cruisers, a light cruiser and seven destroyers, was steaming on course 320° about 18 miles NE of Cardiv 2 and 40 miles NNW of the oilers. The screen was still unequally distributed, all the most powerful gunfire ships being with the van; and it was a very close screen — capital ships only 1.5 kilometers and destroyers only 2 kilometers from the center.[74] Ozawa evidently hoped to compensate with intense antiaircraft fire for his lack of planes. At about 1600 Cardiv 3 (*Chitose, Zuiho* and *Chiyoda*) had launched 16 planes to attack the Americans at a falsely reported advanced position, and this group was just being recovered when the battle broke. Including these and all other would-be strikes, search missions, near and distant combat air patrol, and a pathetic "interception force" of fifteen, Ozawa managed to get about 75 planes airborne to meet the onslaught of 216 from TF 58. The American pilots believed that not over 35 aircraft [75] participated in the interceptions, which were made very close to the ships; but these few Zekes and Hamps did so well, in view of their meager strength, as to create the impression that only experienced pilots had survived the Turkey Shoot.

During the air-surface battle, which lasted about 20 minutes, every Japanese ship maneuvered independently, turning in tight circles and figure S's, and throwing up intense antiaircraft fire in a spectrum of colors — "blue, yellow, lavender, pink, red, white and black. Some bursts threw out sparkling incendiary particles; some

[74] Cardiv 2 Log of Messages and Orders, Pineau trans.; 61st Destroyer Group War Diary (WDC 161,640); *Genyo Maru* Action Report (Same), and data communicated by Capt. Ohmae.
[75] CTF 58 Action Report p. 17. Some American aviators reported that the flight decks of the carriers were completely bare of planes, and others did not sight a single Japanese plane during the attack. Seven of the above-mentioned 16 were shot down when attempting to land.

dropped phosphorus-appearing streamers." [76] Some of the American dive-bombers, including those from *Wasp*, concentrated on the oilers which they encountered first, and managed to disable two, *Genyo* and *Seiyo Maru*, which were abandoned and scuttled that evening.

Dauntless planes, Helldivers, and Avengers from the Clark and Reeves task groups concentrated on the carriers of Admiral Joshima's division. *Lexington's* pilots claimed to have sunk both *Hiyo* [77] and *Junyo* and to have damaged *Ryuho*, making altogether 16 hits. But *Ryuho* was not hit, and *Junyo* not sunk. *Hiyo* was sunk by torpedoes, one of which the Japanese imputed to a submarine; but no submarine was about. Here is the story of what seems to have happened.

Four Avengers from *Belleau Wood* led by Lieutenant (jg) George B. Brown USNR in company with four more from *Yorktown*, all armed with torpedoes, sighted Joshima's division on their port hand and *Zuikaku* to starboard, from 12,000 feet. After circling Cardiv 2 to size it up, the *Yorktown* planes sped over to *Zuikaku* as the biggest target. Lieutenant Brown, thinking that *Hiyo* was good enough game and noting a friendly cloud to dive through, led his four planes to attack her. A 180-degree turn was made in the 50-degree dive to place the setting sun behind the planes. As they broke through the cloud and began leveling off, they turned toward the carrier, spreading out so as to approach from different quarters. *Hiyo* looked, and acted, completely undamaged.

The last thing Lieutenant Brown said before he took off was that he would torpedo a carrier at any cost. He did, and the cost was heavy. His plane was hit several times by antiaircraft fire as he was lowering for a final run; part of the port wing was shot off; fire burst out, filling the center section of the plane with flames

[76] *Bunker Hill* Action Report 13 July p. 23. An exceptionally good air action report, this is supplemented by Lt. R. J. Mead's Narrative.

[77] This carrier in the U.S. Action Reports and in JANAC is called *Hitaka*, which is another reading of the characters for *Hiyo*. There was no Japanese ship named *Hitaka*. A similar confusion arose from misreading *Junyo* characters as *Hayataka*.

which forced the radioman to bail out; and the radioman "booted" the gunner out. As the carrier made a sharp turn to port, Lieutenant Brown, now alone in the Avenger, pressed home his attack. And on the way down the fire burned itself out. His torpedo probably hit; that of his wingman, Lieutenant (jg) Benjamin C. Tate USNR, probably missed; but the third torpedo, dropped by Lieutenant (jg) Warren R. Omark USNR from an altitude of 400 feet, certainly found its mark and exploded.[78]

On the retirement Lieutenant Tate's plane, which had been hit several times by antiaircraft and had lost the use of its wing gun, was chased by two Zekes, but Tate worked his way into a cloud and eluded them. He then joined wing on Lieutenant Brown, flying very low. Brown's Avenger was badly shot up, and the pilot, severely wounded and bleeding profusely, could no longer steer a straight course. Tate finally lost contact with him. Lieutenant Omark, after fighting off two Vals and a Zeke, overtook Brown and led him toward "home" until long after dark; but Brown's plane, steering erratic courses, disappeared when passing through a cloud and was lost, with its intrepid pilot.

The two crewmen of this plane who bailed out during the attack made parachute landings safely, inflated their life jackets and became interested spectators of *Hiyo's* last moments. Battleship *Nagato*, cruiser *Mogami* and several destroyers steamed around her in circles, almost running down the men in the water, and then retired, leaving one destroyer to stand by. Fires spread rapidly over the carrier until she was burning from stem to stern. Three violent explosions were sharply felt by the swimmers, and several smaller explosions followed. As darkness descended, *Hiyo*, down by the bow so that her propellers were out of water, cast a brilliant light on the surrounding waters. About two hours after the hit she disappeared, and the stand-by destroyer swept the area with her

[78] The Japanese list of losses in *Camp. Pac. War* p. 245 states, "One torpedo hit, making steerage impossible. While drifting about ship again incurred torpedo attack by enemy submarine. One torpedo hit, large conflagration broke out. . . ." Bailed-out crewmen in the water said they saw three aërial torpedoes hit, but perhaps only one did. The alleged hit by a submarine torpedo was probably an internal explosion.

searchlight, looking for survivors. Both American crewmen were picked up next day when a part of TF 58 passed through the scene of the battle.[79]

If the five *Enterprise* Avengers led by Lieutenant Van V. Eason that also took part in this attack had been armed with torpedoes, as Lieutenant Brown's had been, they might have sunk *Ryuho;* but they carried only bombs. Approaching in line, they were so tossed about by the antiaircraft bursts — some from *Nagato's* main battery — as to be compared by the "tail-end Charley" of the pilots to a dancing blacksnake.[80] Fighter planes led by Commander "Killer" Kane of *Enterprise* went ahead, strafing.[81] *Nagato* and *Mogami* gave the "Big E" boys so much attention as to suggest they were seeking revenge for Midway. The large quantities of tracers that their anti-aircraft gunners shot upward, and the 5-inch bursts that showered out bouquets of fiery red confetti with white streamers, made beautiful twilight pyrotechnics but fortunately did no damage. Lieutenant Eason claimed eight hits and observed a tremendous explosion on the carrier, with flames 200 feet high. But whatever damage he did inflict was superficial, for it is not mentioned in the Japanese damage report of the battle, and *Ryuho* did not have to go home for repairs.

As the *Enterprise* Avengers pulled out of their dives, four Zekes got after them, but two broke away "to match two Hellcats that came screaming down out of a mêlée higher up." "The ships continued to fire 5-inch shells at us all the way out to the rendezvous area; looking back, the sky was a mass of bursting shells, flaming planes, and the Hellcats and Zekes still fighting it out above." [82]

Commander J. D. Arnold of Air Group 2 from *Hornet* was

[79] Story of crewmen George H. Blatz and Ellis C. Babcock, in *Belleau Wood* Air Action Report and *N.Y. Times* 6 July 1944.

[80] *Enterprise* Action Report, Enclosures, Narratives of Lt. (jg) R. W. Cummings and Lt. Eason.

[81] Cdr. W. R. Kane, when acting as air coördinator during the Saipan landings on 15 and 16 June, had been shot down by AA fire from "friendly transports" and had made a water landing, splitting a gash in his head; but, fitted with a special helmet, he led his fighter squadron on the 20th. Lt. C. D. Farmer's paper.

[82] Narratives by Lts. (jg) J. A. Doyle and E. J. Lawton in *Enterprise* VT–10 Action Report.

deeply concerned lest the biggest carrier escape, as she had at Coral Sea (in which he had fought), through pilots' concentrating on the smaller flattops. He therefore scouted ahead of a group that included *Yorktown's* torpedo-bombers as well as his own, selected *Zuikaku,* and ordered an attack on her. The "Happy Crane" [83] had no Zekes to defend her, but she had not yet run out her luck. All but four of Arnold's Avengers had been armed with 500-pound G.P. bombs instead of "fish," and *Zuikaku* dodged the two torpedoes that were dropped. Dive-bombers from *Enterprise* and *San Jacinto* joined the fray. "*Zuikaku* was also strafed," said Captain Ohmae, "as I well know, since I was on the bridge with Admiral Ozawa when Commander Ishigura, standing by his side, was struck by a machine-gun bullet splinter. The three or four strafing planes were very brave and came in low." In this onslaught the big carrier received several bomb hits and five near-misses. The explosions started several fires on the hangar deck which quickly became unmanageable, and the order Abandon Ship was actually given; but before it could be completely executed the damage control party reported progress, the order was rescinded, and all fires were brought under control. *Zuikaku* returned to Kure under her own power and was repaired in time to get sunk in the 25 October battle off Cape Engaño.[84]

Four Avengers from *Monterey,* accompanied by eight from *Bunker Hill* and four from *Cabot* and eight *Bunker Hill* Hellcats, sighted the oiler group first; but the group leader, Lieutenant R. P. ("Rip") Gift of *Monterey,* radioed to his fellows, "To hell with the merchant fleet, let's go get the fighting Navy!" So they continued westward to attack Kurita's van — the *Chiyoda* group — at the southwest angle of the Japanese trapezoid. These Avengers, too, were armed only with 500-pound G.P. bombs. They made one hit on *Chiyoda* aft, which set her afire and wrecked her flight deck; one hit on battleship *Haruna* of the charmed life, which flooded a

---

[83] See Vol. III of this History, p. 88.
[84] *Hornet* Aircraft Action Report 1 July 1944 II 380–86; Letter from Capt. Ohmae, 1952; Hajime Fukaya "The Shokakus," U.S. Naval Inst. *Proceedings* LXXVIII (1952) p. 641.

magazine; and a near-miss on cruiser *Maya* that caused fires to break out. Encountering only two Zekes over the target, they splashed one and made a fairly peaceful retirement.[85] It was perhaps just as well that nearby *Zuiho* and *Chitose*, who counted battleships *Yamato* and *Musashi* in their screens, were neglected by Lieutenant Gift's formation.

Considering the lack of time to coördinate attacks, the pressure that American pilots were under to hit and run while darkness descended over the sea, they were successful. They had sunk another carrier and downed two thirds of Ozawa's remaining aircraft. Only 20 of the 216 attacking American planes were lost in action,[86] and a number of their pilots and crewmen were later recovered. Undoubtedly the attack would have done even better if more of the Avengers had been armed with torpedoes instead of bombs. But air torpedoing in the United States Navy had never entirely recovered from the beating it had taken at Midway, in spite of the substitution of Avengers for the obsolete Devastators, and of better aërial torpedoes fitted with "pickle-barrel" false heads, enabling them to be dropped from higher altitudes and at greater speeds. Dive-bombing had established itself at Midway as the best method to sink carriers. Moreover, few big ships suitable as torpedo targets had been encountered by the carrier planes for a year. All this added up to neglect of air torpedoing in the United States Navy; but the results of this battle reversed the trend.[87]

As the Americans retired, there was no pursuit, and the only attacks were delivered within sight of the Japanese Fleet. Eight torpedo-bombers from *Cabot* and *Monterey*, and dive-bombers from *Enterprise* and other carriers which were retiring after attacks on *Chiyoda*, *Hiyo* and *Zuikaku*, were jumped by six or

[85] *Monterey* Aircraft Action Report No. 6, compared with *Camp. Pac. War* 245–46, and Lt. (jg) C. A. Dunn's paper.
[86] See end of chapter for total score of the day.
[87] Commander Air Group 25 (Lt. Cdr. G. B. Brown of *Cowpens*) Aircraft Action Report 4 July 1944; cf. Commander Air Group 2 (Cdr. J. D. Arnold of *Hornet*) Aircraft Action Report 29 June.

seven Hamps from high altitude. Commander Ralph L. Shifley and his wingman, Lieutenant (jg) Gerald R. Rian USNR, both flying Hellcats from *Bunker Hill,* saw that the Avengers were likely to get into trouble and went after the Hamps with great skill and energy. They saw one splash and another depart from the scene, smoking; actually only one pilot of this Japanese group returned safely to *Zuikaku,* claiming a bag of 19 American planes for himself and his fellows. They did shoot down two Helldivers before encountering Shifley and Rian, but none of the Avengers were even damaged.[88]

Seven torpedo-bombers, which Ozawa had caused to be launched from *Zuikaku* half an hour before the Americans struck, turned back without finding anything. On their way home they crossed the returning American planes but avoided conflict. The story of a Japanese Val's following our planes and making three attempts to light on *San Jacinto,*[89] though firmly believed on board that "flagship of the Texas Navy," is probably apocryphal, as is the tale of a second enemy plane being waved off from *Wasp.* As far as I can determine, not a single Japanese plane came within sight of Task Force 58 on 20 June.

Ozawa would not yet accept defeat. At 1900, just as the air battle ended, he actually ordered a surface counterattack. Admiral Kurita and the entire van, together with heavy cruisers *Myoko* and *Haguro* and a destroyer squadron, were ordered to head east and seek night action. At the end of two hours, since the position of Task Force 58 was still unknown to him, Ozawa reluctantly canceled the order, and at 2205 Kurita reversed course to rejoin the main body. He never could have reached Mitscher, who at that moment lay about 230 miles to the southeast, recovering planes.

At noon of 20 June, Ozawa had about 100 carrier planes operational in the Mobile Fleet. By nightfall he had lost 65 more, and, of the 27 float planes remaining at noon, 15 were destroyed. His

---

[88] CTG 58.2, *Bunker Hill,* and Commander Air Group 8 (Cdr. Shifley) Action Reports, which agree with Japanese Cardiv 1 log. These were the only enemy planes sighted that day by the TG 58.2 strike group. Lt. (jg) C. D. Smith and Lt. (jg) J. O. McIntire, the two SB2C pilots, were lost.

[89] *San Jacinto* Action Report pp. 78, 85.

own flag log of Operation A-Go ends this day with the significant entry: —

Surviving carrier air power: 35 aircraft operational.[90]

Thirty-five planes out of the 430 which he had had in his hangars and on his flight decks the morning of 19 June!

c. Night Recovery, 2045–2300

Complete darkness fell by 1945. The weather front had moved south during the day, the sky was overcast and the night very dark, and planes returning from the battle were a long way from "home." The pilots knew it was nip-and-tuck whether their fuel would hold out; one, Lieutenant (jg) Milton F. Browne usnr of *Wasp*, had to ditch halfway home, as his gas tank had been punctured.[91] Although TF 58 had slightly closed Ozawa's fleet during the hours subsequent to launching, the carriers had to turn to windward to recover planes. Their distance from the Japanese targets now varied from 240 to 298 miles, depending on the time the planes started to return, and the distance they had to consume while orbiting before having a chance to land.[92] This, and flying at high speed in the hope of beating nightfall,[93] caused many to run out of gas.

Admiral Mitscher opened out his three task groups so that 15 miles lay between them, to give maneuvering room for night recovery. At 1912, for the second time in this operation, he proposed that Admiral Lee's battle line be released from protecting the carriers while they were steaming to windward for plane recovery, and that they push northwesterly at top speed, to be in a position to engage Ozawa's Fleet at daylight. Admiral Lee, apparently, was not consulted, and Spruance a second time refused to allow the

[90] Japanese Monograph No. 91, p. 23 of typescript. This says "25" but that is a mistranslation; the Japanese original says "35."

[91] *Wasp* Bombron 14 Action Report 29 June 1944. Browne and his gunner were rescued two days later by a PBM that had gone beyond the assigned search area.

[92] *Bunker Hill* Action Report 13 July.

[93] Cdr. R. M. Smeeton rn (see chap. xvii note 1) declared that the American aviators wasted gas by unnecessary high-speed flying, but this is not true of all. One bomber pilot from *Bunker Hill*, flying alone in the darkness to conserve fuel, hit the water at 130 knots. He and his gunner were later rescued.

battle line to separate. "Consider Task Force 58 should be kept tactically concentrated tonight," he replied, "and make best practicable speed toward the enemy so as to keep them in air striking distance." [94] He figured out that Lee had no chance of overtaking Ozawa, and wished to keep his battle line within signaling distance in order to dispose of any damaged ships that the aviators might encounter next day.

At 2045 the returning planes began to circle over the American carriers. Task Force 58 turned into the light east wind and bent on 22 knots. Admiral Mitscher then made a decision that endeared him to the hearts of all naval aviators; he gave orders to light up the carriers in bold disregard of enemy submarine or plane menace.

That night recovery, lasting two hours, was the most spectacular event of these two crowded days. Lieutenant Commander Evan P. Aurand, who was sent aloft in a night-fighting Hellcat to help shepherd the flock home, had the best view. The scene made him think of a Hollywood première, Chinese New Year's and Fourth of July rolled into one. The carriers turned on truck lights, glow lights to outline flight decks, and red and green running lights, and flashed signal lights to identify themselves; all vessels of the screen showed red truck lights and their 5-inch guns threw up a liberal supply of star shell. Each group flagship pointed a searchlight vertically as a homing beacon. The night was pitch black with no visible horizon, and about sixty miles to the south a thunderstorm was making up, whose lightning flashes were mistaken by a number of homing pilots for star shell. Aurand made several trips over to the storm, turning on his running lights and rounding up lost fliers.

One of the best accounts of the night landings is by Lieutenant (jg) E. J. Lawton USNR of *Enterprise:* —

We had almost reached the force when we saw the lights come on. It is clear that the task force did all in its power to make it easier for us to get home. Lieutenant Eason led us in over the *Enterprise* but her deck was fouled for some time. We circled for a few minutes, watching the lights of the planes below fan out in the pattern of the landing

[94] CTF 58 Report p. 58.

circle. But there had been too much strain in the last five hours to reduce things to patterns now; and inevitably, landing circles became
crowded, intervals were lost and deck crashes occurred. Many planes
— too many — announced that their gas was gone and they were going
in the water. Others were caught short in the groove. Seen from above,
it was a weird kaleidoscope of fast moving lights forming intricate trails
in the darkness, punctuated now and then by tracers shooting through
the night as someone landed with his gun switches on, and again by
suddenly brilliant exhaust flames as each plane took a cut, or someone's
turtleback light getting lower and lower until blacked out by the waves
closing over it. A Mardi Gras setting fantastically out of place here,
midway between the Marianas and the Philippines.[95]

Lieutenant Eason's tank went dry just as he was approaching the
ramp of *Lexington*. He quickly pulled his wheels up, made an S-
turn to port, landing in the water alongside, and was rescued by a
destroyer within ten minutes. A Helldiver from *Hornet* crash-
landed on *Bunker Hill*, although waved off and given Very signals
indicating foul deck. The plane up-ended with its propeller fast-
lodged in the flight deck; then along came an Avenger from *Cabot*
which, although violently warned to keep off, tried to land,
knocked a wing off on a gun mount, and crashed the immobilized
Helldiver, killing two and injuring four men who were working on
the wreckage.[96] Almost half the aircraft landed on the wrong
carriers, and when noses were counted there were often found
planes belonging to eight or nine different ships on one flight deck.
Desperate pilots made passes at everything afloat. Ensign R. W. Burnett USNR of *Monterey*, waved off from his own carrier, mistook the
red truck lights on a destroyer for those of a landing signal officer
on a flattop, made a pass at the destroyer and splashed alongside. A
boat from the destroyer rescued him and his crewmen before they
were fairly wet. Another pilot, from a light carrier, said to himself
that he wasn't going to land on her short flight deck; he would pick
out the biggest damn carrier there was. He did, and found that it
was his own!

[95] *Enterprise* Action Report, Enclosure on VT–10. Lt. Lawton landed on
Princeton.
[96] *Bunker Hill* Action Report p. 12. The ship's air officer, Cdr. "Wingover"
Smith, was killed.

By 2252 when it was clear that every plane had either landed, splashed, or been shot down, and as the carriers were formed up again into cruising disposition, the sea suddenly took on the appearance of a meadow full of fireflies in June. Pilots and crewmen, swimming or in rubber rafts, were blinking their little waterproof flashlights; and the trilling of the boatswain's whistles that aviators carried to attract attention added hyla-like music to this midsummer scene. Fortunately there was now a flat calm. The destroyers, using their 18-inch searchlights to spot rafts and swimmers, did wonderful rescue work, and all but one were so employed by Admiral Mitscher's orders; anti-submarine screening was completely neglected in favor of saving lives. The great laugh of the evening came at the expense of Lieutenant Commander K. F. Musick, torpedo squadron commander of *Bunker Hill*. He had splashed on an earlier operational flight and had been pulled out by destroyer *Hickox*. This time he ditched again for want of gas and was picked up by the same destroyer, on whose stack, next the painted miniatures of planes shot down, he found a caricature of himself to which a sailor was adding a "hash mark" to celebrate the second rescue!

Because of this hectic night recovery, plane losses on 20 June were much heavier than those of the previous day, but the casualties among aviators were almost the same. According to Admiral Mitscher's report, 6 Hellcats, 10 Helldivers and 4 Avengers were missing, and presumably shot down in combat; 17 Hellcats, 35 Helldivers and 28 Avengers were destroyed by deck crashes or ditching near the task force. The total complement in the lost planes was 100 pilots and 109 aircrewmen, but 51 and 50 were pulled out of the water that night, leaving 49 and 59 unaccounted for by daylight 21 June. An additional 33 pilots and 26 aircrewmen were saved on that and subsequent days. This left the net aviator losses 16 pilots and 33 crewmen.[97] *Hornet*, the lucky carrier, lost 21 aircraft on 20 June but only one pilot and two crewmen, one of whom was killed in a deck crash.

[97] Cf. table at end of chap. xvi. Add 2 officers and 4 enlisted men of CV crews killed in deck crashes. Fifth Fleet War Diary p. 37; Land and Van Wyen Report pp. 6–58.

CHAPTER XVI

Battle of the Philippine Sea, Conclusion

20–24 June

1. Stern Chase, 20–22 June

ADMIRAL OZAWA'S problem of plane recovery differed only in degree from that of Admiral Mitscher. As soon as the last American plane departed, around 1930 June 20, the few surviving Japanese aircraft came home. Even less prepared for night landings than the Americans, the enemy aviators had worse luck, and the few of them that were left could ill be spared. What with splashes and crashes on damaged carrier decks, less than half of the 100 carrier planes that Ozawa had left early that afternoon were recovered; and only 35 of these were in a condition to fly again. But the engineering plant of every ship afloat was intact. So when Ozawa received Admiral Toyoda's order to retire at 2046 June 20, his 6 remaining carriers, 5 battleships, 13 cruisers and 28 destroyers were able to maintain a speed of 20 knots, ample for escape.

Spruance's stern chase had already begun, but it was not a relentless pursuit. As we have seen, he had rejected Mitscher's suggestion at 1912 June 20, to release Lee's battle line immediately in the hope of catching Ozawa.[1] It was a mathematical certainty that

---

[1] Combatdiv 9 (Rear Adm. Hanson) approved this decision: "The high speeds required during the air battle of the 19th, plus those used on the night of the 19th trying to overtake the enemy, made serious inroads on destroyers' fuel on hand. By the morning of the 21st the average fuel supply of the destroyers was 33 per cent; the lowest, 24 per cent. This made a chase at high speed impracticable."

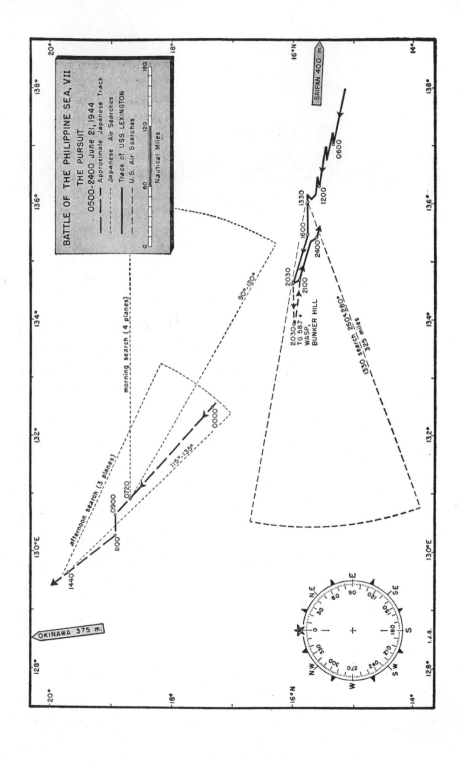

BATTLE OF THE PHILIPPINE SEA, VII
THE PURSUIT
0500-2400 June 21, 1944

———————— Approximate Japanese Track
·················· Japanese Air Searches
——————— Track of USS LEXINGTON
— — — — — U.S. Air Searches

Nautical Miles
0   60   120   180

SAIPAN 400 m.

OKINAWA 375 m.

0600
1200
1330
1600
2030
2100
2400

2030α TG 58.7 +
WASP,
BUNKER HILL

1330 search 250°-280°
325 miles

90°-120°

115°-135°

morning search (4 planes)

afternoon search (3 planes)

0720
0900
1100
1440
0000

even the faster and best-fueled ships could never overtake able-bodied units of the Japanese Fleet this side of Japan. Even if some of the battle line could have sustained a speed of 30 knots, which is doubtful, they would have closed only 120 miles in 12 hours, a little more than one third of the distance to the enemy. At Mitscher's recommendation, a force speed of 16 knots was maintained "in order to retrieve as many pilots as possible," [2] and that was 4 knots less than Ozawa was doing. By 0130 June 21 the two Fleets were 327 miles apart, the Japanese bearing W by N (285°) from the Americans,[3] and during the first three watches of 21 June TF 58 made good only 150 miles. It was actually losing distance on the enemy.

Spruance's only reason for pursuit under these circumstances was the hope of catching cripples or ships standing by them. For aught anybody on the American side yet knew, *Shokaku* and *Hiyo* were still afloat, and nobody was so optimistic as to assume that one torpedo hit had finished *Taiho*. A report received at 0130 June 21, from a PBM which had been shadowing the enemy force for two and a half hours, to the effect that Ozawa's ships were trailing oil, suggested that some were badly damaged. So, in the hope that either Lee's battle line or Mitscher's carrier planes would catch up with these lame ducks and their consorts at daylight, Spruance steamed westward at economical speed.

Task Force 58 recommenced searching only a few hours after recovery was completed. Several long-range night-flying Avengers were sent out from *Bunker Hill* and *Enterprise* between 0200 and 0300. Next, at 0600, each task group launched a deckload strike of Hellcats carrying 500-pound bombs in the hope of finding cripples. The pilots were instructed to return if they found nothing after flying 300 miles. Nothing did they find; but the Avengers picked up the Mobile Fleet and shadowed it until 0743, reporting the enemy to be on a northwesterly course, 360 miles distant from

[2] CTF 58 Action Report p. 60.
[3] From the PBM contact mentioned below, in Fifth Fleet War Diary p. 31. The respective positions at that time were lat. 16°30′ N, long. 132°48′ E, and lat. 15°17′ N, long. 137°07′ E.

TF 58.[4] Ozawa had opened the distance. He was already well beyond the effective radius of American carrier bombers.

When this information reached Spruance, it confirmed his belief that the main body of the Mobile Fleet was pressing homeward at a speed greater than Task Force 58 could possibly overcome. But he still cherished the hope of overtaking a few ships that had been slowed down by battle damage. Leaving Mitscher with orders to search for cripples and to seize every opportunity to strike, Spruance at 1050 June 21 directed Admiral Lee, now reinforced by *Bunker Hill* and *Wasp* for air protection, to push ahead at best speed, and himself at 1126 took *Indianapolis* forward to join the battle line. The carriers followed, making good about 15 knots; destroyers of the screen fished out several airmen en route.

By this time some of the destroyers with the battleships were dangerously low on fuel. So there was a further delay, from 1205 to 1454, while battleships fueled destroyers, steaming at 11 to 14 knots. At 1516 a 15-knot speed was resumed, on course 280°.

The Hellcats launched at dawn had now returned, with no information. The next search group, launched at 1500, combed the empty waters of the Philippine Sea for the hypothetical Japanese cripples. Spruance mentally allowed them four hours to make contact. At 1920 June 21, shortly after the sun went down in a big red ball, Commander Fifth Fleet issued orders that, if the late afternoon search sighted no ships, the entire task force would retire. None did they see, since none there were; so at 2030, when *Lexington* was at lat. 16° N, long. 134°40′ E, the chase was abandoned and course shaped for Saipan. Lee's ships, having reached long. 133°55′ E,[5] right on the edge of the battle area of 20 June, searched carefully for survivors and made a very encouraging haul. Float planes from *Indianapolis, San Francisco* and *New Orleans* picked up nine men. Mitscher, too, sent off an

---

[4] CTF 58 Action Report p. 61; narrative of flight by Lt. R. S. Nelson USNR, attached to *Enterprise* Action Report.

[5] This was 545 miles from Samar and 675 from Saipan, according to Com Fifth Fleet Action Report p. 15. In other words, Lee had had time to gain only about 45 miles on Mitscher.

abundance of low-flying searches and a number of destroyers to cover a wide sector from the position where Ozawa's ships had been attacked. Dumbo Catalinas and PBMs from Saipan were enlisted in the search, and these painstaking efforts were rewarded by the rescue of 59 aviators who otherwise must have perished in the Philippine Sea, so far were they from friendly shores.

At the moment Spruance abandoned the chase, the Mobile Fleet was about 300 miles from Okinawa, toward which Ozawa had shaped his course that morning. That evening (21 June) Ozawa called his senior staff officer, Captain Ohmae, into his cabin and dictated a letter to Commander in Chief Combined Fleet, offering his resignation. He expressed the deepest regret that he had lost this opportunity once more to lead Japan on the glorious path of victory. The defeat he ascribed to his own inadequacy, and to the pilots' want of training. Toyoda, after consulting with the navy minister in the Tojo Cabinet, refused to accept Ozawa's resignation. The veteran retained his command, only to be beaten again by Halsey in the Battle of Cape Engaño and there to lose most of the carriers that had survived the Philippine Sea action.

In the early afternoon of June 22 a defeated and dispirited Mobile Fleet anchored in Nakagasuku Bay, Okinawa [6] — the great harbor which a year later was to be renamed after General Buckner. Four of the six surviving carriers, together with battleship *Haruna* and heavy cruiser *Maya*, had to proceed to Japan either for repairs or for long-needed upkeep. Worst of all, the Fleet had brought back only 35 serviceable carrier planes.

Task Force 58 made for a prearranged fueling rendezvous with a task group of fleet tankers, about 220 miles east of the point where retirement had commenced.[7] At noon 22 June the oilers were encountered; fueling commenced at once, continued at 10-knot speed, until nightfall, and was completed next day.

[6] *Tone* War Diary (WDC 160,144, N.A. 11,841).
[7] The position, according to *Monterey's* log, was lat. 15°32' N, long. 138°29' E. For composition of this oiler group, TG 50.17, see Task Organization in Appendix II.

While Admiral Reeves's group was still fueling, there took place a remarkable single combat between a *Princeton* plane and a Japanese bomber. An Avenger (TBM–1C) piloted by Ensign Warren C. Burgess USNR, on anti-submarine patrol at noon 23 June, sighted a Betty flying low over the water and heading away from the carriers. She was probably engaged in a routine search, from Yap or Palau. By making all possible speed — 245 to 250 knots — Burgess overtook the enemy, then flying only 10 feet above the ocean. He made two low runs, firing with his twin .50-caliber wing-guns; but both times his guns jammed and he had to drop back. To continue with the account by Burgess's squadron commander, Lieutenant Commander F. A. Bardshar:

Burgess decided it was time to change his tactics and splash the Betty without the aid of gunfire. He put his plane about two feet above her and sat there in an attempt to force her into the water. He succeeded in forcing the Betty to hit the water with her belly, but she immediately bounced back up to ten feet, her initial altitude, with no damaging results. Abandoning this procedure, Burgess retired to the Betty's starboard side and during retirement the TBM–1C's stinger was able to fire about thirty rounds into the after port side of the Japanese fuselage.

Burgess next decided to adopt the Russian technique of chewing up the enemy plane with his propeller. This was also unsuccessful, although his prop. came within inches of the Betty's starboard wing. Feeling somewhat frustrated, Burgess flew wing on the Betty with about two feet between wing tips. He looked over and waved at the Japanese pilot, who only toothed back at him. At this juncture the turret gunner of the torpedo plane in desperation opened his hatch and emptied all six rounds of his .38-caliber revolver into the Betty, with unobserved results on the enemy but with great elation to the gunner.

Tiring of this, Ensign Burgess crossed over top of the enemy plane and retired to about a quarter of a mile away on the Betty's port side. He managed to get his starboard wing-gun charged, and made a pass at the Betty's port side. This time his tracers went into the starboard engine and it burst into flames. The flames spread to the starboard wing, Betty lost control, her port wing dipped into the water, and she executed a neat cartwheel. Ensign Burgess saw one survivor in the water, who was picked up almost immediately by a friendly destroyer.[8]

[8] *Princeton* Aircraft Action Report 1 July 1944.

Fueling completed, Admiral Spruance in *Indianapolis*, with the fire support ships that he had borrowed from Turner, took station off Saipan, arriving in the afternoon of 23 June. Three of Mitscher's fast carrier groups were ordered to proceed to Eniwetok for a brief rest; but Admiral Clark had something else in mind.

2. *"Operation Jocko," 24 June* [9]

"Jocko" Clark, who had been O.T.C. at the strikes on Iwo and Chichi Jima the previous week, felt the pressure of unfinished business. Owing to weather and a big battle coming up, he had not had time to give those islands a proper working over. Why not strike them again before retiring to Eniwetok? Accordingly he started north after fueling and at 1400 June 23 "advised CTF 58 by dispatch that unless otherwise directed this Group would strike Iwo Jima . . . morning of 24 June while en route to Eniwetok." Mitscher heartily approved, and thereafter referred to this diversion as "Operation Jocko."

Clark's expectation that there would be plenty of game up north was well founded. The Japanese were trying to reinforce the Tinian and Guam airfields. Owing to foul weather, the squadrons had been so delayed that now there was a backlog of 122 planes on Iwo and Chichi Jima,[10] awaiting word from Admiral Kakuta at Tinian that damaged airfields had been repaired and were ready to receive them.

By 0600 June 24 *Hornet, Yorktown, Bataan* and *Belleau Wood*, with their screen of cruisers and destroyers, had reached a point 235 miles SE by S of Iwo Jima. The weather was rough, but not nearly so bad as on the previous visit. While the first three carriers launched a fighter sweep of 51 Hellcats, each armed with a 500-

---

[9] TG 58.1 War Diary (enclosed in Action Report 14 July); *Hornet* War Diary and Air Action Report; Cincpac Monthly Analysis for June p. 95.

[10] Japanese Monograph No. 91 p. 25: 21 long-range bombers, 59 carrier fighters, 38 bombers, 4 recce planes (Capt. Ohmae). According to Capt. A. Sasaki's interrogation, "Of the pilots employed, only about one third were experienced, the others being students." *Inter. Jap. Off.* II 396.

pound bomb to destroy grounded planes, *Belleau Wood* assumed combat air and anti-submarine patrol for the group.[11]

The 51 Hellcats had an unexpected battle en route. Clark had been snooped by a Japanese patrol plane shortly before reaching his launching position, enabling Admiral Sadaichi Matsunaga, commanding 27th Air Flotilla at Iwo, to fly off all his fighters and a few bombers to intercept. At 0815 they met the Americans about halfway. The Hellcats jettisoned bombs and piled in; then there was a battle royal in the air. At the end of it, 24 Japanese fighters (Zekes and Hamps) and 5 Judys[12] had been shot down, at the cost of 6 Hellcats. Four Hellcats which had clung to their bombs continued to Iwo and dropped them on the airfield; the rest returned to their carriers.

They arrived none too soon. Matsunaga, eager for revenge, had already sent one raid against the carriers, and was about to send a second. The first, consisting of about 20 torpedo-bombers, was completely destroyed — some shot down by C.A.P., others by the task group's antiaircraft fire. Of the second — 9 Jills, 9 Judys and 23 Zekes and Hamps — "The results were vague and the target was not sighted."[13] Intercepted at a good distance from the carrier group by combat air patrol and special scrambles of fighter planes, this raid was turned back after losing 7 Jills and 10 Zekes. Not too vague, after all!

Occasional dogfights continued until 1830. Half an hour later, Clark assumed cruising disposition and proceeded to Eniwetok. A few planes still hovered around, dropping "window" and flares, but no more attacks developed.

This destruction of 66 more planes undoubtedly contributed to the conquest of Saipan. After a third raid on Iwo and Chichi Jima, with which Admiral "Jocko" celebrated the Fourth of July, the Hachiman air group was so weakened by combat and operational

[11] It had been Mitscher's doctrine for some time that the light carriers assume these routine duties, but this had not been practicable during the big battle.

[12] Figures corrected in Japan from original claim of 58 VT and 10 VB shot down in the first interception and 34 to 46 in the second.

[13] Japanese Monograph No. 91.

losses that on the 7th the remnant of 41 Zekes and 13 bombers was sent back to Japan.

Clark's interest in the "Jimas" had become so marked that the aviators caused to be printed a certificate of membership in the "Jocko Jima Development Corporation," offering "Choice Locations of all Types in Iwo, Chichi, Haha and Muko Jima, Only 500 Miles from Downtown Tokyo." Signed by Admiral Clark as "President of the Corporation," one of these diplomas was awarded to every participant.

A similar interdicting action was performed on the southern flank by the XIII Army Air Force, based at Los Negros. Following strikes on Woleai on 20 and 22 June, B–24s flew an average of 21 daily sorties against Yap for five days, 23–27 June. And for five days slightly earlier, 19–23 June, Kwajalein-based Liberators flew high-altitude bombing missions against Truk. These close to 1000-mile bombing missions were costly — two B–24s shot down and 21 damaged in the attacks on Yap.[14]

3. *Victory*

The immediate reaction in Task Force 58 to the Battle of the Philippine Sea was one of disappointment and vexation. Admiral Clark, only ten days after, told this writer, "It was the chance of a century missed." Admiral Mitscher thus concluded his action report: "The enemy escaped. He had been badly hurt by one aggressive carrier strike, at the one time he was within range. His fleet was not sunk." Admiral Montgomery wrote: —

Results of the action were extremely disappointing to all hands, in that important units of the enemy fleet, which came out in the open for the first time in over a year and made several air attacks on our superior force, were able to escape without our coming to grips with them. It is true that our troops on Saipan were well screened and protected against the enemy surface force, but it is considered unfor-

[14] Craven and Cate *Army Air Forces in World War II* IV 687–88.

tunate that our entire strength was deployed for this purpose and therefore not permitted an opportunity to take the offensive until too late to prevent the enemy's retirement.[15]

At naval air headquarters in Pearl Harbor the line was, "This is what comes of placing a non-aviator in command over carriers." Admiral Spruance had never won wings, but that does not prove that he did not know what to do with naval air power. After all, he more than anyone else had won the Battle of Midway. He was not infallible, of course. In warfare, where decisions have to be made promptly on imperfect intelligence of the enemy, mistakes are inevitable; and in considering a commander's actions we should base judgment on his reaction to factors known or legitimately guessed by him at the time, not on the fuller knowledge that reaches an historian years later.

There was no distinction between Spruance and Mitscher in aggressiveness, fighting spirit or desire to come to grips with the enemy. The difference in their respective attitudes was due to the scope of their respective responsibilities. Mitscher was responsible only for TF 58; hence his absorbing passion was to destroy the Japanese carriers that menaced his carriers. Spruance had the overall responsibility for Operation "Forager"; for the Joint Expeditionary Force as well as the carriers; for the troops ashore on Saipan and the Guam assault force, which was still hanging in the bight. His objective was to secure the Marianas. Imbued with a strong sense of that mission, Spruance refused to be diverted; he was unwilling to accept the risk that the Japanese ships reported up to the early hours of 19 June might be only a detachment of the Mobile Fleet.

On the other side, there are three alleged counts against Spruance. First, Mahan is quoted to the effect that the main object of a fleet is to destroy the enemy's fleet.[16] Second, that a powerful striking force as mobile as the fast carriers should never be tied to

---

[15] CTF 58 Action Report p. 62; CTG 58.2 Action Report pp. 9–10.

[16] But where did Mahan say this? The nearest thing we can find is in his *Naval Strategy* p. 199, where, discussing the Siege of Gibraltar, he says, "In war the proper main objective of the navy is the enemy's navy." And on pp. 220–21 his discussion strongly supports the decisions of Spruance in this battle.

the apronstrings of an amphibious operation. Third, that in view of the known strength of Ozawa's Mobile Fleet any possible "end run" could have been dealt with adequately by the ships left to guard Saipan. No danger of a flanking movement actually existed; but, in view of Japanese past performances, the possibility had to be anticipated. Military men never get any credit for guarding against dangers that might occur yet do not; but they are quickly "hanged" if they fail adequately to guard against dangers that do occur — witness Pearl Harbor.

Admiral Spruance, who is able to view his own actions candidly and without emotion, still thought eight years later that he had missed a great opportunity. "As a matter of tactics," he wrote to me in 1952, "I think that going out after the Japanese and knocking their carriers out would have been much better and more satisfactory than waiting for them to attack us; but we were at the start of a very important and large amphibious operation and we could not afford to gamble and place it in jeopardy. The way Togo waited at Tsushima for the Russian fleet has always been in my mind. We had somewhat the same basic situation, only it was modified by the long-range striking power of the carriers." [17]

Yet, would it have been better, as a matter of tactics, to have sought out Ozawa's Fleet on the night of 18–19 June and attacked it next morning? We cannot assume that fortune would have favored the strong — it did not do so at Midway. Our dive- and torpedo-bombers would probably have sunk some of the Japanese carriers; but the Japanese planes might also have sunk some of ours. And the "Turkey Shoot" could never have made such a spectacular score if Mitscher had had to divide his air forces between offense and defense; Ozawa's planes and antiaircraft would probably have doubled or trebled their small bag of American planes and pilots if he had been on the defensive on the morning of 19 June, and had been able on the 20th to employ his full air strength instead of a poor remnant. Moreover, Japanese land-based air forces at Guam could have got into the fight if the battle had been joined

[17] Letter to the writer 20 Jan. 1952.

halfway between Ozawa's position and the Marianas. Spruance, by steering east on the night of 18–19 June, against Mitscher's wishes and his own inclination, put Task Force 58 in about the optimum position to inflict the greatest damage on the enemy. His entire fleet was concentrated. All fighter planes were available for interception, and enemy planes that escaped them encountered the antiaircraft fire of Lee's battle line. And the Japanese planes on Guam were knocked out before they could take the offensive.

We have been discussing the Battle of the Philippine Sea as if it had been simply a carrier-plane battle, but the submarines and the anti-submarine vessels must not be forgotten. By their attrition of the Mobile Fleet even before it departed Tawi Tawi, by sending Spruance the only clear intelligence he had of enemy movements, and by sinking *Taiho* and *Shokaku*, United States submarines contributed heavily to the result. So, too, did the destroyer escorts and destroyers that broke up the Japanese submarine concentration to the south. The I- and RO-boats were then far distant from the Fifth Fleet; but if they had not been smothered by excellent anti-submarine tactics they might well have moved north and done a great deal of damage.

The battle also illustrates the inadequacy of land-based bombing, even when Navy-trained, as compared with carrier-based bombing. It may be conceded that Japanese land-based air *might* have given a better account of itself if General MacArthur's timely invasion of Biak had not caused its redeployment at the crucial moment. But the respectable component left on Guam and Yap before Saipan D-day, instead of wearing down and reducing the strength of the Fifth Fleet according to plan, was annihilated by carrier planes within a space of one week.

One technique in which the Americans fell far short of perfection was air search, on the part of land-based patrol planes as well as carrier planes.[18] Air search should have given the American

---

[18] Cruiser *Mobile* (Capt. C. J. Wheeler) Action Report: "This operation . . . did not show any improvement in our ability to search for, track, and retain con-

commanders adequate intelligence of the enemy's force and movements at least 24 hours earlier. If Ozawa's change of course in the early afternoon of 19 June had been reported, or if long-range night searches had been sent out by TF 58 after dark on the same day, they should have made contacts that would have enabled Spruance to get his fleet in position for a "one-two" strike on the 20th. And the PBM and PB4Y searches were ineffective because of communications failures.

In the matter of planes, the F6F Hellcat fully sustained its high reputation, and the two types of Avengers did well when given their proper weapon, the torpedo; but the new Helldiver (SB2C) was outshone by the two remaining squadrons of Dauntless dive-bombers (SBD). Unfortunately, nothing could be done about it, since the production lines were rolling with Helldivers; here the Dauntless fought her last battle.

Ozawa may be said to have conducted his fleet well. The Japanese plane searches kept him fairly in touch with the movements of Task Force 58 for 24 hours or more before Spruance knew where he was; and he made good use of the lee gauge. Commander Mobile Fleet avoided the usual (and always disastrous) Japanese strategy of feint and parry; he kept his inferior force together and gave battle at a distance that prevented his enemy from striking back immediately. His handling of the fueling problem, in view of the shortage of oil and scarcity of tankers, was masterly. But all this availed him naught because his air groups were so ill trained. As the Japanese post mortem on the battle said, quoting the modern version of a Japanese classic, the "Combat Sutra," chapter 49: "Good tactics should be applied only by a combat force that is well trained. Hence tactics may be compared to sandals. Good sandals should be worn by a strong-footed man. Then he can walk fast and long. A weak-footed man, even if he wears a pair of good sandals, can never walk as well as a strong-footed man." Ozawa had fine ships and good planes, but his aviators

---

tact with the enemy; he excels in all this, and once again took advantage of his superiority to get in the first attack."

were weak-winged through inexperience, and land-based air failed him completely.

Admiral Mahan never said that destruction of an enemy fleet was an object in itself, but a means to the greater ends of victory and a lasting peace. The Battle of the Philippine Sea contributed as much to victory as if Ozawa's fleet had been destroyed; for without its air arm the fleet was crippled, and the six carriers that survived were useful only as decoys to lure another American admiral to do what Spruance had declined to do. Admiral Toyoda had announced on 15 June, "The fate of the Empire rests on this one battle." He was right. It decided the Marianas campaign by giving the United States Navy command of the surrounding waters and air. Thus, the Japanese land forces in Saipan, Tinian and Guam were doomed, no matter how bravely and doggedly they fought. And victory in the Marianas made an American victory over Japan inevitable.

Admiral Spruance compared his tactics to those of Togo at Tsushima in 1905. An historical parallel more remote in time but closer in fact, because amphibious and land operations were involved, was the Yorktown campaign of 1781. In the naval battle off the Capes of the Chesapeake, on 5 September of that year, Admiral de Grasse defeated an inferior fleet under Admiral Thomas Graves RN that threatened to break into the Chesapeake and raise the siege of Yorktown. The battle itself was not tactically decisive since Graves lost but one of his nineteen capital ships, and De Grasse was criticized for not renewing action. But he covered the British in a week's maneuvering at sea, shouldering them away from the Cape long enough for a second French fleet to enter Hampton Roads with Rochambeau's siege artillery, and later to enter himself. In other words, De Grasse's sense of his mission, to support the Allied land campaign against Cornwallis, prevented him from risking the chance of throwing away his advantage. His cautious tactics rendered Cornwallis's surrender inevitable; and so won the War of Independence, although the British Fleet was not destroyed. Spruance's sense of his mission, to protect the amphibious operation against Saipan, precluded his running undue risks; he failed to annihilate the Japanese Fleet, but he won air and sea command, so that the Japanese forces in those islands were sealed off from any hope of reinforcement.

If General Saito, in command of Japanese forces on Saipan, had been a European, he would have emulated Cornwallis; being Japanese, his forces had to be annihilated. Saipan was Japan's Yorktown; and, although Ozawa's fleet was still formidable in fire power, that did not greatly matter after he had lost his air groups.

4. *Plane Losses*

a. Japanese

In view of the wild statements about Japanese plane losses in accounts of this battle published elsewhere, we have made every effort to arrive at the truth. The fixed points are these: —

Mobile Fleet at dawn 19 June [19] had 430 carrier and 43 float planes operational.

Mobile Fleet at dawn 20 June had 100 carrier and 27 float planes operational.

Mobile Fleet on 21 June had 35 carrier and 12 float planes operational.

In other words, Ozawa lost, in two days' searching and fighting 395 (92 per cent) of his carrier planes and 31 (72 per cent) of his float planes.

How these losses were incurred is more difficult to estimate. According to Japanese records of the successive searches and raids on 19 June: —

	No. Planes	*Failed to Return*	*Returned*
Three dawn searches	43	21	22
Raid I	69	42	27
Raid II	130	98	32
Raid III	47	7	40
1000 search	2	2	0
Raid IV	82	73	9
	373	243	130

[19] It had lost 5 CV search planes and 2 float planes on the searches of June 17–18.

In addition to those that failed to return, 22 went down with *Taiho* and *Shokaku*, making a total of 265 that were not back on board for the second day's fight, and 130 that were. If 354 carrier planes were launched 19 June (19 of the search planes were Jakes), 76 were left on board for C.A.P. and reserves. Subtracting the 22 that went down with the two carriers, we must add 54 to the 130 that returned from the raids, making 184 that should have been on board the morning of the 20th. But Japanese carrier records state that only 100 were serviceable. How about the other 84? Probably at least 75 carrier planes, plus 6 Jakes, were too damaged, either by fighting or bad landings, to fly again, and the other three were operational losses from the C.A.P.

Thus, Ozawa lost, in all, 330 of his 430 carrier planes together with 16 of his 43 float planes, on 19 June alone. Of the 354 carrier planes in searches and raids, 233 of which failed to return, 19 (of Raid IV) landed on Guam wrecked, and we may guess that at least 20 more, at one time or another, crashed on Guam or Rota. That leaves 194 "failed to return" planes to account for. The great majority of these must have been destroyed by American interceptions, most of the rest by antiaircraft fire, and a number by operational splashes and crashes. It is impossible from American records to decide exactly how many were accounted for by ships' antiaircraft fire and interceptors respectively; there are so many duplications. But, to those destroyed by enemy action we must add at least 65 of those that returned to their carriers, which were too damaged to fight again.

In addition the Japanese lost 18 Guam-based planes in air action 19–20 June and "about 62" on the ground. About 30 of these were under repair, so we shall not count them, although they were now completely destroyed. Assuming 32 destroyed on the ground plus 18 in the air, Guam-based losses add 50 to the total score.

In the searches and the twilight battle on 20 June, Mobile Fleet lost an additional 65 carrier planes and 15 float planes. Of these, 19 carrier planes were lost in combat and the rest operationally, according to Japanese sources; but it seems improbable that as many as 46 carrier and 15 float planes could have been lost operationally. I believe that at least 40 were shot down by the American raiders, but the Japanese, not knowing exactly what went on at twilight, listed as "operational" all that were not seen from their ships' decks to be shot down.

The certain final score is this: on 21 June the Mobile Fleet had left only 35 carrier planes (25 of them Zekes) and 12 float planes. In the two days' battle it lost 426 planes. Add an estimated 50 from Kakuta's Base Air Force at Guam, and you have 476 total Japanese plane losses in the Battle of the Philippine Sea. The number of aviators lost from the Mobile Fleet was about 445.

b. United States [20]

19 June

	VF	VT, VOS, VB	Total	Aviators
Interception and Search Missions				
Shot down or crashed due to damage	14	1	15	13
Operational losses	1	0	1	0
Shot down by friendly AA fire	1	0	1	1
Bombing Strikes on Guam				
Shot down or crashed due to damage	2	6	8	11
Operational losses	0	5	5	2
Totals	18	12	30	27

20 June

	VF	VT, VOS, VB	Total	Aviators
Missing in action, presumably shot down	6	14	20 ⎫	16 pilots,
Splashed near or crashed on TF 58	17	63	80 ⎭	33 crewmen
Totals	23	77	100	49
Total for 19 and 20 June	41	89	130	76

[20] Result of research by Ens. Pattee, in Action Reports.

CHAPTER XVII

Saipan Secured

21 June–9 July 1944

1. *The Pattern of Air and Naval Support*

WHILE, as Tennyson wrote,

> . . . there rain'd a ghastly dew
> From the nations' airy navies grappling in the central blue,

ground operations on Saipan went doggedly forward. As a result of the naval victory all Japanese forces ashore were sealed off and doomed; but, being Japanese, they forced the United States to pay a heavy price for the island.

The immediate effect of the naval battle was the reverse of what one would expect. When the Marines saw the transports and combatant ships retiring, they felt let-down, fearing Admiral Turner had abandoned them, as the Battle of Savo Island had forced him to do for a short time at Guadalcanal; but they soon learned better. The Japanese, on the contrary, assumed that their Navy had chased Turner away, and their joy was increased by the Tokyo broadcasts claiming eleven American carriers sunk. It took a long time for this optimism to wear off; even General Saito was expecting relief from the air as late as 7 July. It might have been a good idea for Task Force 58 to have put on a victory parade around Saipan after the Battle of the Philippine Sea!

If the Saipan garrison had heard the communiqué that Imperial Headquarters, Navy section, issued 24 June, they would certainly have been less hopeful. The government, changing the tone of bravado with which it had first announced the battle, stepped

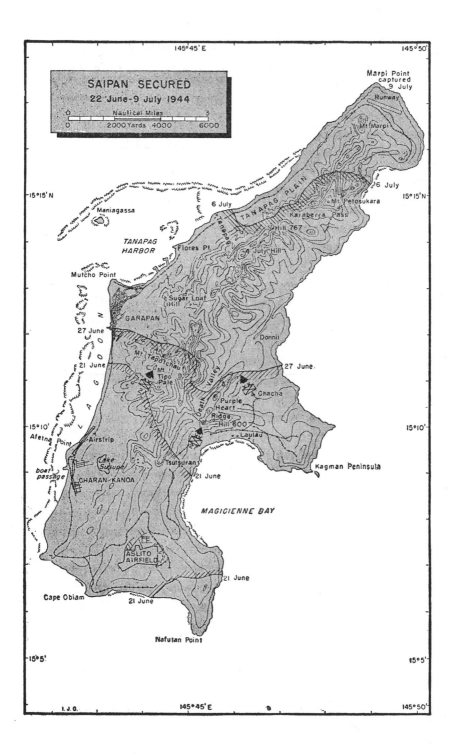

SAIPAN SECURED
22 June-9 July 1944

Nautical Miles

2000 Yards 4000 6000

Marpi Point
captured
9 July

Runway

Mt. Marpi

6 July

15°15'N

Mt. Petosukara

Maniagassa

6 July

TANAPAG PLAIN

Karaberra Pass

Tanapag

Hill 767

TANAPAG
HARBOR

Flores Pt.

4 July Hill

Mutcho Point

Sugar Loaf
Hill

GARAPAN

27 June

Donnii

L A G O O N

Mt. Tapotchau

21 June

Mt.
Tipo
Pale

27 June

Chacha

Death Valley

Purple
Heart
Ridge

15°10'

Afetna Point

Hill 600

Laulau

Airstrip

Lake
Susupe

Tsutsuran

Kagman Peninsula

boat
passage

CHARAN-KANOA

21 June

MAGICIENNE BAY

ASLITO
AIRFIELD

21 June

Cape Obiam

21 June

Nafutan Point

15°5'

I. J. G.

145°45'E

145°50'

down its claims to five carriers and "more than one battleship sunk or damaged," but admitted the loss of only one Japanese carrier. It described Task Force 58 as "the most powerful and destructive naval unit in the history of sea warfare" and the American advance as the greatest of the war, both in strength and in the "fury of fighting morale." It predicted that if the enemy captured Saipan and built an air base there, both the Philippines and Japan would be exposed to long-range bombing. For Japan had already been given a taste of the B–29s, raiding from their Chinese base. This was a new note in Japanese propaganda — preparing the people for the worst.

Pathetic attempts were made to reinforce Saipan. The commander at Tinian tried more than once to send troops across Saipan Channel at night, but the narrow seas were too closely watched for them to get through. Imperial Headquarters on 16 June ordered the 29th Division on Guam to send one battalion, and the 52nd Division, the garrison on Truk, to send two battalions, to help their comrades on Saipan. The commander at Truk replied that he had absolutely no transportation available. General Takashina started off two infantry companies with some artillery, in 13 large landing barges from Guam, on the night of 21–22 June; they made Rota by morning and at Rota they stayed until the end of the war.[1]

On 24 June Admiral Spruance, after conferring with Admiral Turner and General Holland Smith, decided to keep all fire support ships on hand and to maintain Conolly's Guam force at sea as floating reserve, until further notice.

Over two weeks of tough and bloody fighting lay ahead. The infantrymen of one Army and two Marine divisions bore the brunt; but never before had attack troops obtained so much and such good fire support. First, in the soldiers' estimation, was their own field artillery ranging from 75-mm pack howitzers to 155-mm cannon. Their fall of shot was spotted by their own "Grasshop-

---

[1] Japanese Monograph No. 48 (851–55) "Central Pacific Operations Record, Vol. I," p. 41.

pers" flying from the Charan Kanoa strip. The Navy daily provided scheduled, harassing, preparatory, deep-supporting, interdicting, counter-battery, and illuminating fires from the gunfire support ships. These vessels were now at the beck and call of the ground forces, the calls being cleared through shore fire support parties. By this time shore fire control sections of the Marines' "Jascos" (Joint Assault Signal Companies), one attached to each assault battalion and a naval liaison officer with every one, were well organized and working effectively.[2] But that was not all the Navy did, by any means. Certain destroyers such as *Albert W. Grant* were designated "sniper ships" to cruise near the coast and fire on targets of opportunity that presented themselves.[3] On several occasions LCI gunboats were employed to shoot right into the mouths of caves where Japanese troops were hiding. Every few days a gunfire ship was sent to investigate the Ushi Point Airfield on Tinian. A camouflaged Betty and several gun installations were destroyed there on 22 June; next day four planes that had just arrived, one a large transport, were discovered there and destroyed, as were three more new arrivals on the 24th.[4]

In addition to these duties, many of them new and most of them profitable, the gunfire support ships kept a constant watch over Saipan Channel for night barge crossings. Every few days some of the ships were detached to start the softening up process on Tinian and Guam in preparation for the landings on those two islands. And all these services continued right through to the end. Never before had the Navy done so much to help a ground operation, or stayed with it so long.

From the enemy point of view (as reported by prisoners), naval gunfire, especially the white phosphorus bursts over troops in the open, was more feared than field artillery or air bombing. "Major Yoshida stated that the most feared of our weapons was the naval

[2] CTF 56 (Gen. H. M. Smith) Report, Enclosure G, Naval Gunfire Officer (Lt. Col. E. G. Van Orman USMC) Report; starts at p. 1155 of Complete Report.
[3] See above, chap. xiii, §4. John Bishop "Sniper Ship," an account of call-fire activities of destroyer *Albert W. Grant* (under the pseudonym *Hellion*), appeared in *Sat. Eve. Post* 4 and 11 Nov. 1944.
[4] CTF 56 Report, Enclosure G, pp. 18, 36.

shelling which managed to reach the obscure mountain caves where their command posts were located. Second in effectiveness was the aërial bombing, and lastly artillery." Said a captured lieutenant, "The greatest single factor in the American success was naval gunfire." Asked how he differentiated between naval gunfire and land-based artillery, he laughed and said it was not difficult when one was on the receiving end. He said that everyone in the hills "holed up" and waited when a man-of-war started to fire. The ships' being able to get at them from any direction "was another [factor] leading to great respect for naval gunfire." [5] General Saito himself wrote, "If there just were no naval gunfire, we feel that we could fight it out with the enemy in a decisive battle." [6]

Equally impressive was the quantity and quality of air support. At the beginning of the campaign the escort carriers of the expeditionary force, under the command of Admirals Bogan, Sallada and Stump, maintained from dawn to dusk about 16 fighters and 20 bombers orbiting two air stations some eight miles off shore, from which to deliver call strikes promptly. This was a recent wrinkle in amphibious warfare, already used at Roi-Namur and Hollandia. Before 18 June the fast carrier forces also delivered close support, and from the 22nd on it was delivered by both escort carrier planes and Army P-47s based on Isely (ex-Aslito) Field.[7] Captain R. F. Whitehead, a career aviator now Commander Support Aircraft, directed the whole show from *Rocky Mount*, receiving calls from shore fire control parties with the advanced troops and relaying them to orbiting aircraft. A conversation recorded by the writer when listening in on the air net on board *Honolulu* will give some idea of what went on all day: —

COMMANDER SUPPORT AIRCRAFT *to a* SQUADRON COMMANDER: "Mission for you. Over target area 173–U,[8] orbit around so you can see the

---

[5] Same pp. 37–38 (p. 1192 of complete Report).
[6] Hoffman p. 168.
[7] CTF 51 Op Plan A10–44, Annex F; CTF 56 Report, Air Operations Report in Enclosure E, p. 3 (1149 of complete Report). TF 58 planes confined their attentions to Guam and Tinian after the carriers returned from Eniwetok.
[8] In the foothills 1.3 miles east of the boat passage. This conversation took place on 19 June beginning 0757.

whole area pretty good. Enemy troops in that ravine, our troops 200 yards west on crest of hill. Panels are laid out. Ground troops will designate target area with white phosphorus. You tell us when you want it laid out."

SQUADRON COMMANDER: "I can see three white panels. I'm going to take a run in there."

C.S.A.: "I'll have them lay white phosphorus right away."

S.C.: "Have them shoot the 'William Peter' right away."

C.S.A.: "Smoke is on the way."

S.C.: "I can see it now."

(*Silence for a few minutes.*)

S.C.: "Attack completed."

C.S.A.: "Very good. After the first run we got a report you were a little short, but the second one was a direct hit."

That request for an air strike was promptly executed. But the average time lag between call and delivery was over an hour, partly because there were 41 liaison parties competing for Captain Whitehead's ear on one communication circuit, partly owing to the pilots' difficulty in locating the exact areas to be strafed or bombed.[9]

Let us take a look at the scene from aloft, as viewed by a pilot of one of the escort carrier planes. Fire support ships look like ingenious toys blowing out gay powder-puffs of smoke, and the roar of their main batteries is muffled to a series of soft "bo-oo's." Landing craft with their white wakes might be a muster of pollywogs playing an elaborate game on the shore of a golden island set in a sapphire sea. Only a few whiffs of smoke and clouds of dust along the narrow dirt roads indicate that human beings are fighting ashore. It is as if you were poised over a bowl of Venetian crystal with a miniature seascape in the bottom, "set delicately humming by the play of a moist finger around its edge," [10] — the humming of airplane motors and amphtracs' diesels, the vibration of one's own plane, the drum-tap of machine-gun fire; for at 10,000 feet the rude cacophony of war becomes harmonious, in the Aeolian

[9] Isely and Crowl p. 334; Sherrod *History of Marine Corps Aviation* p. 252.
[10] Henry James, "The Jolly Corner."

mode. These fleeting impressions last but a few seconds. A vicious burst of flak rocks the plane and shatters the spell; an urgent call over voice radio orders you to go down and get a fieldpiece that is holding up the troops in Square 191 Q, and you must consult the gridded map and figure out which clump of trees harbors the enemy you are there to kill.

Despite the overwhelming defeat of Japanese air power at the Battle of the Philippine Sea, the enemy was still capable of mounting a diminishing series of small air raids right up to 7 July; some from Iwo Jima, others from Palau, even a few from repaired airfields at Guam. Escort carriers, fast carriers and bombardment ships made every effort to keep the enemy-held fields in Tinian, Rota and Guam neutralized, but they did not completely succeed in keeping Guam out of the picture.

A bold Betty came in after dark 22 June, one of a group of four bombers from Truk [11] to accomplish something. Battleships *Pennsylvania*, *Maryland* and *Colorado* were anchored abreast in Charan Kanoa roads, throwing up star shell; when the enemy plane, completely undetected by human eyes or radar, crossed *Pennsylvania's* bow on a level with sky control, neatly dropped a torpedo that hit *Maryland* well forward, and was off and away before a single gun opened up. *Maryland's* damage control party promptly shored up bulkheads and stopped leaks so that she was able to steam slowly home; but there were many red faces in the battlewagons. Admiral Oldendorf signaled Admiral Turner that unless the ships stopped firing star shell his big ones would have to put out to sea; so out they went, to spend most of the night at general quarters while more Bettys horsed around 8 or 10 miles away, dropping "window."

Shortly before midnight 23 June, a lone Betty, one of seven from Iwo Jima, dropped a stick of bombs in the wake of Admiral Oldendorf's flagship *Louisville*. At 0052 June 24 her companions made a fairly successful high-level bombing attack on the anchorage off Charan Kanoa. They caused minor damage to an LST, an LCT,

---

[11] Capt. Ohmae is our source for Japanese data on these raids.

two PCs and repair ship *Phaon*, and inflicted 18 casualties. That
evening (the 24th) four torpedo planes from Peleliu fueled at
Guam and attacked "what appeared to be a transport," but missed.

By this time the fire support ships had learned how to lay effective smoke screens over the transports, which remained in the
roadstead all night; and Army night fighters based on Isely Field,[12]
as well as Navy night fighters from the carriers, intercepted. Consequently, all later enemy air attacks were little more than nui-
sances. On 26 June at 2318 a low-flying torpedo plane collided
with the jumbo boom of cargo ship *Mercury* and fell apart. Its
torpedo entered the vessel's superstructure, but fortunately failed
to explode; there were eleven casualties. The following night
there was a roughly coördinated attack on the roadstead by three
Bettys from Truk, two Jills from Guam and six Bettys from Palau.
Over twenty bombs, of which one barely missed flagship *Cambria*,
dropped around the transports, and a few hit the ground near
Isely Field; but there was no damage, and two of the attacking
planes were lost. Again, on the nights of 28–29 June and 30 June–
1 July, intermittent attacks by bombers from Truk and Iwo Jima
were delivered on the airfield and the roadstead, but no damage.
As late as the night of 6–7 July, when the Japanese were assembling
for their last banzai charge, three planes from Guam and eight from
Truk attacked ships and ground positions, with complete lack of
success. Two were shot down by night-flying Hellcats of Task
Force 58, and one by destroyer *Hudson*.

The minesweepers, always present in amphibious operations and
seldom given their proper due, first swept Charan Kanoa and
Garapan roadsteads, and then, on 27 June, cleared Magicienne Bay
of 25 contact mines planted in expectation that the principal landing would take place there. Next day *Keokuk*, an auxiliary-net
cargo ship, laid 10,000 feet of anti-submarine net around the
Garapan anchorage. But no Japanese I- or RO-boat ever got a
torpedo past the patrolling destroyers.

[12] On 22–23 June 111 rocket-firing P-47s of VII A.A.F. landed on Isely Field
from escort carriers *Natoma Bay* and *Manila Bay*, which launched them about 60
miles off Saipan. P-61 night fighters came in on 24 June.

2. The Struggle for Mount Tapotchau, 21–26 June

At dawn 22 June the front line of the two Marine divisions extended from a point on the sea about 1000 yards north of Beach Red 1, across the narrowest part of southern Saipan, to about the center of Magicienne Bay. The 27th Division held the shores south and east of Isely Field, but Nafutan Point was still in enemy hands. General Holland Smith left the 2nd Battalion of the 105th RCT, 27th Division, to take care of the Point and ordered the 106th and 165th RCTs to prepare to take their places in the front line. The next advance was to go up and around Mount Tapotchau.

At 0600 June 22, with full naval gun and air support of Task Force 52 available, coördinated with 18 battalions of field artillery,[13] the 2nd and 4th Marine Divisions abreast, and the 27th Infantry Division still in reserve, jumped off in a coördinated attack to the northeast. The first day scored substantial gains on the lower slopes of Mount Tapotchau, including the summit of Mount Tipo Pale, with the right flank resting on the northern bight of Magicienne Bay.

Holland Smith now decided to employ his three divisions abreast. The 27th, less the one battalion on Nafutan Point, was directed to pass through the left of the 4th Marine Division that night, and on the morning of 23 June to join the attack at the center of the line. Major General Ralph Smith of the 27th Division, fearing lest his troops lose their way at night, delayed this maneuver until there was light enough to see; but during the four-mile uphill hike his columns became fouled up, with the result that the three battalions of the 27th started the attack 55 minutes, 2 hours, and 3 hours 15 minutes late, respectively.

This was a bad start for the 27th Division, and it never quite caught up. It was not due to any lack of courage on the part of the infantrymen, or even lack of experience; for the 27th had fought at Makin and Eniwetok. But the Army and the Marines

[13] Hoffman p. 126.

were trained to different tactics. As we have already seen, when they advanced on parallel lines on Eniwetok Island in February,[14] the Marine tactics in land fighting are to "by-pass strong points of resistance for mopping up by reserve elements, in order to press the attack to better ground, to reach and destroy the enemy."[15] But at least this Army Division had been taught to advance slowly and methodically behind a creeping artillery barrage, theoretically leaving little mopping up to do. Such tactics were unsuitable for terrain such as at Saipan, where the fighting led over heavily wooded glens and stony ridges pockmarked with caves where the enemy lay low, and whence he could be got out only by flame-throwers and demolition charges. The Marines had frequently confronted similar terrain and knew what to do; the 27th had fought only on flat coral atolls, and did not. It was too readily held up by one well-concealed machine gun or knot of riflemen. Such tactics were peculiarly exasperating to Marines, who felt that they must keep the enemy moving or he would dig in deep; they were desperately anxious not to let the offense bog down, as the Army had done at Munda.

On 23 June the two battalions of the 165th RCT advanced about 400 yards, the 106th RCT not at all. On their right a regiment of the 4th Division Marines captured Hill 600, overlooking the Kagman Peninsula, against stiff resistance, and on their left another Marine regiment seized a cliff or ridge overlooking "Death Valley," which dominated the route to Mount Tapotchau. But this left the front lines in the shape of a deep U, with the 27th at the bottom. The Marines' situation was rendered precarious by the exposure of their flanks, owing to the inability of the 27th Division to advance. Thus, Holland Smith's planned swift action to take Mount Tapotchau fell off to a standstill.

On Nafutan Point a battalion of the 105th RCT had been given the task of destroying a pocket of enemy resistance; the defenders of Aslito airfield, about 500 in number, had retreated thither. This

[14] See Vol. VII p. 298.
[15] Gen. H. M. Smith Report, Enclosure B, p. 14.

battalion was ordered to attack at daylight 23 June, but it did not start until 1330, and then made negligible progress. To do this unit justice, it was somewhat shaken by its command post's coming under "friendly" naval gunfire with a resulting 6 killed and 33 wounded among key personnel. But there was no improvement next day, 24 June. "A faint-hearted attack was made. The means were available for complete success, had a determined attack been made." [16] This failure of the 105th, as we shall see, paved the way for an enemy break-through on the 26th.

General Holland Smith was "highly displeased," as he expressed it, with the poor performance of the 27th Division on both fronts. He believed that it was due to bad leadership. After consulting the senior United States Army officer on the island (Major General Jarman, the designated Island Commander), and conferring with Admiral Turner in *Rocky Mount* and Admiral Spruance in *Indianapolis*, he was "authorized and directed" by Commander Fifth Fleet to relieve Major General Ralph Smith from command of the 27th Division and appoint Major General Jarman in his place. That was done on the evening of 24 June.

Although five United States Army generals in the Pacific theater alone — one, as we have seen, at Biak — were relieved from their commands during the war, this was the only instance which caused a row; for it was unheard of for a Marine Corps general to relieve an Army general. And, as the 27th Division (a former National Guard unit) had many important friends in politics, the "Smith vs. Smith" controversy was aired in the public press [17] even before there was an official investigation. This writer entertains no doubt

[16] H. M. Smith *Coral and Brass* pp. 171–72, quoting an Army officer's report. The General also expressed his views in *Sat. Eve. Post* 13 Nov. 1948 and was answered in the same number by Capt. E. G. Love USA, official historian of the 27th Div'n. Capt. Love, who has an article in *Infantry Journal* LXIII No. 5 (Nov. 1948) vol. LXIV No. 1 (Jan. 1949), has a symposium on the subject between correspondent Robert Sherrod, who witnessed the campaign, and Capt. Love. Perhaps the most judicious comment is in Isely and Crowl pp. 342–56.

[17] Especially in the Hearst press, starting with the San Francisco *Examiner* 8 July, and ending with a "plug" to have the entire Pacific war entrusted to General MacArthur whose "difficult and hazardous military operations . . . have been successfully completed with little loss of life in most cases." Quotations in Sherrod *On to Westward* pp. 90–91. Cf. Isely and Crowl p. 342.

that General Holland Smith was right. The real trouble with the
27th Division was that it had never been overhauled and the in-
competent and overage company and battalion commanders relieved. It should never have been included in the same attack force
with Marines. The Saipan battle weeded out the unfit, but it also
killed many of the brave and true.

The worst performance was turned in by the battalion of the
105th RCT on the Nafutan Point front. Owing to its feeble advance on 22–25 June, the battalion was still on the 3000-yard-wide
base of the peninsula without enough men to seal it off. The new
commanding officer, Colonel Geoffrey M. O'Connell USA, procured more artillery and the aid of three fire support destroyers in
preparation for a vigorous attack on 27 June. But the enemy anticipated him. Captain Sasaki, commanding the 317th Independent
Infantry Battalion on the Point, determined to break through at
night and join other Japanese forces which he believed to be operating near Hill 500. The password was *Shichisei Hokoku*, Seven
Lives for the Fatherland.[18] Sasaki's force, about 500 strong, had no
trouble in marching around the battalion's right flank, eluding outposts so that scarcely a shot was fired. At 0230 June 27 his columns
hit Isely Field. Seabees and Army Engineers quickly rallied and
prevented them from doing much damage. Sasaki then advanced
toward Hill 500 where, instead of the headquarters of Colonel
Oka, he found two Marine regiments, the 14th and 25th. Mutual
surprise! The Japanese force was wiped out at the cost of 33
Marines killed and wounded.

Sasaki's break-through relieved the 2nd Battalion 105th RCT
of what otherwise would have been a very tough job, cleaning up
Nafutan Point. It secured the point without opposition and reported burying 550 Japanese; but many of these had been killed
by naval and air bombardment.

In the meantime a fierce struggle was going on for Mount
Tapotchau, the summit of which was captured on 27 June by

[18] The sentiment of Masasue Kusunoki, a 14th-century Nathan Hale, wishing
he might be reborn seven times and each time to die for the Emperor. As applied
here, however, it meant to kill seven Americans for each Japanese.

elements of the 2nd Marine Division, commanded by Lieutenant Colonel Rathvon M. Tompkins. His battalion had only 200 men left at the end of the battle. The 27th Division, still in the center, got a foothold on "Purple Heart Ridge" which commanded "Death Valley" between it and the mountain's summit; while the 4th Marine Division overran Kagman Peninsula, taking the formidable defenses of the Magicienne Bay beaches from the rear.

At last, after ten days' fighting, Americans had possession of the highest ground on the island and could fight downhill. Japanese combat strength had been reduced by about 80 per cent in eleven days. General Saito signaled to General Tojo in Tokyo begging him to apologize to the Emperor for his weakness, promising to defend the north end of Saipan to the last man, and blurting out the plain fact: "There is no hope of victory in places where we do not have control of the air." General Holland Smith trudged up a pilgrim's path to the little shrine on the summit of Mount Tapotchau and felt like a modern Moses on the top of Mount Pisgah. The "entire island lay stretched visibly before him, like a huge aërial photograph."

3. *The North End Cleared, 27 June–9 July*

The end was in sight, but there was plenty of fight still in the Japanese. General Saito continued to contest every yard of the way, using the numerous caves and other hiding places on the northern slopes of Mount Tapotchau. He still had a few tanks, two of which charged undetected into a concentration of the 165th RCT, when its battalion commanders were conferring on the next day's plans, and escaped after wounding 61 and killing 12, including Lieutenant Colonel H. I. Mizony USA. His battalion, the 3rd, had already suffered so severely in Death Valley that it was now reorganized into a single rifle company, 100 strong.[19] By 30 June, when the Americans were still contesting the northern foot-

[19] Hoffman pp. 177–78.

hills of Mount Tapotchau, General Saito had withdrawn the bulk of his troops to a "final line of resistance" running from Tanapag Village to the eastern shore, and changed his command post for the sixth and last time.

From 1 July to the final debacle at Marpi Point, enemy resistance was isolated, sporadic and desperate. The American troops had all the air and naval support they could use in the small and diminishing area held by Saito. On 4 July, for instance, the 4th Marine Division had two light cruisers and four destroyers attending to its wants, the 27th had three destroyers, on call, *Cleveland* and *Birmingham* pounded Marpi Point, and *Montpelier* peppered troops moving along the beach with 40-mm fire.[20]

On 3 July the 2nd Marine Division occupied Garapan, now reduced to rubble, and Mutcho Point. The 27th Division took the seaplane base at Flores Point next day. Here the island becomes so narrow that the 4th and 27th Divisions assumed responsibility for the whole, the 2nd temporarily going into reserve. On the same day Saito's "final line of resistance" was overcome with the capture of its strongest point, "Fourth of July Hill." On the 5th and 6th, units of the 27th Division found tough fighting along the western shore near Tanapag Village and Makunsha, and the 4th Marine Division captured Mount Petosukara.

By command of Admiral Nagumo and General Saito, the Japanese on the night of 6–7 July put on the biggest banzai attack of the war, initially directed at the 27th Division which was holding Tanapag Plain and the western shore. The two Japanese commanders promised to fight with their men, who were exhorted each to kill ten Americans.

General Holland Smith had long expected such an attack when the enemy was cornered and desperate. He and General Watson visited the 27th Division command post on 6 July and warned the commanding general[21] that a banzai attack would probably

[20] CTF 56 Report, Naval Gunfire Off. Exp. Troops Report, pp. 61–62.
[21] Maj. Gen. G. W. Griner USA, who had relieved the temporary commander, General Jarman, on 28 June. For other evidence of the warning see *Infantry Journal* LXIV No. 1 (Jan. 1949) pp. 20–21.

come down Tanapag Plain within twelve hours. A Japanese prisoner gave the word too; yet the 27th Division was unprepared; units of the 105th RCT selected comfortable positions for the night without regard to fields of fire in case they were attacked. There was a 300-yard gap between two of their battalions, not even covered by machine guns. Into and through that gap, at 0445 July 7, poured at least 3000 Japanese, like crowds swarming onto a field after a football game. Some were armed only with bayonets lashed to bamboo sticks, some were unarmed, but all were screaming *"Banzai!"* and *"Shichisei Hokoku!"* The 1st battalion 105th was overrun. Its commanding officer, Lieutenant Colonel William J. O'Brien USA, refusing to retreat, strode up and down with pistol in hand until seriously wounded, then manned a .50-caliber machine gun mounted on a jeep, and when last seen alive was standing upright, firing into the enemy hordes.[22] The Japanese spearhead was slowed down, after it had gone 1500 yards, by two batteries (twelve 105-mm guns) of the 3rd Battalion 10th Marine Regiment, sited about 500 yards southwest of Tanapag Village. Both batteries were overrun, but not until they had expended all their shells; the cannoneers continued to fight as infantrymen, the battalion commander, Major William L. Crouch USMC, was killed, and 135 other casualties were incurred. The Japanese survivors lunged ahead to the 105th RCT command post, where the soldiers held firm and fought well. After several hours of close-in fighting at this point, all the Japanese were killed. The two victimized battalions of the 105th, in the meantime, had formed perimeter defense near Tanapag Village. Then came the "unkindest cut of all." Army artillery, assuming this perimeter to be Japanese, fired into it, driving the hard-pressed survivors to the beach and into the water. Many swam out to a reef off Tanapag Harbor, whence they were rescued by destroyers. That attack cost the United States 406 lives, but over 4300 Japanese bodies were found on the field of battle.[23]

---

[22] *N. Y. Times* 28 May 1945.

[23] *Coral and Brass* pp. 195–200. Either the top estimate of the strength of the banzai attack was too low, or 1300 of these Japanese had been killed before the final battle.

By the time this last desperate attack flickered out, both top Japanese commanders were dead. General Saito, knowing the charge to be hopeless, prepared to join his ancestors in the traditional manner. He and his staff were in their headquarters cave, in a spot that they prophetically called Paradise Valley. After issuing a last message to the remains of his army, declaring that he would die with them "to exalt true Japanese manhood," the General dusted off a rock, sat down facing the East, cried *"Tenno Heika! Banzai!* (Hurrah for the Emperor!)" and opened an artery with his own sword. His adjutant then shot him in the head with a pistol. Most of his staff followed suit; the survivors cremated them with gasoline. Saito's ashes, identified by them, were accorded by Holland Smith a military funeral with honors appropriate to his rank.[24]

Not far away from General Saito's headquarters, in another cave, was Admiral Nagumo, with about 60 faithful staff members and yeomen. A survivor who helped to bury the Admiral's body has revealed that on 6 July Nagumo killed himself with a pistol shot.[25] Strange and appropriate fate! The proud commander of First Air Fleet and Pearl Harbor Striking Force, of the crack carriers that had ranged victoriously from Oahu to Trincomalee, met an obscure death just as the sword of Holland Smith pricked the last bright bubble of Japanese dominion.

4. *Conclusion*

Most of the 27th Division was now withdrawn to reserve, and the 2nd Marine Division resumed its place on the left flank. On the following night, at 0430 July 8, remnants of the Japanese launched a second but feebler banzai charge. The American perimeter defense held, and the several hundred assailants were disposed of. About one hundred of the survivors swam out to the reef, refused

[24] A full account of the General's end, by one of his officers taken prisoner, will be found in Hoffman pp. 283–84.

[25] Sakujiro Hikida, in Los Angeles *Rafu Shimpo* 12 Mar. 1953. No marker was erected, lest the Admiral's remains fall into enemy hands. What happened to Admiral Takagi, the submarine commander, is still unknown.

to surrender to patrolling amphtracs, and committed suicide or were killed.

Now the 4th Marine Division advanced along the right flank, fighting most of the way to Marpi Point, overrunning the incomplete airstrip on 9 July. And the 2nd Division drove up the western shore. For at least three weeks after 9 July, the newly arrived Saipan Garrison Force hunted out knots of Japanese soldiers in caves, and for three nights fire support destroyers furnished starshell illumination.

An official flag-raising was held on the morning of 10 July at Lieutenant General Holland Smith's headquarters in Charan Kanoa. Two days later Major General Harry Schmidt USMC relieved Holland Smith as commander of all troops on the island.[26]

A grisly postscript to the capture of Saipan was the suicide of hundreds of Japanese civilians on the northern cliffs of the island on 11 and 12 July. Rejecting invitations by the Marines to surrender, and often threatened by surviving soldiers; men, women and children cut each others' throats, deliberately drowned, or embraced death by any means they could. Parents dashed babies' brains out on the cliffs and then jumped over themselves; children tossed hand grenades to each other. This episode was a grim reminder that the road to Tokyo would still be hard and long.

Very many Japanese soldiers and civilians were still holed-up in caves and ravines, and for two weeks 20, 30, or even 50 surrendered or were killed daily. It was not until 10 August that Admiral Spruance announced the capture and occupation of Saipan to be completed. Months and even years elapsed, before all the enemy hold-outs surrendered or were liquidated.

It was not for want of invitations that the Japanese refused to surrender. Over half a million leaflets, printed in basic Japanese and in Korean, had been dropped on the island by aviators, providing a "surrender certificate," presentation of which entitled the bearer to "honorable treatment as prescribed by the Geneva Convention,"

---

[26] Gen. H. M. Smith retained his overall command of TF 56 (Expeditionary Troops Marines) and of Fleet Marine Forces Pacific. Maj. Gen. Clifton B. Cates USMC relieved Maj. Gen. Harry Schmidt as C.O. 4th Marine Division.

and loud-speakers were brought up to the caves where civilians and soldiers were hiding. These efforts had a limited success; the number who did surrender was greater than that in any earlier operation. The total military was 1780, of whom less than half were Koreans. And over 14,500 civilians gave themselves up. Of these, over 3000 were native Chamorros or Caroline Islanders; they were the first to come in, and the most coöperative. An internment camp was established near the Charan Kanoa airstrip as early as 23 June, and a permanent one later, in the Garapan baseball park. The large number of internees who had to be given shelter and food posed a new problem for the United States forces, and offered good practice for a stiffer one later, in Okinawa.

Owing to the stubborn defense by the enemy, Saipan was a costly operation.

TROOPS EMPLOYED AND CASUALTIES INCURRED IN TAKING SAIPAN [27]

	Total Strength	Killed and Missing in Action	Wounded in Action	Total Casualties
Corps Troops V 'Phib Corps	3,062	22	130	152
2nd Marine Division, reinforced	21,746	1,256	4,914	6,170
4th Marine Division, reinforced	21,618	1,107	5,505	6,612
1st Bn. 29th Marines, reinforced		(see note 27)		
27th Infantry Div. USA, reinforced	16,404	1,034	2,532	3,566
XXIV Corps Artillery USA	3,631	7	18	25
Total	67,451	3,426	13,099	16,525

Number of enemy buried: 23,811
Prisoners of War: 921 Japanese (including 17 officers), 838 Koreans, 21 unidentified; total, 1780
Number of civilians interned by 5 August: 10,258 Japanese, 1173 Koreans, 2315 Chamorros, 814 Caroline Islanders; total, 14,560 [28]

"I have always considered Saipan the decisive battle of the Pacific offensive," wrote General Holland Smith. "Saipan was Japan's administrative Pearl Harbor, . . . the naval and military heart and brain of Japanese defense strategy." [29] Its loss caused a greater dismay in Japan than all her previous defeats put together. "Saipan

[27] CTF 56 Report, G–1 Report p. 4 (p. 1114 of entire Report). Casualties of 1st Bn. 29th Marines are included in those of divisions to which it was attached at various times. Of the wounded, 5873 returned to duty as of 10 August 1944. Total strength does not include 848 replacements to 2nd Division and 845 to the 4th, who arrived before 9 July, or the garrison troops.

[28] Same Report pp. 7–9 (1117–1119).

[29] *Coral and Brass* pp. 181–82.

was really understood to be a matter of life and death," said the German naval attaché at Tokyo in 1945. "About that time they began telling the people the truth about the war." [30]

Even before the island fell, on 26 June, Marquis Kido, the Emperor's most intimate adviser, sent for Foreign Minister Mamoru Shigemitsu, to express the Emperor's wish that he attempt a diplomatic settlement of the war. All three felt that, as an essential preliminary to peace, Tojo must go; and the *jushin,* or elder statesmen,[31] agreed. Tojo tried to compromise by relinquishing some of his several posts to others; but he was unable to persuade any but "yes men" to accept portfolios; and on 18 July, the day that the loss of Saipan was publicly announced, he and the entire cabinet resigned. General Kuniaki Koiso formed a new cabinet, with Admiral Yonai of the *jushin* as deputy premier and Shigemitsu as foreign minister. And, although Koiso took office with a promise to prosecute the war vigorously and issued a defiant statement, everyone who understood Japanese double-talk knew that the change of ministry meant an admission of defeat and a desire for peace. Yet nobody in Japanese military or political circles would accept the onus of proposing peace, so the Pacific war dragged on for another twelve months.

Here is what a young Marine officer, who had fought all through the war with the 2nd Division, thought of the Saipan campaign: —

"David, my boy, the Marines will win this war yet. I have never experienced such a battle. I have never seen such skill in fighting. I have never seen anything more of a tribute to our collective worth to the nation than the ugly, smoking profile of Saipan . . . and the way the Marines took it — confidently, carefully, proudly — was something no one not here can ever know. This battle was transcendent." [32]

[30] Interrogation of Vice Adm. Paul H. Weneker, *Inter. Jap. Off.* p. 285.

[31] Toshikazu Kase *Journey to the Missouri* p. 75. The *Jushin* (literally "principal subjects") included all ex-prime ministers. They succeeded the *genro* or elder statesmen, who were all dead, as an informal but influential consultative body.

[32] Capt. David A. Kelleher USMC to D. W. Mellor 14 July 1944. Capt. Kelleher, who had gone straight from college into the Marine Corps in 1941, was killed at Tinian eleven days after this letter was written.

CHAPTER XVIII

Logistics for the Marianas[1]

1. *Conceptions and Principles*

LOGISTICS problems for the Marianas differed both in degree and in kind from those already worked out for the Gilberts and Marshalls. Not only was "Forager" a more difficult and complicated operation to mount; it required more of everything — troop-lift, fuel, ammunition, provisions and repair facilities — all of which had to be extended, delivered or provided very much farther from continental bases and over a far greater stretch of time. From the first, Cincpac intended to turn the southern Marianas into a major forward military-naval-air base for servicing and staging the Fleet, especially the submarines, for training ground troops, and for bombing Japan by B–29s. Furthermore, we intended to keep them after the war was won.

Momentum is a word that comes up frequently in logistic as in strategic discussions, as the great desideratum. For, the closer that one offensive steps on another's heels, the greater will be the enemy's loss and confusion, and the less one's own. Japan's remarkable series of thrusts to the southwest in early 1942 had proved that. We now intended to turn the same principle of momentum against the Japanese; to keep them continually off balance until they surrendered. The Palau operation was coming up in September; and although in April nobody, not even the Joint Chiefs of

[1] For general sources on Pacific logistics see Vol. VII p. 100 note. Additional sources for "Forager" are CTF 51 Op Plan A10–44 (6 May 1944), Annex G (the initial logistic plan); Turner Action Report 25 Aug. p. 28 and ff; Rear Adm. Hill Action Report p. 69 and ff; Lt. Gen. H. M. Smith Report 10 Sept. 1944, G–4 Annex. Much additional information was obtained orally at the time, and in 1952 Rear Admirals W. R. Carter and H. E. Eccles, logistics experts, read this chapter critically and supplied additional data.

Staff, knew what would be next, everyone knew it would come promptly.

To keep up momentum, base force commanders had to be brought into the discussion of plans, along with assault, theater, and logistic support commanders. Shipping requirements had to be based on unloading capacity at the objective, so that shipping would not be tied up for weeks and months, as had happened early in the war (and was still happening in the Southwest Pacific). Echelons of shipping had to be arranged so that there would be no halt in the flow of supplies.

It is very difficult to change logistic plans for a series of amphibious offensives, after the procession of ship-borne supplies has started. The flow may be slowed down or diverted, if suitable alternate harbors and warehouses are available; it may possibly be speeded up; but it cannot be reversed without immense confusion and waste. Operations of the magnitude and complexity of "Forager" and its successors were so new to American (or to any) logistics planners that few were capable of thinking these principles through, of implementing them, or of planning beyond the assault phase.[2] Fortunately Admiral Spruance was one of these few. He understood that "Forager" was but a means to a further end; and he saw to it that his and Admiral Turner's plans for the assault were coördinated with those for base development. The Marianas campaign was the first in the Central Pacific in which these principles of momentum and what one may call, for want of a better term, "follow-through," were properly appreciated by the top strategic and tactical planners.

The story of base development in the Marianas belongs to a later volume, not this, but the reader must keep in mind that, right through the assault phase, logistic services were planning ahead for the development phase.

---

[2] The planning for "Overlord" (Normandy) may be cited to the contrary. But a cross-Channel operation, under various names, had been in the planning stage since January 1942, when the American troop and logistic build-up in Britain had begun. Pacific Fleet, as we have seen, received its directive for "Forager" only three months before D-day.

The floating and mobile service base (Service Squadron 10), the great contribution to victory of Service Force Pacific Fleet, continued to function. This system of servicing and repairing the Fleet was even better adapted to the Marianas than to the Marshalls operation, because three excellent advanced anchorages were available. Commodore Carter, Commander Service Squadron 10, kept his headquarters afloat at the most active forward area, the lagoon of Eniwetok, leaving representatives at Kwajalein and Majuro.[3]

2. *Food and Fuel*

The Southern Attack Force destined to assault Guam received initial food supply from South Pacific sources, which meant that the bulk of the fresh provisions came from New Zealand. The Northern Attack Force for Saipan and Tinian received initial supply from Hawaiian warehouses and the Pacific Coast of the United States. Both were to be maintained from the West Coast via Hawaii, Majuro, Kwajalein and Eniwetok. As usual, the Navy undertook to feed troops afloat and Marines ashore, while the Army provided rations for its own troops ashore; but the Navy had to find the ships to bring everything out there.

Vice Admiral Calhoun's Service Force, which had the responsibility for all this, found one of its main difficulties to be the lack of "reefers" or provision ships (AFs). These vessels are designed to carry a balanced load of dry and fresh provisions, and to permit "optional discharge" loading; i.e., stowing the items so that one combatant ship after another can be replenished without previously unloading the entire cargo into a warehouse and sorting it out. In May–August 1944 most of the reefers were in the Atlantic Fleet; as one Service Force officer said, "If we had 10 per cent of what they have over there, we could feed the Pacific Fleet caviar." So the nine AFs of the Pacific Fleet had to be supplemented by War Shipping Administration ships, merchant-marine manned. These big vessels,

[3] See Vol. VII p. 106; for composition of Servron 10 see end of Appendix IV.

with 5000 tons' cargo capacity, could carry 348,000 cubic feet of refrigerated food, which would feed 90,000 men for thirty days. But these ships had to unload "solid pack" into storehouses ashore or on the beach; they could not, like the AFs, provision one ship after another, because their holds and hatches were not so organized. And Saipan had no facilities for bulk cargoes until about 15 August. Yet, for two months, the Service Force was able to feed fresh provisions to crews of all combatant ships five days out of six, and to sailors and Marines ashore, one day in three. If a ship's supply officer used his head, he served his crew the more perishable stuff first; a ship could keep the sea 60 days before the sailors began serious grumbling about their food.

Operation "Forager" lasted so long that many battleships, cruisers and destroyers attached to the fast carrier groups were kept at sea over four months. Hence they had to be served by a Stores Issue Ship (AKS). These floating general stores carried some 5000 items in 90 classes, from steel plates for battle damage to toilet paper. Since today's Navy is a floating cross-section of contemporary civilization, about 40,000 different items are required to take care of ships at sea; the 5000 carried by the AKSs were merely the most urgent.

The tanker situation was almost as tight as that of the reefers. Fleet oilers had to be spliced out by commercial tankers, allocated by the Army and Navy Petroleum Board in Washington, to bring replenishment cargoes to Kwajalein and Eniwetok. Operation "Forager" was very greedy of all kinds of petroleum derivatives. Planes drank up avgas like dragons, and the fast carriers charging about the Philippine Sea for days on end, despite holding speed down to an economical 14–16 knots when not engaging the enemy, burned up "black" oil by the million gallons. Weather in the Philippine Sea was relatively calm in June and July, requiring high speed to handle planes; and the Japanese Fleet was both active and aggressive. So, what with one thing and another, the Navy during the Marianas operations burned 43 per cent more oil than had been estimated. Yet no ship or plane missed action for want of fuel.

This unexpected demand was met by sending six fleet oilers and 40 chartered tankers, carrying the colossal total of 4,495,156 barrels of oil, up into forward areas (Majuro, Kwajalein and Eniwetok) in the month of July; while other ships replenished the Hawaiian fuel oil storage with over two million barrels more. These figures are for "black" (fuel) oil only. In addition, these 46 tankers, and three others, brought up into forward areas in July *eight million gallons* of avgas and 275,000 barrels of diesel oil. About 75 per cent of this oil and gas came directly from Curaçao and Aruba in the Dutch West Indies, distant almost half the circumference of the globe from Guam.

The planning of this fueling phase was shared by Service Force Pacific Fleet and Admiral Spruance's staff. Commodore "Gus" Gray of Admiral Calhoun's organization was responsible for getting the oil to Eniwetok, while Captain Burton B. Biggs, an experienced logistics officer on Admiral Spruance's staff, made fueling plans for up through D plus 2 day, and directed the fueling after that. The same "deuces and treys" system of fueling [4] was used as in the Marshalls; only this time the tankers were more often in groups of four and five. Combatant ships of the Expeditionary Force peeled off in echelons according to timetable or, in case of special need, met fleet oilers in designated waters; sometimes so close to Saipan that the mountains could be seen.

Three of these tankers under Captain E. E. Paré, U.S.S. *Saranac*, *Neshanic* and *Saugatuck*, were fueling four destroyers and destroyer escorts at 10 knots in waters about 40 miles southeast of Mount Tapotchau, at 1630 June 18, when they were attacked by five bomber planes from Palau and Yap. This was the first enemy air attack on Navy oilers in the Central Pacific; it had always been a mystery why the Japanese never picked on them instead of going after transports and combatant ships. On this occasion the Japanese were looking for carriers but could not find any. All three tankers were hit; and *Saranac*, which lost 8 killed and 22 wounded, had to proceed to a navy yard for repairs. The bomb that hit *Neshanic*

[4] See Vol. VII p. 107; see end of Appendix II this volume. for list of oilers.

expended itself among the gasoline drums stowed on deck, flames rose masthead high, but the damage control party was so efficient that in seven minutes the fire was quenched. She and *Saugatuck* were repaired at Eniwetok by Service Squadron 10.

3. *Ammunition*

Food consumption of a fleet or an army can be accurately calculated, but to estimate ammunition consumption in advance of a campaign requires a clear crystal ball. Orders for ammunition have to be sent to the mainland depots at least two months in advance, before anyone can tell how long or hard the enemy will fight. In this department, too, there was a scarcity of special auxiliaries (AEs) for replacement supply after combatant ships had exhausted their initial loadings.[5] To old faithful *Lassen, Rainier, Shasta* and *Mauna Loa* were now added *Sangay* and *Mazama*. All but one of these, carrying fleet and aircraft ammunition, anchored in Eniwetok Lagoon, where they were supposed to remain in order to reload a few combatant ships at a time. But the fighting lasted so long and naval gunfire was in such demand by ground forces that this ammunition fleet, starting with *Mazama* 21 June, had to proceed to Saipan while the battle was still being waged; it was a special providence that none was hit by an enemy bomb or shell. Even carriers were rearmed from ammunition ships in Tanapag Roads while Garapan was still in enemy hands. In addition, small amounts of naval projectiles and powder cases accompanied the assault forces in ten different AKAs such as *Almaack*, from which fire support ships reloaded off Charan Kanoa while the air and ground battle waxed fierce. LSD *Ashland* and 26 LSTs also were used for emergency replenishment, and a number of Victory ships were chartered by Service Force to assist. The first of these arrived off Saipan 30 June.

The expenditure of ammunition by the Fleet in the Marianas

[5] Complete list of ships and rounds on board is in CTF 52 (Admiral Turner) Attack Order Annex C Appendix 8.

and the Battle of the Philippine Sea was colossal: 6378 rounds of 14- and 16-inch; 19,230 rounds of 6- and 8-inch; 140,000 rounds of 5-inch, up to 10 July — before Guam was invaded.[6] Any such amounts would have been considered fantastic before 1942, and the problem of delivering them to so remote a place as Guam would have seemed insoluble. Yet even this is not the entire story.

So far we have considered only fleet and aviation ammunition. For the ground troops, seven units of fire (15 for antiaircraft guns) were brought up in the transports to go ashore with the assault waves, and Cincpac had to prepare successive echelons of ammunition supply for the ground forces in addition to what the Fleet needed. In May the Navy procured from the War Shipping Board six more Victory ships, merchant-marine manned, for this purpose. They were loaded on the West Coast for selective discharge on much the same principle as the provision ships, so that the ammunition of any desired caliber could be got at promptly without unloading layers of what was not wanted. This was the first operation in which the Navy tried "optional discharge" loading of ammunition in merchant ships. It worked fairly well in spite of the lack of winchmen and stevedores trained to handle explosives.[7] No combatant ship lacked ammunition at any time, and the only shortage among ground troops occurred the first day or two; that was owing to delay in getting the bullets ashore.

4. *Shipping and Stretchers*

Merchant shipping offers the greatest logistics problem. Attack transports (APAs) and attack cargo ships (AKAs) were now present in the Pacific Fleet in sufficient numbers for lifting troops

[6] Admiral Spruance's estimate in his Action Report.

[7] Naval officers were only partly successful in dissuading zealous port directors from topping off these vessels with miscellaneous cargo for discharge in the warehouses at Pearl Harbor. The Navy wished to route them directly to the Marshalls without calls at Pearl. Oahu was already so full of ammunition dumps that one could hardly take a walk without running into barbed wire; and, as the harbor explosions of Halifax and Bombay had proved, it is highly dangerous to bring loaded ammunition ships into a harbor crowded as Pearl was at this time.

and their assault equipment to the Marianas. At an average of 1250 to 1500 troops per ship, one transport division comprising four APAs and one AKA are required to lift a regimental combat team, thrice as many to lift a division, and four vessels of each type for the extra troops, weapons, vehicles and matériel of an Army corps.[8] But the problem of maintaining troops in the Marianas at a time when over two million Americans were in Europe and Africa, and when several bases in the Gilberts, Marshalls, Aleutians, Admiralties and New Guinea had to be kept going, strained even the war-swollen American Merchant Marine. Every possible method of economizing shipping was studied. Projects were carefully screened to ensure that only the bare essentials were moved; repeated reductions were made in planned facilities for base development in conquered islands, and the times of completion stretched, to avoid shipping demands that would overtax unloading facilities on the beaches and so create "dead" shipping time. The net overall estimates, according to a staff study by Captain J. F. Rees dated 12 April 1944, of the number of ships needed up to 30 July, were 120 cargo vessels (only 18 of which were then on hand), and 58 transports (of which only 22 were then on hand).[9] And, for base development in the Marianas, about 56 more cargo ships would be needed by 30 October.

One cannot employ every ship afloat, all at the same time, to support a single amphibious operation. There has to be a flow of supplies, both military and civilian, into heavily populated and garrisoned areas like Hawaii and Australia as well as into forward bases like Majuro, Kwajalein and Eniwetok. Provision has to be made for moving new divisions from the Continent to islands where they are to receive their final training for the next operation. For instance, when the 2nd Marine and 27th Infantry Divisions were moved out of Hawaii for Saipan, the 81st and 98th Infantry Divisions had to be moved in to train for the Palaus and whatever

[8] Cincpac's "Granite II" plan of 3 June 1944 Appendix G has a five-color chart of how all available transport types were to be employed.

[9] Annex I to the Cincpac-Cincpoa staff study of 12 April, as corrected by Capt. Rees. The numbers are in terms of Liberty ships of 9000 tons.

would come next. Transports had to be found to do this; obviously those engaged in the Marianas could not serve.

The full potentialities of LSTs were first realized in New Guinea and the Marianas. Of the 48 included in the Saipan assault force, 34 picked up assault troops and amphtracs at Eniwetok, as well as priority cargoes of food, water, ammunition and medical supplies. Eight carried the Marines' divisional artillery loaded in dukws, with their ammunition partly loaded in LVTs. Six carried four pontoon barges each, six carried two causeway sections each, and thirty-five carried an LCT each.[10]

A tremendous strain was placed on the Service Force by the length of time that the Pacific Fleet remained concentrated in the Eniwetok-Marianas area. Special cargoes had to be loaded at Pearl Harbor and sent out in fast ships. Many important items were flown by Naval Air Transport Service or Air Transport Command planes to Isely Field, Saipan. Yet there was no shortage serious enough to slow up operations. The fresh water situation was always difficult, as the Expeditionary Force included a large number of small craft and merchant vessels that had no distilling plants; but a number of LCTs and LSTs were told off to transfer water and food from the larger and self-sustaining vessels to the smaller ones.

For the naval campaigns expected in 1945, said Admiral Turner, a forward base must be found within 1000 miles of the scene of operations, where large stocks could be accumulated ashore and a boat and barge pool established. Saipan and Guam were developed for this purpose.

Just in time to keep up the momentum of operation "Forager," a second mobile service base, Service Squadron 12,[11] was organized by Admiral Calhoun. Under the command of Captain Leon S. Fiske, this squadron specialized in harbor improvement and base development. Known in the Fleet as the "harbor stretchers," this squadron

---

[10] CTG 52.2 (Rear Adm. Hill) Action Report p. 69.

[11] For composition of Servron 12, see end of Appendix IV. Later it acquired battleship *Oregon* of 1898 fame, as a storage barge for high explosives. The writer was astonished to see her familiar silhouette, shorn of all superstructure, anchored in Meritzo Harbor, Guam, early in 1945.

took over all the harbor control duties of Servron 10, and it was carefully integrated with Seabee brigades, "Lion" units for airfield construction, and the like.

As a measure of Servron 12's accomplishments, Apra Harbor, Guam, which could accommodate only 16 to 20 small vessels before the war, was so "stretched" that at one time in 1945 over 200 ships were moored there. One of their ingenious devices was to use floating dry docks (ARDs) as freight carriers. By successive flooding at Pearl Harbor the floating dry docks were loaded with barges, harbor dredges and construction material in two or three layers, then pumped out and towed to Guam, Saipan and other places where harbors were being developed. On arrival they were again flooded, and out floated the various craft. Thus the problem of getting these indispensable auxiliaries quickly to work was solved.[12]

[12] Bureau of Docks *Building the Navy's Bases* (1947) I 224.

CHAPTER XIX

The Fight for Tinian[1]

24 July–1 August 1944

1. Plans and Preparations, 12–23 July

THE capture of Tinian was perfectly planned and almost fault-lessly executed by the same Marine and naval units that had won the decision at Saipan. The preliminary bombing and naval bombardment, for once, was adequate; tactical surprise was attained by a wise though risky choice of beaches; landings and follow-up were singularly devoid of confusion; the Marines, unhampered here by slower-moving units, drove ahead with their customary *élan*, and in nine days secured the island, incurring unusually light casualties in the process.

Of the four strategically situated Marianas, Rota, used only as a bombing target, was left in Japanese hands until the surrender. But the same haughty treatment could not be given to Tinian. It lay too close to Saipan; left under enemy control it would have been a nuisance and a danger to the new American base. Tinian is only 10½ miles long with a maximum width of five miles, but it already contained one first-class airdrome with two 4700-foot runways, three more airstrips were under construction, and there was enough even ground to make it the premier B–29 base for bombing Japan. As one approached Tinian, it reminded one of the slopes of Aiea above Pearl Harbor, so intensively was it cultivated with sugar

---

[1] This operation has been adequately covered by the Marine Corps monograph by Maj. Carl W. Hoffman USMC *The Seizure of Tinian* (1951). John Bishop, "The Trick that Won a Steppingstone to Japan" *Sat. Eve. Post* 22 Dec. 1944. *Cincpac Monthly Analysis* August 1944 includes a useful day-by-day account.

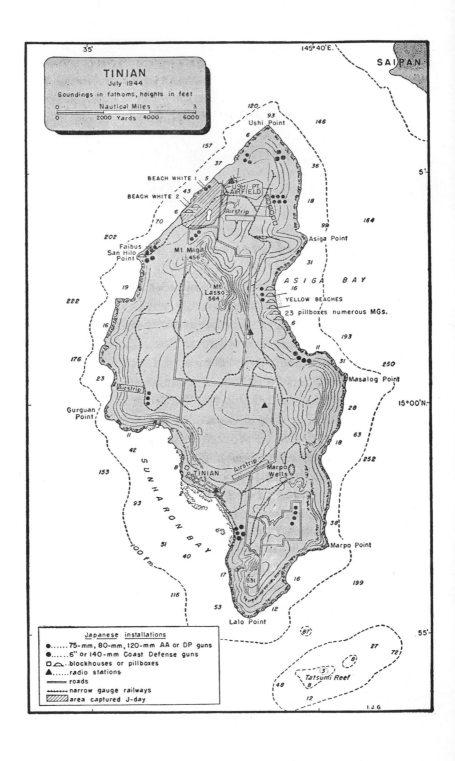

TINIAN
July 1944
Soundings in fathoms, heights in feet

Nautical Miles
0 ... 3
2000 Yards 4000 6000
0

SAIPAN

145° 40'E.

35'

5'

120
93
Ushi Point
146

157

6

37
36

BEACH WHITE I 5
USHI PT.
AIRFIELD
43
18
BEACH WHITE 2
6
Airstrip
99
164

170

202
Faibus
San Hilo
Point
Mt. Maga
456
Asiga Point
31

19
Mt.
Lasso
564
A S I G A   B A Y
16
YELLOW BEACHES
222
23 pillboxes numerous MGs.
16
6
193
176
11
31
250
23
Airstrip
28
Masalog Point
15°00'N
Gurguan
Point
11
63
18
42
8
TINIAN
Airstrip
Marpo
Wells
252
153
93

51
40

100 fm.
17
531
16
199
Marpo Point
116
53
12
Lalo Point
55'
87
27
72
81
3
48
Tatsumi Reef
8
12

S U N H A R O N   B A Y

Japanese installations
● ......75-mm, 80-mm, 120-mm AA or DP guns
● ......6" or 140-mm Coast Defense guns
□ ◠.blockhouses or pillboxes
▲ ......radio stations
——— roads
+++++ narrow gauge railways
▨▨ area captured J-day

I.J.G.

cane; but the individual canefields were much smaller, and the entire island, except the hills and the southern tableland, was divided up checkerboard fashion. Hitherto, American bluejackets had felt no compunctions about shooting up Japanese-held islands; but on approaching Tinian some were heard to express regret that this pretty island had to be "taken apart."

The capture of Tinian by the Northern (Saipan) Attack Force had been in all plans for Operation "Forager" from the first. Detailed planning began only in June because everyone realized that information on the physiography and defenses of this island could be increased tenfold while the fight for Saipan was on.

The concept and tentative operation plan, drafted by Admiral Turner's staff and accepted by General Holland Smith en route from Pearl Harbor, envisaged a shore-to-shore operation from Saipan to the northern part of Tinian. On 5 July, Admiral Turner appointed his second-in-command, Rear Admiral Harry W. Hill, to command the naval attack force (TF 52) for the capture of Tinian. One week later, General Holland Smith designated as commander of ground troops Major General Harry Schmidt USMC, who was then relieved as commanding general of the 4th Marine Division by Major General Clifton B. Cates USMC. That division, and the 2nd (Major General Thomas E. Watson USMC), were chosen to capture the island.

In the meantime air strikes and naval bombardments were softening up the island. Air bombing, started by Admiral Mitscher's fast carrier-based planes on 11 June, continued with few holidays for six weeks. Fire support ships that could be spared from duties on Saipan started bombarding 14 June and omitted never a day thereafter. The XXIV Corps Artillery sited its large-caliber pieces on the southern shore of Saipan as early as 20 June and began systematically pounding the northern half of the island. While the Saipan fight was on, 7571 rounds were fired, and 24,536 more between 9 and 23 July inclusive — an average of over one round a minute for 15 days. Moreover, Tinian was scrutinized from every possible angle between the bird's-eye of high-level air photographers and the fish-eye of underwater demolition teams. The photographs were so thoroughly studied by trained evaluators that the island's defenses became almost as well known to the planning staffs as the features and parts of a Hollywood movie queen are to her fans.

To prevent air interference, Liberators of VB–109, based on Isely Field, Saipan, raided Iwo, Chichi and Haha Jima on 14, 15 and 20 July. They claimed destroying on the ground between 10 and 30 aircraft. During July almost daily missions were flown from Eniwetok against Truk by B–24s, while Southwest Pacific bombers took care of Yap and Woleai. Tinian was effectively sealed off from enemy air interference, except from the Palaus; and they, as we shall see, were attended to by Task Force 58. During the week of 20–27 July, for the first time since Saipan D-day, not one Japanese plane was observed over the central Marianas.[2]

The great question before the planners was, where to land? Tinian breaks off into the water in a series of jagged cliffs, running up to a height of 150 feet, composed of water-carved hard coral which lacerates the flesh and tears the clothing of anyone who tries to negotiate it. Beaches practicable for landing craft and amphtracs, with exits through which vehicles could roll promptly, were few and far between. The best, corresponding to the Charan Kanoa beaches on Saipan, were on Sunharon Bay in front of Tinian Town. But these were too obvious, lying abreast of the principal Japanese concentration. From a mile south of the town, around Lalo, Marpo and Masalog Points to Asiga Bay, the shoreline is a series of high cliffs. But the northern half of the island, where the jagged coral scales off to mere three- to ten-foot heights at the water's edge, had very few beaches. Those designated "Yellow" on Asiga Bay were the best; the only others were two very short beaches, one only 60 yards and the other 160 yards long, on the northwest slope of the island, almost opposite Ushi Point Airfield. These were designated White 1 and 2.

---

[2] Cincpac Analysis of Air Operations, July; VII A.A.F. Intelligence Summary No. 43 p. II–1.

It was necessary to make a decision between White and Yellow. On the nights of 10 and 11 July the amphibious reconnaissance battalion of the V 'Phib Corps and the Navy's two underwater demolition teams that had performed well at Saipan were sent to make a close examination of both; the Marines to explore beaches and their exits, the UDTs to investigate reefs, approaches and underwater obstacles. The Yellow beach parties turned in a most discouraging report. Off shore they had found plenty of anchored mines; over the reef, numerous potholes, boulders and coral heads. Barbed wire was laid along the beaches, which were flanked by jagged 25-foot cliffs; and numerous pillboxes and trenches indicated that the Japanese expected a landing there and were building strong points.

The White beaches were found to be so short that not more than four to eight LVTs or landing craft could land abreast,[3] but no mines or underwater obstacles were discovered; tanks and dukws could roll ashore without drowning; there was no barrier reef as at Charan Kanoa, and the flanking cliffs were so low that troops could easily climb them.

Admiral Turner, after hearing all the arguments, chose the White beaches, and Admiral Spruance backed him up. No two naval officers were more unlike in personality and character than Turner and Spruance, but they always saw eye to eye in military matters, and made a perfect team.

Next day, 13 July, General Schmidt issued his operation plan. Assuming that he could obtain tactical surprise and that the weather would be accommodating, the great problem was to put ashore promptly two divisions, reinforced by tanks and vehicles, with their supplies, over two very narrow stretches of sand. Compared with the 3- to 4-mile front of the Saipan beaches, landing on the 60 yards apiece of White 1 and 2 would be like shooting at the enemy through two portholes instead of using the broadside. The landing force would have to be up-ended, as it were, and sent

---

[3] White 2, though 160 yards long, had only a center section of 65 yards free of coral heads and ledges.

in edgewise, 8 or at most 16 LVTs abreast, instead of the 96 abreast that had roared ashore in each assault wave at Charan Kanoa. A veritable amphibious Thermopylae! Obviously, there would have to be some very prompt fanning out on the beachhead to clear the exits; any pile-up of supplies would put a stopper on the entire movement. "J-day" for the landing, tentatively set at 24 July, was made definite only on the 20th. To support the two Marine Divisions, still short of D-day strength, Admiral Hill had almost all Admiral Oldendorf's fire support ships, but not Admiral Ainsworth's, which would be taking care of Guam.[4] To lift the troops, there were the LSTs, LCTs, landing craft and amphtracs, and two transport divisions of the Northern Attack Force, all that was needed for the short haul.[5]

This plan did not afford the Marines much rest after their struggle for Saipan; but that fight, though hard, had not been enervating, and the Marines had learned so much that they needed no rehearsal or special training to take another island.

The assault plan incorporated two unique features and used two new devices. One was the concentration of XXIV Corps artillery — eight battalions of 105-mm howitzers, three of 155-mm howitzers and two of 155-mm "Long Tom" guns, about 194 cannon in all — on the southwest shore of Saipan, whence they could shell northern Tinian and even send creeping barrages ahead of the troops. The other novelty, dictated by the very short beaches, was an absolute prohibition against leaving ammunition and supplies on the shore; they must be moved by wheeled vehicles and tractors to designated inland dumps without rehandling. This meant not only a ship-to-dump shuttle of amphtracs and dukws, but a Saipan-Tinian ferry service of LCMs carrying preloaded trucks and trailers. The new "gimmick" was a portable LVT landing ramp, to enable vehicles to climb the cliffs on the beaches' flanks. This simple jury rig was carried on an amphtrac and so placed that the forward end could be tilted 45 degrees and slapped down on a

[4] J-day for Tinian was W plus 3 at Guam.
[5] See ships marked T in Marianas Task Organization, Appendix II.

five-foot coral cliff, leaving the after end of the ramp to drop on beach or reef when the amphtrac backed away. These ramps spliced out the effective landing places by as much as 50 per cent. And a new weapon, napalm, was first tried at Tinian.

The Japanese forces on Tinian comprised slightly over 9000 officers and men, divided almost equally between Army and Navy. Nominally the top commander on the island was Vice Admiral Kakuji Kakuta, a stout fellow over six feet tall, who commanded the Base Air Force. After losing almost every plane in the Battle of the Philippine Sea, Admiral Kakuta's offensive operations were, perforce, rhetorical. On 31 July he radioed to Tokyo, "I will make a charge with all forces under my command. All confidential documents have been destroyed. This may be my last communication." So it was. Whether he was killed in action, or bowed out in traditional fashion, is not known.[6]

The actual commander of Tinian was Colonel Kiyochi Ogata of the 50th Infantry Regiment 29th Division, which had been transferred from Manchuria in March. This was a well-trained outfit; most of the Marines said that it fought better than the Japanese troops on Saipan. Ogata had a 75-mm mountain artillery battery of 12 pieces, 6 anti-tank guns and 12 light tanks. He also controlled one battalion of the 135 Infantry Regiment, which belonged on Saipan but was doing an amphibious exercise on Tinian on D-day and never got away.

Captain Goichi Oya commanded all naval units on Tinian, including a guard force of about 2000 men whose main duty was to defend Ushi Point airfield. These sailors had had little infantry training but were fanatically eager to fight. Captain Oya was responsible also for the coast defense guns and most of the anti-aircraft batteries on the island. Of these, the most important were

[6] The Japanese P.O.W. story (4th Marine Div. D-2 Intelligence Report No. 4 of 7 Aug.) quoted in Hoffman *The Seizure of Tinian*, to the effect that Kakuta and staff attempted to evacuate by making rendezvous with a submarine in rubber boats, which were stopped by a U.S. patrol craft, is not corroborated either by Japanese or U.S. sources.

three 140-mm coast defense guns at Ushi Point, the same number at Faibus San Hilo Point, and six 75-mm howitzers commanding the White beaches; four 140-mm coast defense guns and three covered 75-mm dual-purpose on Asiga Bay, commanding the Yellow beaches; three 120-mm DP behind Gurguan Point, commanding the airstrip there; and, south of Tinian Town, four 120-mm DP, two 75-mm howitzers and three English Whitworth-Armstrong naval 6-inch guns. These last, emplaced in a cave, were the only ones that gave United States forces any great trouble. Armored bombproofs, such as had figured heavily in the defenses of the Gilberts and Marshalls, were few and far between. The only important groups were six concrete and steel shelters near the Ushi Point airfield, and about 23 concrete pillboxes along Asiga Bay. The first were partially demolished by artillery fire before the landing, and the second were bypassed.

According to the rules and traditions of Western warfare, there should have been no need to assault Tinian. After the fall of Saipan the situation of the Japanese on Tinian was absolutely hopeless. Colonel Ogata could have surrendered with all the honors of war, as he was invited to do by showers of leaflets and sundry broadcasts. The bourgeois of Quebec observed to the commandant of the garrison in 1759, after the defeat and death of Montcalm, "It is in no way shameful to surrender when it is impossible to win"; and the commandant, a logical Frenchman, capitulated. But surrender under any conditions was contrary to Japanese principles of honor, and Colonel Ogata resolved to defend his island to the last man. Or, as a cynical Japanese soldier noted in his diary, the Navy "took to its heels," leaving the Army to defend Tinian to the last soldier.[7]

Believing that the major landing must come either on Sunharon or Asiga Bays, Colonel Ogata posted most of his defense forces there. But he did not leave the northwestern sector, including the White beaches, altogether defenseless. Each sector commander received a remarkable directive: "Be prepared to destroy the enemy at the beach, but be prepared to shift two thirds of your force else-

[7] Cincpac-Cincpoa trans., Item No. 11,405.

where." For mobile force and reserve he had but one battalion of the 50th Infantry, one battalion of the 135th Infantry, and a dozen light tanks, all well posted on the southern edge of Mount Lasso.

The unfortunate Japanese on Tinian played the rôle of laboratory guinea pigs during the 43 days of preliminary naval gunfire and air bombing. The Americans, with complete control of sea and air, were able to spot almost every shot and keep a daily target-condition record. The air arm tried out the incendiary napalm, which, when incorporated in an aërial bomb, spreads fire over a wide area. These were dropped for the first time on 22 July, two days before J-day, by Army Air Force P–47s based on Isely Field. The results were inconclusive, as the right mixture of napalm powder with gasoline or oil had not yet been worked out; but Tinian proved a good testing ground and napalm later increased the terror and destruction of air bombing to a marked degree. Marine observers embarked in two LCI gunboats to determine whether the 40-mm fire of those craft was sufficiently accurate for close support of troops. They decided that the "Elsie Items" bounced about too much for point firing, so it was decided to use them only to cover the landings. Shore fire-control parties with their naval liaison officers spent days on board the gunfire ships designated to support the landing force, and worked out procedures to improve both the promptness and the quality of naval call fire.

Admiral Hill divided Tinian into five fire support sectors for 23 July (J minus 1 day) with a view to both destruction and deception. Only light firing was directed at the northwestern area, but battleship *Colorado* pounded the three 140-mm coast defense guns on Faibus San Hilo Point, which were well sited both to enfilade the White beaches and to be defiladed from Saipan-based artillery. She completely destroyed this battery with sixty 16-inch shells. The naval vessels also gave heavy attention to Tinian Town, to convince the Japanese that the main landing would take place in Sunharon Bay. Lieutenant Burke's UDT even made a daylight reconnaissance of the beaches off Tinian Town on 23 July to support the deception; and at the same time *Tennessee* and *California* fired 480 fourteen-inch and 800 five-inch shells into the town, which destroyed it.

During three periods of 40 to 60 minutes each on 23 July, naval gunfire over the southern half of Tinian was checked in order to give the air bombers a chance. The attacking planes flew either from the decks of carriers or from Isely Field. Almost 200 sorties were made from *Essex* and *Langley*, over 50 from escort carriers *Gambier Bay* and *Kitkun Bay;* and over 100, eighteen of them armed with the new napalm bombs, from the 318th Air Group, Army Air Force. All day long the XXIV Corps artillery based on Saipan pounded the northern half of Tinian. Fixed emplacements on the island were few, and the Japanese troops stayed in slit trenches or dugouts until the bombardment was over.

By nightfall 23 July the island no longer presented its former pleasant appearance of rural opulence. Numerous fires sent up billows of smoke; dust clouds hovered over spots where high-caliber shells had exploded; Tinian Town was a shambles. Yet even these prolonged shoots and bombings did not quench the enemy's will or destroy his power to fight.

2. *J-day, 24 July*

The one cloud of anxiety that hung over the top commanders and staffs as "Jig-day" approached was the uncertain weather. By 20 July the typhoon season had begun, and any typhoon could have dissipated the delicate plans for the White beach landings, or the logistic follow-up. Nothing could be done about it, except to plan supply by air drop in case a typhoon struck within a few days of the landings. Fortunately none did until 29 July, but rain fell during a part of every day of the operation.

For several days before J-day, and also during part of the night before, embarkation of the landing force went busily forward on the leeward coast of Saipan. Most of the assault division, the 4th, was embarked with its amphtracs in 37 LSTs at the pier in Tanapag Harbor. LSTs also lifted the four 75-mm howitzer battalions preloaded in dukws. Two LSDs, *Ashland* and *Belle Grove*, carried most of the tanks preloaded in LCMs; others were transported directly in LCTs and LCMs, which were formed into groups and escorted to Tinian by patrol craft and LCCs. Since there were not enough LSTs to go around (the Guam operation being but four days old),[8] two regiments of the 2nd Marine Division were embarked in eight transports off the Charan Kanoa beaches; and the third regiment waited for LSTs to return from Tinian. The mess crews of the naval vessels did their utmost for the troops in the matter of food, and their efforts were well appreciated, since the Marines had been living on "C" and "K" rations for weeks. After a hearty supper of good Navy chow, Marines did not particularly mind sleeping topside in the warm rain, as many of them in the LSTs had to do.

The preliminary naval bombardment and air bombing of the area behind the White beaches was like that on Saipan. But the fake diversionary landing was conducted with more histrionics than any previous one of that nature. The show was staged by the transports carrying the 2nd Division, to keep Colonel Ogata convinced that the main landing would take place opposite Tinian Town.[9] At sunup the Marines crawled down cargo-net ladders into their landing craft, which milled about some four miles off the town beaches, and at 0730 headed realistically for the shore. The Japanese opened up with mortar fire which failed to hit, but Colonel Ogata assumed that he had frustrated a landing when the landing craft reversed course a mile off shore and returned to their transports. So, everyone was satisfied. But the Japanese scored heavily on two gunfire support vessels.

Destroyer *Norman Scott*, which was firing 1800 yards from the shoreline, and battleship *Colorado*, about 3000 yards off shore, were

---

[8] An assault battalion of 880 officers and men, with 50 personnel amphtracs and 18 armored amphtracs, filled 4 LSTs.

[9] *New Orleans* and *Montpelier* also fired on the Asiga Bay defense, with a similar end in view.

the targets. At 0740 the three Whitworth-Armstrongs, well concealed in caves at the base of a cliff some 3500 yards southeast of the town pier,[10] opened rapid fire on these two ships. Within 15 minutes *Norman Scott* received six hits, which killed her commanding officer (Commander Seymour D. Owens) and 18 men, wounded 47, knocked out a 5-inch and a 40-mm gun, demolished No. 1 stack, and did other damage. At the same time *Colorado* sustained 22 hits, which inflicted serious casualties among topside personnel, especially the crews of antiaircraft guns. Forty-three officers and men were killed, and 97 wounded badly enough to require hospitalization; seven guns ranging from 20-mm to 5-inch were knocked out and others damaged. The battleship quickly located the battery and fired back; and as a result of her efforts, and those of cruiser *Cleveland* and destroyer *Remey*, that battery was silenced. It was not put out of business until 28 July, when *Tennessee* applied 70 rounds of 14-inch HC and 150 rounds of 5-inch 38-caliber to the task.

These were mere flea-bites, so far as stopping the operation was concerned. The diversionary force soon reëmbarked its troops and withdrew to join the real landings on the White beaches. There the first wave of amphtracs left the line of departure at 0717. At exactly ten minutes before eight o'clock the first wave of 24 amphtracs (8 for White 1, 16 for White 2), tailored to fit these narrow strands, "growled to a vibrating halt, waited while troops debarked, then lurched back to sea,"[11] clearing the beach for Wave Two, only four minutes behind the first. Thirteen more waves followed at close intervals. The Marines were wearing their favorite green coveralls with camouflaged helmets, and they traveled light, without packs, each carrying besides his weapons a poncho, emergency rations, water, a spoon, an extra pair of socks, and (as dictated by Saipan experience) a can of "bug powder."

Of the eight LVTs that carried an assault rifle company of about

[10] This is supposed to have been the same battery that had hit *California* and *Braine* on 14–15 June.
[11] Hoffman *Seizure of Tinian* p. 48.

200 men to Beach White 1, only four could land abreast on the beach itself; the others had to nose against jagged coral cliffs three to ten feet high, up which the troops scrambled. White 1 had been mined, but none of the mines exploded. By 0820 the whole of Major Frank E. Garretson's 2nd Battalion 24th Marine Regiment was ashore. The Japanese defenders resisted with rifle fire, and some of the still untouched artillery on Mount Lasso dropped shells into the area; but only four officers and seven other Marines were killed on both beaches, together with four men who were lost when mines exploded their LVTs on White 2.

That beach, double the length of White 1, allowed eight amphtracs to beach abreast on the sand, and eight more against the coral. This enabled elements of two battalions of the 25th Marine Regiment (the 2nd, Lieutenant Colonel Lewis C. Hudson, and the 3rd, Lieutenant Colonel Justice M. Chambers) to land simultaneously. By 0820 both battalions were ashore. Here the Japanese mines had not deteriorated, and before bomb disposal units and UDTs could eliminate them three amphtracs were blown up. The Japanese had also planted booby traps with attractive bait such as cases of beer and "samurai swords," but the Marines had learned by sad experience to avoid such deadly "souvenirs." More serious was the fact that preliminary bombardment and bombing had failed to destroy two pillboxes so sited as to place bands of fire across Beach White 2. The leading companies of Marines bypassed the pillboxes, leaving them to be captured later, along with 50 dead defenders.

Bulldozers to improve the beach exits arrived in LCTs at 1030 and the first tanks came ashore within an hour. Behind them rattled 75-mm half-tracks of the weapons companies. All were ashore by 1850, and none were lost, although one bulldozer fell into a pothole. The first dukws landed on White 2 at 1315 and rolled immediately to selected positions 300 yards inland, and within an hour the 75-mm pack howitzers that they carried were supporting the infantry. But these were not the Marines' only artillery support. Forward observers, spotting Japanese targets, found they could obtain call fire within a few minutes from the Saipan-based corps artillery.

All day long two thin but powerful streams of weapons, supplies, vehicles, and fighting men flowed through the narrow ports of the two White beaches, fanning out to supply dumps or to establish the beachhead perimeter. The 23rd Marine Regiment, third and last of the 4th Division, landed between 1400 and 1745. And one battalion of the 2nd Marine Division, which earlier had staged the fake landing at Sunharon Bay, came ashore on White 1 from transport *Calvert* between 1700 and 2000. One of the new portable LVT ramps was emplaced at about the same time, and two pontoon causeway piers, towed over from Saipan, arrived about dusk; the one at White 1, on which the naval construction platoon worked all night, was ready next morning to allow loaded trucks to roll directly out of LSTs.

By the close of J-day, 15,614 United States Marines, soldiers and blue-jackets were ashore on Tinian. Tactical surprise, long-protracted bombardment and perfect planning and control had brought about a completely successful landing at a cost of only 15 men killed and about 200 wounded. The planned beachhead was secured, defense lines were well tied in for the night, fields of fire were coördinated to meet counterattack, and barbed wire (brought up by dukws) was strung outside the lines. A combat outpost was set up 400 yards south along the road to Tinian Town, in expectation that an enemy counterattack would come from that direction.

3. *Tinian Taken, 25 July–2 August*

Japanese reaction to the landings developed slowly. So much smoke and dust covered the battlefield that even the artillery posted on Mount Lasso took some time to reply. Colonel Ogata, whose headquarters were near the summit of that 540-foot hill, must have known by noon that the White beach landings were the main show and that he could safely shift forces from Asiga Bay and Tinian

Town to meet the onslaught. But gunfire and air bombing had played hob with his communications, and deployment took time. The only ready means of retaliation were the two infantry battalions posted on the slopes of Mount Lasso, the dozen tanks also awaiting the word there, and the naval ground forces posted around Ushi Point airfield. And all these were thrown into night counterattacks in the very early hours of 25 July.

It was a dark, moonless night with showers, facilitating the kind of fighting in which the Japanese had excelled early in the war; but the Marines had now learned how to meet it. Their dispositions were correct and they had ample artillery support. Several naval vessels, their magazines now well filled with the much-desired star shell, stood by ready to light up the beachhead like a night baseball field. Thrice between 0200 and daylight the Japanese attacked; on the left, in the center, and to the right of the beachhead. The charge on the left, which came first and lasted longest, was made by about 600 naval troops from the airfield. Their élan was praiseworthy but their training slight, and their massed attack was mowed down with canister from 37-mm guns, machine-gun fire, mortar shells and rifle fire. Tanks completed the carnage as day broke, and 476 bodies were counted within a hundred yards of the perimeter. Many of them were officers, wearing their white dress gloves.

Attacks on the center, which began at 0230, looked serious. One penetrated an angle between the two Marine regiments and speared out in two prongs, one of which reached the 75-mm howitzers' firing positions near the beach and killed some valuable men before being shattered. The other ran against an infantry support platoon and was wiped out. About 500 Japanese were lost in this thrust.

On the right flank the enemy's attack was led by five of the dozen tanks in his possession, rolling up the coastal road. Every one was stopped in its tracks by artillery and bazookas. Supporting infantry pressed on but never cracked the Marines' lines. At the close of this attack, around daybreak, the Marines were treated to the weird sight of Japanese bodies hurtling ten to fifteen feet into

New Guinea and the Marianas

the air from individual explosions of their own making. It was later ascertained that they had been carrying magnetic mines to slap in the tracks of American tanks, and, when frustrated, chose this spectacular method of suicide.

In these counterattacks the Japanese expended some 1250 men, one seventh of the island's defense force, while the Marines' losses were less than one hundred killed and wounded.[12]

From daylight 25 July on, the Marines' offensive halted only at nightfall, pushing the enemy back so fast that Colonel Ogata was never able to maneuver for an all-out counterattack. During most of the 25th, shell and mortar fire continued to fall on the beachhead, breaking up one of the pontoon causeways. One 75-mm shell exploded on the tent pole of an artillery fire director center, killing its commanding officer, Lieutenant Colonel Harry J. Zimmer, Captain David A. Kelleher, and nine others. There was a tough fight that day for the cliffy, 390-foot Mount Maga which overlooks the beachhead, and another for Mount Lasso on the 26th; but by nightfall the northern third of the island, from the cove south of Faibus San Hilo Point across to Asiga Point, was in American hands.

Naval gunfire support was consistently excellent throughout this operation. Lieutenant Colonel E. G. Van Orman usmc, the top naval gunfire officer of the expeditionary troops, declared that call fire procedure was carried out much more satisfactorily than at Saipan or Guam because of "experience gathered by all hands at Saipan and exchanged and clarified in meetings . . . both afloat and ashore prior to J-day. Ships and shore fire-control parties acted in far greater mutual understanding than in any prior operation."[13] Air bombing was not as important here as at Saipan for want of suitable targets, but a daily average of 175 air bombing sorties from escort carriers and Isely Field was flown against Tinian. The time lag in obtaining air strikes was not greatly short-

[12] Hoffman p. 68 note 97.
[13] Hoffman pp. 78, 126–30, quoting TF 56 Action Report, Naval Gunfire Section p. 138.

ened, however, and aviators found it difficult to induce XXIV Corps artillery to check fire over an area when they were ordered to strafe it.

Task Force 58 was never idle. Three of Admiral Mitscher's fast carrier groups, after doing their part in the pre-landing bombing of Tinian targets, performed a deep-support mission against possible staging fields for enemy aircraft. Departing the Marianas 23 July, Admiral Clark's TG 58.1 pounded Yap, Ulithi, Fais, Ngulu and Sorol atolls in the western Carolines daily from 25 to 28 July inclusive; while TGs 58.2 and 58.3 (Admirals Montgomery and Reeves) worked over three Japanese airfields in the Palaus and searched the surrounding waters for ships, but ships were scarce.[14] Nowhere did more than one or two planes rise to intercept, but the carrier pilots claimed to have destroyed 58 parked planes on the several airfields attacked — 47 in the Palaus and 11 at Yap.

It was impossible to keep "Jocko" Clark long away from the "Jimas." After the western Carolines strikes, TG 58.2 went to Eniwetok for a brief rest, while Clark's and Reeves's groups refueled and rearmed from the Mobile Service Base off Saipan, and then headed north. Iwo and the southern Bonins were raided on 4 and 5 August. A fairly large convoy was picked up off Muko Jima. The carrier planes sank destroyer *Matsu*, two destroyer escorts, two ramped beaching craft, and five freighters totaling over 20,000 tons. Cruisers and destroyers under Rear Admiral Laurance DuBose cleaned up the small craft. Only about 25 grounded planes were found to be disposed of, and only three arose to be shot down; but, in terms of ships sunk, this fourth and last visit of the "Jocko Jima Development Corporation" was the most profitable.[15]

Ushi Point, the principal airfield on Tinian, was overrun by the Marines on 26 July. The 4700-foot strip, though cluttered with

---

[14] Japanese Monograph No. 116 credits CV planes with only a 123-ton SC at Palau. JANAC credits CV planes (claimed by *San Jacinto*) with having sunk *Samidare* 30 miles N of Babelthuap on 26 July; but Japanese records show this destroyer sunk 26 August by submarine, and *Batfish's* patrol report confirms the fact.

[15] Spruance War Diary, checked by above sources. Our losses were 16 planes and 19 aviators and crewmen, all by antiaircraft fire.

wrecked planes and debris and soggy with rain, had not been very badly holed by the bombardment, and the service unit that moved in promptly had it in operation by 29 July. About a year later, the famous B–29 "Enola Gay" took off from this field carrying the atomic bomb that exploded over Hiroshima.

Throughout July, men and supplies flowed over the White beaches. Although these were the narrowest beaches used in any major amphibious operation in the Pacific, they were the most efficiently controlled. Not one package of supplies was allowed to rest on the waterfront; every truck, dukw, or other vehicle was directed by the "traffic cops" to an assigned dump inland before it could discharge. The speed of unloading over pontoon causeways was phenomenal; one LST discharged 30 ration-loaded trucks on the pier at Beach White 1 in six minutes.

On 28 July came the much-feared break in the weather. A typhoon in the Philippine Sea built heavy swells that broached the pontoon causeways and an LST, halting the train of sea-borne supplies temporarily; but the Seabees had worked on Ushi Field to such good purpose that it could be used as an entry-port for airborne supplies, and in three days Marine Corps and Army transport planes based at Isely delivered 33,000 rations to Tinian.[16]

Every day, steadily and methodically, the Marines moved south in skirmish line behind barrages of their own artillery. Every night they formed defense perimeter and dug in and almost every night rain fell, but that was the least of the Marines' worries. Fortunately for them, most of Tinian was open canefield with slight opportunity for the enemy to take cover. Japanese resistance appeared to be completely disorganized after 27 July; the only stubbornly contested positions were well camouflaged caves along the coast. Gurguan Point airstrip was taken on the 28th. Tinian Town, demolished and completely deserted, was occupied 30 July. Sunharon Bay was promptly mineswept, and soon replaced the White beaches as the principal landing place.

---

[16] A squadron of U.S. Army transport planes (C–47s), alerted at Eniwetok, was moved forward to Saipan to assist the Marine Corps Curtiss Commandos.

In a week's time the two divisions had captured about four fifths of the island. Everyone expected that the enemy would sell the remaining fifth dear. This southern portion of the island rose in a series of cliffs and escarpments to altitudes over 500 feet, and fell off sharply into the sea. Here the enemy made his last counter-attack, in very rough terrain. By the end of 1 August the Marines had reached the cliffs overhanging Marpo and Lalo Points, and General Harry Schmidt announced that Tinian was secured.

But, as the Marines remarked bitterly, the Japanese never seemed to get the word that they were "secured." Organized resistance had ceased, but the caves along the southern end of the island were still full of no-surrender soldiers. Lieutenant Colonel John W. Easley of the 3rd Battalion 6th Marine Regiment was killed in an attack on his command post on 2 August. Sergeant Peter B. Saltonstall USMCR, son of a United States Senator, was killed on the 13th when leading a patrol. Night after night, small groups and even individual Japanese expended themselves in futile attacks. Civilians gave up more readily, but there was a small replica of the Saipan suicide party over the cliffs. For three months the entire 8th Regiment of the 2nd Marine Division engaged in mopping up. In this process they killed 542 more Japanese and themselves suffered 38 killed and 125 wounded.

Even with these added casualties, the capture of Tinian was not too costly. But one cannot say that it was cheap when men like Colonels Easley and Zimmer, Commander Owens, Captain Kelleher and Sergeant Saltonstall paid for it with their lives. During the nine days of combat, the Marine Corps and Navy lost 389 officers and men killed and 1816 wounded; but over 5000 Japanese were buried and 252 were taken prisoner. What became of the unaccounted-for 4000 defenders is not known; most of them, doubtless, committed suicide in caves, but some may have got away in small boats to Aguijan or Rota. Colonel Ogata was last seen alive on 2 August; he and Captain Oya doubtless took leave of life in Japanese ceremonial manner.

So ended the taking of Tinian. Major Hoffman points out that it cannot properly be compared with the Saipan operation for difficulty. At the larger island the attacking forces were projected over a thousand miles from their nearest base; at Tinian they only had to cross a five-mile channel. The numerical superiority of attack to defense was much greater; the terrain, less rugged and difficult; control of air as well as ocean had been secured; prior intelligence was more exact; and preliminary bombardments were protracted beyond those that had preceded any earlier landing. Yet, with all these allowances, Tinian still stands, in General Holland Smith's words, as "the perfect amphibious operation in the Pacific War." [17]

[17] *Coral and Brass* p. 201.

CHAPTER XX

Guam Recovered[1]

June–August 1944

1. A Deferred Operation

GUAM, the most important of the Marianas, an American possession for over forty years before the war, was the last to be taken; but that was not the plan. Operation "Forager" called for an assault on Guam by Rear Admiral Richard Conolly's Southern Attack Force a few days after the invasion of Saipan, and Admiral Spruance had originally set W-day (as Guam D-day was designated) for 18 June. But it had to be postponed; first, to defeat Ozawa's Mobile Fleet; and second, because the unexpected toughness of the Saipan fight convinced everyone that the taking of Guam would require three divisions instead of the somewhat less than two that were on hand. That meant lifting from Oahu the General Reserve, the 77th Infantry Division, and it would take time to find the necessary transportation.

[1] CTF 53 (Rear Adm. Conolly) "Report of Amphibious Operation for the Capture of Guam" 10 Aug. 1944; CTG 53.2 (Rear Adm. Reifsnider) Report 29 Aug.; Comgen Exp. Force (Lt. Gen. H. M. Smith USMC) Report on "Forager" 4 Sept.; Com III 'Phib Corps (Gen. Geiger) Report on Guam Operation 27 Aug.; Comcrudiv 6 (Rear Adm. Joy) Action Reports and War Diaries; 3rd Marine Div. Special Action Report on "Forager" 19 Aug. 1944; 1st Provisional Marine Brigade Report on Guam Operation and Operations Journal, 19 Aug. 1944. A preliminary ms. draft of Maj. O. R. Lodge's Marine Corps monograph *Recapture of Guam* was kindly furnished by Lt. Col. H. W. Edwards USMC, Head of Historical Branch, G–3, Marine Corps. The writer visited Guam early in 1945 and spent some time examining the terrain of the fighting and conversing with officers of the 3rd Marine Division who had taken part in it. *Ours to Hold High, The History of the 77th Division* (1947) is excellent, and Maj. Frank O. Hough USMCR *The Island War* (1947) chap. xi has the best account hitherto published of this operation. The most important Japanese sources are Lt. Col. Hideyuki Takeda "Outline of Japanese Defense Plan and Battle of Guam" 4 Oct. 1946, and Monograph No. 48 "Central Pacific Operations Record, I" (No. 851–55).

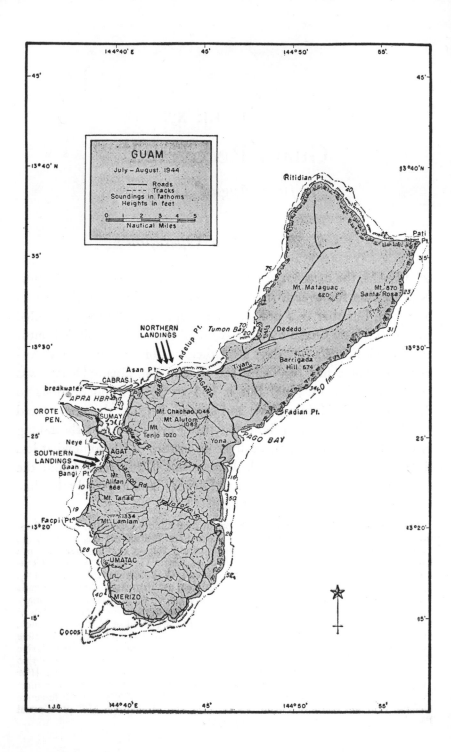

144°40' E   45'   144°50'   55'

45'

13°40' N

GUAM

July — August 1944

———— Roads
- - - - Tracks
Soundings in fathoms
Heights in feet

0 1 2 3 4 5
Nautical Miles

35'

13°30'

NORTHERN
LANDINGS

Adelup Pt.
Tumon Bay
Asan Pt.
CABRAS I
breakwater
APRA HBR
OROTE
PEN.
SUMAY
Neye I.
SOUTHERN
LANDINGS
Gaan Pt.
Bangi Pt.
Facpi Pt.

13°20'

UMATAC
MERIZO

15'

Cocos I.

Ritidian Pt.
Pati Pt.

Mt. Mataguac
620'
Mt. 870
Santa Rosa

Dededo

Barrigada
Hill 674

Tiyan

Mt. Chachao 1046
Mt. Alutom
1082
Mt.
Tenjo 1020
Yona
PAGO BAY
Fadian Pt.

Matson Rd.
Mt.
Alifan
868
Mt. Tanae
Mt. Lamlam
1334

13°40'N

35'

13°30'

13°25'

13°20'

13°15'

I.J.G.   144°40' E   45'   144°50'   55'

The Chamorros of Guam had had a very unhappy experience under Japanese rule.[2] The new rulers changed the name of their beloved island to Omiya Jima, "Great Shrine Island." Japanese became the language of instruction in the schools. With no other employment, the able-bodied were forced to work for a pittance on military projects, especially building airfields — one on Orote Peninsula; one, called Tiyan, near Agaña; and a third, which was never completed, near Dededo.[3] From early 1942 to the spring of 1944, when the island was garrisoned by naval guard units, conditions were not too bad for the natives. They became almost intolerable when Japan decided early in 1944 that she would have to fight for Guam, and sent in army forces from Manchuria. All schools and churches were then closed, forced labor was increased, food was seized and doled out in slender rations, and most of the population was herded into concentration camps where hundreds died of disease and malnutrition. A number were executed for exhibiting "American sympathy," in forms such as looking up with a smile at an American plane. Nowhere, not even in the Philippines, were American liberators received with greater enthusiasm than in Guam.

Japan had better success at getting troops and matériel into Guam than into Saipan. The core of the defense force was the 29th Infantry Division, whose commanding officer, Lieutenant General Takashina, was island commander as well.[4] This was the division waylaid en route by submarine *Trout*, which had sunk transport *Sakito Maru* with 2400 men; but the rest had got through. The naval guard unit was reinforced to 3000 men; the 6th Expeditionary Force, 5100 strong, under Major General Kiyoshi Shigematsu, arrived 20 March; and, what with naval construction forces, artillery and tank units, and personnel of the Base Air Force, there

[2] Stanley Fink "Co-Prosperity on Guam," *Marine Corps Gazette* Oct. 1944.
[3] Tiyan was incorporated in our Agaña Field and the Dededo strip in our Depot Field.
[4] The area commander, Lt. Gen. Obata, was caught on Guam by the Saipan landings, when trying to return to Saipan after an inspection tour to Palau; he supervised the plan for fixed defenses, but left the fighting command to Takashina.

were about 19,000 fighting men on Guam when the Americans landed [5] — appreciably more than the Americans estimated. There were plenty of coast defense guns, with antiaircraft units and fixed emplacements; and the five weeks' grace accorded the defenders by the postponement of W-day enabled them to construct the most formidable underwater beach defenses yet encountered in the Pacific. On the other hand, the same delay gave United States forces a chance to deliver the most intensive and prolonged prelanding air bombing and naval bombardment that any Japanese-held position ever received.

Rear Admiral Richard Conolly's Southern Attack Force (TF 53) for Guam had been a separate entity from the Saipan-Tinian forces right along and, most happily, Cincpac gave Conolly almost the identical "team" with which he had taken Roi and Namur in February.[6] The ground troops selected, the III Amphibious Corps (3rd Marine Division and 1st Provisional Brigade) under Major General Roy S. Geiger USMC, were not the same Marines as at Roi-Namur, but the important thing is that they *were* Marines; and the 77th Division, which had to be committed with them, was new enough to learn from the Marines. "Dick" Conolly [7] had come a long way since the early months of the war when he commanded Admiral Halsey's destroyer screen in his carrier raids on the Marshall Islands and Marcus. Robust and genial, thorough and methodical, he loved planning as well as fighting, and he did a great deal of the planning himself at General Geiger's headquarters at Guadalcanal. The cordial relations thus established at the planning stage, according to the General, cemented the Naval and Marine Corps elements into a homogeneous team. "At no time was there a conflicting opinion that was not settled to the satisfaction of all concerned." [8]

[5] Information from Lt. Col. Hideyuki Takeda of the 29th Div. who surrendered at the end of the war, tabulated by Maj. Lodge and Mr. Wilds of the Office of the Chief of Military History.

[6] Compare Guam task organization in Appendix IV below, with that of Roi-Namur in Vol. VII pp. 345–47.

[7] Brief biography in Vol. VII p. 232*n*.

[8] Gen. Geiger Report p. 4.

Guam on the map somewhat resembles an old sock hung to a line by its top edge (Ritidian and Pati Points); the ankle relatively flat, but the bulbous foot inflated and blown westward by the tradewind. Apra Harbor, our main objective, is formed by a couple of ragged strips off the sock (Cabras Island and the cliffy Orote Peninsula) just below the heel. Since the island is only five miles across at the ankle, between Pago and Agaña Bays, one may wonder why the planners did not select for landings the lightly defended eastern beaches, from which troops could cross to Agaña and Apra. The answer is, first, that surf beating for countless ages on the windward coast had built up a sort of lip to the fringing coral reef that would be impassable for landing craft in any sort of weather, and that bad weather had to be anticipated in July. And, second, that while "hitting 'em where they ain't" is good strategy if you don't want the place where they be, in this case the Marines and Navy wanted Apra Harbor and Orote Peninsula quick, to develop for their own use; and at Munda the strategy of landing somewhere else and fighting through jungle to the wanted airfield had proved slow, costly and discouraging. So it was decided to put the landing force ashore simultaneously at two sets of beaches, Asan and Agat, one on each side of Apra Harbor; and by double-envelopment to secure harbor and airfield promptly. The rest of the island could wait.

Guam was naturally better known to American officers than either Saipan or Tinian; but the prewar maps, though made by Army Engineers and at that time considered excellent, proved to be far short of what was wanted in the sort of warfare developed since 1941. Photographic intelligence, starting with some good low-level shots of the beaches taken by submarine *Greenling* in April, continued almost daily by planes. Yet the map of the island furnished to the attack forces was unsatisfactory, showing large areas bare that actually were heavily forested, and not indicating low hills that were cannily employed by the defense.

For ten days after Saipan D-day, Admiral Conolly's TF 53 jockied around some 150 to 300 miles east of the island. For, although W-day was indefinitely postponed, Turner feared he might need Geiger's Marines on Saipan. On 25 June Spruance sent the transports floating the 3rd Marine Division back to Eniwetok but kept the 1st Provisional Brigade near at hand for five days more. This long wait was enervating to the Marines. In Eniwetok Lagoon, which afforded few facilities for exercise ashore, tents and tarpaulins were rigged over the weather decks of the LSTs, giving the tractor groups the appearance of a low-grade Arab encampment; but the men there were more comfortable than those in steel-sided transports. Something had to be done to keep the Marines occupied, so they were briefed and rebriefed on the objective until they complained that "Guam was coming out of their ears."

Perhaps the worst sufferers from the long shipboard confinement were the Marines' famous dogs, which they had first employed on Bougainville; yet these dogs rendered fair service on Guam. Confidence that a canine sentinel would alert him if snipers approached, helped many a Marine to catch a little sleep. And some of the more vicious and enterprising dogs could be persuaded to inspect caves that might harbor enemy troops.[9] The only Marines not disturbed by weather or anything else were the "Navajo talkers." These Navajo Indians had been recruited and specially trained to operate voice radio sets in their own language, which completely baffled the Japanese listeners.

Since his junior officer days, Admiral Conolly had been noted for the thoroughness and enthusiasm with which he tackled every task. He was most anxious to get going, because the typhoon season was due to break in July. During a five-day conference (29 June–3 July) with Spruance, Turner and General Holland M. Smith at Saipan, Conolly, with Geiger's support, proposed to go ahead with the invasion; but his superior officers insisted that it must wait until the 77th Division could be brought up. He then

---

[9] Conversations with Lt. W. T. Taylor USMC, the 3rd Div. war dog officer, at Guam. Of 60 dogs, 20 were killed or missing. Mongrel dogs proved to be the best and police dogs next; Dobermans were too nervous; dogs of any breed were better than bitches.

Rear Admiral Richard L. Conolly USN

Major General Roy S. Geiger USMC

demanded gunfire ships to start softening up the island. Spruance, who wished to spare Guam from indiscriminate bombardment in order to save the lives of our Chamorro friends, consented on condition that someone be found to plan and conduct a systematic bombardment of enemy positions, beaches, and strong points. Turner then told Conolly to find someone to do it. "Dick" Conolly went down the ladder from Turner's sea cabin in *Rocky Mount*, climbed back immediately, and said, "I have the fellow, Kelly; his name is Conolly!" And Conolly it was who directed the bombardment, in addition to commanding the amphibious assault.

Guam had already been subjected to an air bombing by TF 58 planes on 11–12 June, and again on the day of the famous "Turkey Shoot." By 20 June all Japanese planes based there had been destroyed and the airfields were unusable. And although the runways were repaired and a few planes were staged in to attack our forces at Saipan, these attacks, as we have seen, gradually petered out. Thus enemy air power was no factor in the recapture of Guam. But the island had been bombarded only once, on 16 June, when it was expected that the landings would follow shortly. A fire support unit commanded by Rear Admiral Ainsworth in *Honolulu*, including battleships *Pennsylvania* and *Idaho* and a number of destroyers, pounded installations on the Orote Peninsula, their fire coordinated with bombers from the escort carriers. *Honolulu* — "Blue Goose" as the crew called her — had the honor to drop the first salvo on Guam since the enemy captured the island.[10] At one end of Orote Field were two mock-up Liberators, the purpose of which was disclosed when an American plane, which nosed down to investigate, encountered a tremendous barrage of antiaircraft fire. The aviators also dropped leaflets urging the natives to take to the bush, which they promptly did.

After the Philippine Sea battle, Guam had a respite until 4 July,

---

[10] During this bombardment, I encountered Joe, the Admiral's Chamorro mess boy, gazing anxiously at his own house on the shore near Facpi Point. He wished me to persuade the Admiral to let him and me make a two-man amphibious landing in a rubber boat, to inform his friends that the Yanks were coming. Seemed somewhat premature to me!

when the planes of Admiral Montgomery's TG 58.3 pulled off a daylight bombing and strafing attack, prolonged into the night by destroyers of the screen bombarding Agaña, Asan and Agat. Next day Admiral Clark's TG 58.1 and Admiral Reeves's TG 58.2 took over, fresh from their Fourth of July raid on Iwo Jima, and included Rota in their unwelcome attentions.

The systematic bombardment entrusted to Admiral Conolly was begun 8 July by Rear Admiral Turner Joy's cruisers and Rear Admiral Van H. Ragsdale's escort carriers (Cardiv 24). Dick Conolly in person appeared off the island on the 14th at the head of a scratch task group composed of his command ship *Appalachian*, battleship *Colorado*, three destroyers and a destroyer escort. "Pug" Ainsworth brought his gang back on the 17th. From the 8th until the landings on the 21st a procession of gunfire ships shuttled back and forth between Saipan, Guam and Eniwetok, taking on fuel and ammunition at the already secured islands and spreading devastation on the defenses of Guam. Every day at least one battleship and several cruisers took part; on 19–20 July there were six battleships and four heavy and two light cruisers firing away.[11] Admiral Conolly had the planes of two or three escort carriers at his disposal daily, and usually at least one group of Mitscher's fast carriers. He made a regular siege of it; Guam in his eyes became another Sevastopol which he must batter down to ease the assault of the soldiers. Photographs taken every morning by escort carrier planes or observation planes from Saipan were delivered for development and skilled scrutiny on board *Appalachian*, where a board of six officers — air and gunnery specialists of the Navy and Marine Corps — evaluated the effects and selected targets for next day. The presence of General Geiger and staff in the flagship helped the Navy to place its shells and bombs where they would do the most good from the Marine point of view. And, incidentally, it had the effect of diminishing the decibels of complaint against the naval bombardment after it was over.

During these 13 days of continuous bombardment preceding the

[11] Gen. Geiger Report, Naval Gunfire section p. 3.

landings, battleships expended 6258 rounds of 16-inch and 14-inch ammunition; the heavy and light cruisers, 3862 rounds of 8-inch and 2430 of 6-inch respectively; and all ships, including the destroyers, 16,214 rounds of 5-inch.[12] Not only the most systematically conducted naval bombardment to date, it was the most prolonged of the war; longer than those on Leyte, Iwo Jima or Okinawa. General Geiger declared that casualties incurred in taking Guam would have been far greater but for this excellent "preparation" of the target by the Navy.

In the meantime the Marines were waiting at Eniwetok for the 77th Division to catch up. This reserve infantry division, composed almost entirely of draftees from the New York metropolitan area and reactivated in March 1942, had been well trained for the past two months on Oahu. Under the command of Major General Andrew D. Bruce USA it "fitted smoothly and quickly" into the III 'Phib Corps "and proved itself a reliable and proficient member of the ground force team." [13] Advance units of one of its regimental combat teams, the 305th, left Pearl Harbor 1 July, embarked in the new Transport Division 38 commanded by Captain John B. Heffernan in *Lamar*. The other two RCTs had to wait a week longer for transports to arrive from Saipan. On the 8th, Admiral Spruance set W-day for 21 July. The tractor groups lifting the Marines' assault units folded their tents like the Arabs they then resembled, and silently stole away from Eniwetok on the 15th. Two days later the Marines' big transports, together with the Heffernan division carrying the 305th RCT, sortied from the lagoon just as the rest of the 77th Division entered. These transports topped off with fuel there and arrived at Guam on W-day plus 1, the 22nd. A short voyage it was for the GIs, in contrast to that of the Marines who had been on shipboard ever since 1 June except for an occasional beer and swimming party on the beaches of Eniwetok.

Admiral Conolly's task group, which arrived off Guam 14

---

[12] Lt. Gen. H. M. Smith Report on "Forager," Enclosure on Naval Gunfire p. 71.
[13] Gen. Geiger Report on Guam p. 4. Cf. General Bruce's article "I'm Proud to Belong," *Liberty* 21 Apr. 1945 p. 22.

July, brought up Underwater Demolition Team 3 (Lieutenant Thomas C. Crist USNR). For two days, beginning 14 July, UDT 3 reconnoitered the beaches chosen for assault, and other stretches of the shore that might be wanted for additional or substitute landings. During three nights the "frogmen" slipped overboard from their rubber boats to investigate the reefs and the beaches, while LCI gunboats, destroyers, cruisers and even battleships plastered the shore to prevent the enemy from shooting at the swimmers. Only one member of UDT 3 was killed.

This reconnaissance confirmed what air photos had already revealed, that the Japanese, without benefit of the mines or other boat traps used by the Germans in Normandy, had blocked the beach approaches very effectively. Off Agat they had planted three lines of palm-log cribs filled with coral rocks, linked each to each by wire cables; off Asan they used four-foot cubic wire cages filled with cemented coral, placed so close that no landing craft could pass between them. On 17 July UDTs 4 (Lieutenant William G. Carberry USNR) and 6 (Lieutenant Deearle M. Logsdon USNR) arrived. Trained at blowing up concrete tetrahedrons on the beach obstacle range at Guadalcanal, they found the improvised Japanese obstacles easy to destroy. Demolition started as soon as twilight faded, with UDT 3 helping. During the next three nights these valiant swimmers, with their hand-placed demolition charges, blew up 300 coral-filled cribs off Agat and 640 wire and coral cubes off Asan, where they left a sign, "Welcome, Marines!" on the reef.[14] As Admiral Conolly afterward declared, no landing could have been made at either place but for these clearance operations.

As W-day approached, the bombing and bombardment became heavier and more intense. On 19 July four battleships delivered main-battery fire; and it was then, according to Major Iwano, that the Japanese guessed correctly where the landings would take

[14] An ensign of UDT 3, hearing talking in the water at the right of the beach, swam over to reprove his men for making a noise but discovered in time that the chattering swimmers were Japanese engaged in extending the line of underwater obstacles.

place, from the intensity of fire directed at the Asan and Agat beaches.[15] *Indianapolis* steamed over from Saipan 20 July with Admiral Spruance on board to contribute a few 8-inch salvos. By dawn of W-day, the whole formidable fleet of gunfire and air support ships had assembled — George Weyler's four battleships and seven destroyers; "Pug" Ainsworth's one battleship, three cruisers and eight destroyers; Turner Joy's one battleship, three cruisers and nine destroyers; Bob Hayler's two cruisers and three destroyers; Van Ragsdale's three escort carriers and five destroyers. On W-day morning, before the landings, these ships threw an additional 1494 rounds of 16-inch and 14-inch shell, 1332 rounds of 8-inch, 2430 of 6-inch, 13,130 of 5-inch, and 9000 4½-inch rockets into the landing area. Dozens of planes bombed and strafed. And a new method of simultaneous air bombing and gunfire bombardment on the same target was tried; ships' guns limited their maximum ordinates of shell trajectory to 1200 feet, and pilots were required to pull out of their bombing runs at 1500 feet. So, at this point, let us pause to attempt a summary of the effects of so prolonged a naval bombardment and bombing.

The effectiveness of pre-landing bombardment, as of naval fire support in general, is one of the controversial subjects in modern tactics. In this operation the Navy claims, and the ground troops admit, an almost complete destruction of Japanese protective works and emplaced artillery in the open; the Navy never pretended to be able to catch mobile artillery or to destroy concealed positions or trenches. After an operation is over and the enemy defenses are destroyed, it is almost impossible to assess "whodunit" — ships' gunfire, air bombing or corps artillery. In the case of Guam, however, we have pretty good evidence from a report by Colonel Takeda to the Marine Corps, after the war was over. He stated that *all* coast defense emplacements *in the open*, and about half of those under cover, were "completely demolished before the landings"; and these included a number of 200-mm guns on points that over-

---

[15] Japanese Monograph No. 48 p. 48. But from captured diaries it seems that Takashina guessed right at least ten days earlier.

looked the beaches. He added that "50 per cent of all installations" (pillboxes, blockhouses, and so forth) "built in the inshore area of the landing beaches were demolished." But the power plants, concealed in caves, were not touched; "communications installations were not damaged"; and "antiaircraft gun positions were operational until the very last." Colonel Takeda also admitted that naval bombardment did the morale of his troops no good. This writer concludes that the prelanding naval bombardment was superior to that of any other operation in the Pacific previous to Korea; and that the small amount it fell short of perfection was unavoidable, owing to the "nature of the beast." After all, if naval and artillery fire could do everything, there would be no use for infantry.

Admiral Conolly had an anxious moment on 20 July when he received a signal from Admiral Spruance asking whether he had made any arrangements to postpone the landings on account of an impending typhoon. Sensation! Fortunately, Conolly had a hurricane specialist on his staff, Lieutenant John Fleet, who assured him that the typhoon which had alarmed the Fifth Fleet aerologist would pass several hundred miles to the west of Guam, that its effect in the shape of surf on the west beaches would not be felt for six or seven days, and that W-day would be fair and calm. Conolly snapped this prediction back to Spruance and requested permission to go ahead; presently he received "Permission granted." Lieutenant Fleet was right. W-day dawned clear with slight overcast, light wind and calm sea, perfect for landing; the typhoon ground swell and heavy rain did not strike in until the night of 29 July.

2. First Phase of the Assault, 21–28 July

a. Northern Sector — the Asan Beaches

At 0600 W-day all assault units had reached their assigned areas, troops were nervously making last-minute adjustment of equipment, and planes from *Wasp* and *Yorktown* came in to strike. The landings were organized very much as at Saipan, the main improvements being a much greater use of rocket-equipped LCIs, and a greatly intensified final bombardment. Amphtracs (both armored and personnel) issued from LSTs for the first assault waves; control officers were in PCs and LCCs, marking the lanes to the beaches, big transports stood six miles off shore to lower troop-filled landing craft, LSDs disgorged tank-filled LCMs; dukws loaded with artillery milled around; and over all there was the terrific din of gun and rocket fire, of air bombs bursting, of diesel and gasoline engines roaring, of LST and landing-craft ramps clanking, while flags striped with the beach colors gave the whole spectacle, to an outsider, the air of an utterly confused and inconceivably noisy motorboat race enlarged several dimensions.

What Julian Corbett said of an eighteenth-century affair still holds good. An amphibious operation is difficult and dangerous to a force unfamiliar with the technique, but easy and formidable when both naval officers and troops are at home with the work, "schooled for it, hand in hand, by constant and well-ordered practice." [16] Dick Conolly's and Roy Geiger's units were superbly schooled.

We shall first take up the northern landings on the Asan beaches, and follow the 3rd Marine Division (Major General Allen H. Turnage) through the first phase of the assault.

Although there was no lagoon here as at Saipan, the wide fringing reef presented an obstacle that could be surmounted quickly only by amphtracs. The LVTs, after debarking assault waves, moved out and took troops off landing craft for the final leg over the reef; some even kept LCMs nosed against the reef edge so that tanks could roll ashore. The day before, UDTs had buoyed and flagged the over-reef "paths" for the tanks to follow, and naval bombardment had been very careful not to pothole the reef. All three regiments of the 3rd Division landed abreast on a 2000-yard front, the 3rd on Beaches Red 1 and 2, the 21st on Beach Green

---

[16] *England in the Seven Years' War* II 222.

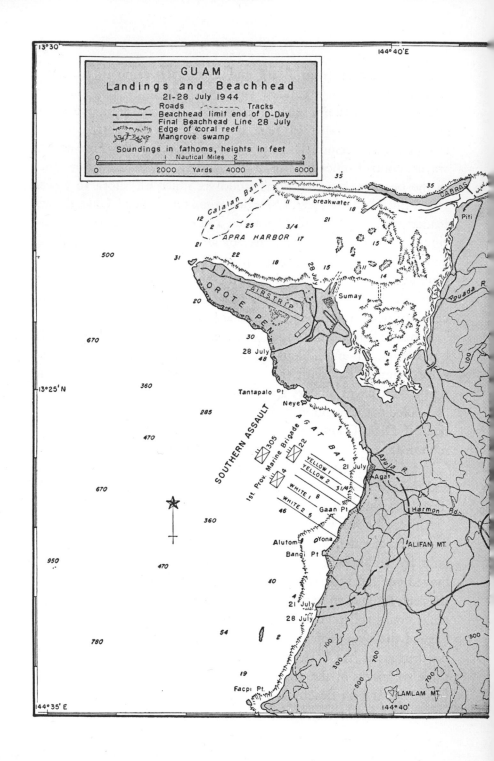

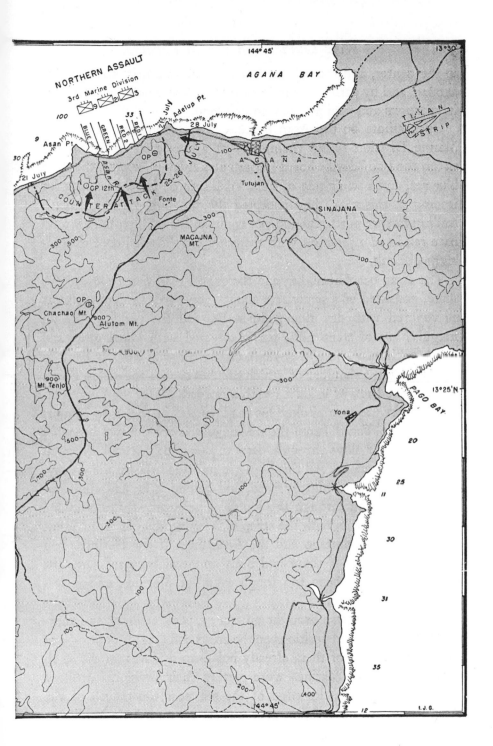

in the center, and the 9th on Beach Blue. The first wave landed at 0829, and by early afternoon practically the whole division with its weapons and vehicles was on dry land.

Once ashore on the Asan beaches, the 20,000 men of the 3rd Marine Division found themselves in a precarious situation between the two "devil's horns" (Asan and Adelup Points), the deep blue sea, and a semicircle of hills. Well briefed for the reasons for landing at this spot, they accepted the situation, realizing that a landing farther north, though not commanded by high hills, would have rendered a junction with the Southern Attack Force exceedingly difficult.

The Asan beachhead, beyond the gravel road that followed the shore, consisted of a semicircle about 1200 yards in depth, almost all covered with dry rice paddies. Beyond the paddies rose an irregular arc of steep hills, partly covered with kunai grass and partly with heavy jungle growth, culminating on the left flank in Chonito Cliff, a shoulder of which touches the sea at Adelup Point. Around the back of it led a rough dirt road, across the Fonte plateau (where Cincpac pitched his headquarters in 1945), to Mounts Chachao and Tenjo. From the middle of this arc the two branches of Asan River flow through narrow, steep defiles and debouch into the rice paddies. All this high ground was held by the enemy. It was accessible to him by road, and behind it he had abundant supplies dispersed through the jungle. The entire setup resembled a miniature Salerno, with the steep hills taking the place of Mount Soprano, Mount Sottano and the Apennines. If the Germans had held Chonito, and if there had been no naval bombardment, the going might have been too tough even for Marines; and it was bad enough anyway.

While the Japanese brought up troops, pack artillery and mortars to their prepared positions on the crests and reverse slopes — and there were plenty of them already holed-up in caves on the steep front slopes — the Marines were getting their divisional artillery ashore and sited on the edge of the sea near the mouth of the Asan River. An observation post was set up on a little knoll that overlooked most of the amphitheater, and regimental command posts were established in dugouts tucked into the base of the cliffs and the defile. The beachhead was so covered with troops that almost every projectile dropped into it by the enemy inflicted casualties, and during the first two days the loss of officers was heavy. But the Marines had certain assets which they exploited to the full: land-based artillery which delivered accurate fire on the reverse slopes of the hills; air-spotted naval gunfire, which pounded every observed enemy concentration and continued harassing fires all night; and an intrepid spirit which did not even consider the possibility of failure. And the enemy had no available air power to bomb and strafe the beachhead.

At daybreak 22 July the Japanese counterattacked in strength but were thrown for a loss. Once that was over, small combat units of the 21st Marine Regiment, supported by their own and naval artillery, began pushing relentlessly up the hills and cliffs, blasting Japanese out of caves and defiles. By the 24th they had reached almost every point of the crest that overlooked their beachhead. Elements of the 9th Regiment performed a smart shore-to-shore operation in LVTs, supported by 40-mm fire from LCI gunboats, to Cabras Island on 22 July, and secured that north prong of Apra Harbor next day. Turning over Cabras to a defense battalion, the 9th then stormed up the Aguada Valley on the beachhead's right flank. On the left flank the 3rd Regiment fought and clawed its way up a steep ridge to ground overlooking the beaches, suffering heavy casualties.

On the night of the fifth day — 25 July — the Japanese delivered their most serious counterattack against the northern beachhead. It had been well planned and expertly prepared, for three days. Toward midnight they began probing and infiltrating all along the line. All night the Marines' left flank was showered by heavy mortar fire, punctuated by occasional banzai charges, and certain small bands of infantry crept down the Asan River valley and almost overran the divisional artillery command post. Several hundred troops reached the rice paddies and engaged in hand-to-hand fighting with the Marines; but these seasoned amphibians dealt with each assault as it came, and by noon 26 July had repelled the attack. The Japanese lost most of their officers in the first assault, and they were unable to reinforce because naval gunfire broke up their troop concentrations in the rear. Every Marine has basic infantry training and keeps his rifle handy, which was fortunate when a Japanese column attacked the 3rd Battalion 21st Regiment command post; it was beaten off by a hastily assembled force of cooks, bakers, clerks and mess attendants. Another group carrying demolition material with which it hoped to destroy the Marines' artillery, was trapped by daylight right in front of the 3rd Division's field hospital. In addition to the corpsmen, ambulatory cases turned out in underwear and pajamas to fight with any weapon they could lay hold of; bed patients fired right from their cots in the tents; 16 Japanese were killed in and around the surgery tent alone.[17]

One Japanese report on the Guam fighting states that this counterattack was thwarted mainly by naval gunfire from off shore and artillery fire from the beach.[18] But Marine combat efficiency was the main factor. After it was over, 3500 enemy dead were counted on the battlefield. This was the decisive battle on Guam itself.

Now the Marines exploited their advantage to secure the Fonte plateau. Lieutenant General Takashina was killed there on 28 July by machine-gun fire as he was trying to retire from his command post. Major General Shigematsu had already fallen, and the elderly Lieutenant General Obata, the Thirty-First Army commander who merely happened to be present, now assumed the responsibility of directing the final defense of Guam. On this northern sector the assault phase ended 28 July when the 3rd Division made contact with the 77th Infantry on the slopes of Mount Tenjo.

Unloading went on over the Asan beaches right along; and it may interest the reader to know what was involved. The 3rd Division comprised 20,324 officers and men, 21.5 per cent of which

[17] Hough *The Island War* p. 273.
[18] Japanese Monograph No. 48, p. 49.

(211 officers and 4231 men) was initially assigned to shore parties. These were responsible for getting almost 25,000 tons of cargo ashore — 14,400 tons of vehicles and organization equipment, 1700 tons of rations, 6000 tons ammunition (7 units of fire for all but antiaircraft weapons, which had 10), and 2130 tons fuel for vehicles and tanks.[19] All this came in over the reef and the beaches in seven days — an average of 3550 tons per diem; a remarkable record, in view of the fact that every pound of supplies had to be transferred from landing or beaching craft to LVT or dukw for transport to inland dumps. It was accomplished only through the prompt anchoring at the edge of the reef of pontoon barges mounting large cranes; these would swing a full cargo net out of landing craft into an amphibian vehicle in a minute's time. Landing on difficult terrain against stout enemy opposition, the 3rd Division not only fought well but unloaded smartly and quickly.

This first week ashore had been costly for the Division. A large majority of its total casualties for the operation (753 killed and missing, 3147 wounded) were then incurred.[20] Casualties both here and at Agat were transferred by LVTs or dukws to specially equipped LSTs until hospital ship *Solace* arrived 24 July. She brought with her the first blood bank waterborne to a fighting front — 100 pints of whole blood contributed by the Marine garrison of Eniwetok. Departing on the 26th with 581 wounded she was relieved by *Bountiful*, which took care of about the same number.

b. Southern Sector — Agat Beaches and Orote

Rear Admiral Reifsnider, Conolly's deputy, had full charge of a difficult landing here by the 1st Provisional Marine Brigade (Brig-

[19] 3rd Marine Div. Action Report, Annex E, Logistics. The Division left behind in Guadalcanal 85 per cent of its tentage and office equipment, 80 per cent of galley equipment, 75 per cent of supplementary equipment, and 50 per cent of its vehicles. There should have been more vehicles, but sufficient quantities of the other equipment were taken. The transports greatly helped the efficiency of the shore parties by sending them hot meals by landing craft.

[20] Maj. O. R. Lodge Marine Corps monograph on Guam chap. v. These figures include casualties for 29 and 30 July, but there were few on those two days.

adier General Lemuel C. Shepherd), which landed two regiments abreast: the 4th (Colonel Alan Shapley USMC) on the White beaches, the 22nd (Colonel Merlin F. Schneider USMC) on the Yellow beaches; while the 305th RCT (Colonel V. J. Tanzola USA) of the 77th Division acted as floating reserve.

These four beaches in Agat Bay, stretching for over a mile between Agat village and Bangi Point, were overlooked by high cliffs on the Orote Peninsula and by two islets, Neye and Yona. Gaan Point stuck out in the middle of the line. Without the long preliminary naval bombardment and air bombing, and the removal of the coral and palm-log cribs by the UDTs, landing would have been impossible. The greatest potential danger was flanking fire from Orote Peninsula, but "Pug" Ainsworth's fire support ships took care of that; *Pennsylvania*, in particular, moved right into Agat Bay, where she could take the entire cliff line under fire; she pumped out a main battery salvo every 22 seconds, and in the final shoot just before the boat waves landed the ancient battlewagon expended over 2000 rounds of 5-inch and over 5000 rounds of 40-mm fire.[21] Behind the beaches the Japanese defenders were driven out of their trench system before the troops landed. Left intact were a row of 25 concealed coconut-log bunkers, one 75-mm gun on Yona Islet, and a concrete blockhouse on Gaan Point (which no photographic interpreter had detected), with one 75-mm and one 37-mm gun, sited to enfilade the beaches.

Initial opposition to the landings was stronger than at Asan. The amphtracs encountered brutally effective mortar and artillery fire as soon as they hit the edge of the reef. Twenty-four of them, more than one in eight of the total, were disabled, mostly by enemy gunfire but some by coral heads. The Marines encountered heavy rifle, machine-gun and artillery fire as soon as they hit the beach. They had little medical aid until the afternoon, as one first-aid station was blown apart and most of the corpsmen killed by a direct hit. Before noon, 75 dead Marines were counted on Beach Yellow 2 alone. But the 1st Battalion 22nd Regiment fought its

[21] War Diary of Capt. John Elliott USMCR on board *Pennsylvania*.

way through the rubble of Agat Village and at 1130 reached its first objective, the Harmon Road that leads to the slopes of Mount Alifan. Fifteen minutes later General Shepherd landed and established his command post in a coconut grove about 200 yards southeast of Gaan Point.

The strong point on Gaan was not disposed of until the afternoon, by a tank attack from the rear. Some tanks were landed on the reef off Beach White 1 as early as 0834, but shell holes, mines, mortar fire, and (it must be admitted) misdirection by a fuddled Navy beachmaster delayed their getting into action. The 4th Regiment, which landed on the White beaches, encountered several pockets of resistance on small hills that were not shown on the map; but they swept on over the canefields at the foot of Mount Alifan and reached their objective line in the early afternoon.

Supplies did not move ashore here as smoothly as had been planned. The loss of 24 LVTs hampered transshipment at the reef's outer edge, and a deposit of silt at its inner edge caused both amphtracs and dukws to bog down. As in all amphibious operations, it was impossible to stop the "assembly line" once started, and only by ingenious expedients such as rubber-boat causeways and ships' life rafts was a dangerous congestion on the reef cleared. Even so, an average of about 3000 tons of cargo per day was unloaded over the Agat beaches during this assault phase.[22]

As early as 1030 the 2nd Battalion of the reserve regiment, the 305th RCT of the 77th Division, was boated and ready to come ashore, but it didn't get the word until 1405. No Marine amphtracs were available (and the 77th had none of its own) when their landing craft hit the reef, and the troops had to wade ashore through waist-deep water, avoiding as best they could the coral heads and potholes. Fortunately the Japanese were then too busy with the Marines to fire on the GIs. At 1530 Colonel Tanzola received a delayed order to land his other two battalions at once. There was another two-hour delay because the boat-control officers, having

---

[22] This figure arrived at by subtracting the 3rd Marine Div.'s figures quoted above from Maj. Lodge's 6650 tons average per diem for both sets of beaches.

received no word, would not let the landing craft leave the line of departure. By this time the 2½-foot tide had risen; water over the reef was chest-high and still there were no LVTs for over-reef transport. Yet the GIs waded and splashed their way through, and Lieutenant Colonel James E. Landrum USA, in charge of the 1st Battalion, located the assembly area ashore and joined the 2nd Battalion (Lieutenant Colonel Robert D. Adair USA) after dark. This was the first of many operations well executed against heavy odds that earned the 77th Infantry its high place in the affections of the Navy and Marine Corps.[23]

Altogether, W-day was a tough one on these Agat beaches — by no means as bad as Tarawa, but worse than Charan Kanoa, Cape Gloucester or Roi-Namur.

At 1830 General Shepherd summed up the results in a message to General Geiger: "Our casualties about 350. Critical shortage fuel and ammunition all types. Think we can handle it. Will continue as planned tomorrow."

The Marines expected a counterattack that night, and at 2230 it came, in the center and on the right. Hill 40, a low, uncharted knoll behind Bangi Point, was wrested from them for a short time but recaptured. On the left flank a column of Japanese tanks followed by mobile artillery rumbled downhill along the Harmon Road at 0230, with the intention of capturing Agat and raking the entire beachhead. A bazooka-armed Marine disposed of the first two tanks before he was killed, and the rest of the Japanese armor was destroyed by Lieutenant James R. Williams's platoon of General Sherman tanks which had been parked near the road for just such a contingency. This Japanese effort was very costly to them — Colonel Suenaga of the 38th Regiment was among the killed — and only less so to the Marines. But their lines held.

As usual, the naval vessels helped with star shell illumination and call fire. "We had been thinking," states a captured Japanese diary, "that we might win through a night counterattack; but when the

[23] The 3rd Battalion, through no fault of its own (its transports were ordered out to sea because of a submarine scare) did not all get ashore until 0600 next day.

star shells came over, one after another, we could only use our men as human bullets. . . . I was horrified by the number of deaths on our side due to the naval gunfire, which continued daily." [24]

On 22 July, the second day, the Brigade captured Mount Alifan, whose northern slopes were honeycombed with caves. Demolition teams sealed the caves, and hand-grenade attacks disposed of coco-nut-log bunkers. The top of the ridge consisted of almost vertical cliffs covered with thick, tangled undergrowth and creepers; but the Marines swarmed up and captured the summit. The 305th advanced somewhat later but tied in with the 22nd Marine Regiment on the left and the 4th on the right for the night, which was marked only by minor attempts at infiltration.

At daybreak 23 July the start of an enemy counterattack on the right flank, between Mount Lamlam and Facpi Point, was spotted by outposts of the 4th Marine Regiment. Shore fire control party being well organized, *Honolulu* was requested to move in, which she promptly did, and spotter planes were launched. At 0930 she began working over the area, aided by planes from the escort carriers. The Japanese quickly decided they did not like it, and retired. A second regimental combat team of the 77th Division, the 306th, waded ashore over the reef and one battalion took position on the front lines, relieving a part of the 4th Marines.[25] All ground units moved ahead that day, and by nightfall the high ground overlooking the Agat beachhead was all secured.

So far, the Marine Brigade and the 77th Division had lost 296 killed or missing in action and 748 wounded. *LCI–365* and *SC–1326* had been hit, losing 9 killed and 22 wounded. *LCI–366* and *LCI–349*, attempting to clean out gun emplacements behind the Neye Islet, lost six men including the skipper and "exec" of *LCI–366*.

Orote Peninsula was the primary objective in this sector. Thrusting out into the ocean, Orote was a natural target for naval gunfire,

[24] Quoted from Cominch Bulletin P-007 "Invasion of the Marianas" III 13, in Maj. O. R. Lodge's monograph on Guam chap. v.
[25] The third RCT, the 307th, landed 24 July with great difficulty in a rising sea; General Bruce then established his command post ashore.

and the Navy gave all it had, pounding selected positions for 30 minutes to an hour every morning while the Marines were eating breakfast. In order to deliver high-trajectory fire and avoid ricochets, heavy gunfire ships like *Pennsylvania* took positions as much as eight miles north or south of the peninsula, arranging the fall of shot to be parallel to the Marines' front lines. All fire was indirect, controlled by air spot, and on occasions a Marine officer rode the spotting plane. The fire was generally admitted to be effective and devastating; but it did not crush resistance by ground troops.

Preceded by an hour of naval gunfire, the 22nd Marine Regiment moved off on 24 July toward Sumay. The road proved to be heavily mined and covered with pre-registered artillery and mortar fire, and the Marines did not get far that day; but by the end of the 25th they had the enemy bottled up on Orote. Commander Asaichi Tamai, senior officer of all naval and army ground troops in this sector, now ordered his men to make a frontal attack, preparing them for the sacrifice by issuing all the beer, sake and synthetic Scotch on the peninsula — and there was plenty; Guam seems to have been a liquor supply center for the Japanese. These interesting preliminaries made so much noise and consumed so much time that the Marine artillery was able to register on all probable approaches. The assault was an amazing spectacle. Sake-crazed troops boiled out of mangrove cover on the front of the 3rd Battalion 22nd Marine Regiment, led by sword-swinging and flag-waving officers, the troops carrying sticks, pitchforks, baseball bats and empty bottles in addition to their rifles. Artillery opened up on them: "Arms and legs flew like snowflakes, Japs ran amuck, screamed in terror until they died. . . . Flares revealed an out-of-this world picture of Nipponese drunks reeling about in our forward positions, falling into foxholes, tossing aimless grenades here and there . . . laughing crazily, to be exterminated in savage close-in fighting. Succeeding waves were caught in a deadly cross fire." [26] At dawn 26 July over 400 bodies were sprawled in front of the Marines' positions.

[26] Hough *The Island War* p. 279.

By this time the 77th Division had taken over so much of the Agat front that most of the Marine brigade was able to pivot on its left flank to drive down the Orote Peninsula. The Japanese had several organized strong points near the airfield which naval gun-fire had not broken up; and, most surprising, the batteries on cliffs adjacent to Neye Islet, which gunfire ships thought they had long since disposed of, came to life and caused the Marines a great deal of trouble.[27] They advanced slowly, the enemy contesting every yard. In taking a strong Japanese position on a ridge overlooking the airfield on 27 July, the 22nd Regiment enlisted the aid of all available aircraft and a terrific barrage from naval vessels and Corps artillery. That did the trick; and, before the astonished gaze of the Marine footsoldiers, the Japanese broke and ran in mad retreat across open country, abandoning their strong defensive position. Two Marine battalions followed them in hot pursuit, seized the dominating ridge and dug in for the night.

This was the turning point in the battle for Orote. On 28 July Sumay and the old Marine barracks (of which only a bronze plaque remained) were taken. By 1400 next day the Marines held the Orote airfield; and that afternoon a tank and infantry patrol that went to the very end of the peninsula found only two Japanese soldiers. There was plenty of mopping-up to do, in the cliffs, but Orote was in American hands. That afternoon Admiral Spruance, Lieutenant General Holland M. Smith, Major General Geiger, and Brigadier General Shepherd assembled on the old parade ground with every soldier who could be spared from the lines. Marines who had helped capture the site furnished an honor guard; "To the Colors" was sounded on a captured Japanese bugle, and at 1530 the American flag again flew over the Orote Peninsula.

Engineers were already at work on the airstrip, which had been so spared by naval gunfire and air bombing that on 30 July a Navy

---

[27] Orote Peninsula was not then, as it became after the capture of Guam, prac-tically one continuous military city. Apart from the airfield, the old Marine bar-racks and rifle range, and the village of Sumay, it was a rolling terrain, covered with heavy undergrowth interspersed with mangrove swamps and an occasional cocoanut grove.

Avenger was able to land. And, as Cabras Island had already been taken by Marines operating from the northern beachhead, the "harbor stretchers" were soon at work improving Apra Harbor.

While the Brigade concentrated on taking Orote, the 77th Division was pushing east and north from the beachhead to join hands with the 3rd Marine Division. Several days were spent profitably in reconnaissance patrols to ascertain where the main enemy strength lay. It was discovered, with the aid of loyal natives, that the entire Japanese force had moved out of the southern massif into the northern half of the island. Accordingly, on 27 July, General Bruce asked permission of General Geiger to seize Mount Tenjo. Permission was readily granted, and by 0830 a company of the 305th reached the summit. That afternoon the 307th Regiment tied in with the 3rd Marine Division, which had already captured Mount Chachao. American lines were now continuous. Final beachhead line had been attained and main objectives secured; it only remained to clear the enemy out of the northern half of Guam.

"The coöperation of the Navy from Admiral Conolly down to LCI gunboats was superb," reported the III 'Phib Corps naval gunfire officer. "No firing problem was considered too much when that was what was wanted by the landing force. Giving the troops what they wanted was the watchword." [28] The same shore fire-control procedures were employed as on Saipan, and on Guam they worked better. Searchlights and star shell were used for night illumination. Every evening General Turnage or General Shepherd would list targets — as many as 25 in each area — for night harassing fires. Many more deep support missions were fired than ever before; spot planes from battleships and cruisers sought out Japanese targets in the interior, far from our own troops' front lines, and directed heavy-caliber fire to them. For close support, the III 'Phib Corps depended more on its own artillery than on that of naval vessels. Call fire [29] was not only good, but versatile; on one occa-

[28] Gen. Geiger Report, Naval Gunfire sec. p. 8.
[29] Lt. Col. R. D. Heinl USMC in his "Case Studies in Naval Gunfire Planning" remarks that the III 'Phib Corps had previously regarded call fire as a "luxury item" since, in contrast to the experience of V 'Phib in Micronesia, its previous

sion, Admiral Conolly ordered *Pennsylvania* in to a position only 600 yards off the Agat beaches to support the Marines with her 40-mm guns. As the Admiral remarked, the old bugaboo that capital ships should never expose themselves to coastal batteries was finally buried at Guam.

Mistakes were made, of course; air observers and cameras could not see everything. An enormous number of rounds was wasted on a brick kiln in the hills, under the impression that it was Japanese headquarters. A Japanese motor transport park under a grove near Sumay was completely "clobbered" because an aviator thought he saw parked planes there. But there was not, I believe, a single instance of American troops being hit by naval gunfire.[30] Very few natives were killed, as most of them sat out the bombardment in the hills. Incidents such as this were common: —

"5 August, *Wichita* plane observed 11 or 12 natives in Area 753 waving white flag; on orders from General Geiger *Wichita* plane dropped following message in English and Chamorro: 'Proceed SW with white flag.' This message brought not 12 but a group of 200 friendly natives through our front lines."

On the quality of close air support there is a difference of opinion. During the assault phase there had to be one coördinator, since planes from fast carriers and escort carriers were involved. Marine Corps officers declared that it was not very good; naturally, as this was one of the earliest occasions when close air support was tried in an amphibious operation.[31] One serious accident occurred on a strike 400 yards in advance of the 3rd Division front lines. Commander Shirley Miller, directing support aircraft from *Appalachian*, briefed Navy planes to perform the mission; just as they completed their run, B–25s from Saipan reported that they had heard the briefing and viewed the target, and proposed to follow up. Miller

---

landings in the Solomons had been lightly opposed and shore-based air power had always been available. But the 1st Provisional Brigade had an experienced Jasco which had functioned under Admiral Conolly at Roi-Namur.

[30] The only reported instances of this were deliberately caused by Japanese artillery salvos, carefully timed to be simultaneous with American salvos to confuse American spotters. Air bombers were victims of the same ruse.

[31] Lodge monograph chap. v, quoting several Marine Action Reports.

gave them permission, and in they went; but a trigger-happy turret gunner of a B–25, without asking his pilot's permission, shot at a presumed enemy target over the nose of his plane, and hit a Marine command post.[32]

3. *Island Secured, 29 July–10 August*

Although the more rugged half of the island and the strategic points around Apra Harbor were now in American hands, and half the Japanese garrison was dead, General Geiger knew well enough that the rest of the campaign would be no pushover. The ruins of Agaña were still in enemy possession. Beyond it lay marshes, from the edge of which a rolling plateau, covered with densely matted jungle growth, sloped up to 600-foot cliffs at Ritidian and Pati Points.

On 29–30 July the American troops had their first opportunity to rest, wash and shave since W-day. From the Fonte plateau, where the buildings of Cincpac advanced headquarters arose a few months later, Marines could look across a steep ravine into the old provincial capital. Men who had binoculars beheld a curious sight — the Japanese garrison putting on a full-dress parade, complete with gleaming bayonets and shining swords, on the Agaña plaza. Whether this was done to frighten the Marines, or to raise Japanese morale, or to impress the natives is not known. The Chamorros certainly were not impressed, for they began swarming to the American lines in numbers embarrassing to their liberators.

General Obata now withdrew the bulk of his forces, for a last stand, to Mount Santa Rosa, overlooking the sea about five miles south of Pati Point, leaving two covering units on the narrow ankle of the Guam sock. Knowledge of this plan would have facilitated General Geiger's task; as it was, he had to guess where enemy troops could be found in the great expanse of jungle that lay ahead. His plan, in brief, was for the 3rd Marine Division to advance with

[32] Conversations with Maj. J. R. Spooner USMC and Cdr. Miller.

three regiments abreast on the left, while the 77th, brought up into position on 29 July, took the right flank. The 1st Marine Brigade now protected the rear. Careful plans were drafted for air, naval and ground artillery support. Admiral Conolly reorganized all supporting arms, with Admirals Ainsworth and Joy under him commanding the two gunfire units.

Both divisions jumped off 31 July. Ruined Agaña was entered by the Marines before noon, while the GIs hacked their way through jungle to the east coast, liberating a concentration camp of Chamorros en route. By nightfall both had reached their objectives. It looked as if the troops would soon outrun the capacity of their supply line; Seabees and Marine Corps engineers (19th Regiment) were put to work improving the dirt roads and trails that had become overgrown during the Japanese occupation. On 1 August they had the Agaña-Pago Bay road open right across the island. General Geiger pushed his troops hard with the object of engaging the enemy before he could organize defensive positions around Mount Santa Rosa. To the same end, Admiral Ainsworth in *Honolulu*, with two battleships, cruiser *New Orleans*, and six destroyers was sent around to the windward coast to help break up enemy concentrations and support the 77th Division, while Admiral Joy's group took care of the west coast and the Marines. On 2 August the Tiyan airstrip was captured, on the 3rd the 77th took Barrigada Village, with a deep artesian well as first prize. Fresh water was a scarce commodity on this half of the island.

Small squads of Japanese with automatic weapons, concealed in the dense foliage on each side of the roads leading north, did their poor best to hold up the invasion. But the first real trouble was encountered on 5–6 August, when the American troops came under artillery fire from the new Mount Santa Rosa strong point. At least seven guns there had escaped destruction by air bombing and naval gunfire. To avoid detection, they were fired by day during rain squalls, or at night. Division and corps artillery could only silence them temporarily. Strong points around Finegayan, the outer bastion of the Mount Santa Rosa defenses, were captured 5 August (along with 100 cases of good Japanese beer), and the attack rolled on.

To the 77th fell the honor of taking Mount Santa Rosa 7–8 August, with a loss of only 41 killed or missing and 104 wounded. That such very light casualties were incurred in storming a major strong point was due largely to the intensive naval shelling — some 2500 rounds of 5- and 6-inch daily for three days. There had been 5000 Japanese troops, seven guns and 13 tanks on the position before the action. All seven guns and five tanks were destroyed, and 530 dead were counted on and around the hill; the survivors slipped away into the jungle.

Marine patrols reached Ritidian Point on the afternoon of 8 August; next day elements of the 77th Division got to Pati Point. And at 1130 August 10, just as *Indianapolis* was steaming into Apra Harbor with Admiral Spruance and General H. M. Smith on board, and as Admiral Nimitz and General Vandegrift were flying over from Saipan, General Geiger announced that organized resistance on Guam had ceased. This was somewhat premature. On the afternoon of 12 August, General Obata's last command post near Mount Mataguac was stormed by units of the 77th; everyone including the General was killed or committed suicide.

Thus, in three weeks after the landing the battle for Guam was won. Admiral Conolly hauled down his flag in *Appalachian* and flew back to Pearl Harbor to plan the Palau operation, leaving Admiral Reifsnider in charge. Most of the naval vessels that had supported the assault departed, and the island commander, Major General Henry L. Larsen usmc, took over on 15 August. At least 9000 Japanese troops were still at large in the jungle, so mopping-up activities continued until after the end of the war.

Before the fighting ended, Seabees and Army engineers were at work on airfields, permanent installations and harbor improvements which, within a few months, transformed Guam into a major advanced base for the liberation of the Philippines. By that time the island population had swollen to over 220,000: 21,838 Chamorros, 65,000 Army, 78,000 Navy and 59,000 Marines. Over 19,000 Japa-

Orote Peninsula and Apra Harbor, Guam

Photo taken 12 June. Cabras Island in background. Note dummy PBYs off right end of airstrip

The Asan beachhead after the landings

Orote Peninsula and Asan Beachhead

Burial at sea

After the Battle, U.S.S. Lexington

nese had been accounted for: 1250 prisoners, the rest killed, including some 8500 killed or captured after 10 August. Attempts of ranking Japanese officers to conduct a die-hard guerilla warfare were frustrated by want of food, aggressive American patrolling, and, as Lieutenant Colonel Takeda admitted, "skillful psychological warfare." The Colonel and 113 officers and men, after hearing their Emperor's order to surrender, gave themselves up on 4 September 1945; but several hundred soldiers still at large perished of hunger in the jungle or surrendered singly over a period of two or three years.

"This campaign was brilliantly conceived, splendidly planned, and precisely executed," wrote a participant of the recapture of Guam.[33] That indeed it was. The month's postponement, unlike most postponements in military history, turned out to be a godsend, since it permitted Admiral Conolly to arrange and carry out the most meticulous bombardment plan of the war. Naval gunfire, air bombing and the UDTs cleared the way for almost faultless landings over difficult reefs. Marines and GIs alike fought with skill and courage against a tenacious enemy, where terrain was all on his side. Casualties,[34] though heavy, fell short of those on Saipan. In short, Guam was a fitting climax to the great Operation "Forager," completed in exactly two months from the first shot, after three land campaigns and the greatest carrier action of the war. On 12 August 1944, the Philippine Sea and the air over it, and the islands

[33] CTG 53.5 (Rear Adm. Ainsworth) Action Report.
[34] Ground Forces engaged and Casualties at Guam: —

	Total Engaged	Killed in Action	Missing in Action	Wounded in Action	Total Casualties
3rd Marine Division	20,328	679	74	3,147	3,900
1st Prov. Marine Brigade	9,886	403	51	1,745	2,199
77th Infantry Division	17,958	193	20	704	917
III 'Phib Corps Troops	6,719	15	0	52	67
Totals	54,891	1,290	145	5,648	7,083

Japanese dead by burial count to 1 Sept.: 10,693; *prisoners:* 98. CTF 56 (Lt. Gen. H. M. Smith) Report on Forager, 1 Sept. 1944, Enclosure F.

of Saipan, Tinian and Guam, were under American control. May they never again be relinquished!

We have now followed the fortunes of the Pacific war through six volumes, from the assault on Pearl Harbor to the securing of Dutch New Guinea and the Marianas. Allied forces, over 90 per cent of them American, had achieved in two and a half years what almost everyone on the morrow of Pearl Harbor thought would take at least five and possibly ten. The second Japanese offensive, in 1942, had been thrown back at the Battles of the Coral Sea and Midway. A long and bitter struggle for Guadalcanal had become the starting point for capturing the rest of the Solomons, while Southwest Pacific forces secured the Papuan Peninsula, and from both sides massive air and naval attacks neutralized the island fortress of Rabaul. The Gilberts and Marshalls and the recovery of lost Aleutian islands followed in quick succession, so that by early 1944 all was ready for a swift advance along Dutch New Guinea and into the Marianas. New techniques, new weapons, new methods had been worked out. And through all these weary months United States submarines had continued their war of attrition against Japanese shipping.

With the Japanese defensive perimeter cracked and broken, the air groups of the Japanese Navy destroyed, and the Tojo government fallen from power, we can take a breather from the Pacific war and return to operations on the other side of the world. For in Sicily, Italy and France, and throughout the Atlantic Ocean, the Atlantic Fleet of the United States Navy had been doing its utmost to implement the great strategic decision of 1941: to beat the European Axis first.

Hollandia Task Organization

Naval Forces Engaged at Aitape — Tanahmerah Bay — Humboldt Bay
22 April — 13 May 1944

Units and ships that later participated in the Wakde, Biak, Noemfoor, and Sansapor operation are marked (W), (B), (N), and (S).

SUPREME COMMANDER, ALLIED FORCES, SOUTH-WEST PACIFIC AREA
General Douglas MacArthur

SEVENTH FLEET
Vice Admiral Thomas C. Kinkaid

TF 77 ATTACK FORCE, Rear Admiral Daniel E. Barbey

Embarking for Aitape, 163rd Regimental Combat Team (reinforced), 41st Division, Brig. Gen. J. A. Doe USA; Tanahmerah Bay, I Corps Headquarters, Lt. Gen. Robert L. Eichelberger USA; 24th Infantry Division, reinforced (less 1 RCT), Maj. Gen. F. A. Irving USA; Humboldt Bay, 41st Infantry Division (less 163rd RCT, reinforced), Maj. Gen. H. H. Fuller USA.

TG 77.1 WESTERN ATTACK GROUP, Rear Admiral Barbey in destroyer SWANSON, Cdr. E. L. Robertson (B)(N)(S).

Transports, Capt. P. A. Stevens
HENRY T. ALLEN, Capt. John Meyer (W); H.M.A.S. MANOORA, Cdr. A. P. Cousins RANR (W); H.M.A.S. KANIMBLA, Cdr. H. H. Shaw RAN; LSD CARTER HALL, Lt. Cdr. F. J. Harris USNR; cargo ship TRIANGULUM, Lt. Cdr. F. W. Parsons USNR.

16 LCIs, Lt. Cdr. J. P. Hurndall USNR (W)(B)(N)(S); 7 LSTs, Cdr. T. C. Green (W)(B)(N)(S).[1]

Screen, Cdr. W. S. Veeder (W)(B)(N)
DDs: HOBBY, Cdr. G. W. Pressey (W)(B)(N)(S); NICHOLSON, Cdr. W. W. Vanous (W)(B)(N)(S); WILKES, Cdr. F. Wolseiffer (W)(B)(N)(S); GRAYSON, Lt. Cdr. W. V. Pratt (W)(B)(N)(S); GILLESPIE, Cdr. J. S. Fahy (W)(B)(N)(S); KALK, Lt. Cdr. H. D. Fuller (W)(B).

[1] *LST-220*, Hollandia only.

Special Service Vessels, Capt. N. D. Brantly

Ocean Tug H.M.A.S. Tug RESERVE (W); *SC-743* (W), *SC-738; LCI-31* (W) (B) (N); *YMS-8, YMS-10*.

TG 77.2 CENTRAL ATTACK GROUP, Rear Admiral William M. Fechteler (B) (N) (S).

Group Flagship: DD REID, Cdr. S. A. McCornock (W) (B) (N).

Transports, Cdr. A. V. Knight RANR

H.M.A.S. WESTRALIA, Cdr. Knight; LSD GUNSTON HALL, Cdr. D. E. Collins; AK GANYMEDE, Lt. Cdr. G. H. Melichar.

Destroyer Transports, Lt. Cdr. F. D. Schwartz

HUMPHREYS, Lt. Cdr. M. J. Carley USNR; BROOKS, Lt. Cdr. C. V. Allen USNR; SANDS, Lt. Cdr. L. C. Brogger USNR; GILMER, Lt. Cdr. J. S. Horner USNR; HERBERT, Lt. Cdr. J. N. Ferguson (B) (S).

16 LCIs, Cdr. H. F. McGee (W) (B) (N) (S); 7 LSTs, Capt. R. M. Scruggs (W) (B) (N) (S).[2]

Destroyers, Capt. R. F. Stout (W) (B)

STEVENSON, Cdr. F. E. Wilson (W) (N) (S); STOCKTON, Lt. Cdr. W. W. Stark (W) (B) (N) (S); THORN, Cdr. E. Brumby; ROE, Cdr. F. S. Stich (W) (B) (N); WELLES, Cdr. D. M. Coffee (W) (B) (N) (S); RADFORD, Cdr. G. E. Griggs (N) (S); TAYLOR, Cdr. N. J. F. Frank.

Special Service Vessels, Capt. Bern Anderson (W) (B) (N)

DMSs HOGAN, HOVEY; *SC-703* (W) (B), *SC-743; LCI-34* (W) (B) (N) (S); *LCI-73* (W) (B) (N) (S); *YMS-46, YMS-47;* tug SONOMA (W) (B).

TG 77.3 EASTERN ATTACK GROUP, Capt. A. G. Noble (W) in destroyer LAVALLETTE, Cdr. W. Thompson (N) (S).

Transports, Cdr. D. L. Mattie (B)

APDs: KILTY, Lt. L. G. Benson (B) (S); WARD, Lt. Cdr. F. W. Lemly USNR (B) (S); CROSBY, Lt. W. E. Sims (B) (S); DICKERSON, Lt. Cdr. J. R. Cain USNR(S); TALBOT, Lt. Cdr. C. C. Morgan USNR; SCHLEY, Lt. Cdr. E. T. Farley USNR (B) (S); KANE, Lt. F. M. Christiansen USNR; DENT, Lt. Cdr. R. A. Wilhelm USNR; NOA Lt. H. W. Bond; LSD BELLE GROVE, Lt. Cdr. M. Seavey USNR; AK ETAMIN, Lt. Cdr. G. W. Stedman USCG.

Screen, Capt. A. D. Chandler (Desdiv 41)

DDs: NICHOLAS, Cdr. R. T. S. Keith; O'BANNON, Cdr. R. W. Smith; JENKINS, Cdr. P. D. Gallery (N) (S); HOPEWELL, Cdr. C. C. Shute; HOWORTH, Lt. Cdr. E. S. Burns. 7 LSTs, Lt. Cdr. D. M. Baker USNR(W).

Special Service Vessels, Capt. J. W. Jamison

DMSs HAMILTON, PERRY; SCs *742, 981* (B), *637, 648;* YMSs *48, 51;* ocean tug CHETCO.

TG 77.4 FIRST REINFORCEMENT GROUP, Capt. E. M. Thompson

Western Unit, Capt. Thompson

AKA VIRGO, Cdr. C. H. McLaughlin USNR; DDs: STEVENS, Lt. Cdr. W. M. Rakow; HARRISON, Lt. Cdr. W. V. Combs; frigate CORONADO, Cdr. M. W. Sprow; 6 LSTs Cdr. F. D. Higbee USCG.[3]

---

[2] *LST-118*, Hollandia only.   [3] All but one also (W)(B)(N)(S).

Central Unit, Cdr. J. J. Greytak

DDs: MCKEE, Cdr. Greytak; JOHN RODGERS, Cdr. H. O. Parish; frigate SAN PEDRO, Lt. Cdr. C. O. Ashley; 5 LSTs, Lt. Cdr. J. E. Van Zandt USNR (W) (B) (N) (S).

Eastern Unit, Capt. H. O. Larson (Desdiv 42)

AKA BOÖTES, Lt. Cdr. H. P. Bacon USNR; DDs FLETCHER, Lt. Cdr. J. L. Foster (N) (S); MURRAY, Cdr. P. R. Anderson; frigates GLENDALE, Cdr. H. J. Doebler USCG; LONG BEACH, Lt. Cdr. T. R. Midtlyng USCG; 6 LSTs, Lt. Cdr. A. Schlott USNR (W) (B) (N) (S).

TG 77.5 SECOND REINFORCEMENT GROUP, Capt. J. B. McGovern

Western Unit, Capt. McGovern

APAs: ZEILIN, Cdr. T. B. Fitzpatrick; WINDSOR, Cdr. D. C. Woodward USNR; DDs: SIGSBEE, Cdr. B. V. Russell; DASHIELL, Lt. Cdr. E. A. Barham; DEs: LOVELACE, Cdr. R. D. de Kay USNR (W); MANNING, Lt. J. I. Mingay USNR (W).

Central Unit, Cdr. H. Crommelin (Desdiv 50)

DDs RINGGOLD, Cdr. Crommelin; SCHROEDER, Cdr. J. T. Bowers; 5 LSTs, Cdr. E. A. McFall.

TG 77.6 Floating Reserve, Capt. G. E. McCabe USCG.

APAs ORMSBY, Capt. L. Frisco USNR; HARRY LEE, Cdr. J. G. Pomeroy; AKA CENTAURUS, Capt. McCabe.

TF 78 ESCORT CARRIER GROUPS, Rear Admiral Van H. Ragsdale.

TG 78.1 Cardiv 22, Rear Admiral Ragsdale; SANGAMON, Capt. M. E. Browder; SUWANNEE, Capt. W. D. Johnson; CHENANGO, Capt. D. Ketcham; SANTEE, Capt. H. F. Fick.

Destroyer Squadron 2, Capt. E. A. Solomons (W) (B) (N) (S). MORRIS, Cdr. Gordon L. Caswell; ANDERSON, Lt. Cdr. J. F. Murdock; HUGHES, Lt. Cdr. E. B. Rittenhouse; MUSTIN, Cdr. M. M. Riker; RUSSELL, Lt. Cdr. L. R. Miller; ELLET, Lt. Cdr. E. C. Rider; LANSDOWNE, Lt. Cdr. W. S. Maddox; LARDNER, Lt. Cdr. O. C. Schatz.

TG 78.2 Cardiv 24, Rear Admiral R. E. Davison.

NATOMA BAY, Capt. H. L. Meadow; CORAL SEA, Capt. H. W. Taylor, CORREGIDOR; Capt. R. L. Bowman; MANILA BAY, Capt. B. L. Braun.

Destroyer Squadron 48, Capt. J. T. Bottom. ERBEN, Lt. Cdr. M. Slayton; WALKER, Cdr. H. E. Townsend; HALE, Cdr. Donald W. Wilson; ABBOT, Cdr. M. E. Dornin; BULLARD (Desdiv 96, Cdr. C. E. Carroll on board), Cdr. B. W. Freund; KIDD, Cdr. A. B. Roby; BLACK, Lt. Cdr. E. R. King; CHAUNCEY, Lt. Cdr. L. C. Conwell; STEMBEL, Cdr. W. L. Tagg.

TF 74 COVERING FORCE "A," Rear Admiral V. A. C. Crutchley RN (W) (B) (N) (S).

Heavy Cruisers H.M.A.S. AUSTRALIA, Capt. E. F. V. Dechaineux RAN; H.M.A.S. SHROPSHIRE, Capt. J. A. Collins RAN; destroyers H.M.A.S. WARRAMUNGA, Cdr. N. A. MacKinnon RAN; H.M.A.S. ARUNTA, Cdr. A. E. Buchanan RAN; AMMEN, Cdr. H. Williams; MULLANY, Cdr. B. J. Mullaney.

TF 75 COVERING FORCE "B," Rear Admiral Russell S. Berkey (W)(B)
(N)(S).

Light Cruisers PHOENIX, Capt. J. H. Duncan; NASHVILLE, Capt. C. E. Coney; BOISE,
Capt. J. S. Roberts; Destroyer Squadron 24, Capt. K. M. McManes; HUTCHINS, Cdr.
J. B. Cochran; BACHE, Lt. Cdr. R. C. Morton; DALY, Cdr. R. G. Visser; ABNER READ
(Cdr. J. B. McLean, Desdiv 48), Cdr. T. B. Hutchins; BUSH, Cdr. T. A. Smith.

The following vessels, joining VII 'Phib after the Hollandia operation, took part
in the assault phases of succeeding operations as indicated: —

Wakde: DD TRATHEN, Cdr. F. L. Tedder; DEs JAMES E. CRAIG, Lt. Cdr. H. M.
Ericsson; EICHENBERGER, Lt. Cdr. N. Harrell; NEUNEDORF, Lt. Cdr. J. N. McDonald;
SC-699, SC-738.
Biak: DDs SAMPSON, Cdr. T. M. Fleck; WARRINGTON, Lt. Cdr. R. A. Dawes; BALCH,
Cdr. H. N. Coffin.
Noemfoor and Sansapor: *PC-1120, PC-1132, PC-1133, PC-1134;* ocean tug
YUMA; *LCI-543, LCI-544.*
Sansapor: Destroyer STACK, Lt. Cdr. R. E. Wheeler.

Task Force 58 of the Pacific Fleet participated in the Hollandia Operation; its
organization was almost identical with that described in Appendix III for the
Battle of the Philippine Sea.

LAND-BASED AND TENDER-BASED AIR

TF 73 AIRCRAFT SEVENTH FLEET

Commodore Thomas S. Combs (Comfairwing 17) (W)(B)(N)(S)

TG 73.1 SEEADLER HARBOR GROUP, Commodore Combs [4]

VP-33, 13 PBY-5 (Catalinas), Lt. Cdr. R. C. Bengston, based on tender TANGIER,
Cdr. R. M. Oliver; VP-52, 13 PBY-5, Lt. Cdr. H. A. Sommer, based on tenders
SAN PABLO, Cdr. S. B. Dunlap, HERON, Lt. J. M. Norcott USNR; VB-106, 11 PB4Y-1
(Liberators), Lt. Cdr. J. T. Hayward.

TG 73.2 LANGEMAK BAY GROUP, Cdr. W. O. Gallery

VP-34, 10 PBY-5, Lt. Cdr. T. A. Christopher, based on tender HALF MOON.

[4] R.A.A.F. Squadrons 11 and 20 (Catalinas) of the 78th Wing were attached 14-21
April 1944. The R.A.A.F. performed numerous patrol and bombing missions in the Banda,
Timor and Arafura Seas, as well as successful mining operations in the harbor at Balik-
papan. See Craven and Cate *The Army Air Forces in World War II* IV 601.

Naval Forces Engaged in the Capture of Saipan and Tinian[1]

(Operation "Forager")

June–August 1944

PACIFIC FLEET

Admiral Chester W. Nimitz, at Pearl Harbor

FIFTH FLEET

Admiral Raymond A. Spruance in *Indianapolis*

TF 51 JOINT EXPEDITIONARY FORCE

Vice Admiral Richmond K. Turner in *Rocky Mount*,
Capt. S. F. Patten
Headquarters Support Aircraft, Captain R. F. Whitehead

TF 52 NORTHERN ATTACK FORCE, Vice Admiral Turner

TG 52.2, Rear Admiral Harry W. Hill (Second in Command)
Commanding General of Expeditionary Troops and Northern Troops and Landing Force, Lieut. General Holland M. Smith USMC; Brig. General G. B. Erskine USMC, Chief of Staff, in *Cambria*, Capt. C. W. Dean USCG (T).

TG 52.3 Transport Group "ABLE," Capt. H. B. Knowles
Embarking 2nd Marine Division, Maj. Gen. T. E. Watson USMC.
Transdiv 18, Capt. Knowles: APAs MONROVIA, Cdr. J. D. Kelsey; FREDERICK FUNSTON, Cdr. C. C. Anderson; AP WARHAWK, Cdr. S. H. Thompson USNR; AKA ALCYONE, Cdr. H. P. Knickerbocker; LSD LINDENWALD, Capt. W. H. Weaver USNR.
Transdiv 10, Capt. G. D. Morrison: APAs CLAY, Capt. E. W. Abdill; NEVILLE, Capt. B. Bartlett; ARTHUR MIDDLETON, Capt. S. A. Olsen USCG; FELAND, Cdr. G. M. Jones USNR; AKA ALHENA, Cdr. M. D. Sylvester; AKs JUPITER, Lt. Cdr. T. A. Whitaker; HERCULES, Cdr. W. H. Turnquist USNR.
Transdiv 28, Capt. H. C. Flanagan: APAs BOLIVAR, Cdr. R. P. Wadell; DOYEN, Cdr. J. G. McClaughry; SHERIDAN, Cdr. J. J. Mockrish USNR; AP COMET, Lt. Cdr. T. C. Fonda USNR; AKA ELECTRA, Cdr. C. S. Beightler; LSD OAK HILL, Cdr. C. A. Peterson.

[1] Units and ships which participated in capture of Tinian are marked (T). C.O.'s here listed were in command 15 June 1944.

TG 52.4 Transport Group "BAKER," Capt. D. W. Loomis
Embarking 4th Marine Division, Maj. Gen. Harry Schmidt USMC[2]

Transdiv 20, Capt. Loomis: APAs LEONARD WOOD, Capt. H. C. Perkins USCG; PIERCE, Capt. F. M. Adams; JAMES O'HARA, Cdr. E. W. Irish; AP LASALLE, Cdr. F. C. Fluegel USNR; AKA (T) THUBAN, Cdr. J. C. Campbell USNR; LSD (T) ASHLAND, Lt. Cdr. W. A. Caughey USNR.
Transdiv 26, Capt. R. E. Hanson: APAs CALLAWAY, Capt. D. C. McNeil USCG; SUMTER, Capt. T. G. Haaf; LEON, Capt. B. B. Adell; AP STORM KING, Capt. H. D. Krick; AKA ALMAACK, Cdr. J. Y. Dannenberg; LSDs WHITE MARSH, Cdr. G. H. Eppelman USNR; (T) BELLE GROVE, Cdr. M. Seavey USNR.
Transdiv 30, Capt. C. A. Misson: APAs (T) KNOX, Cdr. J. H. Brady, (T) CALVERT, Cdr. E. J. Sweeney USNR; (T) FULLER, Cdr. N. M. Pigman; APs (T) JOHN LAND, Cdr. F. A. Graf; GEORGE F. ELLIOT, Cdr. A. J. Couble; AKA BELLATRIX, Cdr. E. J. Anderson USNR.

TG 52.8, EASTERN LANDING GROUP,[3] Cdr. C. J. McWhinnie

Embarking 1st Battalion 2nd Marine Regiment, Col. W. B. Kyle USMC.
Transdiv 12, Cdr. McWhinnie: APDs (T) WATERS, Cdr. McWhinnie, (T) STRINGHAM, Lt. Cdr. R. H. Moureau USNR; (T) GOLDSBOROUGH, Lt. W. J. Meehan USNR; (T) MANLEY, Lt. R. T. Newell USNR; (T) OVERTON, Lt. Cdr. D. K. O'Connor USNR; NOA, Lt. Cdr. H. W. Boud USNR.

TG 52.12 Transport Screen, Capt. R. E. Libby (Comdesron 56)

Destroyers (T) NEWCOMB, Cdr. L. B. Cook; (T) BENNION, Cdr. J. W. Cooper; (T) HEYWOOD L. EDWARDS, Cdr. J. W. Boulware; (T) BRYANT, Cdr. P. L. High; PHELPS, Lt. Cdr. D. L. Martineau; SHAW, Cdr. R. H. Phillips; (T) PRICHETT, Cdr. C. T. Caufield; (T) PHILIP, Lt. Cdr. J. B. Rutter; (T) CONY, Cdr. A. W. Moore; MUGFORD, Lt. Cdr. M. A. Shellabarger; SELFRIDGE, Lt. Cdr. L. L. Snider; (T) CONYNGHAM,[4] Lt. Cdr. Brown Taylor; (T) PATTERSON, Lt. Cdr. A. F. White; (T) BAGLEY, Cdr. W. H. Shea; (T) RENSHAW, Cdr. J. A. Lark; APD KANE, Lt. F. M. Christiansen USNR; PCEs *1396, 1404, 1457, 1460.*

TG 52.5 Tractor Flotilla, Capt. A. J. Robertson in *PC(S)-1402*
Tractor Group "ABLE," Capt. J. S. Lillard

LST Unit 1, Lt. Cdr. J. L. Harlan: LSTs *451, 31, 130, 213, 218, 242, 263, 271;* LST Unit 2, Lt. Cdr. S. A. Lief USNR; LSTS (T) *484, 34* "PB,"[5] (T) *278,* (T) *341, 390,* (T) *450* "PB," (T) *461,* (T) *485;* LST Reserve "ABLE," Lt. E. C. Shea USNR; LSTs (T) *486,* (T) *120* "PB," *127,* (T) *131, 166,* (T) *246.*

Tractor Group "BAKER," Capt. Robertson

LST Unit 3, Cdr. W. S. Whiteside: LSTs (T) *226,* (T) *19,* (T) *42,* (T) *45,* (T) *84, 126, 223,* (T) *273;* LST Unit 4, Lt. Cdr. J. B. Hoyt USNR; LSTs (T) *225,* (T) *128* "PB," (T) *129,* (T) *222,* (T) *224, 269* "PB," (T) *275, 487;* LST Reserve "Baker," Cdr. R. W. LaJeunesse: LSTs *354,* (T) *23, 121,* (T) *340;* Support Artillery Group, Lt. R. J. Buchar USCG; LSTs *272,* (T) *40, 124, 169, 240, 277,* (T) *483.*

[2] Relieved by Maj. Gen. Clifton B. Cates USMC 12 July and assumed command of Northern Troops and Landing Force.
[3] So designated because detailed to a separate landing on Magicienne Bay, which was not carried out.
[4] Replaced *Ralph Talbot,* whose bow was damaged in collision with *California* on 12 June en route to Saipan.
[5] "PB" indicates that the LST carried a Pontoon Barge Unit, these units being under command of Cdr. C. E. Anderson.

Appendix II

TG 52.6 CONTROL GROUP, Commodore P. S. Theiss
14 SCs, 7 LCCs, 25 LCIs, 3 APDs

TG 52.17 FIRE SUPPORT GROUP ONE (all T), Rear Admiral J. B. Oldendorf

Unit 1, Rear Admiral H. F. Kingman: BBs TENNESSEE, Capt. A. D. Mayer; CALIFORNIA, Capt. H. P. Burnett; CA INDIANAPOLIS, Capt. E. R. Johnson; CL BIRMINGHAM, Capt. T. B. Inglis; DDs REMEY (Desron 54, Capt. J. G. Coward on board), Cdr. R. P. Fiala, WADLEIGH, Cdr. W. C. Winn; NORMAN SCOTT, Cdr. S. D. Owens; MERTZ, Cdr. W. S. Eastabrook.

Unit 2, Cdr. P. H. Fitzgerald: DDs ROBINSON, Cdr. E. B. Grantham; BAILEY, Cdr. M. T. Munger; ALBERT W. GRANT, Cdr. T. A. Nisewaner.

Unit 3, Capt. H. B. Jarrett: DDs HALSEY POWELL, Cdr. W. T. McGarry; COGHLAN, Lt. Cdr. B. B. Cheatham; MONSSEN, Cdr. B. A. Fuetsch.

Unit 4, Rear Admiral Oldendorf: CA LOUISVILLE, Capt. S. H. Hurt; BBs MARYLAND (Rear Admiral T. D. Ruddock on board), Capt. H. J. Ray; COLORADO, Capt. W. Granat; DDs MCDERMUT (Cdr. D. C. Varian on board), Lt. Cdr. C. B. Jennings; MCGOWAN, Cdr. W. R. Cox; MCNAIR, Cdr. M. L. McCullough; MELVIN, Cdr. W. R. Edsall.

Unit 5, Rear Admiral R. W. Hayler: CLs MONTPELIER, Capt. H. D. Hoffman; CLEVELAND, Capt. A. G. Shepard; DDs YARNALL, Cdr. B. F. Tompkins; TWINING, Cdr. E. K. Wakefield; STOCKHAM, Cdr. E. P. Holmes.

TG 52.10 FIRE SUPPORT GROUP TWO (all T), Rear Adm. W. L. Ainsworth [6]

Unit 6, Rear Admiral Ainsworth: CL HONOLULU, Capt. H. R. Thurber; BBs PENNSYLVANIA, Capt. C. F. Martin; IDAHO, Capt. H. D. Clarke; DDs ANTHONY (Cdr. E. B. Taylor on board), Cdr. B. Van Mater; WADSWORTH, Cdr. J. F. Walsh; HUDSON, Lt. Cdr. R. R. Pratt; APD DICKERSON, Lt. Cdr. J. R. Cain USNR; seaplane tender WILLIAMSON, Lt. Cdr. J. A. Pridmore; minesweeper HOGAN, Lt. Cdr. W. H. Sublette.

Unit 7, Rear Admiral G. L. Weyler: BB NEW MEXICO, Capt. E. M. Zacharias; CAs MINNEAPOLIS, Capt. Harry Slocum; SAN FRANCISCO, Capt. H. E. Overesch; DDs HALFORD, Lt. Cdr. R. J. Hardy; TERRY, Lt. Cdr. J. M. Lee; BRAINE, Cdr. W. W. Fitts; APD TALBOT, Lt. Cdr. C. C. Morgan; minesweeper STANSBURY, Lt. Cdr. D. M. Granstrom USNR.

Unit 8, Rear Admiral C. T. Joy: CAs WICHITA, Capt. J. J. Mahoney; NEW ORLEANS, Capt. J. E. Hurff; [7] CL ST. LOUIS, Capt. R. H. Roberts; DDs FULLAM, Cdr. W. D. Kelly; GUEST, Cdr. M. G. Kennedy; BENNETT, Lt. Cdr. P. F. Hauck.

TG 52.14 CARRIER SUPPORT GROUP ONE (all T), Rear Admiral G. F. Bogan

Unit 1, Rear Admiral Bogan: CVEs FANSHAW BAY, Capt. D. P. Johnson with Composite Squadron 68: 16 FM-2 (Wildcat), 12 TBM-1C (Avenger), Lt. Cdr. R. S. Rogers; MIDWAY, [8] Capt. F. J. McKenna with Composite Squadron 65: 12 FM-2, 9 TBM-1C, Lt. Cdr. R. M. Jones USNR; DDs CASSIN YOUNG, Cdr. E. T. Schrieber; IRWIN, Cdr. D. B. Miller; ROSS, Cdr. B. Coe.

[6] This Group belonged initially to TF 53, the Southern Attack Force, being intended for the bombardment of Guam; but as it was first used for the bombardment of Saipan and Tinian, it is entered here as reorganized in Crudiv 9 (Rear Adm. Ainsworth) Operation Plan 2-44.
[7] Relieved Capt. J.D.H. Kane who died ashore on 13 June.
[8] Name subsequently changed to *Saint Lo*.

Unit 2, Capt. O. A. Weller: CVEs WHITE PLAINS, Capt. Weller with Composite Squadron 4: 16 FM–2, 3 TBF–1C, 9 TBM–1C, *Lt. Cdr. R. C. Evins: KALININ BAY, Capt. C. R. Brown with Composite Squadron 3: 14 FM–2, 9 TBM–1C, Lt. Cdr. W. H. Keighley USNR; DDs PORTERFIELD, Cdr. J. C. Woelfel; CALLAGHAN, Cdr. F. J. Johnson; LONGSHAW, Cdr. R. H. Speck.

* Killed in this operation. Lt. E. R. Fickenscher became C.O.

TG 52.11 CARRIER SUPPORT GROUP TWO (all T), Rear Admiral H. B. Sallada

Unit 3, Rear Admiral Sallada: CVEs KITKUN BAY, Capt. J. P. Whitney with Composite Squadron 5: 12 FM–2, 8 TBM–1C, Lt. Cdr. R. L. Fowler; GAMBIER BAY, Capt. H. H. Goodwin with Composite Squadron 10: 16 FM–2, 12 TBM–1C, Lt. Cdr. E. J. Huxtable; DDs LAWS, Cdr. L. O. Wood; MORRISON, Cdr. W. N. Price; BENHAM, Cdr. F. S. Keeler.

Unit 4, Rear Admiral F. B. Stump: NEHENTA BAY, Capt. H. B. Butterfield with Composite Squadron 11: 12 FM–2, 9 TBM–1C, Lt. Cdr. O. B. Stanley; DDs BULLARD (Cdr. C. E. Carroll on board), Cdr. B. W. Freund; KIDD, Cdr. A. B. Roby; CHAUNCEY, Lt. Cdr. L. C. Conwell.

TG 52.13 MINESWEEPING AND HYDROGRAPHIC SURVEY GROUP (all T), Cdr. R. S. Moore USNR

Unit 1, Cdr. W. R. Loud: HOPKINS, Lt. A. L. C. Waldron; PERRY, Lt. Cdr. I. G. Stubbart; LONG, Lt. Cdr. R. V. Wheeler; HAMILTON, Cdr. R. R. Sampson.

Unit 2, Lt. Cdr. H. L. Thompson: CHANDLER, Lt. Cdr. Thompson; ZANE, Lt. Cdr. W. T. Powell; PALMER, Lt. W. E. McGuire USNR; HOWARD, Lt. O. F. Salvia.

Unit 3, Cdr. Moore: CHIEF, Lt. Cdr. J. M. Wyckoff USNR; CHAMPION, Lt. Cdr. J. H. Howard USNR; HERALD, Lt. E. P. Dietrich USNR.

Unit 4, Lt. Cdr. J. R. Fels USNR: ORACLE, Lt. Cdr. Fels; MOTIVE, Lt. Cdr. G. W. Lundgren USNR; HEED, Lt. Magruder Dent USNR.

Units 5 and 6 and Mobile Hydrographic Unit: 5 YMS, 2 LCC, 6 LCV.

TG 51.1 JOINT EXPEDITIONARY FORCE RESERVE, Rear Admiral W. H. P. Blandy in FREMONT

Embarking 27th Infantry Division, U.S. Army, Maj. Gen. Ralph C. Smith USA [9]

(Most of these also used for Tinian)

Transdiv 7, Capt. C. G. Richardson: APAs CAVALIER, Capt. R. T. McElligott USCG; J. FRANKLIN BELL, Capt. O. H. Ritchie USNR; HEYWOOD, Capt. P. F. Dugan; AP WINGED ARROW, Cdr. J. E. Shomier; AKA FOMALHAUT, Cdr. C. A. Printup. Transdiv 32, Capt. M. O. Carlson: APAs FREMONT, Cdr. C. V. Conlan; HARRIS, Capt. M. E. Murphy; CUSTER, Cdr. W. Terry; AP HERALD OF THE MORNING, Cdr. H. A. Dunn; AK AURIGA, Cdr. J. G. Hart USNR. Screen, Capt. W. F. Petersen: DDs WALLER, Lt. Cdr. W. T. Dutton; PRINGLE, Lt. Cdr. J. L. Kelley; SAUFLEY, Lt. Cdr. H. G. Bowen; SIGOURNEY, Lt. Cdr. Fletcher Hale; DEs SEDERSTROM (Lt. Cdr. J. G. Urquhart on board), Lt. J. P. Farley USNR; FLEMING, Lt. K. F. Burgess USNR. Fleet tug CHICKASAW, Lt. L. C. Olson USNR. Transdiv 34, Capt. Charles Allen: APs PRINCE GEORGES, Lt. Cdr. W. J. Lane USNR; KENMORE, Lt. Cdr. O. H. Pitts USNR; DE GRASSE, Lt. Cdr. William Jordan USNR; LIVINGSTON, Cdr. L. J. Alexanderson USNR; LEONIS, Lt. Cdr. A. J. Barkowsky USNR. LCI Gunboat Group 8, Lt. Cdr. T. Blanchard USNR: 7 LCIs. Screen, Capt. J. R. Phal: DDs CONWAY, Lt. Cdr. J. H. Besson; EATON, Cdr. Fritz Gleim; DEs TISDALE, Lt. Cdr. Theodore Wolcott; EISELE, Lt. S. C. Ranta USNR; BARON, Lt. Cdr. J. W. Stewart; ACREE, Lt. Cdr. C. O. Davidson. Net-layer MIMOSA, Lt. W. M. Hupfel USNR; net cargo ship KEOKUK, Lt. Cdr. J. L. McLean.

[9] Detached 24 June; Maj. Gen. George W. Griner USA assumed command 28 June.

TG 52.7 SERVICE AND SALVAGE GROUP, Capt. S. E. Peck

Net-layer CINCHONA; tugs TEKESTA, TAWASA, MOLALA; repair ship PHAON; salvage vessel PRESERVER; seaplane tender BALLARD; landing craft repair ship AGENOR; salvage vessel CLAMP; 8 YMS.

TG 50.17 FUELING GROUP, Capt. Edward E. Paré
(Also covered Tinian operation)

Unit 1: DD PAUL HAMILTON, Cdr. L. G. May; DEs SAMUEL S. MILES, Lt. Cdr. H. G. Brousseau USNR; SWEARER, Lt. K. H. Hannan USNR; AOs NESHANIC, Cdr. A. C. Allen; SAUGATUCK, Cdr. F. S. Kirk; SARANAC, Cdr. J. G. Cross. Unit 2: DD CAPPS, Cdr. B. E. S. Trippensee; DEs BANGUST, Lt. Cdr. C. E. MacNish USNR; WEAVER, Lt. Cdr. R. S. Paret USNR; AOs LACKAWANNA, Cdr. A. J. Homann; MONONGAHELA, Cdr. F. J. Ilsemann; NEOSHO, Lt. Cdr. F. P. Parkinson. Unit 3: DD JOHN D. HENLEY, Cdr. C. H. Smith; DEs RIDDLE, Lt. Cdr. R. H. Cramer; WATERMAN, Lt. Cdr. J. H. Stahle USNR; AOs CIMARRON, Cdr. A. H. Kooistra USNR; KASKASKIA, Lt. Cdr. W. F. Patten; SABINE, Lt. Cdr. H. C. von Weien. Unit 4: DD HALL, Cdr. L. C. Baldauf; DEs LAMONS, Lt. Cdr. C. K. Hutchison; WESSON, Lt. Cdr. Henry Sears; AOs CALIENTE, Lt. Cdr. A. E. Stiff USNR; GUADALUPE, Cdr. H. A. Anderson; PLATTE, Cdr. F. S. Gibson USNR. Unit 5: DEs FAIR, Lt. D. S. Crocker USNR; HILBERT, Cdr. J. W. Golinkin USNR; AOs PECOS, Lt. Cdr. G. W. Renegar USNR; SCHUYLKILL, Cdr. F. A. Hardesty; TALLULAH, Lt. Cdr. W. F. Huckaby USNR. Unit 6: DEs MANLOVE, Lt. Cdr. H. P. Foster USNR; MITCHELL, Lt. Cdr. J. K. Carpenter USNR; AOs ASHTABULA, Lt. Cdr. Walter Barnett USNR; CAHABA, Lt. Cdr. J. Birnbaum USNR; TAPPAHANNOCK, Cdr. C. A. Swafford. Unit 7: DEs WHITMAN, Lt. R. G. Coan USNR; WILEMAN, Lt. R. M. Tanner USNR; AOs KENNEBAGO, Lt. Cdr. C. W. Brockway USNR; MARIAS, Cdr. J. G. Olsen USNR; SUAMICO, Cdr. A. S. Johnson. Unit 8: AOs CACHE, Lt. Cdr. C. R. Cosgrove USNR; KANKAKEE, Cdr. E. V. Raines; MASCOMA, Lt. Cdr. H. P. Timmers USNR. Unit 10: CVE COPAHEE,[10] Capt. Dale Harris; DD EVANS, Cdr. F. C. Camp. Unit 11: CVE BRETON, Capt. F. M. Trapnell; DD DAVID W. TAYLOR, Cdr. W. H. Johnsen. Unit 12: CVEs MANILA BAY, Capt. B. L. Braun; NATOMA BAY, Capt. H. L. Meadow; DDs HALLIGAN, Cdr. C. E. Cortner; HARADEN, Cdr. H. C. Allan.

Hospital ships: RELIEF, Lt. Cdr. J. C. Sever USNR; SOLACE, Cdr. E. B. Peterson; BOUNTIFUL, Cdr. G. L. Burns USNR; SAMARITAN, Cdr. C. W. Scribner USNR.

[10] *Copahee* and *Breton* provided replacement carrier aircraft; *Manila Bay* and *Natoma Bay* were employed to transport the P-47s (Thunderbolts) provided as initial garrison aircraft on Saipan.

Forces Engaged in the Battle of the Philippine Sea[1]

1. *United States, 19–20 June 1944*

FIFTH FLEET
Admiral Raymond A. Spruance in *Indianapolis*

TF 58 FAST CARRIER TASK FORCE
Vice Admiral Marc A. Mitscher in *Lexington*

TG 58.1 CARRIER TASK GROUP ONE, Rear Admiral J. J. Clark

| CV 12 | HORNET | Capt. W. D. Sample |

Air Group 2: 1 TBM–1C (Avenger) Cdr. J. D. Arnold

VB–2	33 SB2C–1C (Helldiver)	Lt. Cdr. G. B. Campbell
VF–2	36 F6F–3 (Hellcat)	Lt. Cdr. W. A. Dean
VT–2	4 TBF–1C, 14 TBM–1C (Avenger)	Lt. Cdr. L. M. D. Ford
VF(N)–76 (det. B)	4 F6F–3N	Lt. R. L. Reiserer

| CV 10 | YORKTOWN | Capt. R. E. Jennings |

Air Group 1: 1 F6F–3, Cdr. J. M. Peters

VB–1	40 SB2C–1C, 4 SBD–5 (Dauntless)	Lt. Cdr. J. W. Runyan USNR
VF–1	41 F6F–3	Lt. Cdr. B. M. Strean
VT–1	1 TBF–1C, 16 TBM–1C	Lt. Cdr. W. F. Henry
VF(N)–77 (det. B)	4 F6F–3N	Lt. A. C. Benjes

| CVL 24 | BELLEAU WOOD | Capt. John Perry |

Air Group 24: Lt. Cdr. E. M. Link

VF–24	26 F6F–3	Lt. Cdr. Link
VT–24	3 TBF–1C, 6 TBM–1C	Lt. R. M. Swensson

| CVL 29 | BATAAN | Capt. V. H. Schaeffer |

[1] Sources for this organization were Cincpac "Operations in Pacific Ocean Areas, June 1944," Ships' Roster Section, Bupers, and the individual Action Reports and War Diaries of all participating units and ships. The number of planes are from Comairpac "Aircraft Availability Report, 24 June 1944," with date of this information received from 5–13 June 1944.

Air Group 50: Lt. Cdr. J. C. Strange USNR

| VF–50 | 24 F6F–3 | Lt. Cdr. Strange |
| VT–50 | 9 TBM–1C | Lt. Cdr. L. V. Swanson |

Crudiv 10, Rear Admiral L. H. Thebaud: CAs BOSTON Capt. E. E. Herrmann; BALTIMORE Capt. W. C. Calhoun, CANBERRA Capt. A. R. Early, CLAAs SAN JUAN Capt. G. W. Clark, OAKLAND Capt. W. K. Phillips.
Screen, Capt. G. W. Clark: destroyers IZARD Cdr. M. T. Dayton, CHARRETTE Cdr. E. S. Karpe, CONNER Cdr. W. E. Kaitner, BELL Cdr. J. S. C. Gabbert, BURNS Cdr. D. T. Eller. Desdiv 92, Capt. W. M. Sweetser: destroyers BOYD Cdr. U. S. G. Sharp, BRADFORD Cdr. R. L. Morris, BROWN Cdr. T. H. Copeman, COWELL Cdr. C. W. Parker. Desdiv 11, Capt. E. G. Fullinwider: destroyers MAURY Lt. Cdr. J. W. Koenig, CRAVEN Lt. Cdr. R. L. Fulton, GRIDLEY Cdr. P. D. Quirk, HELM Lt. Cdr. S. K. Santmyers, MC CALL Lt. Cdr. J. B. Carroll.

TG 58.2 CARRIER TASK GROUP TWO, Rear Admiral A. E. Montgomery

| CV 17 | BUNKER HILL | Capt. T. P. Jeter |

Air Group 8: 1 F6F–3, Cdr. R. L. Shifley

VB–8	33 SB2C–1C	Lt. Cdr. J. D. Arbes
VF–8	37 F6F–3	Lt. Cdr. W. M. Collins
VT–8	13 TBF–1C, 5 TBM–1C	Lt. Cdr. K. F. Musick
VF(N) 76 (det. A)	4 F6F–3N	Lt. Cdr. E. P. Aurand

| CV 18 | WASP | Capt. C. A. F. Sprague |

Air Group 14: 1 F6F–3, Cdr. W. C. Wingard

VB–14	32 SB2C–1C	Lt. Cdr. J. D. Blitch
VF–14	34 F6F–3	Lt. Cdr. E. W. Biros USNR
VT–14	15 TBF–1C, 3 TBF–1D	Lt. Cdr. H. S. Roberts USNR
VF(N)–77 (det. C)	4 F6F–3N	Lt. J. H. Boyum

| CVL 26 | MONTEREY | Capt. S. H. Ingersoll |

Air Group 28: Lt. Cdr. R. W. Mehle USNR

| VF–28 | 21 F6F–3 | Lt. Cdr. Mehle |
| VT–28 | 8 TBM–1C | Lt. R. P. Gift USNR |

| CVL 28 | CABOT | Capt. S. J. Michael |

Air Group 31: Lt. Cdr. R. A. Winston

| VF–31 | 24 F6F–3 | Lt. Cdr. Winston |
| VT–31 | 1 TBF–1C, 8 TBM–1C | Lt. E. E. Wood USNR |

Crudiv 13, Rear Admiral L. T. DuBose: CLs SANTE FE, MOBILE, BILOXI. Desron 52, Capt. G. R. Cooper: OWEN, MILLER, THE SULLIVANS, STEPHEN POTTER Cdr. L. W. Pancoast, TINGEY. Desdiv 104, Cdr. H. B. Bell: HICKOX, HUNT, LEWIS HANCOCK, MARSHALL. Desron 1, Capt. E. R. McLean: MACDONOUGH, DEWEY, HULL.[2]

[2] Commanding officers of ships in screen are not repeated if they are given in Appendix II.

TG 58.3 CARRIER TASK GROUP THREE, Rear Admiral J. W. Reeves

CV 6   ENTERPRISE   Capt. M. B. Gardner

Air Group 10: Cdr. W. R. Kane

VB–10	21 SBD–5	Lt. Cdr. J. D. Ramage
VF–10	31 F6F–3	Lt. R. W. Schumann
VT–10	9 TBF–1C, 5 TBM–1C	Lt. Cdr. W. I. Martin
VF(N)–101 (det. C)	3 F4U–2 (Corsair)	Lt. Cdr. R. E. Harmer

CV 16   LEXINGTON   Capt. E. W. Litch

Air Group 16: 1 F6F–3, Cdr. E. M. Snowden

VB–16	34 SBD–5	Lt. Cdr. Ralph Weymouth
VF–16	37 F6F–3	Lt. Cdr. Paul D. Buie
VT–16	17 TBF–1C, 1 TBM–1C	Lt. N. A. Sterrie USNR
VF(N)–76 (det. C)	4 F6F–3N	Lt. W. H. Abercrombie USNR

CVL 30   SAN JACINTO   Capt. H. M. Martin

Air Group 51: Lt. Cdr. C. L. Moore

VF–51	24 F6F–3	Lt. Cdr. Moore
VT–51	6 TBM–1C, 2 TBM–1D	Lt. Cdr. D. J. Melvin

CVL 23   PRINCETON   Capt. W. H. Buracker

Air Group 27: * Lt. Cdr. E. W. Wood

VF–27	24 F6F–3	Lt. Cdr. Wood
VT–27	9 TBM–1C	Lt. Cdr. S. M. Haley USNR

CA INDIANAPOLIS; CLAA RENO Capt. R. C. Alexander. Cruadiv 12, Rear Admiral R. W. Hayler: MONTPELIER, CLEVELAND, BIRMINGHAM. Desron 50, Cdr. C. F. Chillingworth: CLARENCE K. BRONSON, COTTEN, DORTCH, GATLING, HEALY. Desdiv 100, Cdr. W. J. Miller: CAPERTON, COGSWELL, INGERSOLL, KNAPP. Desdiv 90, Cdr. F. L. Tedder: ANTHONY Cdr. Blinn Van Mater, WADSWORTH Cdr. J. F. Walsh, TERRY, BRAINE.

TG 58.4 CARRIER TASK GROUP FOUR, Rear Admiral W. K. Harrill

CV 9   ESSEX   Capt. R. A. Ofstie

Air Group 15: 1 F6F–3, Cdr. David McCampbell

VB–15	36 SB2C–1C	Lt. Cdr. J. H. Mini
VF–15	38 F6F–3	* Lt. Cdr. C. W. Brewer
VT–15	15 TBF–1C, 5 TBM–1C	Lt. Cdr. V. G. Lambert
VF(N)–77 (det. A)	4 F6F–3N	Lt. R. M. Freeman

CVL 27   LANGLEY   Capt. W. M. Dillon

Air Group 32: Lt. Cdr. E. C. Outlaw

VF–32	23 F6F–3	Lt. Cdr. Outlaw
VT–32	7 TBF–1C, 2 TBM–1C	Lt. D. A. Marks

CVL 25   COWPENS   Capt. H. W. Taylor

* Lost in this action.

Air Group 25: Lt. Cdr. R. H. Price

VF–25   23 F6F–3   Lt. Cdr. Price
VT–25   3 TBF–1C, 6 TBM–1C   Lt. R. B. Cottingham USNR

Crudiv 11, Rear Admiral L. J. Wiltse: CLAA SAN DIEGO Capt. L. J. Hudson. Crudiv 14, Rear Admiral W. D. Baker: CLs VINCENNES Capt. A. D. Brown; HOUSTON Capt. W. W. Behrens; MIAMI Capt. J. G. Crawford. Desron 12, Capt. W. P. Burford: LANSDOWNE Lt. Cdr. W. S. Maddox; LARDNER Lt. Cdr. J. D. Parker; MCCALLA Lt. Cdr. E. K. Jones; CASE Lt. Cdr. R. S. Willey. Desdiv 24, Cdr. J. L. Melgaard: LANG Cdr. Harold Payson; STERETT Lt. Cdr. F. J. Blouin; WILSON Lt. Cdr. C. J. MacKenzie; ELLET Lt. Cdr. E. C. Rider. Desron 23, Capt. T. B. Dugan: CHARLES AUSBURNE, STANLY Lt. Cdr. J. B. Morland; DYSON. Desdiv 46, Cdr. R. W. Cavenagh: CONVERSE Cdr. J. B. Colwell; SPENCE Cdr. H. J. Armstrong; THATCHER Cdr. L. R. Lampman.

TG 58.7 BATTLE LINE, Vice Admiral W. A. Lee in WASHINGTON

Batdiv 6, Vice Admiral Lee: WASHINGTON Capt. T. R. Cooley; NORTH CAROLINA Capt. F. P. Thomas. Batdiv 7, Rear Admiral O. M. Hustvedt: IOWA, NEW JERSEY. Batdiv 9, Rear Admiral E. W. Hanson: SOUTH DAKOTA, ALABAMA. Batdiv 8, Rear Admiral G. B. Davis: INDIANA Capt. T. J. Keliher. Crudiv 6, Rear Admiral C. T. Joy: CAs WICHITA, MINNEAPOLIS, NEW ORLEANS Capt. J. E. Hurff; SAN FRANCISCO. Desdiv 12, Cdr. K. F. Poehlmann: MUGFORD, RALPH TALBOT Lt. Cdr. W. S. Brown; PATTERSON, BAGLEY. Desdiv 89, Cdr. E. B. Taylor: HALFORD, GUEST, BENNETT, FULLAM, HUDSON. Desdiv 106, Cdr. Thomas Burrowes: YARNALL, TWINING, STOCKHAM, MONSSEN.

TENDER-BASED AIR AT SAIPAN

AVD 10   BALLARD   Lt. Cdr. G. C. Nichandross USNR

VP–16   5 PBM–5 (Mariner)   Lt. Cdr. W. J. Scarpino

LAND-BASED AIR AT MOKERANG FIELD, LOS NEGROS

VB–101 [3]   12 PB4Y–1 (Liberator)   Cdr. J. A. Miller

TF 17 PATROL SUBMARINES, Vice Admiral Charles A. Lockwood
In support of the Marianas Operation, 12–22 June 1944

Bonin Islands: PLUNGER Lt. Cdr. E. J. Fahy; GAR Cdr. G. W. Lautrup; ARCHERFISH Cdr. W. H. Wright; PLAICE Cdr. C. B. Stevens; SWORDFISH Cdr. K. E. Montrose.
SE of Formosa and Eastward: PINTADO Lt. Cdr. B. A. Clarey; PILOTFISH Lt. Cdr. R. H. Close; TUNNY Cdr. J. A. Scott.
E and SE of Marianas: ALBACORE Cdr. J. W. Blanchard; SEAWOLF Lt. Cdr. R. B. Lynch; BANG Cdr. A. R. Gallaher; FINBACK Lt. Cdr. J. L. Jordan; STINGRAY [4] Lt. Cdr. S. C. Loomis.
Ulithi-Philippines: FLYING FISH Lt. Cdr. R. D. Risser; MUSKALLUNGE Cdr. M. P. Russillo; SEAHORSE Lt. Cdr. S. D. Cutter; PIPEFISH Lt. Cdr. W. N. Deragon; CAVALLA Lt. Cdr. H. J. Kossler.
Off Surigao Strait: GROWLER [5] Cdr. T. B. Oakley.

[3] Relieved VB–106 at Mokerang 2 June.
[4] On lifeguard duty off Guam until D plus 4.
[5] On lifeguard duty off Saipan until D minus 3.

SEVENTH FLEET SUBMARINES
Rear Admiral Ralph W. Christie

SE of Mindanao: HAKE Cdr. J. C. Broach; BASHAW Lt. Cdr. R. E. Nichols; PADDLE Lt. Cdr. B. H. Nowell.
Tawi Tawi: HARDER Cdr. S. D. Dealey; HADDO Cdr. C. W. Nimitz, Jr.; REDFIN Cdr. M. H. Austin; BLUEFISH Cdr. C. M. Henderson.
Off Luzon: JACK Cdr. A. E. Krapf; FLIER Cdr. J. D. Crowley.

2. *Japanese Forces in Operation A-Go,*[6] *1–20 June*
(Carrier plane complements as of departure from Tawi Tawi)

MOBILE FLEET
Vice Admiral Jisaburo Ozawa in TAIHO

VAN FORCE, Vice Admiral Takeo Kurita in ATAGO

Cardiv 3, Rear Admiral Sueo Obayashi
CVLs CHITOSE, CHIYODA, ZUIHO; 62 Zekes, 9 Jills, 17 Kates
Batdiv 1 (Vice Admiral Matome Ugaki): YAMATO, MUSASHI
Batdiv 3 (Vice Admiral Yoshio Suzuki): HARUNA, KONGO
Crudiv 4 (Vice Admiral Kurita): ATAGO, TAKAO, MAYA, CHOKAI

Desron 2, Rear Admiral Mikio Hayakawa in CL NOSHIRO
Desdiv 31: NAGANAMI, ASASHIMO, KISHINAMI, OKINAMI
Desdiv 32: TAMANAMI, HAMAKAZE, FUJINAMI, SHIMAKAZE, * HAYANAMI

"A" FORCE, Vice Admiral Ozawa

Cardiv 1, Vice Admiral Ozawa
CVs * TAIHO, * SHOKAKU, ZUIKAKU; 79 Zekes, 70 Judys, 7 Vals, 51 Jills
Crudiv 5 (Rear Admiral Shintaro Hashimoto): MYOKO, HAGURO

Desron 10, Rear Admiral Susumu Kimura in CL YAHAGI
Desdivs 10 and 17: ASAGUMO, URAKAZE, ISOKAZE, * TANIKAZE
Desdiv 61: HATSUZUKI, WAKATSUKI, AKIZUKI, SHIMOTSUKI, * MINAZUKI

"B" FORCE, Rear Admiral Takaji Joshima

Cardiv 2, Rear Admiral Joshima
CVs JUNYO, * HIYO; CVL RYUHO; 81 Zekes, 27 Judys, 9 Vals, 18 Jills
BB NAGATO; CA MOGAMI
Desdiv 4: MICHISHIO, NOWAKI, YAMAGUMO
Desdiv 27: SHIGURE, SAMIDARE, * SHIRATSUYU, HAYASHIMO, HAMAKAZE, AKISHIMO * HARUSAME

* Sunk or lost in this operation; for details consult index.

[6] Prepared by Capt. Ohmae who was on Admiral Ozawa's staff; earlier printed lists are inaccurate. I have included all DDs sunk after the start of A–Go. The carriers' plane complements are as of the morning of 19 June. In *Chitose, Zuiho* and *Ryuho,* all VBs, and in *Junyo* and *Hiyo* 9 out of 27 VBs, were Zeke fighters equipped as bombers.

SUPPLY FORCES

1st SUPPLY FORCE

AOs HAYASUI, NICHIEI MARU, KOKUYO MARU, * SEIYO MARU
DDs HIBIKI, HATSUSHIMO, YUNAGI, TSUGA

2nd SUPPLY FORCE

AOs * GENYO MARU, AZUSA MARU
DDs YUKIKAZE, UZUKI

SUBMARINE FORCE (6th Fleet)

* Vice Admiral Takeo Takagi, at Saipan

* I-5, * I-10, I-38, I-41, I-53, * I-184, * I-185; * RO-36, RO-41, * RO-42,
RO-43, * RO-44, RO-47, RO-68, * RO-104, * RO-105, * RO-106, * RO-108,
RO-112, RO-113, * RO-114, RO-115, * RO-116, * RO-117.

* Sunk or lost in this operation; for details consult index.

Naval Forces Engaged in the Capture of Guam

21 July–10 August 1944

TF 53 SOUTHERN ATTACK FORCE

Rear Admiral Richard L. Conolly,[1] in APPALACHIAN

Including SOUTHERN TROOPS AND LANDING FORCE,
Major General Roy S. Geiger USMC

TG 53.1 NORTHERN ATTACK GROUP, Rear Admiral Conolly

TG 53.3 NORTHERN TRANSPORT GROUP, Capt. Pat Buchanan
Embarking 3rd Marine Division, Maj. Gen. Allen H. Turnage USMC.
Transdiv 2, Capt. H. D. Baker: APAs PRESIDENT JACKSON Capt. A. F. Junker; PRESIDENT HAYES Cdr. H. E. Schieke; PRESIDENT ADAMS Cdr. M. C. Erwin; AP PRESIDENT MONROE Cdr. J. M. Payne USNR; AKA TITANIA Cdr. H. E. Berger. Transdiv 8, Capt. F. R. Talbot: APAs CRESCENT CITY Cdr. L. L. Rowe; WARREN Cdr. W. A. McHale USNR; WINDSOR Cdr. D. C. Woodward USNR; AP WHARTON Capt. J. J. Fallon; AKA LIBRA Capt. F. F. Ferris. Transdiv 24, Capt. Buchanan: APAs DU PAGE Capt. G. M. Wauchope USNR; ELMORE Cdr. Drayton Harrison; WAYNE Cdr. T. V. Cooper; hospital transport RIXEY Cdr. P. H. Jenkins; AKA AQUARIUS Capt. R. V. Marron USCG. LSDs EPPING FOREST Cdr. Lester Martin USNR; GUNSTON HALL Cdr. D. E. Collins USNR.
Screen, Capt. E. M. Thompson: DDs JOHN RODGERS Cdr. H. O. Parish; STEVENS Lt. Cdr. W. M. Rakow; HARRISON Lt. Cdr. W. V. Combs; MCKEE Lt. Cdr. R. B. Allen; SCHROEDER Lt. Cdr. R. W. McElrath; COLAHAN Cdr. D. T. Wilber; HAGGARD (Cdr. J. H. Nevins on board), Lt. Cdr. D. A. Harris; HAILEY Cdr. P. H. Brady; DMSs HOGAN Lt. Cdr. W. H. Sublette; STANSBURY Lt. Cdr. D. M. Granstrom USNR; HOPKINS Lt. D. P. Payne USNR; minesweepers SKYLARK Lt. Cdr. G. M. Estep USNR; STARLING Lt. R. C. Biles USNR.

TG 53.16 TRACTOR GROUP THREE, Capt. G. B. Carter

LST Unit 3, Cdr. V. K. Busck: 16 LSTs.
Control Unit, Capt. Carter: DD STEMBEL Cdr. W. L. Tagg; 9 SCs.
LCI(G) Unit, Cdr. W. R. McCaleb: 7 landing craft infantry gunboats.*

* *LCI–468* sunk in this operation.

[1] For officers higher in chain of command see Appendix II. C.O. of flagship: Capt. J. M. Fernald.

TG 53.9 MINESWEEPING AND HYDROGRAPHIC GROUP,
Lt. Cdr. G. M. Estep

SKYLARK, STARLING, 6 YMSs. Salvage and Service Unit: ocean tug APACHE; salvage vessel GRAPPLE; net layers AGENOR, ALOE; repair ship HOLLY. Reconnaissance and Demolition Unit, Cdr. R. A. Wilhelm USNR: APD DENT Cdr. Wilhelm.

TG 53.2 SOUTHERN ATTACK GROUP,
Rear Admiral L. F. Reifsnider

TG 53.4 SOUTHERN TRANSPORT GROUP, Capt. J. B. McGovern

Embarking 1st Provisional Marine Brigade (4th and 22nd Regiments), Brig. Gen. Lemuel C. Shepherd USMC; Corps Artillery, Brig. Gen. Pedro A. del Valle USMC; 305th RCT of 77th Division, U. S. Army.

Transdiv 4, Capt. McGovern: APAs ZEILIN, ORMSBY; GEORGE CLYMER Capt. M. T. Farrar; AP PRESIDENT POLK Cdr. C. J. Ballreich; AKA VIRGO. Transdiv 6, Capt. T. B. Brittain: APAs, FAYETTE Cdr. J. C. Lester; HARRY LEE; WILLIAM P. BIDDLE Capt. L. F. Brown USNR; LEEDSTOWN Cdr. Harold Bye; CENTAURUS.

Transdiv 38, Capt. J. B. Heffernan: [2] APAs LAMAR Capt. B. K. Culver; ALPINE Cdr. G. K. G. Reilly; APs GOLDEN CITY Cdr. C. M. Furlow; STARLIGHT Cdr. W. O. Britton USNR; AKA ALSHAIN Cdr. R. E. Krause; LSD CARTER HALL Lt. Cdr. F. J. Harris.

Screen, Capt. W. P. Burford: DDs FARENHOLT Lt. Cdr. K. S. Shook; SIGSBEE Lt. Cdr. G. P. Chung-Hoon; DASHIELL, MURRAY; JOHNSTON Cdr. E. E. Evans; FRANKS Cdr. N. A. Lidstone; PRESTON Cdr. G. S. Patrick; ANTHONY Lt. Cdr. C. J. Van Arsdall; WADSWORTH Cdr. J. F. Walsh; WEDDERBURN Cdr. J. L. Wilfong.

TG 53.17 TRACTOR GROUP FOUR, Cdr. E. A. McFall

DD BLACK Lt. Cdr. E. R. King. LST Unit 4, Cdr. R. W. Cutler USNR, 14 LSTs. Control Unit, Cdr. Henry Crommelin: DD RINGGOLD Lt. Cdr. T. F. Conley; 7 SCs. LCI(G) Unit, Lt. H. B. Rabenstein: 9 LCI(G)s. Seaplane Servicing Unit, Lt. Cdr. J. A. Pridmore: tender WILLIAMSON Lt. W. H. Ayer; *APc–46* Lt. R. M. Rosse USNR.

TG 53.6 MINESWEEPING AND HYDROGRAPHIC UNIT,
Cdr. R. R. Sampson

Sweep Unit 3, Lt. Cdr. W. B. Porter: minesweepers SHELDRAKE, Lt. T. W. Cross USNR; SWALLOW Lt. (jg) M. McVickar USNR. Sweep Unit 4, Lt. E. E. McCarthy: 6 YMS. Sweep Unit 6, Cdr. Sampson: DMS HAMILTON Lt. Cdr. John Clague USNR; PERRY Lt. Cdr. I. G. Stubbart; LONG Lt. S. Caplan USNR. Salvage and Service Unit, Cdr. E. C. Genereaux: tug LIPAN Lt. N. R. Terpening. Reconnaissance and Demolition Unit, Lt. F. M. Christiansen: APDs CLEMSON Lt. W. F. Moran USNR; KANE Lt. Christiansen.

TG 53.5 SOUTHERN FIRE SUPPORT GROUP, Rear Admiral W. L. Ainsworth

Identical with TG 52.10 in Appendix II, plus battleships COLORADO, TENNESSEE, CALIFORNIA; cruisers NEW ORLEANS, INDIANAPOLIS, ST. LOUIS; destroyers FULLAM, GUEST, MONAGHAN, DALE, AYLWIN, MURRAY, DASHIELL, HARRISON, MCKEE, JOHN RODGERS, STEVENS, JOHNSTON.

[2] Embarking the 305th RCT. The rest of the 77th Division, RCTs 306 and 307, was embarked in Transdivs 18 and 28 of the Transport Group "Able," Northern Attack Force (see Appendix II).

TG 53.7 CARRIER SUPPORT GROUP, Rear Admiral V. H. Ragsdale

Cardiv 22, Rear Admiral T. L. Sprague

CVE 26   SANGAMON   Capt. M. E. Browder
Air Group 37; Lt. Cdr. S. E. Hindman
VF-37 22 F6F-3   Lt. Cdr. Hindman
VT-37 1 TBF-1C, 8 TBM-1C   Lt. Cdr. P. G. Farley USNR

CVE 27   SUWANNEE   Capt. W. D. Johnson
Air Group 60; Lt. Cdr. H. O. Feilbach USNR
VF-60 22 F6F-3   Lt. Cdr. Feilbach
VT-60 8 TBM-1C, 1 TBF-1   Lt. Cdr. W. C. Vincent USNR

CVE 28   CHENANGO   Capt. Dixwell Ketcham
Air Group 35; Lt. Cdr. F. T. Moore
VF-35 22 F6F-3   Lt. Cdr. Moore
VT-35 8 TBM-1C, 1 TBF-1C   Lt. C. F. Morgan USNR

Screen, Capt. J. T. Bottom: destroyers ERBEN, WALKER, ABBOT, HALE

Cardiv 24, Rear Admiral F. B. Stump

CVE 58   CORREGIDOR   Capt. R. L. Thomas
VC-41 14 FM-2, 4 TBM-1, 8 TBM-1C   Lt. A. P. Kolonie USNR

CVE 57   CORAL SEA   Capt. P. W. Watson
VC-33 14 FM-2, 2 TBF-1   Lt. Cdr. Richard Gray
6 TBF-1C, 4 TBM-1C

Screen, Cdr. C. E. Carroll: destroyers BULLARD, CHAUNCEY, KIDD

TG 53.19 CORPS RESERVE GROUP, Capt. H. B. Knowles

Transdiv 18, Capt. Knowles: APAs MONROVIA, FELAND, FREDERICK FUNSTON; AP WAR HAWK; AKA ALCYONE; AP CHINA VICTORY. Transdiv 28, Capt. H. C. Flanagan: APAs BOLIVAR, SHERIDAN, DOYEN; AP COMET, AKA ALMAACK, AP CLAREMONT VICTORY. Screen, Cdr. W. R. Edsall: DDs MELVIN, SHAW, SELFRIDGE, AULICK; DMSs PALMER, ZANE; DEs BARON, ELDEN.

MOBILE SERVICE BASES

Servron 10, Commo. W. R. Carter: survey ship HYDROGRAPHER, repair ships AJAX, VESTAL, HECTOR, LUZON; tenders PHAON, CASCADE, MARKAB, PRAIRIE; DMS DORSEY; 5 floating docks; Degausser YDG-6; auxiliaries ARGONNE, ORVETTA; tugs ARAPAHO, KEOSANQUA, MATACO, ONTARIO, ATR-44, -46.

Servron 12, Capt. L. S. Fiske: survey ship BOWDITCH; net ships SAGITTARIUS, TUS-CANA, PAPAYA, CHINQUAPIN; dredges TUALATIN, HAINES, INDIANA; salvage vessels CLAMP, GEAR; Coast Guard cutters WOODBINE, TUPELO, PAPAW; tugs PAKANA, ZUNI; freighters WM. W. BURROWS, ALKES, CITY OF DALHART; 2 floating docks.

TANKER GROUPS

Oilers MONONGAHELA, TAPPAHANNOCK, NEOSHO, CAHABA, ASHTABULA, LACKAWANNA; water tankers OKLAWAHA, NIOBRARA; store ship BOREAS; aux. cargo ship AZIMECH; misc. unclassified ELK, BEAGLE.

Index

Index

Names of Combatant Ships in SMALL CAPITALS
Names of Lettered Combatant Ships, like LSTs and RO-boats, and of
Merchant Ships, and of all *Marus*, in *Italics*

In the Appendices, only Flag and General Officers have been indexed.

A

ABNER READ, 127
Adachi, Lt. Gen. H., 66–7, 72–4
Adair, Lt. Col. R. D., 392
Admiralty Is., 3, 6, 29, 39; as air-naval
base, 45, 50, 59, 80, 88–9, 95–6, 106 7,
141, 156*n*, 164, 223, 227–8, 241, 256,
260, 313, 348
Afetna Pt., 183, 194–8, 203
Agaña, 150–1, 282, 373, 375, 378, 398–9
Agat Beachhead, 375, 378–81, 389–98
Agingan Pt., 152, 194–5, 198, 208
"A-Go" Operation, 13–14, 94, 117–18,
130–2, 213–21; plane deployment for,
219; chart, 153
Aguijan, 150, 369
Ainsworth, Rear Adm. W. L., 171–3,
180–1, 207, 210, 356, 377–8, 381, 390,
399, 409, 419
Aircraft, U.S., types of: B-29, 5–8, 157,
209, 324, 341, 351, 368; F6F, 38, 175–7,
242*n*, 311–12, 317; F6F(N), 154, 286;
P-47, P-61, 209, 329*n*; PB4Y (B-24),
49n, 164–5, 285; PBM, 210, 242, 254–5,
264, 285–6, 317; PBY, 49–50, 136*n*;
SB2C, 274–6, 292, 295, 303–4, 317;
SBD, 274, 295, 317; TBF, TBM, 32,
285–6, 290, 295–300, 303–10, 317
Air photos, *see* Photography
Air-sea rescue, 21–2, 33, 39, 49*n*, 50,
308–9
Air search, Jap. and U.S., 50, 106, 219–
20, 233–4, 241–2, 245–9, 254–8, 265,
271–2, 284–90, 307–10, 316–17; chart,
242–3
Airsols, 156, 164

Air support of amphib. ops., New
Guinea, 34–8, 61, 68–70, 82–4, 92,
96–8, 107, 110; Marianas, 174–9, 190,
203–5, 326–7, 330, 333–5, 353–4, 358–
61, 365–7, 377–8, 381–3, 390, 397
Aitape, 61–4, 67–74, 78–9, 83, 87, 95*n*,
96, 145; chart, 71
AKASHI, 32
AKIGUMO, 19
ALABAMA, 40, 269*n*, 270, 282*n*
Alamo TF, 47, 57, 64–5, 73, 102, 115, 136
ALBACORE, 19, 265, 269, 278–81, 285
ALBERT W. GRANT, 325
Aleutian Is., 17, 251*n*, 348
Allen, Cdr. B. C., Jr., 55
ALMAACK, 346
AMMEN, 66, 74, 97, 127
Ammunition expenditure and supply,
82, 108, 180, 200, 212*n*, 346–7, 353,
359–62, 379, 381, 390, 400
Amphibian Engineers, *see* Engineer
Special Brigades
Amphibious assault tactics, 54–6, 196–7,
356–7, 364
Amphtracs, *see* LVT
Anami, Lt. Gen. K., 66*n*, 67, 132
Anatahan, 152, 175*n*
Anderson, Capt. Bern, 45*n*, 64–5, 81,
87, 98, 111–12, 116, 123–4, 135
Anderson, Cdr. C. E., 201*n*, 208
Andrews, Cdr. C. H., 21
ANGLER, 21–2
Anti-submarine ops., 222–3, 230–1, 312,
316, 329
AOBA, 118–20, 125, 130–1
APOGON, 24, 155
APPALACHIAN, 378, 397, 400

Apra Harbor, 350, 375, 387, 396–8, 400
ARCHERFISH, 30
Arle, Lt. H. F., 255
Army Air Forces, U.S., V, 34–7, 47, 57, 61, 66–7, 92–8, 107, 116, 120, 124, 136, 141–2, 156; VII, 156, 164, 329n; XIII, 50, 96, 106, 110, 143, 156n, 313
Army, U.S., Corps, I, 63; XI, 72–4; XXIV, 353–6, 360, 367
Army, U.S., Infantry divs., 6th, 135, 141–3; 24th, 63, 75–7, 86–8; 27th, 160, 171, 202, 208–9, 330–7, 348; 32nd, 63, 70–3, 96; 41st, 63, 79, 82, 95–6, 103; 43rd, 72–3; 77th, 160, 371, 374–9, 390–5, 399–401
Arnold, General H. H., 5n, 6
Arnold, Cdr. J. D., 297–9n
ARUNTA, 73, 97, 127–9
ASAGUMO, 120, 131
Asan Beachhead, 375, 378–80, 382–90
ASANAGI, 23
ASHIZURI, 220
ASHLAND, 346, 361
Aslito Airfield, see Isely
ASPRO, 23
ATAGO, 249n, 290–1
Aurand, Lt. Cdr. E. P., 302
Australia, in SW Pac. Command, 46–7, 70, 97
AUSTRALIA, 47, 73, 97, 123–6

B

BABCOCK, E. C., 297n
Babo, 89, 143, 219
BACHE, 74, 110, 127
Baker, Lt. Harry, 193
Baker, Rear Adm. W. D., 239, 415
BALAO, 17
BALLARD, 242n
BANG, BARB, 23–4, 278
BANGUST, 229
Barbey, Rear Adm. D. E., 47, 55–6, 63–4, 68, 76–9, 81, 85–6, 94–5, 403
Bardshar, Lt. Cdr. F. A., 310
Barnes, Brig. Gen. E. W., 143
Base development, 341–2, 349–50, 400
BASHAW, 30
BATAAN, 36, 174, 238, 250, 292, 311
Batchelder, Col. M. J., 187n, 198
BATFISH, 367n
Battleships, in bombardment, 179–83
Beach obstacles, 380
Beach parties, 53, 70

Beaching craft, types, 54–6, 68n
BEALE, 66, 127
BELLE GROVE, 361
BELLEAU WOOD, 36, 154n, 174, 238, 250, 262, 292, 295–7, 311–12
BENNINGTON, 150
Berkey, Rear Adm. R. S., 47, 81, 91, 96–7, 106, 122, 136, 406
Biak, 37, 50, 86, 89, 91, 95–7, 103–35, 145, 220–1, 260, 316; charts, 109, 128
Biggs, Capt. B. B., 345
BILOXI, 37
BIRMINGHAM, 197, 335
BLACKFISH, 30
Blair, Capt. L. N., 22
Blair, Lt. W. K., 273
Blakely, Lt. Cdr. E. N., 23
Blamey, Gen. Sir Thomas, 46–7
Blanchard, Cdr. J. W., 278–80
Blandy, Rear Adm. W. H. P., 160, 171–2, 410
Blatz, G. H., 297n
Block, Lt. Col. Edward, 73
BLUE RIDGE, 63, 135
BLUEGILL, 17n, 23
Bogan, Rear Adm. G. F., 326, 409
BOISE, 47, 97, 108, 123–8
BONEFISH, 217–18
Bonin, Lt. Cdr. R. A., 24
Bonin Is., 18, 23, 149, 157, 219, 367; see Chichi, Haha
Borneo, 214, 217
Bosnik, 103–24
Bougainville, 12, 66, 156, 219, 223–4, 376
BOUNTIFUL, 200, 389
Bowling, Cdr. S. S., 47, 57
BOYD, 239
Brady, Cdr. P. H., 223
BRAINE, 182, 362n
BRETON, 230
Brewer, Lt. Cdr. C. W., 266–8, 276–8
Brindupke, Cdr. C. F., 31
Broach, Cdr. J. C., 120
Brown, Cdr. Gaylord B., 273, 276
Brown, Lt. (jg) George B., 295–7
Browne, Lt. (jg) M. F., 301
Bruce, Maj. Gen. A. D., 379, 393n, 396
Bruce, Lt. (jg) J. L., 276
Buie, Cdr. P. D., 257n
BUNKER HILL, 32, 37, 154, 174, 250, 264n, 268–76, 292, 298, 300–4, 307–8
BURDEN R. HASTINGS, 229
Burgess, Ens. W. C., 310
Burke, Rear Adm. A. A., 274n, 286n

Burke, Lt. R. F., 184, 359
Burnett, Ens. R. W., 303
BURRFISH, 23

C

CABOT, 37, 174, 250, 262, 292, 298–9, 303
Calhoun, Vice Adm. W. L., 158, 343–5, 349
CALIFORNIA, 180–2, 197, 200, 360–2
CALVERT, 364
CAMBRIA, 186, 329
Carberry, Lt. W. G., 380
Carney, Rear Adm. R. B., 10*n*
Caroline Is., 20–9, 367; *see* Palaus, Ponape, Truk, Woleai, Yap
Carr, Lt. (jg) G. R., 267
Carrier operations, Feb.–Apr., 1944, 27–41, 85–6, 154–7; "Forager," 131, 172–9; Battle Phil. Sea, 213–321; later, 353, 360, 367, 378, 383
Carriers, wanted in SW Pac., 95, 124, 144–5; comparative table, 233; escort carriers, 49, 68, 95, 180, 203, 207–9, 231–2; 252; in killer ops., 178, 227–8; call fire, 326–8; plane replacements, 230, 329*n*; Tinian and Guam, 360, 366, 377–8
Carter, Capt. G. B., 207
Carter, Commo. W. R., 341*n*, 343, 420
CARTER HALL, 77
CASCO, 255*n*
CASSIN YOUNG, 212
Cates, Maj. Gen. C. B., 338*n*, 353, 408
CAVALLA, 17*n*, 241–4, 265, 280–1, 285
Chamorros, 149–52, 158, 173, 339, 373, 377, 398–400
Chandler, Capt. A. D., 228
CHANDLER, 230
CHARRETTE, 239
Chichi Jima, 24*n*, 219, 232, 237–40, 311–13, 354
Chihaya, Cdr. Masataka, 11*n*
CHILDS, 49*n*
China, 4–9, 24, 66, 90, 107
CHITOSE, CHIYODA, 217–18, 247, 263, 288, 294, 298–9
Christie, Rear Adm. R. W., 20, 48, 217–18, 416
CHUYO, 16*n*
Claggett, Cdr. B. D., 75
Clarey, Lt. Cdr. B. A., 23
Clark, Lt. Cdr. A. H., 17
Clark, Rear Adm. J. J., biog., 238*n*; 36–7, 40–1, 174–5, 239–40, 286; com-

mand, 412; strikes on Iwo, etc., 232, 237–40, 243, 260, 311–13, 367, 378; in Battle Phil. Sea, 250, 258, 272, 295
CLEVELAND, 182, 335, 362
Collins, Commo. J., 73–4, 136
COLORADO, 180, 328, 359, 361–2, 378
Coman, Commo. R. G., 47
Combined Chiefs of Staff, 4–7, 46
Combined Fleet, 214–15
Combs, Commo. T. S., 47, 49–50, 120, 123, 406
CONNER, 240
Conolly, Rear Adm. R. L., 159, 170–2, 219, 324, 371–401, 418
CONVERSE, 240
Convoys, Jap., 17–23, 90, 107*n*, 117, 167–8, 175, 218
CORAL SEA, 207
COWPENS, 36, 174, 238, 250, 268, 273, 299*n*
Coye, Lt. Cdr. J. S., 22
Cramer, Lt. Cdr. R. H., 230
CREVALLE, 21–2
Crist, Lt. T. C., 380
CROAKER, 17*n*
Crowe, Lt. Col. H. P., 193
Crutchley, Rear Adm. V. A. C., 47, 76, 91, 96–7, 106, 122–30, 136, 220, 405
CURRITUCK, 50–1
Cutter, Lt. Cdr. S. D., 17

D

DACE, DALY, 66, 75, 127
Dana, Lt. (jg) Paul, 178
Darwin, Port, 22, 28, 97, 107
DAVID W. TAYLOR, 230
Davis, Cdr. J. W., 21
Davis, Rear Adm. G. B., 415
Davison, Rear Adm. R. E., 405
Day, Cdr. D. H., 84, 111
Dealey, Cdr. S. D., 19, 33, 220
Del Valle, Brig. Gen. P. A., 419
Destroyer Escorts, 55, 223–31, 316, 345, 378
Dive-bombing, 299–300
Doe, Brig. Gen. J. A., 63, 72, 96, 403
Dogs, Marine Corps, 376
Driniumor R., 71–4
DuBose, Rear Adm. L. T., 367, 413
Dukws, 53–4, 106, 110–12, 195, 209, 356, 361–3, 383, 389
DYSON, 240

E

EASON, LT. V. V., 297, 302–3
Eccles, Rear Adm. H. E., 341*n*
Eichelberger, Gen. K. L., 63, 75–9, 85–7, 94, 133, 403
Eisenhower, General Dwight D., 161
Ellison, Lt. (jg) W. D., 195
Embick, Lt. Gen. S. D., 8*n*
Endo, Vice Adm. Y., 67, 88–9
Engineer Special Brigades, 51–3, 70, 77–9, 85–7, 100, 106, 113, 137–8
ENGLAND, 224–30
Eniwetok, 156, 160–4, 170–2, 185, 190, 229–30, 242, 311, 330–1, 343–9, 354, 367–8, 376–9, 389
ENTERPRISE, 37, 154*n*, 174–6, 179, 250, 256, 268, 271, 283, 290–2, 297–9, 302, 307
Escort vessels, 55
ESSEX, 154, 174, 238, 240, 250, 266–9, 272–3, 276, 360
ETAMIN, 69, 71
Evans, Cdr. E. E., 223
Explosions, 85, 171

F

FANSHAW BAY, 207
Fast carrier forces, 28–9, 33, 82, 161, 219, 223, 232, 239, 311, 314, 326–8, 353, 367, 378
Fay, Lt. Cdr. E. B., 229
Fechteler, Rear Adm. W. M., biog., 64*n*; ops., 64–5, 81–6, 95–6, 103–14, 125, 135–6, 141–3, 404
Felix, Lt. Cdr. D. T., 255*n*
Fifth Amphibious Corps and Force, 159–61, 197, 209, 355, 396*n*
Fifth Fleet, as organized for "Forager," 159–62
Fighter-directors, 116, 125, 261–2
FINBACK, 250, 254, 278
Fiske, Capt. L. S., 349
Fleet, Lt. John, 382
Fleming, Cdr. M. K., 123
FLETCHER, 127–30
FLYING FISH, 23, 231, 241–3
Foltz, Ens. R. E., 270
"Forager" Operation, 149 and ff; chart, 153; size of, 160; logistics for, 341–50
Fowler, Ens. R. E., 267

Fowlkes, Col. B. C., 113
Frank, Cdr. N. J., 228
FRANKS, 223
Fuel problems, 214–16, 222, 235, 317, 344–6
Fuller, Maj. Gen. H. H., 63–5, 81–3, 95, 103, 106, 113–16, 123–5, 133, 403
FUSO, 118–20

G

GALVIN, ENS. J. R., 33
GAMBIER BAY, 207, 360
GAR, 30
Garrison, Lt. Cdr. M. E., 17–18
Geelvink Bay, 27, 60–1, 86, 143; chart, 105
Geiger, Maj. Gen. R. S., 159, 170, 374–400, 418
GEORGE, 224–8
Gift, Lt. R. P., 298–9
Gilbert Is., 3–6, 12, 19, 66, 156–7, 165–6, 169, 185, 190, 330, 341, 348, 358, 392
Gill, Maj. Gen. W. H., 72–3
GILLESPIE, 116
Ginder, Rear Adm. S. P., 32, 239
Gray, Commo. A. H., 345
Gray, Cdr. J. S., 286*n*
GRAYBACK, 17
Greene, Cdr. R. O., 164*n*
GREENLING, 375
Griffin, Col. Raphael, 187*n*
Griner, Maj. Gen. G. W., 335*n*, 410*n*
Guadalcanal, 123, 159–64, 170–1, 176, 244, 253, 322, 374, 380
Guam, history and descr., 149–52, 375; in strategy and air strikes, 8–10, 174–5; plans for, 157–64; airfields in Jap. strategy, 232–4, 248–51, 311, 377; W-day, 172, 197, 241, 371, 379; the operation, 371–99; casualties, 388–9, 400–1; bases and logistics, 343, 388–9, 400; charts, 372, 384–5
GUARDFISH, GUDGEON, 19, 24
Guerrillas, Filipino, 21
Guimaras Str., 221, 231–2, 241
GURNARD, 21, 90, 218

H

HADDO, 22
HAGGARD, HAILEY, 223
HAGURO, 118–20, 130–2, 282, 287, 300

Haha Jima, 239, 313, 354
Haines, Capt. J. M., 48
Hains, Cdr. Hamilton, 224-8
HAKE, 120
Hale, Capt. W. A. O., 139
Hall, Maj. Gen. C. P., 72-4
Halmahera, 16, 90, 95, 107, 116-18, 141-4, 219
Halsey, Admiral W. F., 10*n*, 161, 224, 309, 374
HAMILTON, 69
HAMMERHEAD, 25
Hansa Bay, 8, 10, 66
Hanson, Rear Adm. E. W., 269*n*, 305*n*, 415
HARDER, 19, 22, 33, 220
HARDHEAD, 17*n*
Harlfinger, Lt. Cdr. F. J., 20
Harrill, Rear Adm. W. K., biog., 238*n*; command, 414; 174-5, 239-42, 249-50, 258, 265, 272; strikes on Guam, 282-3
Harris, Cdr. D. A., 223
Harris, Lt. G. C., 75
HARUNA, 298, 309
HARUSAME, 125-6
HATAKAZE, 20
Hawaii, 16, 170-1, 180, 343, 348, 379
Hayakawa, Rear Adm. M., 416
HAYANAMI, HAYATAKA, 220, 295*n*
Hayler, Rear Adm. R. N., 381, 409, 414
HAZELWOOD, 227
Heavey, Brig. Gen. W. F., 51-2
HEERMANN, 227*n*
Heffernan, Rear Adm. J. B., 10*n*, 379
Heinl, Lt. Col. R. D., 200*n*, 396*n*
Hencey, Clarence, 211
HENRY T. ALLEN, 77, 135
HERRING, 16, 24
HF/DF, 251-4, 278, 285
HICKOX, 304
Hill, Rear Adm. H. W., 186, 211, 256, 353, 356, 359, 407
HIYO, 217, 249, 264, 272, 294-6, 299, 307
HOBBY, 112
Hoel, Lt. Cdr. R. W., 268
HOEL, 227*n*
Hoffman, Maj. C. W., 5*n*, 167*n*, 186*n*, 200*n*, 351*n*, 357*n*, 362*n*, 369
Hogan, Cdr. T. W., 217-18
HOGAN, 82
HOGGATT BAY, 227-8
HOKAZE, 120*n*
HOLLAND, 26
Hollandia, charts, 62, 80; in strategy,

6, 9-10, 28, 60; airfields, 34-8, 326; plans, 34-6, 45-6, 56, 61-5; the operation, 68-89; as base, 102-45, 217, 223
Holmes, Cdr. E. P., 270
HONOLULU, 181-2, 284, 326, 377, 393, 399
Hoover, Vice Adm. J. H., 156, 158, 164, 242
Hopkins, Capt. H. V., 49*n*
HORNET (1943), 32, 36, 174-6, 205, 238-40, 250, 262, 272-6, 292, 297, 303-4, 311
Hospital ships, 200, 389
Hough, Maj. F. O., 371*n*
HUDSON, 329
Humboldt Bay, 79-87; see Hollandia
Hustvedt, Rear Adm. O. M., 415
HUTCHINS, 66, 108-10, 127

I

I-BOATS: *I-5, -10, -16, -176, -184, -185,* 222-30; *I-42,* 30
IDAHO, 18, 377
IKAZUCHI, 19
ILLUSTRIOUS, 154*n*
Imperial Headquarters, strategy, 11-14, 65-6, 134, 213; and New Guinea, 66-7, 89, 94, 107, 117-18, 145, 220; and A-Go, 213-21, 223, 232; and Saipan, 183, 322-4
INAZUMA, 217
INDIANA, 41*n*, 268-70
INDIANAPOLIS, 177, 197, 243, 257*n*, 308, 311, 332, 381, 400
IOWA, 40, 270
Irving, Maj. Gen. F. A., 63, 75-9, 403
Isely, J. A., 186*n*
Isely, Lt. Cdr. R. H., 178
Isely Field, 152, 168-9, 178, 206-9, 326, 329-33, 349, 354, 359-60, 366-8
Ishigura, Cdr., 298
Ito, Rear Adm. Y., 117-19, 122, 130
ITSUKUSHIMA, 119, 131
Iwano, Maj. M., 380
Iwo Jima, 237-40, 311-13, 328-9, 354, 367, 378-9

J

JACK, 21, 90
Jamison, Capt. J. W., 69-70
Japan, plans to defeat, 4-9; strategy, 10-14; cabinet crisis, 340; see Imperial Headquarters

Japanese Naval Air Arm, carrier training, 235, 317; plane production, 11; in SW Pac., 89, 117–24, 132, 136, 216; Base Air Force, 207, 218–19, 233–5, 245, 260, 289–90, 321, 357, 373; raids on Saipan, 328–9; losses, 319–21

Japanese Navy, in SW Pac., 117–32; reorganization, 214; fuel shortage, 214–16, 222, 235, 317; losses, 416

Jarrell, Cdr. A. E., 127–30

Jascos, 325

Jautefa Bay, 80–6

JENKINS, 127

Johnsen, Cdr. W. H., 230

JOHNSTON, 223

Joint Chiefs of Staff, 6–11, 36, 46, 51, 52*n*, 66, 140–1; directive of 12 Mar. '44, 9–10, 45, 61, 91, 95, 154, 157–8, 341–2

Jones, Lt. Col. G. M., 139

Jones, Col. L. R., 187*n*, 199

Joshima, Rear Adm. T., 217, 249, 264, 295, 416

Joy, Rear Adm. C. T., 181, 378, 381, 399, 409, 415

JUNYO, 217, 249, 264, 272, 294–5

K

KAKUTA, ADMIRAL K., 219*n*, 234–5, 260, 289–90, 311, 321, 357

KALK, 111, 116, 132

Kamiri, 135–6, 139

Kane, Cdr. W. R., 297

KANIMBLA, 77

Kauffman, Cdr. D. L., 165–6, 184

Kavieng, 8–10, 60

KAZAGUMO, 120

Kelleher, Capt. D. A., 340, 366, 369

Kelley, Col. G. W., 206

Kendall, Lt. E. F., 261*n*

Kenney, Maj. Gen. G. C., 34–7, 46–9, 61–7, 87, 92, 156

KEOKUK, 329

Kido, Marquis, 340

Kimmel, Cdr. M. M., 24

King, Adm. E. J., and strategy, 5–6, 11, 19; on explosion, 171*n*; on ENGLAND, 228

Kingman, Rear Adm. H. F., 197, 409

Kinkaid, Vice Adm. T. C., 28, 45–9, 55, 63–4, 73, 91–5, 122–6, 135, 403; and A-Go, 217

KINU, 118, 120, 125, 130–1

Kiralfy, Alexander, 10–11, 28, 173

KITKUN BAY, 360

Klamano oilfield, 140

Knowles, Capt. H. B., 193*n*, 201*n*

Koehler, Lt. Cdr. J. T., 166

Koga, Admiral M., 12–13, 27, 94, 173, 217, 253*n*

Komatsu, Sakio, 269, 279

"KON" Operation, 118–32, 145, 168, 220–1; chart, 121

Korea, 17, 24, 382

Korim Bay, 126–7, 130

Kornasoren, 135, 138–9

Kossler, Lt. Cdr. H. J., 280–1

Krueger, Lt. Gen. Walter, 46–8; staff work, 63–4, 72, 75; and operations, 82, 87, 94–6, 102, 133–6, 141

Kumamba Is., 101

Kurile Is., 8, 18, 23

Kurita, Vice Adm. T., 216*n*, 249, 254–6, 263–5, 269, 288, 292, 298, 300, 416

Kusaka, Vice Adm. R., 215–16

Kuykendall, C. W., 31

Kuzume, Col. N., 107–8, 118, 132–3

Kwajalein, 28, 34, 156, 166–72, 190, 219, 260, 313, 343–8

L

LAMAR, 379

Landing craft, types used in SW Pac., 53; in Marianas, 356

LANGLEY (1943), 37, 174, 238, 250, 265, 360

Laning, Cdr. C. B., 108–10

LAPON, 21

LASSEN, 346

Latta, Cdr. F. D., 22

Lautrup, Lt. Cdr. G. W., 30

LAVALLETTE, 127

Lawton, Lt. (jg) E. J., 297*n*, 302–3

LCIs, 53–6, 68, 84, 96–100, 106, 111–16, 138–9, 143, 166, 383

LCI gunboats, 56, 190, 209–10, 325, 359, 380, 387, 396

LCI-31, *-34*, *-73*, 100, 111, 114; *-468*, 207; *-349*, *-365*, *-366*, 393

LCTs, 53–5, 86, 106, 111, 125, 137, 171, 349, 356, 361–3

LCT-248, 122

Lee, Vice Adm. W. A., 28, 37, 40–1, 179, 242–3, 249–51; command, 415; reaction to Mitscher's proposal, 244–5;

in "Turkey Shoot," 258, 262, 265, 268; later, 283, 301–2, 305–8, 316

Leeson, Lt. Cdr. R., 73

LEXINGTON (1943), 32, 37–8, 174–9, 213n, 243, 249–50, 257–8, 265–71, 274, 282–3, 292, 295, 303, 308; track chart, 275

Lidstone, Cdr. N. A., 223

LINDENWALD, 196

Lockwood, Vice Adm. C. A., 16, 19, 24, 158, 241, 252, 278, 285, 415

Lodge, Maj. O. R., 371n, 374n

Logistics, 160, 341–50

Logsdon, Lt. D. M., 380

LONG, 82

Los Negros, *see* Admiralties

LOUISVILLE, 197, 200–1, 328

Love, Capt. E. G., 332n

LSDs, 54, 361, 383

LSTs, in SW Pac., 53–114, 119, 125, 135, 138, 143; in Marianas, 170–1, 190–5, 200, 209, 346, 349, 356, 361, 364, 376, 383, 389

LST–84, 207; *–353, –485*, 171; *–456*, 113; *–487*, 119

Lucas, Lt. J. G., 200n

Luzon, 4, 9, 17, 157, 231

Luzon Strait, sub. battle in, 25

LVTs, in SW Pac., 54, 77–86, 104–11, 138, 143; in Marianas, 165, 190–202, 209, 327, 349, 355–7, 361–4, 383, 387–92

MAC and MC

MACARTHUR, GENERAL DOUGLAS, AND STRATEGY, 3–10, 20, 27; command, 45–8, 52, 91, 403; New Guinea ops., 34–6, 56, 60–145, 220–2; support of Marianas, 114, 161, 241, 253, 316

McCampbell, Cdr. David, 269–73, 276–8

MCCORD, 227

McCornock, Cdr. S. A., 120

McCuskey, Lt. Cdr. E. S., 263n, 278n

MACDONOUGH, 39, 178

McGee, Cdr. H. F., 55

McIntire, Lt. (jg) J. O., 300n

McLean, Cdr. J. B., 127

McManes, Capt. K. M., 127–30

M

MAFFIN BAY, 92–7, 102

Magicienne Bay, 179n, 183–97, 209–10, 329–30, 334

Mahan, Admiral A. T., 314, 318

Majuro, 29, 34–41, 154–6, 172, 219, 229, 343, 348

Manila, 9, 21, 28, 90, 217

MANILA BAY, 209, 329n

Manokwari, 86, 118, 120n, **126**, 129, 132–4, 143

MANOORA, 77

Manus, *see* Admiralties

Marcus I., 220, 374

Marianas, chart, 163; hist. and descr., 149–54, 165; in strategy, 5–9, 13, 19, 118–21, 145, 157–66, 216, 219–21, 339–40; air strikes on, 17, 149–83; reinforced, 17–23, 167–9; natural defenses, 165; base development, 341–2, 349–50; secured, 401–2

Marine Corps, 157–8, 160–2, 169, 184; aviation, 156, 164n; tactics, 331; uniform, 362; 1st Prov. brigade, 160, 374–401; 2nd, 3rd and 4th divs., 159–60, 170, 186–208, 330–9, 348, 353–401

Marshall Is., 3–19; the, by-passed, 156; reconnoitered, 220–1; sub. missions to, 222–31; *see* Eniwetok, Kwajalein, Majuro

Martin, Cdr. W. I., 176–8, 184

Martineau, Lt. Cdr. D. L., 210–12

MARYLAND, 180–2, 328

MASSACHUSETTS, 40

MATSU, 367

MATSUKAZE, 24n

Matsunaga, Admiral S., 312

Maui, rehearsal at, 171

MAUNA LOA, 346

MAYA, 299, 309

MAZAMA, 346

MELVIN, 231

Menado, 122

Merchant shipping, U.S., 343–8; Jap., 13–16, 21–6, 48

MERCURY, 329

Miller, Cdr. J. A., 285n

Miller, Cdr. Shirley, 397

MINAZUKI, 220

Mindanao, 7–9, 13, 23, 45, 50, 91, 101, 118, 217

MINEKAZE, 19

Minelaying, by aircraft, 32

Minesweeping, 69, 180n, 329

MINNEAPOLIS, 269

Mios Soe Is., 141

Mios Woendi, 116, 132, 137

MISSISSIPPI, 180

Mitscher, Vice Adm. M. A., biog., 236; 27, 36–9, 85–6, 154–8, 161, 172–4, 179, 213n, 216; command, 214n, 412; westward proposal, 241–5, 252, 264; battle disposition, 249–51; during "Turkey Shoot," 258–66, 271–4; later decisions, 282–6, 290–92, 300–8; search procedures, 286–90, 307–9; later raids, 353, 367, 378; summary, 313–16

Mizony, Lt. Col. H. I., 334

MOBILE, 37, 273, 316n

Mobile Fleet, 214–21, 231–3; movements before battle, 231–2; plane losses, 289, 300–1, 305

Mobile service and supplies, 34, 211, 343–50, 367

MOCHIZUKI, 49n

MOGAMI, 264, 271, 294–7

Mokmer, 104, 107–10, 113–16, 122, 132–3

MONSSEN, 201

MONTEREY, 37–9, 174, 250, 258n, 260, 292, 298–9, 303, 309n

Montgomery, Rear Adm. A. E., biog., 237n; command, 413; 32, 37–8, 154, 174, 178, 243, 250, 258, 270–1, 276, 367; report, 313–14; Guam, 378

MONTPELIER, 182–3, 276n, 335, 361n

Mooney, Ens. W. R.,

Moore, Rear Adm. C. J., 10, 253n

Moore, Cdr. J. A., 17

Moore, Cdr. R. S., 180n

Morotai, 47, 144

Motor Torpedo Boats, 47, 56–8, 66, 73–4, 91, 132, 136, 142–3

MULLANY, 66, 97, 127

Mumma, Cdr. M. C., 57n

Murray, Lt. Col. R. L., 193

MUSASHI, 13, 27, 31, 131–2, 217–18, 299

Musick, Lt. Cdr. K. F., 304

MUSTIN, 120–5

Myers, Lt. R. F., 261n

MYOKO, 118–20, 130–2, 300

N

NAGAISHI, CAPT. M., 234n

NAGARA, NATORI, 17n

NAGATO, 264, 294–7

Nagumo, Vice Adm. C., 167–8, 185, 201n, 216, 254, 335–7

Nakamura, Capt. T., 182n, 201n

Napalm, 357–60

NARWHAL, NAUTILUS, 22

NASHVILLE, 47, 78, 83, 97, 108, 123–4, 126n

NATOMA BAY, 209, 329n

Navajo Indians, 376

Naval Air Transport, 349

Naval gunfire support of amphib. ops., New Guinea, 76–7, 81–2, 91, 110–6; Saipan, 197–200, 206, 211, 324–6, 330, 335; Tinian, 353, 359–66; Guam, 387–8, 392–6

Naval shore bombardment, Carolines, 40–1; New Guinea, 69, 74–7, 82–3, 96–9, 108, 137–9; Marianas, 179–83, 190, 194, 333, 353, 361, 377–83, 390

Nelson, Lt. R. S., 290–1, 308n

NESHANIC, 207n, 345

Netherlands East Indies, 4, 9, 60, 65, 140, 219

Netherlands forces in SW Pac., 46–7

NEWCOMB, 230

New Guinea, in strategy, 3–12; description, 59–61; conquest of, 45–145

NEW JERSEY, 40

NEW MEXICO, 180

NEW ORLEANS, 181, 308, 361n, 399

NICHOLSON, 115

Nimitz, Admiral C. W., and strategy, 3–11, 15, 28–9, 34–8, 46, 63, 86, 95, 145; Marianas, 158, 161, 219–23, 241, 400, 406

Noble, Capt. A. G., 64, 69, 70, 91n, 96–8

Noemfoor, 91, 132–40, 145; chart, 137

NORMAN SCOTT, 361–2

NORTH CAROLINA, 27n, 30n, 39–40, 269n

NOSHIRO, 131–2, 218

NOWAKI, 131

O

OAK HILL, 196

Obata, Lt. Gen. H., 12, 167, 373n, 388, 398, 400

Obayashi, Rear Adm. S., 217, 247–51, 263–5, 288, 416

O'Brien, Lt. Col. W. J., 336

Ogata, Col. K., 357–8, 361, 364–6, 369

Ohmae, Capt. J., 292n, 298, 309, 328n

Oi, Capt. A., 11n, 14n

O'Kane, Cdr. R. H., 24, 155

OKINAMI, 131

Okinawa, 17, 217, 253, 309, 339, 379

Oldendorf, Rear Adm. J. B., 40, 170, 180–1, 200, 210, 328, 356, 409

Olsen, Lt. Cdr. R. I., 21
Omark, Lt. (jg) W. R., 296
ORCA, 50, 123
O'Regan, Capt. W. V., 24
OREGON, 349*n*
Orote, 175, 262-3, 273-7, 283, 373-7, 389-98
OTORI, 175
Owens, Cdr. S. D., 362, 369
Owi, 50, 116, 120, 123-4, 131-3
OYODO, 31
Ozawa, Vice Adm. J., biog., 216; command, 416; and KON, 117, 131-2; and A-Go, 214-21, 231-45; battle plan, 246-9, 254, 260; locates enemy, 246, 265, 271-2; dispositions, 263, 292; dis. charts, 264, 293; raids in "Turkey Shoot," 263-74; movements after, 284-9; loses flagship, 279-82; and 20 June battle, 288-301; defeat, 305-9, 315-9

P

PACIFIC FLEET, reorganization, 161-2; *see* Fifth Fleet
Pagan, 152, 167, 175, 240
Page, Lt. Cdr. J. E., 224
Palaus, in strategy, 9, 12, 157, 215, 232; sub. patrols, 22-3; air raids on, 29-33, 174, 367; as Jap. base, 13, 20, 27, 65, 114, 234, 246*n*, 260, 328-9, 345
Paquet, Freeman, 33
Parai, 104, 114-15
Paratroops, 139
PARCHE, PARGO, 23-5
Paré, Capt. E. E., 37, 345
Parece Vela, 154, 285*n*
Parks, Cdr. L. S., 25
Patrick, Brig. Gen. E. D., 135, 139
PCS-1452, 192
Pearl Harbor, explosion at, 171; *see* Hawaii
Peleliu, 341, 348, 400; *see* Palaus
Pendleton, Lt. Cdr. W. B., 224-5
Pennebaker, Lt. Col. E. P., 164*n*
PENNSYLVANIA, 180-2, 328, 377, 390, 394, 397
PERRY, 69
Peters, Cdr. J. M., 277*n*
Peterson, Capt. G. E., 23
PHAON, 211, 329
PHELPS, 201, 210-12

Philippine Is., strategy, 3-9; sub. patrols, 20-2
Philippine Sea, Battle of, 11, 14-15, 24, 133, 209, 322, 328; preliminaries, 213-56; sources, 213*n*; "Turkey Shoot," 239, 257-80, 283-7, 294, 315, 377; 2nd day's battle, 288-304; chase, 305-9; forces engaged, App. III; summary and losses, 313-21
PHOENIX, 47, 97, 108, 123, 126
Photo recce. and interp'n, 29, 37, 61, 75, 95, 104, 141, 154-5, 158, 164-5, 353-4, 375, 378-80
PILOTFISH, PINTADO, 22-3, 168
Pineau, Roger, 213*n*
PIRANHA, 24
POCOMOKE, 242*n*, 255
POGY, POLLACK, 19-20, 23
Ponape, 8, 38-41, 156, 222
Pownall, Rear Adm. C. A., 28, 34
PRESERVER, 211-12
PRINCETON, 37, 174, 248, 250, 268, 271, 282, 303*n*, 310
PUFFER, 16, 218, 220
Puluwat, 156, 174

R

RABAUL, 6, 11-13, 30, 39, 49*n*, 60, 156, 263*n*
RABY, 224-8
Radar, in Battle Phil. Sea, 262, 282, 285
RADFORD, 127
Ragsdale, Rear Adm. V. H., 68, 378, 381, 405, 420
RAINIER, 346
Ramage, Cdr. L. P., 25
RANGER, 237
RATON, RAY, 16, 21-3, 218
REDFIN, 19, 22, 221, 237
Rees, Capt. J. F., 348
Reeves, Rear Adm. J. W., biog., 237*n*; 32-3, 37, 174, 178-9, 235, 243, 250, 258, 271, 286, 295, 310, 367, 378; command, 414
REID, 82, 114-15, 120-5
Reifsnider, Rear Adm. L. F., 371*n*, 389, 400, 419
REMEY, 362
Reynolds, Cdr. L. K., 223
Rian, Lt. (jg) G. R., 300
RIDDLE, 230
Ridgway, Lt. Cdr. D., 261*n*
Riseley, Col. J. P., 186*n*, 194

RO-*15*, *-36*, *-41*, *-42*, *-44*, *-104*, *-105*, *-106*, *-108*, *-111*, *-114*, *-116*, *-117*, 222–31; RO-*45*, 39
ROBALO, 24
Rocket fire, 53–6, 84, 98–9, 111, 114, 120, 383; from planes, 178, 209, 329n
ROCKY MOUNT, 186, 202, 210, 242, 326, 332, 377
ROE, 99
Roscoe, Theodore, 15n, 24n, 278n
Rota, 149–51, 154, 233, 248–9, 258, 271–4, 282–91, 320, 324, 328, 351, 369, 378
Ruddock, Rear Adm. T. D., 409
RUSSELL, 120, 123, 125
Russia, 7–8, 11–12
RYUHO, 217, 249, 264, 272, 294–7

S

S-*47*, 141
Sabin, Ens. G. E., 230
SAILFISH, 16n
ST. LOUIS, 181
Saipan, 234, 238, 242, 319; in strategy, 5, 8–9, 23, 145; hist. and descr., 149–52; attack on, 154–212; defense of, 167–9, 179, 318, 324; secured, 322–38; forces and casualties, 339; charts, 188–9, 204, 323; as base, 359–61, 364, 376–8
Saito, Lt. Gen. Y., 167–9, 183–7, 202–3, 208–10, 216, 319, 322, 334–5; on naval gunfire, 326; death, 337
Sakito Maru, 17, 167, 373
Sakonju, Rear Adm. N., 118–20, 125–31
Sallada, Rear Adm. H. B., 326, 410
Saltonstall, Sgt. P. B., 369
Samate, 120
SAMIDARE, 125–6, 130, 367n
SAMPSON, 114
San Bernardino Str., 202, 231, 241–3
SAN CARLOS, 50
SAN DIEGO, 154n
SANDLANCE, 17–18, 22
SAN FRANCISCO, 308
SANGAMON, 29
SANGAY, 346
SAN JACINTO, 174, 178, 205, 250, 288n, 292, 298, 300, 367n
SAN PABLO, 49–50
Sansapor, 74, 91, 140–5; chart, 142
SANTA FE, 37
SARANAC, 207n, 345
SARATOGA, 154n, 218

Sarmi, 36–7, 88–97, 101–2
Sasaki, Capt. A., 311n, 333
Satawan, 38–41, 156, 174
SAUGATUCK, 345–6
Saunders, Capt. W. V., 227
Sawar, 36–7, 92–7, 102
SAZANAMI, 19
SC-*648*, 69; *-699*, 114; *-703*, 99, 100; *-743*, 81; *-1326*, 393
Scarpino, Cdr. W. J., 255n
Schmidt, Maj. Gen. Harry, 187n, 338, 353–5, 369, 408
Schouten Is., 103–4
Scott, Cdr. J. A., 30
Scott, Lt. Cdr. James, 224
Scruggs, Capt. R. M., 56, 112
Seabees, 209, 333, 350, 368, 399–400
SEAHORSE, 17, 241–3
SEARAVEN, 155
Seiyo Maru, 231, 295
Selby, Lt. Cdr. F. G., 218
Senda, Rear Adm. S., 107
Sentani, Lake, 60–3, 74–8, 84–9, 94–5, 126
Service squadrons, 34, 211, 343–6, 349–50, 367
Seventh Amphibious Force, 47, 53–6, 64, 91, 95, 104, 110, 141
Seventh Fleet, 47–8, 95, 110, 116, 119; air arm, 49–50, 120, 123
Shapley, Col. Alan, 390
SHARK, 22–3, 168
SHASTA, 346
SHAW, 211
Shelby, Lt. Cdr. E. E., 155
Shepherd, Brig. Gen. L. C., 390–2, 395–6, 419
Sherman, Rear Adm. F. C., 154, 238
Sherman, Rear Adm. Forrest, 9
Sherrod, Robert, 186n, 195
Shifley, Cdr. R. L., 300
Shigematsu, Maj. Gen. K., 373, 388
Shigemitsu, Hon. M., 340
SHIGURE, 118, 125, 130
SHIKANAMI, 118, 125–6, 130–1
Shimada, Admiral, 214
SHIMAKAZE, 131
Shimizu, Col., 136, 139–40
SHIRAKUMO, 19
SHIRATSUYU, 125–6, 130, 231
SHOKAKU, 17n, 217–8, 249, 264, 271, 280–1, 285, 307, 316, 320
Shore fire-control parties, 197, 200, 203, 206, 325, 359, 393, 396

Shore parties, 52–3, 84–5, 113, 208, 389*n*
SHROPSHIRE, 47, 73, 97, 126
Sibert, Maj. Gen. F. C., 142–3
Sibutu Passage, 217–18
SILVERSIDES, 22–3
Sims, Lt. (jg) C. A., 274
SKIPJACK, 19, 155
Small, Rear Adm. E. G., 29
Smith, Lt. (jg) C. D., 300*n*
Smith, Lt. Gen. H. M., 159, 170, 186, 202, 206, 209; in Marianas, 324–5, 330–9, 353, 370, 376, 395, 400, 407
Smith, Maj. Gen. Ralph C., 160, 171, 203, 330–2, 410
Snowden, Cdr. E. M., 178*n*, 205*n*, 285
SOLACE, 200, 389
Somerville, Rear Adm. Sir James, 154*n*
SONOMA, 114
Sorong, 37, 86, 89–90, 107, 117–22, 125, 130, 140–1
SOUTH DAKOTA, 40, 269–70, 282*n*
Southwest Pacific command, 4, 8, 28, 45–8
SPANGLER, 227–8
SPEARFISH, 23
Sprague, Rear Adm. T. L., 420
Spruance, Adm. R. A., Com. Fifth Fleet, 28–9, 158, 161; command, 407, 412; character, 232*n*, 235–6; conferences, 202–3, 242, 324, 332; conduct of battle, 237–45, 250–60, 282–4, 290–1, 313–9; pursuit, 290*n*, 301, 305–9; later decisions, 324, 338; and logistics, 342, 345; Tinian and Guam, 355, 371, 376–82, 395, 400
STEELHEAD, 25
STEPHEN POTTER, 39
Stevens, Capt. P. A., 77
Stewart, Maj. J. L., 197
STINGRAY, 252–3, 278
STOCKHAM, 262, 268–70
STOCKTON, 114
Stone, Cdr. L. T., 21
Stout, Capt. R. F., 97
Strategic plans of May 1943, 4–5; of Dec. 1943, 7–10; of 12 Mar. 1944, 9–19, 45, 61, 91, 95, 154, 157–8, 341–2; Japanese, 10–14
Streett, Maj. Gen. St. C., 50
Stroh, Cdr. R. J., 164*n*
Stuart, Col. W. J., 186*n*
Stump, Rear Adm. F. B., 207*n*, 326, 410, 420
STURGEON, 23

Submarines, Jap., 16, 24, 30, 39, 222–31, 316, 329; chart of ops., 226
Submarines, U.S., patrols, 14–26, 167–8, 214, 217–20; rescue, 21–2, 33, 39; in SW Pacific, 48, 66; Palaus, 30–1; Marianas, 155, 375; in Bat. Phil. Sea, 231, 241–4, 250, 278–81, 316
Sulu Sea, 4, 7, 16, 20–1
SUNFISH, 155
Surigao Strait, 202, 241
Sutherland, Maj. Gen. R. K., 7–8
SUWANNEE, 230
SUZUKAZE, 19
SWORDFISH, 24*n*

T

TAIHO, 217–18, 221, 249, 264, 269, 279–82, 285–9, 307, 320
Takagi, Vice Adm. T., 167, 222, 229, 337, 417
TAKASAKI, 220
Takashina, Lt. Gen., 373, 381*n*, 388
Takeda, Lt. Col. H., 371*n*, 374*n*, 381–2, 401
Tamai, Cdr. A., 394
Tami, 61, 87
Tanahmerah Bay, 61–3, 68, 74–9, 85, 94–6; charts, 62, 76
TANG, 24, 30, 39, 155
TANGIER, 49–50
TAKASAKI, 220
Tanzola, Col. V. J., 390–1
Tapotchau, Mt., 152, 179*n*, 190, 197, 208, 345; struggle for, 330–5
Tarakan oil, 119, 214–7, 281
Tarr, Ens. Thomas, 276–7
Task Force 58, defined, 161; comp. table, 233; dispositions, 242–3, 249–51, 258–9; numbers and organization, 258, 412–15; operations, 27–41, 84–6, 154–5, 172–9; 214*n*, 232*n*, 238–43
Tate, Lt. (jg) B. C., 296
TATSUTA, 18
Taussig, Cdr. E. D., 150
TAUTOG, 19, 23
Tawi Tawi, 94, 116, 131, 173, 185, 216–21, 235
Taylor, Lt. W. T., 376*n*
TAYLOR, 228–9
TENNESSEE, 180–2, 187, 197–8, 360–2
Teshima, Lt. Gen. F., 66–7
Thebaud, Rear Adm. L. H., 413
Theiss, Commo. P. S., 192, 196, 409

Third Amphibious Corps and Force, 161, 170, 374, 396, 401
Third Fleet, 161
Thorwall, Cdr. C. A., 224n, 227–8
THRESHER, 24
Tinian, hist. and descr., 149–54, 354; the taking of, 351–70; bombardment, 179–81, 359–61; concealed battery, 157–62, 182, 362; numbers and casualties, 364, 369; chart, 352
TINOSA, 22
Titus, Lt. Cdr. J. C., 22n
Toem, 92, 97–9, 102, 137, 143
Tojo, Gen. H., 309, 334, 340
Tompkins, Col. R. M., 334
Torpedoes, U. S., sub., 15–16; air, 299
Toyoda, Admiral S., biog., 13n; and KON, 117, 120, 131–2; and A-Go, 13–14, 94, 173, 215–21, 231, 248n, 290, 305, 309, 318
TRATHEN, 127
TRIGGER, 20
Troop lift, 348–9
TROUT, 17, 167, 373
Truk, in strategy, 4–10; strikes on, 34, 38–9, 156, 174, 313; as Jap. base, 29, 207, 219, 222, 260–3, 290, 324, 328–9
TSUGARU, 119, 131
TULLIBEE, TUNNY, 30–1
"Turkey Shoot," 257–84, 294, 315, 377; Jap. "score," 287; chart, 270–1
Turnage, Maj. Gen. A. H., 383, 396, 418
Turner, Vice Adm. R. K., plans for "Forager," 158–61, 166, 170–2, 179n, 349; Saipan, 184–6, 190, 193n, 200–9, 324; Tinian and Guam, 353–5, 376–7

U

UGAKI, VICE ADM. M., 131–2, 221, 231, 241, 416
Ulithi, 367
UMIKAZE, 19
Underwater demolition teams, 165–6, 183–4, 195–6, 208, 354–5, 363, 380, 383, 390, 401
URAKAZE, 280–1
URANAMI, 118, 125, 130–1

V

VAN ORMAN, LT. COL. E. G., 325n, 366
Vetter, Capt. J. P., 165n
Vogelkop, as Jap. base and objective, 6–12, 59–66, 89, 94–7, 107, 134–6, 168, 219; foothold gained, 140–2; charts, 105, 121

W

WADLEIGH, 230
Wagner, Rear Adm. F. D., 50–1
Waigeo I., 140–1
WAKATAKE, 32
WAKATSUKI, 282
Wakde, 36–7, 50, 72, 88–102, 107, 110, 116, 119–20, 124–6, 135–7, 141–3, 241; chart, 100
Wakde-Sarmi, 88–102; chart, 93
Wake I., 220
Walker, Lt. Cdr. F. D., 21
Ward, Lt. Cdr. R. E. M., 16n
WARRAMUNGA, 73, 97, 127
WASHINGTON, 244
WASP (1943), 250, 265n, 271–3, 292, 295, 300–1, 308, 383
Watson, Maj. Gen. T. E., 186n, 335, 353, 407
Weather, 257, 288, 360, 368, 382
WESTRALIA, 84
Wewak, 10, 49n, 61, 66–7, 72–4, 87
Weyler, Rear Adm. G. L., 381, 409
Weymouth, Lt. Cdr. Ralph, 274, 285n
Wheeler, Capt. C. J., 316n
Whelchel, Cdr. D. L., 25
Whitehead, Maj. Gen. E. P., 47, 64n, 92
Whitehead, Capt. R. F., 326–7
WHITE PLAINS, 207
WICHITA, 181, 269n, 397
Widhelm, Capt. W. J. ("Gus"), 285
WILKES, 78, 99, 115–16
Wilkinson, Rear Adm. T. S., 161
Williams, Lt. J. R., 392
Williamson, Lt. J. A., 228n
WILLIAMSON, 180
Wilson, Vice Adm. Russell, 8n
Wiltse, Rear Adm. L. J., 415
Windissi, 143
"Window," 262, 312, 328
Winston, Lt. Cdr. F. L., 261n
Woleai, 19, 28, 33, 49, 156, 174, 215, 313, 354
WRIGHT, 50

Y

YAHAGI, 218
YAMAGUMO, 131

Yamamoto, Fleet Adm. I., 10
YAMATO, 131–2, 218, 221, 299
Yap, strikes on, 32–3, 174, 313, 367; as Jap. base, 179n, 208n, 219, 232–3, 245, 290, 345
YARNALL, 262, 268
YORKTOWN (1943), 37, 154, 174, 238, 250, 257n, 262, 270–2, 276, 282, 292, 295, 298, 311, 383
Yoshida, Maj. K., 168n, 325

Young, Lt. L. V., 141
YUBARI, 17n

Z

"Z" PLAN, 12–3, 173, 217, 253n
Zamboanga, 19, 118–19, 217
Zimmer, Lt. Col. H. J., 366, 369
ZUIHO, 217, 247, 263, 288, 294, 299
ZUIKAKU, 217–18, 249, 264, 272–3, 285n, 287–300